Promise to Pay

American Beginnings, 1500–1900

A series edited by Hannah Farber, Stephen Mihm, and Mark Peterson

Also in the series:

Flowers, Guns, and Money: Joel Roberts Poinsett and the Paradoxes of American Patriotism
by Lindsay Schakenbach Regele

Banking on Slavery: Financing Southern Expansion in the Antebellum United States
by Sharon Ann Murphy

A Great and Rising Nation: Naval Exploration and Global Empire in the Early US Republic
by Michael A. Verney

Trading Freedom: How Trade with China Defined Early America
by Dael A. Norwood

Wives Not Slaves: Patriarchy and Modernity in the Age of Revolutions
by Kirsten Sword

Accidental Pluralism: America and the Religious Politics of English Expansion, 1497–1662
by Evan Haefeli

The Province of Affliction: Illness and the Making of Early New England
by Ben Mutschler

Puritan Spirits in the Abolitionist Imagination
by Kenyon Gradert

Trading Spaces: The Colonial Marketplace and the Foundations of American Capitalism
by Emma Hart

Urban Dreams, Rural Commonwealth: The Rise of Plantation Society in the Chesapeake
by Paul Musselwhite

Building a Revolutionary State: The Legal Transformation of New York, 1776–1783
by Howard Pashman

Sovereign of the Market: The Money Question in Early America
by Jeffrey Sklansky

A complete list of series titles is available on the University of Chicago Press website.

Promise to Pay

The Politics and Power of Money in Early America

KATIE A. MOORE

The University of Chicago Press
Chicago and London

Publication of this book has been aided by a grant from the Bevington Fund.

The University of Chicago Press, Chicago 60637
The University of Chicago Press, Ltd., London
© 2024 by The University of Chicago
All rights reserved. No part of this book may be used or reproduced in any manner whatsoever without written permission, except in the case of brief quotations in critical articles and reviews. For more information, contact the University of Chicago Press, 1427 E. 60th St., Chicago, IL 60637.
Published 2024
Printed in the United States of America

33 32 31 30 29 28 27 26 25 24   1 2 3 4 5

ISBN-13: 978-0-226-83581-5 (cloth)
ISBN-13: 978-0-226-83583-9 (paper)
ISBN-13: 978-0-226-83582-2 (e-book)
DOI: https://doi.org/10.7208/chicago/9780226835822.001.0001

Library of Congress Cataloging-in-Publication Data

Names: Moore, Katie A., author.
Title: Promise to pay : the politics and power of money in early America / Katie A. Moore.
Other titles: Politics and power of money in early America | American beginnings, 1500–1900.
Description: Chicago ; London : The University of Chicago Press, 2024. | Includes references and index.
Identifiers: LCCN 2024016853 | ISBN 9780226835815 (cloth) | ISBN 9780226835839 (paperback) | ISBN 9780226835822 (e-book)
Subjects: LCSH: Money—North America—History—18th century. | Money—Social aspects—North America. | North America—History—Colonial period, ca. 1600–1775. | North America—Economic conditions—18th century. | North America—Social conditions—18th century.
Classification: LCC HG508.M667 2024 | DDC 332.4/9709033—dc23/eng/20240515
LC record available at https://lccn.loc.gov/2024016853

♾ This paper meets the requirements of ANSI/NISO Z39.48-1992 (Permanence of Paper).

Contents

	Introduction: Early American Monetary Practice	1
1	From Coin to Currency	14
2	The Sinews of War	42
3	Accounting for Politics	64
4	Coined Land	88
5	Money and Blood	120
6	Money on the Margins	151
7	From Currency to Coin	187
	Epilogue: The Currency Act Crisis	213

Acknowledgments 229
List of Abbreviations 233
Notes 235
Index 295

INTRODUCTION

Early American Monetary Practice

On October 2, 1704, thirty-eight-year-old Sarah Knight set out from her home in Boston to New York City to settle her brother's estate. She traveled by horseback, accompanied by the postman or a local guide, and ate and slept in taverns and private homes. A sophisticated, enterprising woman, Knight marveled at the rough manners and customs of rural Connecticut, where, she recounted in her journal, "They give the title of merchant to every trader." She was particularly bemused by the prevailing monetary practice of pricing store goods differently according to the form of payment. A promise to pay within a year or so was known as "*Trust*," essentially credit. Knight identified three ways of paying up front: "*Pay*" meant grain, pork, beef, and other farm products at the legal values set by the colonial assembly that year (also known as commodity money); "*Pay as money*" (or country pay) involved farm products at a one-third discount from their official values to account for discrepancies between market prices and those the government decreed; and "*mony* . . . or Good hard money, as sometimes silver coin is termed by them," included Spanish pieces of eight (pesos), Massachusetts "pine tree shillings," and wampum shell beads for small change. Suppose a buyer came in asking for a sixpenny knife, "in pay it is 12d [pence]—in pay as money eight pence, and hard money its own price, viz. 6d. It seems," Knight concluded, "a very Intricate way of trade and what *Lex Mercatoria*"—European merchant law— "had not thought of."[1]

Knight poked fun at country life, disparagingly referring to those whom she met as bumpkins, yet there was nothing crude about the commercial practices she witnessed on her journey through the English colonies of North America. A woman of high rank, she could afford to pay her travel companions in good Spanish silver and perhaps even thought of money *as* silver. But most European colonial settlers had to navigate a more complex monetary landscape in order to participate in markets, one where foreign coins and credit instruments circulated alongside commodity monies and verbal promises. This "Intricate way" of early American monetary practice resists easy description and unsettles what economics textbooks say about money and its history. Its heterogeneity contradicts not only money's purported uniformity, but also the fairytale of its progressive development from barter to coin and then bills. So too, the colonial state's role in designating monetary forms and values belies the myth that money is natural, an organic byproduct of "human economy." Lastly, the presence of trust as a mediating factor within colonial American communities, whereby, Knight remarked, the country folk "are constantly almost Indebted" to the merchants, collapses the dichotomy between money and credit, rendering the comparison a distinction without a difference.[2]

Whereas mainstream economics defines money as a set of functions—unit of account, mode of payment, and medium of exchange—*Promise to Pay* considers early American money as a practice and a relationship as much as a thing. It accordingly draws insights not just from historians but also from anthropologists, sociologists, legal scholars, and economists. In his 1930 *Treatise on Money*, the economist John Maynard Keynes offered a historical and sociological explanation of money's origins in ancient Babylonia. Drawing from the rich body of work on money produced by the German historical school around the turn of the century, Keynes argued that states first claimed the right to name the "Money-of-Account" in which debts had to be expressed, before also seizing "the right to declare *what thing* corresponds to the name." He identified this era of monetary history as "the Age of Chartalist or State Money."[3]

Yet straightforward explanations, even unorthodox ones, often fall short in describing complex social phenomena, most of all money. For indeed, the most salient feature of early American monetary practice was its multiplicity. English (British after 1707) colonial governments borrowed gold or silver specie (coin) from wealthy individuals or issued paper currencies known as "bills of public credit" receivable for local taxes. European settlers tendered and accepted wampum, corn, wheat, tobacco, and sugar denominated in pounds (£), shillings (s), and pence (d). A handshake and verbal IOU typically sufficed among family and friends, as households maintained running tallies of their credits and debits with other households over months or even years, a practice historians once called "bookkeeping barter."[4] Some monies were official, others informal; some interregional, others local. And while colonial governments designated the standard money of account within the territories they claimed, gave physical monies authenticity by making them legal tender for taxes and debts, and in some cases even made their own money, not all of it was "State Money."

Money as Trust

A growing body of research on money and finance in the nineteenth-century United States, together with the broadly interdisciplinary literature on money, debt, and credit in early modern England, has in the past few decades transformed historians' understanding of money in the Anglophone world from a frictionless medium produced by a disembodied market to a constitutional project made by societies and states.[5] Increased public scrutiny of how and under what conditions governments make money arising from the student debt crisis, COVID-19 relief, and soaring military outlays—all in the face of a worsening climate emergency—has more recently been the context of greater scholarly interest in the local paper currencies that financed imperial wars and shaped local economies in colonial North America. Not content to take money for granted as an impersonal instrument for facilitating the exchange of goods, epiphenomenal to productive processes and indifferent to human relations, early American historians instead depict colonial currency as "a cultural signifier of oppression or liberation," as "a powerful policy tool and political weapon," and as "a technology of imperial formation," to quote three studies from 2021.[6] Eschewing orthodox conceptions of money for unconventional framings offered by social scientists, these historians are now rightly situating paper money in networks of power and the social relations of debt, as they interrogate the extent to which early American money reduced moral obligations to monetary calculations.[7]

Promise to Pay contributes to this scholarship on the history of money by emphasizing the constellation of promises that made up early American monetary practice and within which an array of power and exchange relations proliferated. The notion that money is simply debt (and therefore credit) is not a particularly new one. Writing in 1914, the economist and credit theorist Alfred Mitchell Innes pointed out that all money—even the almighty dollar—is just debt, "a promise to 'pay,' a promise to 'satisfy,' a promise to 'redeem.'"[8] As the sociologist of money Geoffrey Ingham put it more recently, "the *origin* of the power of money [lies] in the promise between the issuer and the user of money—that is, in the issuer's self-declared debt."[9]

English colonial settlers in North America had their own name for this promise: "publick faith." In seventeenth-century England, *public faith* referred to the king's duty to protect the weight and fineness of the precious metal coinage. Colonists who invoked public faith, however, were describing the trust between colonial governments and their constituents that gave paper bills their value in exchange. "For those who take the Bills in the Circulation of them, have the Publick Faith to rest upon, and the Authority of the

Government," a popular minister declared in 1721.[10] "The *Bills* have a twofold Promise: An *explicit* Promise on the Face of them . . . *That the Government will receive them in all publick Payments*" as well as "an *implicit* Promise founded in the *common Consent* of the Colonies where they pass," a paper money advocate reiterated in 1740.[11] Separated by a generation, these authors did not subscribe to the liberal illusion then emerging in Britain of money arising through the market, the purview of private wealth creators, whose value in the economy derived from the value of its commodity content. Nor did they describe it as a product of magisterial fiat. In their telling, paper bills embodied a mutual agreement between the government, which pledged to receive the bills in payment of taxation, and the governed, who gave their mutual consent to take as money what was payable as taxes.

Yet even when a state imposes money through the fiscal process, the coercion of this process is not always enough to enforce its value in exchange. Drawing on anthropology, "heterodox" economists are now emphasizing the role of social trust in making money meaningful.[12] Thus for economists Michel Aglietta and André Orleans, monetary transactions involve multiple registers of confidence, at once hierarchical, habitual, and ethical.[13] Following Aglietta and Orleans, the political scientist Stefan Eich defines money as "an ambivalent project suspended between trust and violence."[14] Writing of colonial African and Asian monetary systems, furthermore, the historian Akinobu Kuroda observes that money's acceptability in markets derived more from "a shared recognition among dealers along a trade circuit of an item as money" than from "any enforcement by the authorities," demonstrating that "money works as a social circuit connecting transaction demand."[15] Seen in this light, money is about more than a state's relations with individual citizens or subjects; as the anthropologist Keith Hart describes, it is "an expression of trust between individuals in a society . . . residing in both personal responsibility and the shared memory of communities."[16] This description applies well to the early American context, where people's trust in money pivoted not only on what they thought of its validity, but also on their judgments of the people who offered it, making the monetary process as much about social interactions and relationships as about the faith placed in the authority of the issuer.

As the classical image of money as a "neutral veil" persists in the historical imagination, however, so the interplay between early American money and systems of domination has eluded some historians.[17] While nineteenth-century US historians have carefully demonstrated the links between chattel slavery and finance, similar connections in the colonial era are just beginning to be drawn.[18] Historians of early American and Atlantic economies have recently shown how marginalized persons participated in the growing world of trade, markets, and money against powerful odds.[19] But with some notable exceptions, current historians tend to avoid the conflicts between farmers and merchants, sailors and captains, tenants and landlords, and enslaved people and enslavers that animated New Left and Neo-Progressive histories and shaped early America "from the bottom up."[20] Historians of the Atlantic world and racial capitalism, inspired by the Black radical tradition, meanwhile, have interrogated the relationship between new ideas about money and value, on the one hand, and emerging hierarchies of difference, on the other, reading with and against the grain of the colonial archive to unearth the stories of enslaved men and women, and how they responded to the economic changes happening around them.[21] Another vein of scholarship, using the tools of literary criticism, has focused on money's relation to language and an emerging public sphere as well as the changing conceptions of economic and moral value money signified, while political and intellectual histories have situated early American currency in the crosshairs of rival European empires and clashing colonial factions.[22]

More so than historians of political economy, economic historians have long been interested in colonial currency and the phenomenon of inflation, engrossed in either upholding or debunking the "quantity theory of money" in early American history.[23] Since the late nineteenth century, economists and historians alike have pointed to British North America as an exemplar of how the overissue of currency leads to inflation, despite there being no statistical link between the quantity of paper money and prices in early America.[24] *Promise to Pay* corrects this misconception by restoring to the history currency depreciation and the inflation that occasionally accompanied it. Colonial economies were far more likely to suffer from deflation than inflation, but when and where prices rose, contemporaries often linked it to war and violence: the fiscal policies local assemblies implemented to mobilize armies or, as in early eighteenth-century South Carolina, poor military outlooks and outcomes.[25] In other instances, commentators blamed depreciation on a colony's worsening balance of trade and payments with Britain—its merchants were importing more than they were exporting—which raised the sterling exchange rate (the expression in colonial pounds of £100 sterling) and diminished the local currency's value in turn.[26] In New England, some colonists linked depreciation and inflation to money scarcity and the marketing practices of greedy merchants, from engrossing goods to price gouging to predatory lending. People living at the time attributed depreciation and inflation more to the conscious decisions of political and individual actors than to the "natural laws" of economics, a discipline (and with it, for that matter, an obsession with inflation) that had yet to fully emerge.[27]

While not a conventional economic or business history, this study explores the role of money in mediating exchange, shaping markets, and distributing value on the cusp of a commercial world in flux, an early capitalist system that relied on both personal reputation and financial credit in order to establish and assess trustworthiness—a colonial capitalism that commodified and "coined" Indigenous homelands and African captives as it reified traditional European hierarchies based on deference and obligation.[28] As English colonial society grew in size and complexity, what people understood as giving money its worth did not so much evolve as multiply: the commodity content of a Spanish piece of eight, the stamp on the face of a pine tree shilling, the fiscal pledge accompanying the first bills of public credit, the real estate mortgage that secured money borrowed from a colonial loan office or land bank. Doubtless the images on paper currency—from colonial seals and nature prints of leaves to representations of navigation and agriculture—had a naturalizing effect, giving holders the impression that value inhered in the money itself rather than in the political process that underwrote it. For some Atlantic merchants, money was the equivalent of property—a form of wealth in and of itself—and thus debts contracted in British sterling ought to be protected by law from the depreciation of local currencies. But notions of ownership over money were far from absolute. Anthropologists Keith Hart and David Graeber identified a fundamental tension at the heart of both historical and modern money—between money as a social relation and money as a commodity—and colonial currency is no exception.[29] The increasing multiplicity and malleability of early American money and its meaning over time complicates the grand narrative of money's linear development from socially embedded "primitive money" to commodity coin to market-driven credit, even as it offers a window onto a society careening, if not always headfirst, toward capitalist transformation.

The study of money offers a new approach to early American history. Drawing on the pioneering work of sociologist Viviana Zelizer, *Promise to Pay* considers money as socially created, "subject to particular networks of social relations and its own set of values and norms."[30] While paper money expressed the reciprocal promise between colonial governments and their constituents known as public faith, informal and extralegal currencies reflected long-established customs and newly emerging practices alike. If book credit represented the mutual trust between neighbors, payment in kind harked back to traditional labor relations based on dependency and duty. A counterfeit bill of public credit depended as much on the reputation of the authentic bill as on that of the person who passed it. In Virginia, warehouse receipts for tobacco grown by enslaved African laborers circulated as currency, engendering a monocrop culture and reinforcing what the historian T. H. Breen identified as a "tobacco mentality."[31] Gifts to and from Indigenous peoples in the form of wampum shell beads, guns and powder, and fur pelts were no less money than the supposedly universal precious metal coins and the bills of exchange—the main financial instruments colonists used to settle debts in Britain, analogous to modern checks—that crossed transatlantic trade routes and crisscrossed European empires. But this did not mean that Native and European people had a common understanding of either gifts or money, or that either group viewed objects such as wampum in strictly monetary terms.[32] As one scholar has written in a different context, colonial monetary systems "encompassed the coexistence . . . of multiple currencies circulating in different circuits and performing different functions . . . the result of convergence of different systems of value and monetary practices."[33] A look at cross-cultural currencies illuminates the links among peoples with radically different systems of value, linkages that helped shape the social and political landscape of early America.

Early American money involved an array of currencies and monies of account that different groups and individuals marked for various purposes, not all of them strictly economic, from giving a gift to hiring laborers to paying a debt.[34] While a Boston shop note could only be redeemed for local store goods, Georgia "Lighthouse Certificates" and Pennsylvania "Bettering House Money," both issued by the colonies' assemblies in 1769, were allocated for rebuilding the lighthouse on Tybee Island and for maintaining the Philadelphia poor, respectively.[35] Crees and Ojibwes used a standard money of account, the "Made Beaver," when they purchased goods from the Hudson's Bay Company, and Illinois Country traders kept accounts in both "Peltry" and French livres until 1760, when the British government declared that the denomination of the livre tournois be abolished and replaced by the New York pound.[36] In the mid-Atlantic, Lenapes accepted silver ornaments from colonial governments and European traders in exchange for fur.[37] For free and enslaved Black people living in New York City, meanwhile, secondhand clothing was a valuable currency in its own right that could be pawned in the informal economy or sold for gold and silver specie.[38] Cash, whether metal or paper, was a lifeline for those who struggled to create claims to credit owing to legal or marital status or to poverty, reflecting how nascent systems of race, gender, and class structured access to certain forms of money.[39] Both within and among early American cultures, monetary practice deviated from the emerging principles of European political economy.

Metal coins and paper bills formed but part of a semiotic system in which cash, credit, and commodities combined to supply the total amount of money in British North America. Connecting them all was the money of account. For indeed, to overstress the "'money-stuff' of actual media of exchange," Geoffrey Ingham maintains, would be to miss "the central importance of money of account."[40] In the English colonies, where reasonably priced coins were often scarce and the expansion of trade and markets outpaced the growth of the paper money supply, interpersonal book credit was the crux of all exchange. The money of account—the currency written on the pages of personal account books and merchant ledgers rather than circulating in space—was just as essential to early American monetary practice as money in its physical forms.[41] Contemporaries sometimes referred to the money of account as the "ideal" or "imaginary" money, the language in which the relative values of goods and services was expressed. Britain had the pound sterling, France the livre tournois, Holland the gulden (or guilder), and the like. The colonies, too, denominated foreign coins, export commodities, public debts, and paper bills in their own pound-based monies of account: Massachusetts pound, Pennsylvania pound, South Carolina pound, and so on, each of which was allowed to "float" (fluctuate freely in value) according to supply and demand relative to the supply and demand for the metropole's sterling. Local, colonial, and imperial monies therefore coexisted in a complementary rather than a substitutive relationship, whereby floating currencies provided colonists with "a flexible means of exchange in transactions between the end-users."[42] For colonial settlers, the money of account offered a shared grammar for buying, selling, borrowing, and lending—whether or not any "money-stuff" changed hands.

A Revolutionary Currency

Melding the "chartalist" conception of money as a creature of states with anthropologists' and sociologists' understanding of money as a social phenomenon, *Promise to Pay* analyzes the complex interplay between money, politics, and power in the English colonies of early America. It does so by focusing primarily, though not exclusively, on the colonial paper monies known as bills of public credit (or simply bills of credit), their early use as a means of war finance, and their apotheosis as state monies whose acceptability in markets stemmed from the power of the purse—the power to tax and spend—of colonial legislative assemblies. Their development was a critical part of the process of colonization in eastern North America over the half-century from 1690 to 1740, the so-called era of salutary neglect when Britain left the colonies to their own devices.

The very concept of money—what constituted it and who authorized it—played a critical ideological role in the rationale and justification for early modern colonization itself. For the seventeenth-century English philosopher John Locke, the creation of property in land, the invention of money, and the establishment of laws formed the basis of all civil government. Yet "there are still *great tracts of ground* to be found" in America, held Locke, "which (the inhabitants thereof not having joined with the rest of mankind, in the consent of the use of their common money) *lie waste*, and are more than the people who dwell on it do, or can make use of, and so still lie in common; though this can scarce happen amongst that part of mankind that have consented to the use of money," that is, gold and silver. Well aware that Indigenous people had their own forms of money (elsewhere he contrasted "the wampompeke of the *Americans*" with "the silver money of *Europe*"), Locke submitted that only English colonists with their precious metal coin could appropriate land beyond that which their labor turned into property, including the vast acres of "waste" land that Indigenous people inhabited in common. While gold and silver money gave Englishmen a right to enlarge their possessions beyond what they needed for their subsistence, the argument went, Native people's supposedly inferior currencies limited their claims to land to relatively small parcels.[43]

Far from the halls of English imperial power, colonial governments flouted Locke's pronouncements when they deployed paper bills instead of precious metal as a key tool of territorial expansion. The conflict of imperial policy and colonial practice is accordingly an essential thread in the story that follows, but this does not mean that the British government necessarily or always opposed colonists' monetary heterodoxy. On the contrary, the central argument put forth in favor of paper money was a mercantilist and imperial one: colonial traders received plenty of gold and silver coins through trade with other countries and colonies, as it happened, but quickly diverted whatever specie arrived on North American shores to Britain in order to pay colonial debts or to purchase British goods. Paper currency was an "inside money," a vernacular medium for financing colonial wars and promoting local trade, and, according to its proponents, a tool for economic development that ultimately benefited the metropole.[44] The spread of paper and its circulation as money in the colonies may itself be seen as an extension of the "regime of inscription" then transforming British knowledge production and political life.[45] The British Board of Trade—a committee of the Privy Council that advised the Crown on imperial trade policy and acted as an intermediary between colonial officials and British merchants—approved of paper money as long as it served Atlantic commerce and facilitated the colonial wars fought to protect it.[46] By eschewing gold and silver for paper, the Scottish philosopher Adam Smith wrote in 1776, America had been able to increase "its wealth, the exchangeable value of the annual produce of its lands and labor," in turn facilitating "the trade which they carried on with Great Britain."[47] For a time, commentators on both sides of the Atlantic saw paper currency as the key to early American and, by extension, British prosperity.

What some Britons and a growing number of colonial elites opposed was how paper bills complicated ascendant British notions of money as fixed and universal. Certainly, British Members of Parliament (MPs) were cognizant of paper money's distributive effects by 1739, when, concerned by the growing cry of creditors on both sides of the Atlantic for the protection of sterling debts against the depreciation of local currencies, the House of Commons launched a decade-long inquiry into the colonial currencies. Advocates of imperial monetary reform got a boost during the War of Jenkins' Ear and War of the Austrian Succession (1739–48) and again during the Seven Years' War (1754–63), when the increased presence of British officers, troops, and resources in North America revealed the extent to which the colonial currencies fluctuated, both in terms of sterling and relative to each other, and the confusion that arose in paying provincial soldiers because of the fluctuation. In this context, imperial reformers proposed placing all of the colonial paper monies on a single standard of value "pegged," or fixed by law, against sterling, "which, 'tis hoped," the Philadelphia printer Benjamin Franklin wrote in 1741, "would effectually remove the Prejudices which the Merchants in *England* seem to have conceived against a Paper Currency in the Colonies."[48] Parliament went beyond the proposed reform when it passed the Currency Acts of 1751 and 1764 restricting the colonies' bills of credit. Together with the more famous Stamp Act of 1765, the Currency Acts embodied the liberal archetype of imperial political economy in which money was silver, creditors' rights were sacrosanct, and private interests combined to amount to the interest of the empire. They played no small part in the economic and constitutional crises that roiled the colonies in the 1760s and 1770s.[49]

In contrast to Britain, where the Bank of England's establishment in 1694 and John Locke's "Great Recoinage" in 1696 appeared to place the production of money outside of politics by dispersing it to numerous private agents and by redefining money as trader's silver, in early America colonial assemblies made and managed money in public view, crafting it for local circulation and tying it to provincial taxes. As a "mode of governance," the legal scholar and historian of money Christine Desan powerfully argues, the assemblies used paper currency to assert authority and cultivated a shared identity around a common set of terms, symbols, and ideas in the process. No idea was more persistent than the notion that the "liberty" of making money and the authority to spend that money were constitutive of the assemblies' power to tax, indeed of common consent to taxation as enshrined in the Magna Carta and English common law.[50] The Second Continental Congress drew on this shared identity when, in May 1775, it authorized the first Continental Currency of the United Colonies to pay the initial costs of the American Revolutionary War (1775–83). While this book is not a study of the causes and course of the American Revolution, its findings may provide some of the answers long sought by historians of the revolutionary era. Rather than viewing the colonial period of the United States as the prologue to a national history, this book considers it on its own terms and from the perspectives of those living at the time.[51]

In doing so, *Promise to Pay* scrutinizes a period that historians of American capitalism have long overlooked. A previous generation of social historians, influenced by the nineteenth-century philosopher and economist Karl Marx and the historian E. P. Thompson, dated the "transition to capitalism" from at least the early nineteenth century, in part because they deemed early American farmers insufficiently profit-oriented, but also because they assumed that colonial America lacked a "commodity form" of money.[52] Conceived as credit as much as a commodity, money provides a window into the overlooked legal and economic changes of the colonial era that created the conditions for capitalist transformation in the late eighteenth and early nineteenth centuries, changes predicated on the political and historical process that Marx identified as "the so-called primitive accumulation." Through laws and customs legitimating the colonization of Native land and the enslavement of African people and through culturally specific appeals to the "intrinsic" value of land and labor, colonial governments and individual actors alike engendered the capitalist transition in eastern North America.[53] Interdisciplinary scholarship has recently shown that the practice of offering property in expropriated lands and enslaved human beings as collateral for credit was well under way by the end of the seventeenth century. Before money's transformation into capital, the end of exchange rather than its means, European colonial settlers turned valuable capital assets into money, making stolen land and stolen lives liquid in order to purchase more land and people, capital and labor that transformed a continent.[54]

Money and Belonging

While money has tended to reproduce hierarchies of power, it has also unsettled and reconfigured them. *Promise to Pay* argues that early American money formed a terrain of contestation over the nature of value, the distribution of resources, and the terms of public belonging. Every society must justify what space it governs, who belongs to the community it constitutes, and how it structures its relations with other communities.[55] Like the legal order from which it emerged, colonial currency helped delineate "the borders of belonging," to borrow from the legal historian Barbara Young Welke.[56] Just as much as laws, maps, and deeds, bills of credit extended colonial claims to territory and articulated authority over growing settler populations. As claims on an imagined "public," the bills apportioned shares of membership in the body politic, and not everyone was invited to join. Most of the claimants were men and women of European lineage who ranged in status from soldiers and war widows to colonial judges and even royal governors, but bills could also be passed to more marginal members of society, counterfeited, or stolen.

A paradox of early American money—whether in the form of book credit or in its more physical manifestation as metal coins or paper money—was that it simultaneously aggrandized and democratized. European and Native, rich and poor, free and enslaved people all deployed money to their own ends, even as the ubiquity of transactions using the standard money of account reinforced colonial authority over market relations. But colonial monetary regimes were not imposed, unchallenged, from above. Power struggles between colonial authorities and imperial administrators over monetary standards, Indigenous monetary practices and resistance to colonial incursions, conflicts within settler communities over access to money and credit, and the persistence of customary modes of exchange all informed currency practices, revealing that colonial monetization was, as in other colonial contexts, a nuanced and complex process characterized by combinations and collisions of different systems of value rather than a swift and smooth transition.[57]

The chapters that follow, then, offer a treatment of money, variously construed, as fundamental to the politics of day-to-day life. Like money itself, colonial households were sites of struggle over value, resources, and belonging between husbands and wives, fathers and sons, and masters and servants. The enslaved likewise encountered struggles over money and value, in ways both similar and singular. Although their participation in the economy was violently circumscribed by dependence and obligation, enslaved people nevertheless earned wages and owned property, negotiating exchange relations within and outside the household and creating social ties that seemed contradictory to many colonial settlers. Sarah Knight confronted such a contradiction on her journey through rural Connecticut, having heard the story of a local farmer who had failed to make good on a promise to a man he held in bondage. The enslaved man took the matter to a judge, Knight recounted, who ordered the farmer to pay forty shillings to the man and admit his fault. Knight thought that New England farmers were "too Indulgent . . . to their slaves," but stopped short of wondering what the money might have meant to the enslaved person, himself property with a price, or, more threatening still, how he might have used it.[58]

Money was central to the formation and development of colonial spaces and the conflicts that arose within them. If colonial governments used paper money to articulate a shared set of values and norms, debates over monetary and fiscal policy reveal fissures within colonial society over what money was, who should have it, and to what end. How people discussed money in the public sphere is therefore a recurrent theme in this book. The topic of paper money dominated legislative sessions, instigated disputes between governors and assemblies, and drove perhaps hundreds of petitions and protests on both sides of the British Atlantic. Of the countless schemes for a medium of exchange in early America, the most intriguing are those that charted alternate courses of development that were never fully realized. Alternatives always abounded. An examination of the commentary reveals that proponents of paper money envisioned it as a tool for managing and administering the eighteenth century's major social and economic changes—the expansion of chattel slavery, the shift to commodity production, the transformation of labor relations, and the consumer revolution—and thus, to return to Keynes, as "a subtle device for linking the present to the future."[59] Opponents of paper bills foresaw the future as well, only they warned of the potential detrimental consequences of too much colonial currency and public debt on private contracts and public trust, and advocated a "return" to a metallic monetary standard that had never really existed. Accordingly, policy debates evoked competing notions of dependency and obligation, as ordinary colonists worked out what it might mean to sell their produce for a bill of credit instead of a shop note, to borrow money from a loan office instead of a wealthy merchant, or to have a recurring claim on the public purse for a wartime disability. At stake was not simply the material or immaterial of money, but the terms of the social, political, and economic relationships it embodied and expressed.

This book returns money to history and history to money. It is a history of early American money as experienced by its users and a history of early Americans as seen through the lens of their money. It resists the temptation to provide a transhistorical theory or any general principles of money, while recognizing that people living at the time sometimes sought to do just that. Instead, it sees early America as a place where different systems of money and value competed for dominance, and those systems reflected contradictory models of resource distribution and political belonging. Promises to pay were made, broken, and reconfigured along the way, conditioned, as all money is, by the fluid dynamics of politics and power.

1

From Coin to Currency

On May 14, 1692, the Puritan minister Increase Mather and the former privateer William Phips arrived in Boston bearing a royal charter for the "Province of the Massachusetts Bay." The new charter, a compromise between the original 1629 Massachusetts Bay Company charter and the Dominion of New England government in power from 1686 to 1689, gave Massachusetts colonists the same rights and privileges as freeborn Englishmen, including that most cherished right of common consent to taxation. Instead of a General Court controlled by church members, the royal charter provided for an assembly of representatives elected by freemen with the power to make laws "for the good and welfare of the province," provided the laws were not repugnant to those of England. Most importantly, the charter authorized the assembly "to Impose and leavy proportionable and reasonable Assessments Rates and Taxes . . . for Our service in the necessary defence and support of our Government of our said Province or Territory and the Protection and Preservation of the Inhabitants there."[1]

The Massachusetts assembly so cherished the power to tax because the power to tax was the source of the power to make money. Taxing and money creation led to numerous other privileges, from the exclusive right to frame money bills and the discretion to examine and audit the public accounts, to control over the appropriation of public funds and the authority to order money from the treasury.[2]

This chapter examines the role that tax redemption mechanisms played in anchoring early American monetary regimes, with an emphasis on America's first paper money: the Massachusetts bills of credit of 1690. In doing so, it troubles orthodox conceptions of money as market-borne. Building on the earlier insights of both chartalism and Keynesianism, mid-twentieth-century "heterodox" economists argued that a modern state can designate anything it chooses as money if it is "willing to accept the proposed money in payment

FROM COIN TO CURRENCY 15

of taxes and other obligations." Everyone owing taxes to the state would be willing to sell goods and labor for said money up to the amount they owe, while everyone else would be willing to accept it with the knowledge that taxpayers will take it in due course.[3] This description bears comparison with English North America, where colonial governments sought to authenticate new forms of money by promising to accept them in payment of taxes, duties, and fees.

Although the Massachusetts experience did not portend modern fiat currencies, neither did it emulate the "financial revolution" then happening across the Atlantic. This chapter considers America's first paper money on its own terms, on the terms of those who used it. The imposition of paper bills was not quick and did not go unchallenged. It was an extended and fraught process made possible by changing economic and political contexts, the colonial government's coordination with local elites, and its cooptation of existing social relationships based on dependency and obligation.

The Money Name and the Money Thing

In his 1930 *Treatise on Money*, the economist John Maynard Keynes suggested that the fundamental building block of ancient monetary systems was the "Money-of-Account," the shared language "in which Debts and Prices and General Purchasing Power are *expressed*." Leaders or ruling bodies first claimed the right to name the money of account in which debts were to be made and settled. Only subsequently did they also seize "the right to declare *what thing* corresponds to the name." The authorities made "Money-Proper" when they put an official value in terms of the money of account (in this case the silver shekel) on the thing (namely, barley) in which subjects were to pay taxes and tribute. Actual coinage came thousands of years later.[4]

A similar observation holds true for English North America, where each colony established a standard money of account, based on but invariably worth less than the English pound sterling, for calculating taxes and debts and keeping track of resources. Massachusetts had the Massachusetts pound, South Carolina the South Carolina pound, and so forth. European settlers referred to the local money of account as currency or current money to differentiate it from other colonies' currencies and from sterling, such as Massachusetts currency or the current money of South Carolina. Along with naming the money of account, colonial governments assigned legal values to locally produced crops for the payment of taxes, known as commodity money. In certain cases, the crops were made legal tender for debts as well. They treated foreign coins the same.[5]

In every colony, the physical money supply involved a wide array of agricultural products grown—willingly or otherwise—by the inhabitants. In 1619, the Virginia House of Burgesses set the value of tobacco at three (Virginia) shillings per pound for the best grade and eighteen shillings per pound for the lower grade.[6] Bermuda, Maryland, and North Carolina followed suit. Later, Virginia colonists would pass tobacco notes—warehouse certificates that inspectors issued to planters when their crop passed inspection.[7] In the 1640s, the Massachusetts General Court published the standard values of farm products, fixing the value of wheat at four shillings per bushel, rye and peas at three shillings fourpence, and corn at two shillings sixpence.[8] Sugar cultivated by enslaved African laborers was legal tender for debts in the Leeward Islands, where "good, dry well-cured merchantable Muscovado Sugar" passed at twelve shillings sixpence per hundred pounds from 1670 to 1700.[9] A Connecticut farmer could pay his taxes for the year 1709 "in Port at Fifty Shillings per. Barrel, or Beef at Thirty Shillings per Barrel, Winter Wheat at Four Shillings per Bushel, Rye at Two Shillings and Four pence per Bushel, and Indian Corn at Two Shillings per Bushel."[10] Across English North America, colonial treasuries accepted animal skins, barley, corn, wheat, peas, tobacco, dried fish, shells, livestock, cheese, milk, tobacco, sugar, molasses, rum, cotton, wool, timber, musket balls, nails, rice, or indigo in public payments. Colonial legislative assemblies regularly revised produce and coin values to manipulate the money supply or reflect market conditions.[11] Although money did not yet grow on trees, at this time it did in fact grow.

The wampum trade deserves special mention. From the moment Dutch colonizers first arrived on the mid-Atlantic coast, Dutch, English, and French traders had exchanged European kettles, pipes, knives, and other manufactured goods for wampum, tiny white and purple beads that coastal Algonquian peoples crafted from clam and whelk shells. The Europeans would sell the beads to visiting Haudenosaunees in exchange for furs that they would then ship across the Atlantic. The ships would return with goods that Native traders prized, and the process would repeat. Among Native peoples, however, wampum had long signified high status. It was given in marriage dowries, buried with the dead, and used to form alliances or retrieve captives. But as wampum became the standard trade currency of northeastern North America between and among European and Indigenous people, its exchange value secured not only by Haudenosaunee demand but by the steady value of beaver in Europe, Native people were swept up in a consumer revolution. They began using European tools to increase production of the beads, hunting animals for the sale value of their skins, and growing surplus corn to sell to colonial settlers. Wampum now had symbolic value and purchasing

FIGURE 1.1. String of purple wampum clam shell (quahog) beads, 1600–1775. 1922.21.1. Courtesy American Numismatic Society. http://numismatics.org/collection/1922.21.1.

power—prerequisites for money—and both European and Indigenous leaders competed to control its flow.[12]

Over time, intensifying European demand for wampum fostered Native dependence on European traders, weakening Native traders' economic position and, in turn, shifting power relations between and within Indigenous societies. But growing European competition placed the Pequot of present-day Connecticut in a position to monopolize the wampum trade. Against this backdrop, English settlers used Native retaliation against colonial encroachment as political cover for punishing the Pequots and extorting wampum payments. Then in 1637, just after the New England colonies fixed the value of wampum at three beads per penny and began accepting it in payment of taxes—effectively making it money—the colonies declared war on the mint masters. Within months, the English had massacred or driven from their homes 1,500 men, women, and children. The conquest of the Pequot and Europeans' exaction of shell beads from other Indigenous societies sent wampum's value soaring to six beads per penny. By 1645, wampum was circulating in all of the New England colonies, plus New York, Pennsylvania, and New Jersey. And from the 1630s to 1664, New England colonists extorted wampum payments amounting to more than £5,000 sterling. These payments, acquired through the threat of violence rather than with European goods, not only enabled Massachusetts merchants to satisfy their English creditors and start making profits, but also facilitated the inflow of gold and silver coins that the colony would later meld into its own money.[13]

As Native lands replaced Native wampum as the principal means of colonial expansion, however, Massachusetts demoted the monetary status of the shell beads. European colonists, no longer obliged to accommodate Indigenous currencies and customs, sought to discredit wampum as money, to relegate it to a mythical land of truck and barter, and thus to deny their dependence on Native peoples and currencies during the early years of colonization.[14] By defining money as gold and silver, the colonists endeavored to become their own mint masters. Massachusetts would subsequently become the first English colony to produce its own money, first in the form of commodity coin and then as fiscal currency. In both cases the colony's creation of money arose out of specific geopolitical conditions in the English Atlantic world: the English Civil War (1642–51), and later the Glorious Revolution of 1688. Yet even as coin and currency came to serve as English settlers' primary means of paying taxes and debts, the finite supply of physical money and the intimate nature of trade relations meant that they would continue to make most of their day-to-day transactions on book credit, with agricultural products, and even with wampum.[15] A heterogeneous monetary landscape in which multiple monies coexisted in a complementary relationship was the result.

Taxation and Tax Collection in the Dominion of New England

Governor Edmund Andros arrived in Boston on December 20, 1686, to assume the reins of power over the Dominion of New England, the newly formed administrative territory that stretched from Maine to New Jersey. The Dominion's establishment marked the latest phase of a twenty-five-year campaign by the English king Charles II and his successor, James II, to regulate colonial trade. The explosion of smuggling between New England and Spanish and Dutch merchants, along with New England's growing prosperity, had convinced Charles II and the Lords of Trade that to profit from American commerce, they needed to streamline colonial administration. This meant eliminating the colonial assemblies and, if necessary, revoking the colonies' original charters. Responsibility for colonial governance would then fall to Andros, who had previously overseen the transition of the province of New York from Dutch to English rule.

For the Massachusetts Bay Colony, whose original 1629 charter had been annulled two years before, Andros's arrival carried the threat of not just unwanted regulation of the colony's trade but also a fundamental reorganization of its internal economy. In the summer of 1686, the Dominion government established a new vice-admiralty court in Boston to enforce the Navigation Acts and collect the accompanying taxes and duties. These acts aimed to increase economic benefits for the English state and English merchants by directing colonial merchants to ship goods using only English ships manned by English crews and by requiring "enumerated" commodities, such as tobacco and sugar, to be shipped directly to England. At the same time, the acts intended to limit the northern colonies' access to non-English European goods by permitting them to import commodities only from England or other English colonies. Massachusetts's failure to take the acts seriously, even as its merchants benefited from the elimination of Dutch economic competition, was high on the list of reasons for the revocation of the colony's charter.[16]

The next order of business was taxes. The Crown authorized Governor Andros to "impose and assess and raise and levy such rates and taxes, as you shall find necessary for the support of the Government," and "to continue such taxes and impositions as are now laid and imposed upon the inhabitants."[17] Taxes remained payable in foreign coins or in commodity money including wheat, barley, rye, peas, corn, and oats at set ratios to pounds sterling. Andros kept the property tax at a penny per pound but raised taxes on cattle and horses. He also doubled the duty on wine, increased the excise, and tried, but failed, to impose royal quitrents. The tax burden was significantly lower than it had been during King Philip's War (1675-76; or Metacom's War, after the Wampanoag sachem who defied colonial incursions), when the property tax soared to thirty-five pence per pound and all taxes had to be paid in specie.[18] Nevertheless, when Andros announced the taxes in the spring of 1687, several towns in Essex County claimed that the taxes infringed on their liberties as Englishmen and refused to appoint commissioners to assess and collect the money.

One of the towns was Ipswich, thirty miles northeast of Boston, where the local minister, John Wise, led a tax revolt the following September on behalf of his community of small farmers, shopkeepers, and fishermen. The son of an indentured servant, Wise graduated from Harvard College in 1673 and became the pastor of Chebacco Parish, a position he would hold until his death in 1725. Wise rejected the consolidation of royal property and power that Andros's appearance in the colony portended. At a more basic level, his revolt was about the principle, enshrined in the Magna Carta and English common law, that taxes could not be levied without the consent of those taxed. The Dominion government had usurped the assemblies of the colonies it had absorbed, but it was by those assemblies that colonists had agreed to be taxed. Wise argued that the right of freeborn Englishmen to be taxed by their own representatives extended to English subjects in North America and could not be abrogated by a governor. The Dominion retorted that colonists had left their rights as Englishmen behind when they left England. As one official bluntly stated, the colonists had "no more priviledges left them" but to not be "bought and sold for slaves."[19] Andros arrested Wise and other town selectmen who had participated in the revolt on charges of high misdemeanor and held them in the Boston jail without habeas corpus. They were eventually released, but not before Andros slapped them with hefty fines and banned them from holding any office.[20]

Popular resistance to Andros's taxes was about more than just "taxation without representation." It was a response to the money scarcity that the taxes brought to the fore. Shortly before Andros's arrival, the Dominion of New England council had remarked on "the great decay of trade, obstructions to manufactures and commerce in this Country, and multiplicity of debts and suits thereupon, principally occasioned by scarcity of coyne."[21] Massachusetts colonists had been complaining about a dearth of gold and silver specie since at least 1669, when it became more profitable for local merchants to send coins abroad than to keep them in the colony. Then Metacom's soldiers destroyed more than half of all the colonial towns, wiped out two generations of capital investment in colonization, and pushed English settlement nearly back to the coast. The war's devastation may well have fast-tracked the revocation of Massachusetts's charter. For the Wampanoag, Narragansett, Nipmuc, and other peoples who resisted English colonialism, the results were more traumatic. While the war cost the New England governments of Massachusetts, Rhode Island, Connecticut, and Plymouth nearly £100,000 sterling, they offset the expense by selling Native captives into Atlantic and Caribbean slavery and using the proceeds to pay soldiers' wages.[22] Hardly a decade later, rumors of a war with the French and the outbreak of hostilities with the Wabanakis of present-day Maine, where some Metacom's War survivors had taken refuge, threatened to stall New England's economic recovery.

In the spring of 1688, it was again time for the New England towns to compile lists of their taxable inhabitants and what they owed. But some towns refused to appoint commissioners to assess property values, while those that did struggled to raise the one shilling eightpence poll tax and penny per pound property tax from the inhabitants.[23] Payments routinely came up short and rarely included specie. Dominion officials expected Boston to contribute £125 to its coffers, but actual collection totaled less than £84.[24]

The Connecticut River Valley towns faced the additional obstacle of shipping their residents' contributory corn down the Connecticut River and around Cape Cod to Boston. "I have done my best to gather the rates ordered unto me," explained a Suffield, Connecticut, constable to the Dominion treasurer, but "it is mostly Indian Corn, I could get little else, the people are very poor and have little else." The constable added, with equal parts frustration and resignation, "I have done as much as I could to [have] it fraighted to Boston by some vessel, but could not as yet, the vessels refuseth the carrying of it. I know not what course to take to get it down to you . . . [but] am endeavouring what I can continually, to get it down with all speed."[25] Another constable paid five pounds out of pocket for transporting the twenty-five pounds' worth of corn he had collected from the people of Springfield, Massachusetts, including two pounds for horses and men "to carry the Corne to the Wharfe" and three pounds "to the Boatmen that boated the corne to Hartford" in Connecticut. Having "truly & honorably disposed of the country corne in my hand," he informed the treasurer, "I would request your Honor to owe me some pay."[26] Perhaps some towns opposed Andros's taxes on constitutional grounds, but more likely the inhabitants simply lacked the means to pay them. Over the decades and across the colonies, groups and individuals would repeat the constables' lament: how could they be expected to pay their taxes when they had no money?

The Rise and Fall of the Boston Mint

In addition to imposing taxes, the Crown charged Governor Andros with enforcing England's 1684 ban on colonial minting. The ban applied to all the English colonies but had been precipitated by the existence of a mint in Boston, established in 1652, that produced pine tree shillings out of the silver plate and Spanish pieces of eight that merchants and pirates brought into Massachusetts. The northern colonies had attracted specie by engaging in what a nineteenth-century historian described as "competitive over-valuation of Spanish silver in terms of sterling."[27] Colonies that "cryed up" (raised the value of) Spanish coins relative to their weight or fineness enjoyed a competitive advantage over colonies that did not raise the value of their coinage. By this means, they drew full-bodied (or heavy) coins that merchants used to pay for imported goods. Ordinary colonists used them to pay local taxes and debts, and to conduct internal trade. By the mid-seventeenth century, however, the colonial coinage had become a hodgepodge of heavy pieces of eight and clipped (or light) coins. While merchants continued to use full-bodied coins to make payments abroad, settlers passed clipped coins at the customary rate of five shillings. In an effort to keep heavy coins inside Massachusetts, the colony raised the value of a full-bodied piece of eight from five shillings to six. But in addition to the large quantity of clipped coins, the 1640s brought news of a scandal at the Potosí mint in Spanish Peru, creating concerns about irregularities in the coinage, outside the colony's control.[28]

English revolutionaries created a political situation that made the Boston Mint possible. In 1642, war broke out in England between Royalists and Parliamentarians. While many settlers in New England were avowed Parliamentarians, Massachusetts colonists were anxious to preserve their charter rights and avoided taking any actions that could later be construed as acknowledging Parliamentary supremacy.[29] Cut off from the metropole, however, New England merchants soon found themselves in dire economic straits. The price of local produce plummeted, and silver money grew scarce. Only after the merchants started doing business in southern Europe, the Atlantic islands, and the Caribbean did their commercial prospects improve and specie return to the colony. In addition to exporting cod, lumber, and ships' stores to Atlantic markets, they began building their own vessels, and shipbuilding and shipping replaced wampum and beaver as the basis of the economy. Before long they were sending provisions and livestock to Barbados and Jamaica plantations in exchange for sugar, molasses, and credits drawn on London merchants. They built distilleries for transforming the molasses into rum and used the credits to pay for English goods.[30] Rather than align itself with either Royalists or Parliamentarians, then, Massachusetts seized the opportunity to expand into the wider Atlantic economy and start acting like a sovereign state—and nothing the colony did came closer to a declaration of statehood than making a circulating coinage.[31]

In May 1652 Massachusetts passed an act for minting its own coins in one shilling, sixpence, and threepence denominations. The coins would be made "of good silver" of the same alloy, or quality, as English money but would be 22.5 percent lighter than English coins, for an exchange rate of £130 colonial money for £100 English money. They would be legal tender for taxes and debts at face value equal to sterling; thus, by law, the coins' value as money would exceed the commodity value of their silver content.[32] Finally, they would be stamped with the letters "NE" on one side and the denomination on the other. The second round of coins—the famous pine tree shillings

FIGURE 1.2 AND FIGURE 1.3. Massachusetts Bay Colony silver pine tree shilling, dated 1652. 1944.94.2. Courtesy American Numismatic Society. http://numismatics.org/collection/1944.94.2.

celebrating the colony's growing shipbuilding industry—would have a double ring around the edge to deter clipping and included a pine tree on one side and the date "1652" on the other.³³

On June 22, the General Court appointed John Hull, a Puritan merchant and silversmith, as mint master and voted to build a "mint howse" on his family's homestead "At the Countries charge."³⁴ According to a recent estimate, Hull would produce an annual average of 55,000 shillings over his thirty-year tenure.³⁵ Investing his 5 percent fee in European commerce, he joined the generation of New England merchants that helped raise Massachusetts's stature in the Atlantic economy. While there is validity to one historian's claim that Hull's career typified the changing relationship between religion and commerce, whereby "puritan legitimizations of civil law and economic expertise as providential mandates [replaced] the corporate discipline of the congregation," such a characterization understates the political economic vision that the mint represented.³⁶

In that vision, the demands of engagement with the expanding Atlantic economy were balanced with the tight-knit commonwealth ideal of Puritan New England. Pine tree shillings advanced both goals while mediating the tensions between them. If most merchants were concerned with the coinage's commercial expediency, Puritan clerics were more interested in its political and religious significance. Either way, Massachusetts colonists now had a trustworthy local currency that was connected, by virtue of its silver content, to the widely circulating gold and silver coins of Mexico, Peru, and

Europe.³⁷ Despite the General Court's efforts to keep the pine tree shillings in the colony, they made their way as far east as the Atlantic islands and the Mediterranean. Such a currency bridged the gap between commodity monies, such as barley and corn, whose cash value derived from the authority of the colonial government, and foreign coins, such as the Spanish piece of eight, the French louis d'or, the Portuguese cruzado, or the German "rix dollar," whose values and availability fluctuated with supply and demand. Unlike either agricultural products or foreign coins, moreover, pine tree shillings symbolized prominent colonists' aspirations for commercial, political, and religious autonomy.³⁸

The Restoration government took more than two decades to suppress the mint. In 1664, a royal commission visited Massachusetts to investigate the colony's alleged disrespect for English laws. The commission declared that coining was a royal prerogative and therefore the mint act was "Contrary & derogatory to the king's authority & Government."³⁹ Charles II summoned Governor Richard Bellingham to London to answer to the charges, but subsequent events—a revolt in Scotland, the Great Fire of London, and war with the Dutch and French—took precedence. The king finally returned his attention to colonial affairs following the Third Anglo-Dutch War (1672–74), sending Edward Randolph to be his eyes and ears in Massachusetts.⁴⁰ The mint figured prominently in Randolph's representations of the colony's rebelliousness. The General Court coined money "as a mark of sovereignty," he described in his report dated October 16, 1676, stamping them with "Massachusetts. and a Tree in ye Center, on the one side, and New England with the year 1652" on the other, "that year being the Era of their Comonwealth, wherein they erected themselves into a free state."⁴¹

Colonial leaders responded strategically, with moderation and supplication. After apologizing for the infraction and denying Randolph's accusations of pretensions to independency, they sought approval for a new mint that would not flout the king's authority, offering to stamp the coins with the royal impress. In doing so, they emphasized the necessity of a uniform coinage for the support of local trade.⁴² The colony had been suffering from a shortage of specie since 1669, when it became more lucrative to export pieces of eight than to bring them to the mint to be made into pine tree shillings. In 1672, the General Court had fixed the value of seventeen pennyweight pieces of eight at six shillings and instructed John Hull to stamp the letters "NE" on Spanish coins "of right alloy and due weight." Specie was so scarce following Metacom's War that the colony had considered "making the mint free." Proponents of free minting, whereby people could bring specie to the mint in return for a slightly lesser amount of metal in the form of coin, argued that it would increase the amount of specie in circulation and so stimulate the local economy.⁴³

Through continued entreaties to the king, the mint operated under colonial authority as late as 1682, when Hull's contract expired.⁴⁴ That year, finding that the recent measures to keep coins in the colony had been ineffective, Massachusetts reduced the price of silver from 84.7 pence per ounce to 80 pence per ounce, lowering the value of a seventeen pennyweight piece of eight from six shillings to five shillings eightpence.⁴⁵ Randolph, not unreasonably, accused the colony's agents of pretending "to begg His Ma[jes]ties pardon" for coining while proceeding to "carry on the Mint."⁴⁶ He later recalled that the colony's practice of "Coining money without his Matyes permission" had been atop the list of reasons "for his Matye to proceed against the Charter," even above its defying the Navigation Acts.⁴⁷ The annulment of the old charter in June 1684 effectively banned the Boston mint by invalidating all the laws associated with it, but that did not stop colonists from petitioning the Crown for its reinstatement for at least another seven years.

But there was a new king after 1685. In February of that year, James II appointed Joseph Dudley as interim president of the Dominion of New England council until Edmund Andros arrived. Dudley, who had served as a colonial agent in London, seized the opportunity to convince Randolph to throw his support behind the mint. A political moderate, Dudley and other landholding and mercantile elites favored accommodation with England in the charter struggle, and they were willing to sacrifice some political and religious autonomy in exchange for favorable commercial policies. Then there were the conservatives, Puritan hardliners such as Increase Mather who opposed compromise with the Stuarts and conspired to have the old charter restored. As interim president, Dudley worked closely with Randolph to establish Boston's vice-admiralty court and introduce Anglicanism to the colony. Dudley persuaded Randolph to support the resumption of coining under royal authority, and they used their connections with imperial officials such as William Blathwayt, Secretary of the Committee for Trade and Foreign Plantations, to try to procure the king's license and impress for establishing a new mint.⁴⁸

Dudley and Randolph put forth an economic rationale for a mint, and Andros happened to agree. In 1686, Andros explained to the Lords of Trade that a mint was necessary to turn "pieces of Eight . . . of unequal weights and value" into "silver moneys to be currant in that Country as the standard and measure of trade [in] all payments."⁴⁹ The chief complaint the royal mint officers had levied against the Boston mint upon inspecting the pine tree shillings was not that the coins themselves usurped royal authority. Rather, it was that they circulated at a lower weight than English shillings of the same alloy.

This had not only transgressed the sovereign prerogative to alter the quality of the coinage, but also drew coins away from the king's other dominions. Should the king decide to permit the reestablishment of the mint under royal authority, the mint officers had advised, the coins should "be made in weight and fineness answerable to his Matys. Silver Coines of England."[50]

Andros responded that the mint had not drawn silver away from England or other colonies. On the contrary, pine tree shillings were "frequently brought into England for want of other returns." New England merchants shipped fish and lumber to Spain and the Caribbean in exchange for sugar and foreign coins that they sent to England to pay for imported goods. Pine tree shillings routinely made up the balance. He warned that bringing the coinage "to the standard of Old England" would "ruyne the Tenant and Debtor, [Destroy] the Trade of that Country and bring no advantage, but loss to the King." A decade before England's "Great Recoinage" of 1696—the calling in of old coins and reminting them at the original standard of weight and fineness—Andros predicted that revaluing, or strengthening, the coinage would sharply reduce the amount of coin in circulation and impoverish those who owed debts in money that was suddenly worth much more than it was when the debts were contracted.[51]

In the end, the Lords of Trade sided with the royal mint officers. As a concession to the New England merchants, they gave Andros the authority to regulate the value of pieces of eight and other foreign coins "for the benefit of Trade & Commerce in those parts."[52] In March 1687 he raised the official silver price to 82.3 pence per ounce, higher than the 80 pence per ounce the General Court had legislated in 1682 but lower than the 1672 value of 84.7 pence per ounce. Andros moreover defined a full-bodied piece of eight as 17.5 pennyweight, a heavier coin than the old 17 pennyweight piece of eight. Knowing that the merchants would set aside most of the specie that came into New England to make returns to the metropole, he accommodated colonists by agreeing to receive their taxes in commodity money, including even pails of milk. Massachusetts agents would renew their solicitations for "the liberty of coinage" after the Glorious Revolution and overthrow of the Dominion of New England government, but the new monarchy would have little interest in sharing the royal prerogative to coin money with the boisterous colony in America.[53]

"Here is a project on foot of passing Bills"

Pine tree shillings and paper money both arose in periods of heightened political instability. In April 1689, following the ousting of James II, a Catholic, by his Protestant daughter Mary and her Dutch husband William of Orange, former Massachusetts magistrates arrested Governor Andros and restored their old government. The magistrates declared their loyalty to the new king and queen, formed themselves into a "Council of Safety," and reappointed Simon Bradstreet as governor. One of Bradstreet's first actions was to dismantle the string of forts and garrisons that Andros had erected in Maine and depose his commanders. New England soldiers deserted their posts on the colonial frontier and returned home, and colonists followed, abandoning entire towns and exposing other English settlements to Wabanaki attacks. News of a war between England and France—the Nine Years' War (1688–97), known as King William's War in North America—arrived soon thereafter. In New England, the Glorious Revolution ushered in a series of English wars with the French that overlapped and intersected with longstanding conflicts both with and among Indigenous peoples.[54]

The royal defenses protecting colonial settlers collapsed following the return of the old government. A reconstituted General Court spent a year trying to raise soldiers and money for the defense of New Hampshire, where Pennacooks fell on Dover in June, and the exposed Maine settlements, including Pemaquid (today Bristol), North Yarmouth, and Falmouth, all targeted in the summer of 1689. But few people volunteered, and most colonists refused to pay taxes—thirty-seven in all in 1689–90, each one more regressive than the last—to a government that went unrecognized in England.[55] As a Boston resident pithily commented, "some questioned their pay, some authority for the press, and few or none went."[56]

In November 1689 alone, the General Court enacted six levies "for the paying of the soldiers, and other public charges, that have arisen since the Revolution by reason of the War."[57] A Dominion of New England loyalist, Benjamin Bullivant, wrote in his diary that the taxes were "hardly dijested by the people" and "many went to prison for refusall" to pay, while Samuel Farlow of Billerica, Massachusetts, for his part, declared that the provisional government was illegitimate and threatened to shoot any constable who tried to collect his taxes, proclaiming that "the Curse of God had followed us ever since they took sir Edmond down and that the Government was not worthy to kiss sir Edmond's arse."[58] Farlow was hardly the only colonist who missed Andros. The following spring, Andros's old soldiers were on the verge of mutiny, gathering in the streets of Boston and "crying out, God blesse King William, God blesse Sir Ed. Andros, & dam all pumpkin states." The General Court ordered a loan, to be repaid out of the first taxes collected, and instructed constables to issue promissory notes to the soldiers in lieu of money, but when the soldiers tried to redeem them, the constables would only honor them at a 25–50 percent discount from face value.[59]

The problem was that the colony had no money and no way of getting any. Other New England governments did not even bother trying to tax their constituents. Connecticut encouraged colonists to make voluntary contributions to the war effort, while Plymouth leaders reported that "Several of our Towns . . . renounce and disclaim any authority that we have here—& forceably refuse to pay the Rates made for the payment of the soldiers."[60] Massachusetts prevailed on the wealthy judge Samuel Sewall "to lay down Thirty pounds Money to ye Treasurer, in behalf of Cambridge for what was unpd of ye Rate." The authorities assured Sewall that his loan would be repaid with interest.[61]

Then in May 1690, erstwhile treasure hunter William Phips led a fleet of seven ships carrying 700 colonial troops in sacking the poorly defended French settlement of Port Royal in Nova Scotia. On his return to Boston with plunder from the settlement's Catholic chapel, he set his sights on the much larger and more brazen target of Quebec in French Canada. Capitalizing on the Port Royal success, Massachusetts rallied Plymouth, Connecticut, and New York to the cause and plotted an ambitious expedition. Members of the Haudenosaunee Confederacy, then engaged in their own struggle against the French and their Indigenous allies, would join them. New York lieutenant governor Jacob Leisler coordinated a simultaneous overland attack on Montreal from Albany, for which he conscripted Fitz-John Winthrop of Connecticut to lead an army of Connecticut and New York militia and Haudenosaunees across Lake Champlain. But the 2,500 men Leisler promised Winthrop never arrived, and the General Court delayed Phips's departure for months in the hope that munitions would appear from England. Meanwhile, Boston teemed with more than two thousand restless soldiers. After finally setting sail in late summer, the expedition was a total disaster. Following a humiliating defeat by the French, a third of the soldiers perished on the journey home from drowning or disease, smallpox having spread through the fleet during the advance. Some were shipwrecked and never found. Phips absconded to London with his tail between his legs, where he quietly joined Increase Mather's efforts to get Massachusetts's old charter reinstated.[62]

The expedition's failure produced an enormous public debt. Most accounts estimated the cost at £50,000 sterling, though a Boston merchant put the loss at closer to £200,000.[63] As the death toll rose, the magistrates announced a new round of taxes.[64] Thomas Savage, whose father had commanded the Massachusetts forces in Metacom's War, recorded the aftermath in an essay published in London the following year. "The General Court laid grievous taxes," he lamented, "which they force from those who refuse to pay."[65] Samuel Myles, the rector of King's Chapel, Boston, begrudged the secrecy that shrouded the appropriation of the revenues. Most soldiers remained unpaid, leaving taxpayers to wonder what became of their money; he suspected it was being diverted to Mather and Phips in London.[66] By Christmas, as the future Massachusetts governor Thomas Hutchinson later chronicled in his two-volume history of the colony, the survivors of the expedition were on the verge of mutiny "for want of their wages."[67]

"Here is a project on foot of passing Bills," Samuel Sewall informed Increase Mather just before the new year, taking care to dispel the rumors then circulating that William Phips had proceeded with anything less than "Activity and Courage" on the Quebec expedition.[68] Squeezed by the public debt, the General Court had issued £7,000 in paper promises in December 1690, enlarged to £40,000 the following spring, for the payment of the soldiers and other public creditors. Not quite money but certainly more than promissory notes, bills of credit transformed the public debt into a public quasi-currency. But the currency's value was highly unstable, soon plunging in terms of sterling, and critics were quick to blame the provisional government. In January 1691, a Boston merchant lamented that the bills circulated at a 50 percent discount.[69] The same month, John Usher, then the royal governor of New Hampshire, received a letter accusing Mather of conspiring—from London, apparently—to defraud the soldiers of their full pay. "It has been a sad thing for the country," the author wrote of the Canada debacle, "and now, to cheat the men, we have paper-money of which you may buy £20 with £13 in cash."[70] In February, an observer slammed the General Court for "stopping the mouths of soldiers and seamen by a new mint of paper-money. Not many will take it, and these that will scarce know what to do with it."[71]

Concomitantly, the General Court authorized a £24,000 tax, to be levied over four years "either in Bills of credit . . . or in grain or provision."[72] The fundamental problem with the bills, some commentators argued, was that they were only good for paying taxes. Consequently, many colonists were leery of accepting them from soldiers. Thomas Savage observed that the bills did "not pass in Trade between Man and Man . . . nor can these poor soldiers and seamen get any thing for them above half their value, they being only used to pay rates with."[73] That spring the provisional government attempted to enhance the bills' value in exchange by promising to receive them in payment of taxes at 5 percent above face value, but the measure predictably encouraged taxpayers to hoard the bills they had acquired from soldiers at a fraction of that value. Hutchinson later suggested that while the provision benefited "those who paid their taxes in notes . . . it did not restore to the poor soldier what he had lost by the discount."[74]

According to Increase Mather's son and the minister of Boston's North Church, Cotton Mather, it was not because of, but rather in spite of, their acceptability in payment of taxes that the bills of credit depreciated. Recalling the event in his 1702 history of New England *Magnalia Christi Americana*, Mather explained that the expected revenues from the new taxes constituted the very "*credit*" on which the bills were "rendered *passable* among the people." Knowing that the taxes would "fetch into the treasury as much as all the bills of credit thence emitted would amount to," people were "willing to be furnished with bills, wherein it was their advantage to pay their taxes, rather than in any other specie." While granting that the bills' original holders had been unable to get "more than fourteen or sixteen shillings in the pound" for them in trade, Mather attributed the discount more to the uncertainty preceding the arrival of the new royal charter in 1692 than to the notion that they were only good for paying taxes. "Had the government been so settled, that there had not been any doubt of any obstruction, or diversion to be given to the prosecution of the tax-act, by a total change of their affairs, then depending at White-Hall," he maintained, "'tis very certain, that the bills of credit had been better than so much silver."[75] People owing taxes would have been willing to sell goods and services to soldiers for bills equal to sterling up to the amount they owed, while everyone else would have been willing to accept the bills with the knowledge that taxpayers would take them in due course. But if the General Court could not enforce the tax, then it could not guarantee the value of what was payable as taxes. Claiming the authority to tax but lacking the capacity to implement that authority, the provisional government's promise to accept the bills "in all publick payments" in value equal to "money" rang hollow.

Archival evidence from the intercharter years actually reveals a partially successful monetary endeavor. Consider Jacob Melyen, a Boston trader who had sold a cargo of flour to Massachusetts "for the Canada Expedition" and received paper bills in return. He complained that the colony, "not able to raise the money presantly, have made papers to Bills of Credit" and wondered who would be willing "to Receive it of me."[76] But if Melyen's reservations were well founded, Samuel Sewall's account book tells a rather different story, reflecting how status and class influenced monetary transactions. Between January 1691 and April 1692, Sewall, a prominent merchant and landlord, recorded dozens of dealings in paper money. On January 20, 1691, Elizabeth Drake, "a poor woman whose Husband was slain at Casco" in the Battle of Falmouth the previous year and who subsequently sought refuge in Boston, gave Sewall a ten-shilling bill to procure "a Load of Wood" for her; the wood cost six shillings sixpence, and so, he noted, he owed her three shillings sixpence. Perhaps Drake had claimed the bill as part of a widower's pension. And perhaps she, too, had worried about being able to spend it. The following day, Richard

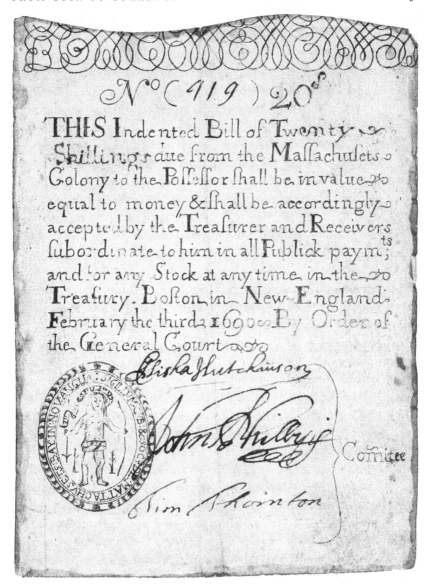

FIGURE 1.4. Massachusetts Bay Colony twenty-shilling bill of credit (altered), 1690. National Numismatic Collection, Smithsonian Institution.

Tally of Boston paid Sewall five pounds fifteen shillings "in Money-Bills" for forty-three bushels of rye, and on January 30, Sewall's tenant, Abraham Hill, paid him two pounds in bills in partial payment of rent. That spring Reverend Solomon Stoddard of Northampton gave Sewall twenty-one pounds in bills in repayment of what the judge had "advanced towards paying ye Indians," but to what end Sewall did not note. On November 16, 1691, Mrs. Usher paid him ten pounds in bills and twenty pounds in specie "for Rent of her House in Boston."[77]

Sewall offered bills of credit in payment of all kinds of goods and services too, including even land. On June 9, 1691, he paid Thomas Hale of Newbury twenty-four pounds one shilling, in bills in denominations ranging from two shillings to ten pounds, for a thirty-acre lot on the banks of the Merrimack River. The following December he gave his brother-in-law Moses Gerrish four twenty-shilling bills and two ten-shilling bills in partial payment of some malt. In June 1692, he purchased "Eight skains of flaxen Thred" at twelvepence per skein from Joseph Bulward of Medfield and gave him a ten-shilling bill, "so that he promises to bring or send me two more such skains in a fortnight or two."[78] Whether Hale, Gerrish, and Bulward received the bills cheerfully or out of deference to their social superior is unknown.

Surely, though, as one of the colony's most prominent settlers, Sewall's involvement in the imposition of bills of credit would have been vital for cultivating monetary trust. He not only accepted and offered the bills in his private dealings at face value but served as a commissioner of currency emissions in his community as well. In some instances Sewall delivered debentures, or bonds redeemable for bills in the future, to public creditors. Unlike bills, the debentures were not transferable and did not come in denominations, though the holder could technically sign them over to a third party. Sewall's account book reflects the personal and makeshift nature of the payments. For example, on January 16, 1691, he gave Stephen Greenleaf "all ye Debentures of ye Canada Company of Capt Stephen Greenlef except Joshua Moodey & Edward Budd," which he carried to Budd's brother-in-law the next day.[79] In May of that year, Major Elisha Hutchinson, a "commissioner of war for disbursements," gave Sewall more than £240 in freshly signed bills to pay out. Of that sum the General Court had earmarked more than £200 for the Canada expedition; four pounds four shillings one penny for Thomas Harris; thirty pounds for "[William] Stoughton & Sewall" (half of which Sewall pocketed); two pounds for a Mr. Barton; and one pound three shillings fourpence for John Aquitticus, an elderly Natick man who lived on the reservation at Skaucoononk near present-day Worcester. For the task, Hutchinson gave Sewall bills of varying denominations: fifteen ten-pound bills, ten five-pound bills, six three-pound bills, fourteen twenty-shilling bills, ten ten-shilling bills, eight five-shilling bills, six two-shilling sixpence bills, and six two-shilling bills.[80] Sewall also used bills to pay his taxes. In July 1691, he paid thirty-three pounds to a Boston constable on his and his mother's behalves.[81]

It was owing to bills of credit that any taxes were gathered at all. Certainly, some towns refused to pay their portions of the £24,000 tax until better prices were given for grain. Such was the case of Northampton in the Connecticut River Valley. Other towns sent mostly commodity money, vexing their constables.[82] The constable of Wrentham later attested that he had been "at a very considerable" personal expense for carrying 176 bushels of grain "to the Treasurers office in Boston, for which he hath not yet been allowed any thing by the Treasurer."[83] A Springfield constable reported having to house and transport the corn he had received from the people, making eight trips to Hartford and two more to Boston at "very great" expense and labor.[84] But other towns took the monetary experiment in stride. Consider Ipswich, the site of the tax revolt against the Dominion of New England, where in June 1691 one constable collected £176 14s. 9d. in paper bills alone.[85] Just a year earlier, the provisional government had instructed the Ipswich selectmen to send wheat, rye, oats, corn, peas, and barley.[86] In all, £10,000 in bills "returned unto the treasury" that year, which the treasurer burned and thus "discharged the debts for which they were intended."[87] This process of deliberate incineration, of casting bills and so the debts they represented into oblivion, would be repeated across half a century.

Boston, the colonial capital, fueled a secondary fiscal circuit, accepting bills of credit in payment of town taxes and using them to finance municipal expenditures. For the year 1691, town treasurer James Taylor discharged eighty-nine claims, nine of them with paper money—a small but significant portion. He gave one pound to Deacon James Allen of the First Church in Boston "for work abut the schoole house"; eighty pounds to the prominent merchant and official Samuel Shrimpton, for what we do not know; twelve pounds to "D[e]acon Elliot," probably Jacob Eliot Jr.; and twenty pounds to the town overseers of the poor.[88] Although the evidence is fragmentary for much of the decade, it suggests that paper money was in motion in southeastern Massachusetts, circulating as a claim on the public and connecting its users in both traditional and novel ways.

Making Money, Spending Money

How, then, did paper money hold up under royal scrutiny? English officials turned a blind eye to the 1690 bills of credit because, according to the prevailing wisdom, they were not money. Rather, they were promises to pay. The bills were technically convertible to specie at the treasury, but everyone knew the colony's coffers were empty. Another option would have been to back them with land. During Metacom's War, Massachusetts had pledged soldiers land, and it would later pay wartime debts in Indigenous homelands. In the 1680s, Native land deeds served as the foundation of two financial schemes: John Woodbridge's proposed "fund of lands," and John Blackwell's short-lived "bank of credit" (discussed in chapter 4). But land could not secure the bills because all titles, including Native deeds, had been voided by Edmund Andros in 1688 and remained up in the air during the intercharter years. Instead, taxes backed the bills. Because of this, some contemporaries called them "treasury notes," that is, monetized public debts that were extinguished when the treasurer accepted them from colonists in payment of taxes.[89]

Given the ongoing charter negotiations, the new money needed to appear as if it was not money at all. The result was quasi-private debt instruments that were transferable from person to person, but not legal tender for debts. Colonists were not required to accept them in payments, and if they did, they did not have to take them at face value equal to sterling.[90] In practice, however, the bills were less like the inland bills of exchange commonly used by English merchants in trade and more like medieval-era tallies, notched wooden sticks given by the Crown to royal creditors as receipts of payment to the Exchequer, or like European siege monies, handwritten notes issued by beleaguered cities to soldiers that circulated as currency and could later be redeemed for gold and silver.[91] They also bore a resemblance to the "playing-card money" that French colonial authorities gave to soldiers in Canada beginning in 1686.[92] Despite the bills' similarity to other public and historic credit currencies, the magistrates eschewed such comparisons for invocations of private bills of exchange and the famous merchant banks of Venice and Holland. The bills were emblazoned not with a pine tree and the year "1652" but with the Massachusetts Bay Colony seal originally adopted under royal authority in 1629. This seal depicts a Native man holding a bow and arrow and uttering the plea "Come Over and Help Us," a reference to the so-called Macedonian Plea that a figure voiced to Paul in a dream in Acts 16:9.[93]

If pine tree shillings had embodied aspirations of political independence, then bills of credit symbolized the "Protestant Interest." Such was the argument Cotton Mather and John Blackwell, who had served as Oliver Cromwell's war treasurer and advised Dudley's council on financial matters, made in two pamphlets published in Boston in 1691. Situating the bills' creation in the context of the Anglo-French rivalry, Mather and Blackwell appealed to colonists' sense of Christian duty and English patriotism. They argued that when people accepted the bills from soldiers for less than face value, "the poor *Soldier* is horribly *injured* . . . and the *Government* made *contemptible* as not worthy to be trusted."[94] Insisting that the bills were a product of the charter negotiations and so constitutive of royal authority, Mather and Blackwell maintained that the taxes payable in them were levied by the consent of the people "in a General Assembly"; that the assembly had a mandate from "the Crown of *England*"; and that since their issue, the bills had enabled the colony to repel the Catholic French as well as "ready *Silver*." To discount them was "in Effect to leave the Country without all manner of defense" against the French and thus to repudiate the English Crown.[95] With Parliamentary supremacy secured in England and the rights of Englishmen extended to the colonists, the historian Philip Haffenden argued, the 1691 charter sanctioned a semi-autonomous provincial political community within the English nation.[96] Materially and symbolically, the bills united colonists behind an emergent Protestant empire.

Politically speaking, the royal charter transformed paper promises into paper money because it gave the assembly the power to tax. The assembly (at that time still known as the General Court) set about redesigning the colony's tax system. In June 1692, it passed acts for "collecting and paying in the arrears" of all colonial taxes levied since October 1, 1689, and all town and county taxes enacted after May 1, 1689; introduced a ten-shilling poll tax on all males over the age of sixteen and a 25 percent annual estate tax, to be apportioned to the towns; and authorized an impost on imported wine and duties on sugar, molasses, and tobacco.[97] The assembly passed additional acts to enforce tax collection and made elected town constables, most of them ordinary men, liable for the arrears; town officials were to overhaul old assessment lists. All the new taxes were to be paid in the 1690 bills of credit.[98] Finally, the assembly appointed a committee to receive "those Bills of Credit that are brought into ye Treasury . . . and to cause them to be burnt."[99] The power to tax and the liberty to make money went hand in hand because whatever the colony declared to be acceptable in payment of taxation was, in effect, money. Moreover, the acts epitomized the transfer of authority from the Puritan colony to the royal province at a time when the old guard was under increasing scrutiny for its botched handling of the infamous Salem witchcraft trials of 1692–93.

In July, another committee began an audit of all debts still owed by "the late Massachusetts Colony." It was soon apparent, however, that many debts remained unaccounted for. Dozens of claimants came out of the woodwork, including individuals who had contributed goods or labor to the Dominion of New England.[100] The committee reviewed claims such as the one made by David Edwards and John Endicott, according to whom Edmund Andros had impressed their small boat for "the Country's Service" for six months, costing them "above one Hundred forty & seven pounds." They asked the General

Court to consider their affairs so "that each may have their due."[101] In another example, John Gardner of Nantucket Island asked for nine pounds five shillings after New York governor Benjamin Fletcher had ordered the islanders to send a sloop with a messenger to Martha's Vineyard "in order to obtain a list of their pols and Estates," an endeavor that Gardner said personally cost him thirty shillings. He insisted that the payment would cover some of the "Extraordinary Charges" townspeople had incurred "for their Defence," including fifteen pounds for two guns.[102] Other claimants attested to not being able to redeem for bills of credit the noncirculating debentures they had received in 1690 for supplying money and ships for the Canada expedition.[103]

The colony needed money not only to settle its outstanding debts but also to mobilize resources for the ongoing war. The assembly seized the opportunity to formalize its control over the appropriation of public funds, in the process claiming another privilege related to the power to tax: the authority to spend. While issuing bills of credit to public creditors was one matter, dictating how public funds were to be used was quite another. According to the royal charter, the latter fell under the governor's and council's purview. The assembly nevertheless enacted that any time the governor and council asked the representatives for money, "the said house of representatives ought particularly to be advised what uses and improvement such money is to be raised for." In doing so, it affirmed that it possessed an "undoubted right to all the liberties and priviledges of an English assembly." The governor and his council were still to dispose of public funds, though only "for the uses and intents of and according to the acts by which the said money is raised." The assembly still required a warrant from the governor to draw money from the treasury, but the warrant had to specify "for what particular service."[104] The representatives' de facto control over the appropriation of public funds wedded the authority to spend and the power to tax, and the liberty to make money completed the union. The authority to spend made the power to tax meaningful, since it was through spending in the first place that the assembly created the money in which taxes were to be paid. As the legal scholar Christine Desan explains of this process, a government "gains the capacity to spend and tax *in* money *as* it makes money."[105]

Early on, moreover, Massachusetts established a pattern of reissuing some of the bills of credit that had returned to the treasury in payment of taxes to service outstanding debts or to finance military expenses instead of burning them. In December 1693, the assembly ordered £1,500 in bills from the treasury for clothing and provisions, £500 of which it earmarked for building and outfitting a ten gun galley. The following June, the assembly ordered an additional £700 "for the equipping and setting forth of the said province galley." The same day it made the bills ordered the previous December acceptable "in all publick payments."[106] Each time old bills were reissued, new taxes were enacted as a "sinking fund" for retiring them from circulation yet again. Hence, on June 22, 1694, the assembly ordered £5,000 in bills from the treasury "upon the fund and credit" of import and export duties and the tonnage duty, as well as the poll and property tax. That October it authorized a tax of £4,841 to be "granted as a fund" for an additional £3,000 reissued. And the following March, it levied a tax of £3,189 as a fund for another £4,000 in bills to be reissued.[107] The assembly issued more bills in June 1695; March, June, and December 1696; March 1700; April and June 1701; and June 1702. The treasury left as much as £15,000 in bills in circulation at any given time. Taxes assessed from 1692 to 1702 averaged about £11,000 annually, meaning issues and reissues may well have totaled more than £110,000.[108]

The power of the purse meant not only the power to tax and the authority to spend but the liberty to make money as well. The transformation Massachusetts began in 1690 diverged from the English past in two ways. First, it curtailed executive authority over money matters, a shift commensurate with the English financial revolution then happening on the other side of the Atlantic. In addition to designating the money of account and the means of payment, medieval and early modern monarchs had claimed seigniorage, or the profits that come from making money. But after the Glorious Revolution, the rejection of the divine right of kings, the rise of commercial banking, and the expansion of warfare produced a dramatic transformation in how money was made. While the Crown retained the prerogative to mint coin and to define the money of account, the English state stopped charging individuals for coin from the mint and began minting coin free of charge. Concomitantly, the state started borrowing money from wealthy investors in the form of bank notes through the new Bank of England. The investors multiplied money further by lending to individuals on the basis of the coin and public debt the bank held.[109] Second, the transformation allocated control over the creation of money, and thus seigniorage, to the assembly rather than to a bank. In this way, the Massachusetts experience departed from England's financial revolution. Indeed, bills of credit were a clear alternative to the Bank of England. While the new United States would later adopt the British model of state-sponsored commercial banking, colonial Massachusetts situated the liberty to make money in the assembly, in the process imagining a new kind of seigniorage based on fiscal capacity rather than on royal prerogative or commercial finance.[110]

The office of the treasurer occupied a special place in the early American monetary landscape. The treasurer served as the intermediary between colonial taxpayers and the colonial government, on the one hand, and between the government and public creditors, on the other. Beginning in 1691, the legislative assemblies wielded significant control over the office. The Massachusetts assembly had the power to appoint treasurers, but others wrested the power from the governor or simply assumed it. The assemblies believed that choosing the person tasked with collecting and disbursing public funds was a natural corollary of the power to tax and the authority to spend. It is "a received Opinion among them," South Carolina representative Thomas Nairne wrote of his constituents in 1710, "that the Power of appointing, examining, censuring, and displacing those who have the public Money in their Hands, is much better lod'gd in the [Carolina] House of Commons, who have so great an Interest in the Colony, than in the Hands of any Governour, for Reasons generally known in America."[111] In addition, the assemblies routinely selected special officers to help with the collection of taxes and duties, and appointed commissioners, officers, and committees to aid in the disbursal of public funds. "In the colonies," the British official Thomas Pownall described on the eve of the American Revolution, "the treasurer is solely and entirely a servant of the assembly."[112] Assemblies' control over the office of the treasurer, together with the power to tax and the authority to spend, reduced governors' already limited control over colonial finances to a mere formality.

The Return of Money Scarcity

That towns on the front lines of King William's War continued to scramble to pay their taxes suggests that America's first paper money did not initially circulate beyond southeastern Massachusetts. Springfield suffered the same geographical obstacles in sending to Boston the corn its inhabitants had contributed that it had experienced under the Dominion of New England. In June 1693, Springfield constable Benjamin Davis petitioned the assembly not to penalize him for losing "a Boate Load of Corne" and "about 130 bushels of pease or more" in the Connecticut River. "By ye pvidence of God, in goeing downe ye falls," he explained, the boat "became wholy lost or altogether unserviceable." Apparently, it was not the first time such a mishap had occurred, "as also once before some loss was in a loading of Corne sent from thence for ye Treasurer." Davis "humbly suggested" that he "may have Credit for such miscaryed Paymts, truly made by him, as if they had not miscaryed." The assembly responded that it would grant the petition if the constable swore to the treasurer that the loss was truly an act of providence and not the result of his own negligence.[113]

Other constables reported being unable to collect the arrears of taxes levied to redeem bills of credit and asked for the amount to be offset or the tax suspended. They explained that they were poor or that the inhabitants were cloistered in garrisons and unable to tend to the harvest.[114] Others sought, and were granted, reimbursement for storage and transportation.[115] Dartmouth constable James Samson had been powerless to collect the arrears because several of the inhabitants no longer lived there and others were too poor to pay. He begged the assembly that he "not be forced to lye in prison to make good yt wch I was not capable to come at." The assembly agreed to bear nine pounds eight shillings eightpence of the arrears but insisted that the town "make good" on the remaining six pounds.[116] In March 1695, Springfield constable David Morgan's property was seized "for satisfaction of ye remainder of sd Rates," despite his having expended considerable time and money storing and transporting the corn he had managed to collect from the people. On examination of Morgan's receipts, however, the assembly determined that it owed him forty-one pounds fifteen shillings sixpence for storage and transportation, nearly twice the twenty pounds fourteen shillings tenpence that remained of the arrears.[117] In May 1695, Amesbury constable John Hoyt was jailed for failing to collect the town's portion of the arrears for the year 1691. He explained that it had been impossible to collect any payments from the inhabitants, as two months after receiving his orders, "ye enemy came upon our town, & did us much damage." Hoyt lost a house, tools, bedding, and four cattle in the raid, and his wife caught "ye malignant fever," leaving him little "time to collect ye rates & provide for my family." Now "Ancient & sickly," he pleaded for his release from prison "some abatement of sd rates . . . and a little longer time for ye payment of ye mony."[118] The assembly allowed Hoyt's family to post bond for his release, but he was killed in another raid less than a year later, at which time the assembly granted the request of his son, Joseph Hoyt, to forgive the debt.[119]

By the summer of 1696, so much of the arrears of taxes were yet unpaid that Massachusetts passed several acts to facilitate and enforce tax collection, including one affirming the treasurer's ability to draw money into the treasury. Another act fixed the value of 17 pennyweight pieces of eight at six shillings per piece, a lighter coin than Edmund Andros's 17.5 pennyweight piece of eight.[120] Then in October 1697, "Upon consideration of the scarcity of money within this province and upon the many difficulties arising thereby, not only with respect to trade and commerce, but also for carrying on the publick affaires of the government, necessary for his majesty's service, more especially during the rebellion and troubles with the Indians," the colonial government prohibited colonists from exporting more than five pounds in specie.[121]

With claims piling up faster than taxes could be collected, the colony again resorted to granting debentures to public creditors. Such a system, however, quickly proved unsustainable. Four years after the end of King William's War, in March 1701, a committee to consider "proposals for supplying the scarcity of mony" issued a set of recommendations, including fixing the value of gold coins and minting copper pennies. A third recommendation called for chartering "a Bank of Credit . . . to make & Emit Bills of Credit." The bank would loan bills in amounts ranging from two shillings to three pounds and be permitted to charge up to 3 percent annual interest. For the duration of the bank's charter, it would have a monopoly on "making any of the Like Bills of Credit." The proposal, which would have established a bank like the one John Blackwell organized in 1686, was dismissed, but colonists would propose comparable schemes in 1714 and again in 1720.[122]

In the end, the assembly reissued bills of credit that had returned to the treasury and, at one point, even issued new bills. In April 1701, it passed an act for reissuing a thousand pounds "for the paying and discharging of debts already due from the province, and the future growing charge of the same." But when, on June 30, the representatives ordered the treasurer, James Taylor, to issue an additional six thousand pounds, he replied "that he hath not Bills sufficient in his hands to Emitt sd. sum." Consequently, they directed Taylor "to Imprint & Emitt so many Bills of Credit in Suitable Sums . . . [as] shall make up the aforesd Sum of Six Thousand Pounds."[123] A year later, the assembly authorized him to issue another three thousand pounds, half of which it earmarked for completing the fortifications and barracks on Castle Island.[124] This was the final paper money emission before the outbreak of the War of the Spanish Succession (1702–13; known as Queen Anne's War in North America) prompted the assembly to make a new, more permanent currency known as "Province Bills."

Despite the makeshift way of disbursing the 1690 bills of credit, the political uncertainty preceding the arrival of the royal charter, and the practice of reissuing rather than burning bills that had returned to the treasury in payment of taxes, America's first paper money rebounded after the initial depreciation and retained its value relative to sterling for the duration of King William's War. Thomas Hutchinson later argued that the bills "continued their value" because "the sum was small," but the size of the currency was comparable to subsequent emissions.[125] The 1690 bills succeeded because they had a limited sphere of circulation and because they flowed through existing social channels based on hierarchy, dependence, and reciprocity: a captain and his soldier; a landlord and his tenant; longtime neighbors. Perhaps some bills made their way to distant settlements such as Northampton in the Connecticut River Valley. However, the available evidence suggests that colonists living in those settlements barely had enough corn with which to pay their taxes. In contrast, people in and around Boston saw and handled paper money on a regular basis. They trusted it out of deference or obligation or, increasingly, because they knew that they, or someone else, would eventually use it pay their taxes.

Whereas the pine tree shillings that Massachusetts minted from 1652 to 1682 took the familiar form of commodity coin, the 1690 bills of credit had a fiscal basis. By issuing non-interest-bearing bills for paying the public debts and for financing military expenses, the colonial assembly claimed seigniorage, long the province of kings and queens. In the process, it bound the liberty to make money to the power to tax and the authority to spend, a fiscal triumvirate that other colonies would emulate as the experimentation of the 1690s gave way to a complex world of public finance. The next two chapters look more closely at the material and social basis of paper money's value, the debates over depreciation and inflation that punctuated its early history, and the changing market relations it shaped as it snaked its way from provincial treasuries to hinterlands and back again.

2

The Sinews of War

Five months after the end of Queen Anne's War (1702–13) in North America, Massachusetts governor Joseph Dudley reflected on the necessity of bills of credit as a means of war finance. On December 1, 1713, Dudley wrote a letter to the Board of Trade assuring their Lordships that "without this method I could never have subsisted nor cloathed the Forces, that have defended and secured these Colonyes as well as our neighbours, but must have left all to ruin and mischief."[1] Eight years later, the Ipswich minister and tax resister John Wise gave credit where it was due. In his 1721 essay, *The Freeholder's Address to the Honourable House of Representatives*, Wise declared that province bills "have paid our Expences thro' a long and Bloody War; without which we should never have been able to submit; for these Men face the fiercest of Enemies." As Dudley and Wise well knew, and as others would come to know, paper money not only fed the colonial war machine, but "like so many Phoenixes out of their ashes," to quote Wise, the whole colonial project rose from a smoldering paper foundation.[2]

The colonies paid for wars rather differently than Britain did. New York governor William Burnet drew upon this contrast in a 1724 letter to the board. Burnet reminded the Lords that Parliament can always borrow money from the Bank of England or East India Company and tax the population later to pay the debt. But in the colonies, he pointed out, "there is no other possible way left to make distant Funds provide money, when it is necessarily wanted, but making paper Bills, to be sunk by such funds." While Britain summoned the money it needed from wealthy investors in the form of interest-bearing loans, the colonies spent the money they needed into existence, cost-free. "Without this," Burnet insisted, "Carolina would have been ruined by their Indian war, Boston could not now support theirs, nor could any of the Provinces have furnished such considerable Sums to the Expeditions against Canada."[3]

The political process that underwrote the colonial currencies also runs counter to the conventional narrative about money's origins. In the myth of barter, money magically appears from an autonomous and self-regulating market. But in history, states make money to pay for wars of conquest, colonialism, and enslavement—and money, in turn, shapes markets.[4] After Massachusetts created America's first paper money to pay the costs of King William's War (1688–97), other colonies followed suit. First was South Carolina in 1703, to pay for the siege of St. Augustine in Spanish Florida the previous fall; followed by New York, New Jersey, Connecticut, and New Hampshire (all in 1709), for expenses related to the joint expedition to Quebec that year; then Rhode Island (1710), to finance military and other public expenses; and, finally, North Carolina (1713), to pay the costs of the Tuscarora War (1711–15).

This chapter argues that the colonies had to use bills of credit as a means of war finance before colonists could use them as a medium of exchange and means of payment. Military aims and exigencies more than market demands thus informed whether, when, and how colonial assemblies issued the bills. Once paper money entered circulation, however, how much stock individuals put in the money and how they used it depended as much on social trust as on faith in the issuing assemblies' authority. Ultimately, paper bills formed new binding ties in colonial contexts. Far from the halls of British state power, they not only offered European settlers a shared language of belonging, but also were the vehicle by which assemblies extended claims to lands and over people. Who received paper money, for what debts, and in what amounts reflected assemblies' priorities, articulated their claims to power, and delimited the boundaries of the colonial political community.

Monetary Circuits and Social Hierarchies

Bills of credit followed a politically constituted circuit that began and ended at provincial treasuries. But the bills were not created by decree, as in the case of a Roman denarius or an English sovereign. Instead, they began their lives as receipts of in-kind contributions to the "public" (hence the official name, bill of *public* credit). An assembly made money when acting on the public's behalf, it mobilized settlers' goods and labor in return for paper bills redeemable in payment of colonial taxes. The practice provided an effective means of organizing resources because it entailed real value, as each bill represented actual contributions—from guns and ships to food and clothing—that established the bill's "fiscal value." Given to a soldier, however, a bill was merely a receipt. One more step was required to make it into money: the assembly had to promise to accept it from anyone holding it in payment of taxes. Then the bill could pass from person to person and retain its worth as a claim on the public. Separate from but related to their fiscal value, the bills held cash value because they offered a transferable means of payment. Public creditors could hold on to their bills to pay taxes later, or they could pass them to someone else in exchange for goods or labor. Because anyone could use the bills to pay taxes, everyone recognized them as a standard of value and mode of payment for transactions in the colony.[5]

That, at least, was the idea. But seldom was the process so straightforward in practice, as after bills of credit entered circulation, they had to navigate a complex social world where monetary transactions were as much about communal relationships and interactions as about public trust in assemblies' claims to authority. And just as bills had to be used as a means of war finance before they could be used as a medium of exchange, they had to follow established social ties founded on reciprocity and kinship before they could foster new economic relations centered on calculations of profit and loss. If the system seemed novel, colonial treasurers disbursed bills in ways that reinforced customary labor relationships based on deference and obligation. In seventeenth- and eighteenth-century European armies, captains fed and clothed soldiers at their own expense, for which the authorities reimbursed them, generously, from the soldiers' wages.[6] Similar relationships could be found throughout colonial North America, where officers assumed responsibility for feeding and clothing soldiers and for distributing their wages, usually after they took a cut for themselves. In turn, the captains helped cultivate trustworthiness in the money in which wages were paid.

But even as these and other traditional social relationships persisted, new ones arose. The late seventeenth and early eighteenth centuries saw the emergence of wartime structures of committees and commissioners to process public creditors' claims, draw up warrants and debentures for payment, and deliver bills of credit to the claimants. Almost anyone could be a public creditor with the right claim, from day laborers and boatmen to doctors and the wealthiest merchants. Consider some of the roughly 110 payments ranging from nine shillings to £500 that Massachusetts treasurer James Taylor discharged between June 1693 and June 1694. One Mathew Austin, whose "Canue [was] Imprest," was paid one pound seven shillings sevenpence. A Jasper Pullman collected two pounds five shillings fivepence "for hire himselfe & Boat to fetch provisions at several times for the souldiers posted at York" in present-day Maine, then under Massachusetts's jurisdiction. Six stonecutters earned six pounds total "for worke done by themselves and servants in building of the Fort at Saco" near York, to be paid out by Benjamin Woodbridge. Nathaniel Hall, a doctor, claimed more than sixty-two pounds "for services & medicines." And several colonists received the sum of £280 10s. for "provisions souldiers' wages and subsistence at the Garrison at Deerfield" in the Connecticut River Valley.⁷

The relationship between colonial governments and their constituents also changed, with colonists increasingly turning to the assemblies to mitigate their suffering. Entire towns petitioned the Massachusetts assembly for relief, as was the case of Lancaster in Worcester County, a besieged village on the front lines of King William's War. Town clerk John Houghton described how the inhabitants were "so long Necessitated to live in Garisson where neither men nor women can doe but very little towards ye supply of theire families . . . whereby many are brought to extreame poverty not knowing how to get either food or cloathing for themselves or famillys; also the great Charge expended in building Repairing & maintaining so many garrisons." In answer to Houghton's plea, the representatives voted to allocate twenty pounds to the town out of the next tax collection.⁸

Wounded veterans petitioned the assembly with growing frequency. Ambrose Dawes lost an eye serving "as a soldier and as a workeman" at Pemaquid, and since then not only had been "unable to gitt a Livelihood," but had also fallen deep into debt paying for medical care. It would be four long months before the representatives voted to grant Dawes ten pounds "in consideration of damage sustained in their ma[jes]ties. Service by the loss of one of his Eyes." How he managed in the meantime is unknown.⁹ The assembly determined which petitions to pursue, which claims to settle, and the going rate for everything from labor to medicine to lost or maimed body parts, establishing a process and a precedent that would be replicated in a dozen other colonies and repeated over five decades. Colonial-era appropriations for poverty-stricken widows, wounded soldiers, and besieged towns may well have presaged the administrative state.¹⁰

Pension claims reflect the larger poverty problem that gripped Massachusetts at the end of Queen Anne's War and give some insight into what colonial families experienced on the home front. As much as a quarter of the white men who participated in the military campaigns perished, most pressed into service from the laboring classes. Consequently, a significant portion of public creditors were wounded veterans or war widows and their children. Soldiers of European descent injured in the line of battle received between three pounds and ten pounds per year, but that was far below what was needed to support a family. After 1715, poor pensioners regularly petitioned the assembly for increases commensurate with the rising cost of living.¹¹

The experiences of two pensioners, Nicholas Picket of Marblehead and Hugh Pike of Newbury, show how common soldiers had to scrounge, year after year, for their due. Pickett's life changed forever in the spring of 1697, when two colonels arrived in Marblehead to fit out an expedition to recover two fishing shallops from the French. John Calley commanded the two-vessel fleet and force of forty local men, including Pickett, virtually all impressed. They received ten shillings per week, noticeably below the prevailing wage for laborers. At some point the men skirmished with the French and someone shot Pickett in the leg. He later told the assembly that the wound had immobilized him "and by that means he became frozen and thereby hath suffered extreme delirious and exquisite pains and torment and at last for the preservation of his life was forced to endure the cutting off his foot." He described himself as "very weak and utterly incapable of doing anything to help himself; or fall into any way to gain a livelihood; and he being a very poor man; having neither housing, land, or other estate to relieve him; and in a very poor, miserable, and deplorable Condition." In October 1697, the assembly allowed Pickett ten pounds plus a pension of five pounds, "as also the charge of his cure be defrayed by the publick."[12] A few years later, the assembly increased his pension to seven pounds, and in 1714 he successfully petitioned for an additional twenty pounds "to pay the Surgeons for their Operation in cutting of his Legg & ye: cure thereof."[13]

Hugh Pike, who was dangerously wounded in the 1707 Port Royal expedition serving as an ensign, also initially received a "yearly Pension of £5." In 1714 he successfully appealed to the colonial government for more money to help pay his medical bills, receiving "the further sum" of three pounds fifteen shillings "to pay his Sergeons Bill." But Pike's health continued to decline. He was unable to work and had a family to support. Every year from 1720 to 1725 like clockwork, Pike petitioned the assembly for more money. The petitions followed a precise formula. Like Pickett and others who successfully solicited the assembly for pension increases, Pike would have known to emphasize his inability to support his wife and children. And most years he managed to procure an additional fifteen pounds, except for 1722 and 1723, when he received an extra ten and five pounds, respectively.[14] If petitions provide a detailed picture of colonial life, however, the treasurer's accounts where payments were recorded were the instruments that transformed poor soldiers' suffering into numeric values, reducing a bloody ten-year war to a succinct record of quantifiable "facts" that could, in turn, circulate as money.[15]

The accounts of James Taylor's successor, Jeremiah Allen, shed light on a world of public finance that extended beyond war costs and far beyond the defensive measures local officials swore were necessary to save the colonies from ruin. Like other early American treasurers, Allen used the account charge and discharge—what the historian of accounting William T. Baxter called "the system of stewardship"—charging himself with tax receipts, outstanding bills of credit, and bills remaining in his hands, and discharging himself of payments to public creditors. The former involved, in part, tallying the amount of money collected from each town and subtracting the total from the sum supposed to have been raised according to the corresponding tax act, reflecting the decentralized nature of tax collection and reliance on local relationships.[16] Disbursals of bills to public creditors, on the other hand, were made by order of the governor in accordance with assembly acts. Allen kept thorough records of these payments, down to the details of infrastructure projects and corresponding assembly votes; the types, locations, and dates of military ventures; and the names of vessels employed in the colony's service.

Paper money made the payments possible. Governors, council members, representatives, postmasters, clerks, printers, army chaplains, colonial agents, lighthouse keepers, jailers, drummers, watchmen, and Harvard College presidents all received their wages in bills of credit—and at conspicuously higher rates than Pike and Pickett. For the year 1714, Allen paid £500 to Governor Joseph Dudley and eighty pounds to Secretary Isaac Addington for their salaries. Samuel Sewall collected a handsome reward for serving as a commissioner of currency emissions, a position he had held on and off since 1690. In 1714, Sewall received fifty pounds for serving as a judge on the Superior Court. Even the doorkeeper to the governor and assembly, Samuel Maxwell, earned a twenty-pound stipend. Other colonists earned cash for one-off jobs, such as Richard Pullen, the keeper of the Green Dragon in Boston, who made eighteen pounds eight shillings for hosting the "Election Dinner for the Gentlemen of her Majesties Council" that May.[17]

In addition to generous salaries for officials, the assembly spent lavishly on infrastructure projects, partnering with private individuals to handle the funds and hiring for construction projects that transformed the physical landscape. A thousand pounds went to a committee for building a lighthouse on Beacon Island at the mouth of Boston Harbor. Another £220 was marked for erecting a bridge over Pawtucket Falls that would connect travelers from Boston to Pawtucket, Rhode Island. The assembly regularly hired painters, carpenters, blacksmiths, and masons to service and repair fortifications, churches, and other public buildings.[18] Though not exactly the double-entry accounting associated with the rise of merchant capitalism, Allen's books "rendered the recorded information inviolable," to borrow the literary scholar Mary Poovey's description of early modern accounting, so that a judge's labor really was worth a thousand times more than that of a common soldier.[19]

The Travels of a Bill of Credit

From the treasury in Boston, Massachusetts bills of credit traversed the New England countryside. Evidence of paper money exchange crops up in the personal account books of early eighteenth-century farmers and artisans, illustrating how settlers worked paper bills into existing reciprocal trade ties based on community and kinship. John Fearing, a Hingham, Massachusetts, weaver, is a good case in point. Fearing made a living producing cotton household goods for his family and friends in exchange for livestock, tools, labor, clothes, and imported commodities such as molasses, indigo, and salt. He recorded his dealings in the money of account, including whenever paper bills changed hands. For example, during 1706 and 1707, he paid six shillings sixpence in "paper mony" to his relative Rebecca Wilder, received "a bill Credit" of five shillings from John Colson for combing and weaving some yarn, took "a bill of" ten shillings from Hannah Bacon for spinning and weaving crepe, and accepted "a paper bill" of five shillings from Isaac Johnson "for weaving 19y and half of spotted stuf." In August 1709, Fearing paid "ten shillings in paper money" in his dealings with Anna Wilder, for whom he had previously combed half a pound and woven eighteen yards of cotton, and from whom he would later receive pork, beef, and a cow. Bills did not replace book credit; they complemented and expanded it.[20]

Fearing valued bills of credit not only because they offered a mode of payment for transactions in his community, but also because he and his neighbors could use them to pay their local taxes. Hingham and other towns enhanced the bills' fiscal value by accepting them in payment of town taxes and in the process augmented the towns' fiscal capacities. The change over time is noteworthy. Prior to 1690, Hingham townspeople had paid their taxes almost entirely in corn. By 1709, however, town rates were "to be paid two thirds of it in money or province bills & the other part thereof in merchantable corn."[21] Towns that accepted bills in payment of town taxes disbursed them to ministers and schoolmasters for their salaries, who could in turn use them to purchase their necessities from producers like Fearing. For example, Haverhill minister John Brown received paper bills for his salary forty times over the course of his twenty-five-year tenure beginning in 1718. Though he typically took the bills from the town treasurer, he occasionally accepted them directly from the constables who had collected them from taxpayers.[22]

Paper money took on new meanings in the growing world of trade and markets. Although Henry Tebbets, the owner of a New Hampshire general store, could not use Massachusetts bills of credit to pay New Hampshire taxes, the shopkeeper still accepted and offered them in payments. In May 1707, for instance, he lent three pounds five shillings in "paper money" to an associate.[23] Thus, paper bills transcended the polities that created them. Fifteen years later, New Jersey yeomen who marketed their produce in New York and Pennsylvania had little choice but to accept their neighbors' "paper bills for their produce" when New Jersey bills were scarce, even though New York and Pennsylvania bills were "not a legal Tender in Taxes or debts between man and man in Jersey."[24] Transferable from person to person, paper money delivered cash services to taxpayers and nontaxpayers, residents and nonresidents alike.

Colonial elites played a crucial role in nurturing trust in the monetary system, in large part because of the prevalent credit culture. Consider the example of John Stoddard of Northampton, Massachusetts. The second son of Solomon Stoddard, the pastor of Northampton Church, the younger Stoddard occupied various high-ranking positions in the colonial government and later helped establish the Stockbridge mission community. He served as an agent of British imperialism, fighting in Queen Anne's War, making deals with Schaghticoke and Haudenosaunee officials, and negotiating for English captives in Canada, all of which earned him handsome monetary rewards. In 1714, the assembly paid Stoddard hundreds of pounds in bills of credit for the trouble and expense of traveling to Canada and recovering twelve prisoners of war. For the people of Hampshire County, however, he was more like a village squire than a provincial statesman. In the early eighteenth-century world of hierarchy and deference, when local elites like Stoddard offered bills, they communicated social trust in paper money to those with whom they themselves were bound by ties of obligation and dependency. Trustworthiness in a monetary system that could potentially erode such bonds had to be cultivated, ironically, by those same elites.[25]

Cross-referencing the treasurer's accounts with Stoddard's own account book provides a window onto that world. In 1727 Jeremiah Allen paid £204 12s. 5d. in bills of credit to Stoddard "for a Supply for his Honr. and Attendance in their Voyage Eastward" to meet the Penobscots at the close of Governor Dummer's War (1722–25), or the Fourth Anglo-Wabanaki War.[26] Stoddard recorded the receipt of the bills in his account book under credits as "Bills Recvd, of Mr. Treasurer Allin for supplies for His Honr, Council and Attendants in their Journey" to Wabanaki country. On the opposite and subsequent pages, Stoddard recorded payments to the colony's creditors, from whom he, or possibly other officials, had borrowed money or purchased supplies for the expedition on the colonial government's behalf. Thus, he "repaid to Majr Mascarene" eleven shillings for "money advanced for Fish & Greens," eight shillings sixpence for "money [Colonel Taylor] advanced for cheese," and one pound eleven shillings for lemons from Colonel Wainwright. Stoddard additionally paid Elizabeth Graves seven pence for washing services, a Mr. Piggott ten shillings "to buy fowle & greens," the servants ten shillings, and the entertainers at Nantasket one pound fifteen shillings.[27] The total expenditures, paid between July 12 and August 1, 1727, amounted to just over £206. Whether Stoddard satisfied the colony's debts to Mascarene, Graves, and the others in the bills from the treasurer (presumably he did), or whether he issued them book credit, is beside the point. Through his earmarking of cash from the treasurer for specific payments, Stoddard not only further differentiated and particularized it, but also integrated public money into private debt relations.[28]

Other powerful men likewise dispensed paper money they would have received in payment of their salaries to ordinary colonists in exchange for labor or as individual "gifts." For instance, Chief Justice Benjamin Lynde, who along with his fellow judges received an annual salary of £100 by 1727, gave "£3. Prov. Bills" to Edward Esty "for his getting 200 cedar rails carted this month to Milton landing place," a "5s bill" as a donation to the minister of Boston's New South Church, "3 new 2s bills to Col. Thaxter's three grand children who live with him, and 6s more to the maid and servants."[29] The historian Margaret Newell observed that Lynde's successor on the Superior Court, Samuel Sewall, "carried an inexhaustible supply of small bills of credit with him to disburse as tips to servants and as presents to his children, grandchildren, and lady friends."[30] For their generosity, Sewall and Lynde expected nothing but respect and obedience in return.

If Sewall supported the use of bills of credit as a means of war finance, however, he opposed a 1712 act making them legal tender for debts. The assembly thus "Comand & Compell men to Lend them at that value," he lamented, while "privat creditors are forc'd to take the publick Faith in payment for their Comodity."[31] Sewall resented having to take the bills from anyone who offered them in trade or as payment for debts, preferring the right to demand satisfaction in gold or silver that he could use to pay his British creditors. This did not mean that he did not value the bills, but that how he assessed and used them was defined less by their market function than by their social meaning. When the assembly gave Sewall paper money, it was akin to an honor or reward, a totem of his public contributions. When he passed that money to a servant or child, it served as an unreciprocated gift, a representation of their unequal relationship. Its value owed less to calculations of profit and loss than to the customs, rituals, and hierarchies that structured the early eighteenth-century world.

Money as a Means of Imperial Intrusion

Money helped shaped the process of English colonization, and it offers a window into colonial constructions of Indigeneity. The earliest New England settlers had adopted Native currencies and imbued them with "cash assumptions," insinuating themselves into Indigenous economies and subsequently profiting from the differences between Native and European conceptions of money and exchange. The trade and power asymmetries resulting from colonists' deployment of those differences to their advantage paved the way for later generations to create currencies and economies based not on contact or conquest but on exclusion.[32] Compared to other colonial contexts, then, bills of credit were not a "*settler* currency," whereby, one scholar theorizes, "the expansion of a currency's domain beyond its national jurisdiction can provide another mode of economic intrusion that facilitates the dispossession of the client country's sovereignty."[33] Rather than introduce colonial paper money to Indigenous populations with the aim of integrating them into colonial labor markets or imposing on them colonial taxes, early American assemblies used it to finance murderous attacks on Native peoples, to pay for the construction of forts on Native lands, and to underwrite Anglo–Native diplomacy. The money was not so much imposed as inflicted.[34]

Through the early eighteenth century at least, however, the persistence of Indigenous power in some quarters of eastern North America shaped colonial governments' ability to obtain Indigenous lands and resources—with or without paper bills. In some instances, the colonies made money in order to meet Indigenous communities' demands for tribute. Beginning with the arrival of Europeans in North America, gifts had served as the bedrock of political and social ties between European and Indigenous people. Early colonial leaders had sought to assimilate Native customs, ritually exchanging gifts with sachems as signs of mutual friendship and protection. In the early seventeenth century, different iterations of what European and Indigenous actors co-conceived as money—from wampum shell beads to animal skins to silver coins—had offered further means of crossing cultural divides and maintaining relationships. As the century progressed, the gifts increasingly included firearms, another form of currency. Guns and ammunition were essential to Indigenous politics, assuring a brisk arms trade (despite periodic bans of it) between Europeans and Native people.[35]

By a conservative estimate, Massachusetts spent the equivalent of hundreds of pounds sterling on guns, provisions, trade goods, guides, treaty commissioners, and entertainment just for the Wabanaki and the Haudenosaunee during King William's War and Queen Anne's War. Colonial leaders learned that if they did not provide the Wabanaki with military support, then Canada would. The French not only had supplied the formidable eastern New England confederacy with weapons and provisions, but had also accompanied them on raids on English settlements. After Massachusetts had initially refused to supply the Wabanaki with ammunition and powder, Governor William Phips traveled to present-day Maine in the summer of 1693 to negotiate a ceasefire with several sachems.[36]

Paper money put a new twist on gift exchange following King William's War, or the Second Anglo-Wabanaki War. Some seventeenth-century treaties and land deeds between Massachusetts and Wabanaki sagamores had stipulated "quitrents" of corn or other gifts.[37] Now, the colonial treasurer would offer bills of credit to Boston merchants in exchange for "Provisions Cloathing and all other supplies suitable for a Trade with the sd Indians"—from peas, corn, and molasses to pipes, kettles, and knives to shirts and thread.[38] Captains and other salaried officials would take and sell the supplies to Wabanaki leaders, taking care to underprice the French, in exchange for animal skins and furs. Once in possession of the skins, the treasurer would unload them to the highest bidder, "the bennefitt thereof to be returned to the publick treasury."[39] To sweeten the deal, the governor could order "Presents out of the publick Treasury . . . for engaging the sd Indians more firmly to the English Interest and obliging them to abandon that of the French."[40] (The assembly drew the line at then acting governor William Stoughton's 1701 proposal to send a gunsmith to live with the Wabanaki and mend their guns "gratis.")[41] Guns, provisions, trade goods, and even military commissions that paper money paid for were crucial to the sachems' shift in loyalty from the French to the English. For their part, the Wabanaki continued to view corn, trade goods, and other items as gifts or tribute, expressions of a reciprocal relationship, which, like treaties and land deeds, could be renegotiated when the needs of the participants changed.[42]

Massachusetts adopted similar tactics in its increasingly desperate attempts to win over the powerful Haudenosaunee of present-day New York. For a longer duration, and to a greater degree of success than the Wabanaki, the Haudenosaunee exploited the Anglo-French rivalry as a means of securing their own survival and prosperity. Massachusetts blamed its failure to obtain Haudenosaunee military aid on New York traders, whom they believed needed the Haudenosaunee to remain neutral in order to continue their contraband trade with Quebec. Haudenosaunees leveraged this belief to wring trade goods and presents from the New England colony—from lead, powder, and shirts sent to Albany to dinners, drinks, and lodging for Mohawk visitors.[43]

One did not have to be a colonial official, however, to benefit from the large sums of money that Massachusetts expended on maintaining relationships with its Indigenous neighbors. During the fragile peace between the close of Queen Anne's War and the outbreak of the Fourth Anglo-Wabanaki War, the treasurer generously reimbursed white men and women who had provided meals and gifts to Native envoys or contributed goods and provisions for diplomatic journeys "to the Eastward." Sarah Battesbe received nine pounds four shillings threepence for hosting Lieutenant Joseph Bean and the Kennebec sachem Bomazeen and "his brother Indians" for two weeks in June 1716, while Bean, an interpreter, collected twelve pounds ten shillings "for his time and trouble." The Boston physician, Maine land speculator, and outspoken paper money advocate Oliver Noyes fetched more than twenty pounds for supplying shirts and coats for Bomazeen's party. Like the merchants who supplied the trade goods for the trade with the Wabanaki, men and women who gave hospitality to Wabanaki visitors served as adjuncts of the colonial state in establishing a payment landscape that facilitated colonial intrusion into, rather than interpenetration with, Indigenous spaces.[44]

The extent to which Native communities "behind the frontier" in southern New England were incorporated into the colonial monetary landscape via military service is less clear.[45] Nearly every Algonquian male living under Massachusetts jurisdiction fought in the wars against the French, often in all-Native units specializing in scouting and guerilla tactics, where their wages for serving as agents of English imperialism would have been slightly more than half of those of their white counterparts. Far from making a decent living, most Native soldiers barely eked out a subsistence, and many ended their lives in debt, forced to sell ancestral land to English settlers to support their families or pay for medical treatment. With the assistance of their towns' selectmen or their captains, some injured Indigenous veterans petitioned the governor or assembly for relief, with mixed success.[46] Among those who received monetary payments were Ben of Scituate, whom the French had shot in the hand during Queen Anne's War, leaving him "utterly disabled," and whom the assembly allowed three pounds plus forty shillings per year for two years, to be paid out by the Scituate selectmen; and Simon Sinkawah of Natick, who had lost both feet to frostbite "in his Scouting in the Service" in the winter of 1705–6 and who received six pounds out of the treasury.[47]

Like their white counterparts, Native veterans could press for years for relief. Such was the case of William Jeffrey of Harwich, who described his condition as "Poor and miserable," having been shot in the arm and had his wrist bones shattered in an attack on St. George's Island (now Monhegan) in the spring of 1724. One of only three men to survive the attack, Jeffrey had been "disabled from doing any Labour" to support himself. After petitioning Governor William Dummer for relief in 1724 (evidently unsuccessfully), in 1727 he appealed to the assembly, which granted him ten pounds plus five pounds per year until 1736, to be paid out by Captain Edmund Freeman. Five years after the payments had stopped, Jeffrey, "now being grown old," again petitioned the assembly for relief and was allowed twenty-five pounds.[48] Men like Ben, Sinkawah, and Jeffrey who joined colonial troops did so as one strategy to ensure their families' economic survival in the face of colonialism. But although some Indigenous communities were able to leverage their members' military service to secure land and autonomy, the gains were small compared to the terrible toll that service took in the long term. Deadly diseases combined with wartime casualties and debilitating injuries to shatter Native Massachusetts.[49]

Monetary Plurality

No colony emulated the Massachusetts money experiment more successfully than New York, where the colonial currency intersected with other monetary forms and systems. On June 8, 1709, the New York assembly authorized the emission of £5,000 in bills of credit to finance that summer's expedition to Canada. The timing was ideal because the colony needed a medium of exchange not only to purchase supplies for the upcoming expedition, but also to help grease the wheels of its growing economy. By 1700, New York City had surpassed Boston as the English empire's premier North American port, as the declining supply of furs and the expansion of Atlantic commerce drew colonists away from trade relations with Native peoples and into exchange networks run out of merchant houses. Meanwhile, the outbreak of war with the French and Spanish opened new avenues for business, including military contracting and piracy. Although seventeenth-century settlers had relied on specie for paying taxes and debts, the colony was drained of coin during the Anglo-French conflicts due to its worsening trade and payments balance with Britain. Worried that New York would be unable to pay the costs of Queen Anne's War, Lieutenant Governor Richard Ingoldesby urged the assembly to issue paper money redeemable by direct taxes the following year.[50]

The colony's printer, William Bradford, designed the bills of credit and stamped them with the coat of arms of New York City. In contrast to the biblically inspired Massachusetts Bay Colony seal adorning the 1690 paper money, the more commercially oriented New York City arms depicted a European sailor, a Lenape hunter, a windmill, a beaver, and flour barrels.[51] Then a committee of four prominent colonists numbered, dated, signed, and issued the bills "towards the discharging of Such provisions and necessaries

THE SINEWS OF WAR   55

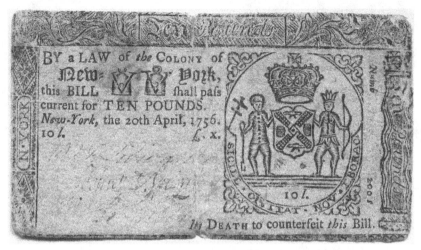

FIGURE 2.1. Colony of New York ten-pound bill of credit, 1756 (obverse). The bill shows the seal of New York City and a counterfeit warning. 0000.999.29178. Courtesy American Numismatic Society. http://numismatics.org/collection/0000.999.29178.

bought for the said Expedition." These signatures reveal a commercial world in flux, a nascent capitalism that relied on personal and financial credit alike to establish and ascertain trustworthiness.[52] As well as making the bills acceptable at the treasury, the assembly declared them legal tender for debts "as if the current Coyn of this Colony had been offered and tendered."[53] Five months later, £4,000 more rolled off Bradford's presses to pay the nearly five hundred soldiers the colony had conscripted for the Canada undertaking on their return, followed by an additional £4,000 to fortify western New York that winter and to reimburse all other individuals "to whom money is due for provisions and other Necessarys by them" for the expedition. The assembly determined whom to pay, for what, and how much. The treasurer, Abraham de Peyster, oversaw the disbursements.[54]

Although there are no surviving treasurer's accounts for the years prior to 1721, the 1709 paper money acts provide some detail regarding how the assembly allocated the latter £4,000. This included £1,312 for supplies for the Canada expedition, £216 for seventeen sawyers and thirteen carpenters who had served on that expedition, and twenty-five pounds for Albany mayor David Schuyler and colonial interpreter Lawrence Claessen for their journey to Onondaga the previous spring. The assembly earmarked £471 total for seven commissioners for procuring supplies and signing bills of credit and for their clerks, and £147 for the lieutenant governor for candles for the fort in New York City. Nearly £750 went toward the defense of the western part of the colony, counting the £221 for fifty Haudenosaunee troops for sixty days at the rate of eighteen pence per day, to be paid out by the commissioners of Indian affairs; £263 for wages for white and Native scouts to guard the frontiers, to be paid out by the same commissioners; £146 for candles for the Albany and Schenectady garrisons; and £61 for building a new blockhouse in Albany. Two years later, the assembly issued another £10,000 to help pay for the disastrous Walker Expedition to Quebec.[55]

Whereas the Massachusetts representatives had snubbed their governor's request to settle a gunsmith among the Wabanaki, the New York assembly granted it several times over. The Haudenosaunee secured the services of New York blacksmiths as part of the many concessions they extracted from the colony. In the fall of 1709, the assembly earmarked forty-nine pounds for "Such as shall perform and do the work and Mistery of Black Smiths & will Inhabite and reside this Winter with the Indians and mend their Arms."[56] In return, the colony sought approval to build military forts on Haudenosaunee lands. Along with "free" blacksmithing services, Haudenosaunees drew gifts of powder and shot, muskets, flints, lead, and trade goods from New York. In August 1714, the assembly appropriated the sum of 1,000 ounces of plate in Spanish coins or the equivalent "in Bills of Credit . . . to be laid out for Presents to the five Nations of Indians at Albany" and for the governor's "Expences in going thither to treat with them."[57] By playing off the British against the French, threatening to throw their loyalty to one or the other, Haudenosaunee leaders were able to wring concessions from both sides and maintain a steady supply of munitions for decades, with devastating long-term consequences for the Indigenous people of the region.[58]

Under the auspices of Governor Robert Hunter, in the summer of 1714 the assembly reported on the as yet unpaid claims of men and women who had contributed goods and labor to the colony since the outbreak of King William's War. Many of the claims had already been documented by warrants drawn and signed by former governors and disbursed to public creditors. Although the warrants were not designed to circulate as currency (similar to the early debentures of Massachusetts seen in the previous chapter), they were technically payable "to order," and many of them had indeed "passed in the nature of Bills of Credit," entitling the holders to payment even if they were not the original recipients. The colony's adoption of paper money also brought new claimants to the fore. The assembly discharged the claims with £27,680 in freshly printed bills of credit, exchanging old debts with new bills. In doing so, the assembly proclaimed its power over the purse strings.[59]

The array of claimants reflects both the province's history as a former Dutch colony with ties to the Haudenosaunee and the opportunities that wartime offered to Indigenous and European women. Take Hilletie van Olinda, a well-regarded "Interpretess to the Indians" of Mohawk and Dutch parentage whose estate New York owed money for her contributions during King William's War and Queen Anne's War. Van Olinda straddled two worlds as an interpreter, first for the Mohawks and later for the English. In 1667, for her services to the Mohawks, the Mohawk sachems conveyed to her the "Great Island" in the Mohawk River at Niskayuna. She was living with her Dutch husband and their children in Schenectady when she caught New York officials' attention. In August 1692, when an Anglo-Haudenosaunee expedition was fitting out from Schenectady to attack the French, Van Olinda translated languages and made wampum belts for colonial officials to present to Native sachems. The purple and white shell beads had long served as the standard trade currency between and among Native peoples and Europeans, but wampum had powerful cosmological and political meanings for the Haudenosaunee, who used it in "the resurrection of names" of the dead, as a "medium of all peacemaking," and "as a way of opening up channels of communication," as the anthropologist David Graeber described.[60] Van Olinda continued to serve as a cultural mediator on and off through at least 1704. In the summer of 1702, she attended Governor Cornbury's conference with Haudenosaunee leaders in Albany. Two years later, after helping to negotiate the Indian deed for the Kayaderosseras Patent, she successfully petitioned officials for a 400-acre "tract of woodland." At her death in 1707, she had outstanding claims on the public purse of seventy-five pounds.[61]

Van Olinda tendered and accepted various forms of payment in her capacity as an interpreter, from the wampum she presented to Haudenosaunee leaders to the land she received from colonial officials. In 1714 the treasurer discharged the colony's debt to her estate in bills of credit. But while wampum and land preserved a connection to the past, and bills forged a link to the future, wampum, land, and bills were not mutually exclusive. All three were means of mobilizing resources, based not on a calculus of profit and loss but on the collective demands of a society at war.[62] As one historian has explained, moreover, when Van Olinda and others like her "translated and explained disparate languages and rituals infused with cultural meanings and values, they acted as brokers, mediating the confrontation of European and Indian cultures," including, in many cases, selecting the appropriate presents and whom to give them to. Van Olinda's acumen as an interpreter not only of multiple languages but also of multiple monies strategically positioned her to shape the exchange of ideas, goods, language, and money in the colony and beyond.[63]

Other colonists whose claims the colony discharged with paper money included Hendrick Bleecker, who received five pounds six shillings sixpence "for his Service as Armourer of the Regiment commanded by Colonel Peter Schuyler" on the expedition to Canada in 1709; Jean Garreau, a New York City doctor, tax collector, and French Huguenot refugee who received six pounds "for his Service as Surgeon on Board a Ship" in 1705; Elias Peltreau, who claimed more than £121 for supplying 1,950 "Pounds of Candles" to the fort in New York City at the start of Queen Anne's War; and Henry Swift, who received thirteen pounds nine shillings "for Lodging and Entertaining the French Gentlemen that came from Canada with a Flag of Truce, and for Entertaining an Indian Sachem, and his Company" in 1708.[64]

Many recipients of paper money were women whose husbands had died in battle or who had themselves contributed goods and labor during the Anglo-French conflicts. Grace Lucretia Hegeman, a New York City widow, for example, successfully petitioned for a survivor's pension of twenty-five pounds "for Three Years Service and Sufferings of her Husband" Denys. Denys had been captured by the French on a mission to free Grace Lucretia, who had been taken prisoner by Wabanakis in the 1689 siege of Pemaquid in Maine, where the couple were living at the time. Deborah Fielding likewise claimed fifteen pounds for the service of her late husband, Nicolas Fielding. Annetie Daniels redeemed a warrant drawn by Governor Cornbury in December 1700 "for tending Sick Soldiers." Margaret Stokes received twenty-six pounds "for Provisions and other things bought" by herself and her late husband Richard for Cornbury's trip to Albany.[65]

The degree to which the colony's growing population of enslaved Africans had claims on the colony is as yet unclear. Laws regulating the militia suggest that enslaved Black men could serve as drummers and trumpeters at the rate of twenty and ten shillings per year, respectively.[66] New York sometimes hired enslaved laborers, but the wages would have gone to their enslavers. In 1727, for instance, the assembly moved to defray the charges of building, supplying, and defending the large stone trading house at Oswego on Lake Ontario, for which it earmarked more than sixty pounds total for forced labor.[67]

Black and Indigenous New Yorkers were technically entitled to the wolf bounty: five pounds for each wolf killed in Suffolk, Queens, and Kings Counties. The bounty for Orange County initially distinguished between "every person or persons," on the one hand, and "any Indian or Slave," on the other, with so-called "persons" allowed four shillings sixpence and Native and enslaved individuals permitted three shillings.[68] In later years, all were allowed the same sum of six shillings. To claim their prize, they needed to carry the head of the animal to a justice of the peace, who would give them "a Certificate to the [County] Treasurer," who in turn would pay the reward upon receipt thereof.[69] But as one historian has noted of the disbursal of wolf bounties in New England contexts, bureaucratic red tape and racist views discouraged Native persons from claiming them. A wolf hunter had to present the head to a local official and swear that he had killed the animal within the town's boundaries. Then the official would have to vouch for the hunter and the town treasurer would pay the bounty.[70]

When New York settled its last war debts in 1717, a lone person of color, referred to only as Jacob Salomon's free Black servant, received fifteen pounds (a considerable amount in those days) for an unspecified task. Yet the same act promised satisfaction to the tune of twenty pounds each in bills of credit to the enslavers of nineteen rebellious Africans whom colonial officials had tortured and executed in the aftermath of the 1712 New York City slave revolt.[71] Eight months after a slave conspiracy that left several buildings destroyed, eight white people dead, and a dozen more wounded, the assembly had passed a bill restricting gatherings of unfree laborers, limiting enslaved people's ability to buy or sell goods, and curbing slave manumission.[72] Governor Hunter had criticized the bill, "which cutting off all hopes from those slaves who by a faithful and diligent discharge of their duty, may at last look for the reward of a manumission by their masters will, will make 'em not only careless servants, but excite 'em to insurrections more bloody than any they have yet attempted." He had finally convinced the assembly to revise it to permit manumissions where surety of at least £200 was given.[73] But if his protests had slowed the drift to slavery as a lifelong status, five years later the assembly affirmed the principle of enslaved people as private property when it allowed compensation for "the Owners of Said Nineteene Negroes" or their heirs, which it promptly disbursed, setting chilling precedents for property in people and the power of the purse.[74] Judicial violence and fiscal power were mutually supporting forces of political and monetary legitimation, including the legitimation of certain forms of negotiable property—and not just the enslaved themselves, but the slips of paper that made their enslavers financially whole.

Proxy Wars

Money creation and militarization went hand in hand in South Carolina more than anywhere else in colonial North America. In the summer of 1702, after England declared war on Spain, South Carolina governor James Moore and his antiproprietary allies, the "Goose Creek Men," seized the opportunity to set an aggressive military agenda. Since the 1680s, the Goose Creek Men had monopolized the trade in Indigenous captives and deerskin, partnering with willing Savannahs and Yamasees to pummel the Spanish colony of Florida from the mid-1680s into the early 1700s. English traders used the outbreak of

Queen Anne's War as political cover to enslave the Indigenous allies of Spain and France. For the Savannah and the Yamasee, the war was a chance to expand their power and build up their armaments.[75]

That August Governor Moore asked for the assembly's blessing of an assault on the Spanish fort at St. Augustine "before it be strengthened with french forces." The assembly initially hesitated, reasoning that it would be better to prepare the colony "for a Defensive war" against the French than to "make a Offensive war against ye Spaniards."[76] In less than a week, however, it was raising volunteers to attack the Spanish town, "the Encouragement to be free Plunder and share of all Slaves." To pay for the expedition, the assembly levied 2,000 pounds "on Reall and Personall Estates, and on Places & offices of Trust." In October, an army of 500 European militia, 300 Indigenous troops, and dozens of enslaved Africans set out from Charles Town.[77] The soldiers arrived in St. Augustine a month later and "possessed themselves of the town with littel or know resistance, and made themselves masters of their Churches and Abbe" and forced all the inhabitants to flee "into the Castell," reported English captain Michael Cole to William Blathwayt of the Board of Trade on December 22.[78] Their good fortune soon ran out. The army besieged the fort for eight weeks while it waited for reinforcements and ammunition from Jamaica, but the relief never came. Instead, two Spanish men-of-war from Havana appeared, and the siege collapsed. After setting fire to their own boats, the defeated soldiers returned to South Carolina on foot.[79]

The St. Augustine debacle mirrored Massachusetts's 1690 Canada failure. Instead of enriching enslavers, the expedition plunged South Carolina into debt. Cole informed Blathwayt that "the charge of this expedition will amount to 7,000*l*."[80] Following Massachusetts, the colony moved to make paper money. Carolina trader and representative Thomas Nairne, writing in 1710, insisted that there had been no avoiding it, as the costs of the expedition had been so great "that they created some Uneasiness, and the Assembly finding it was in vain to struggle with the Difficulty, by raising annual Taxes, which could not have been levied soon enough to answer the present Exigency, they concluded to stamp Bills of Credit."[81]

In the spring of 1703, the South Carolina assembly ordered the public receiver (similar to a treasurer) and three commissioners "to make or cause to be made" £6,000 in paper bills, redeemable in payment of direct taxes and indirect duties spread over two years.[82] After stamping the bills, leaving blank spaces for the amounts, the commissioners carried them to a room adjoining the assembly, where the bills were numbered, signed, and sealed by a joint committee of two members of the governor's council and three representatives. From there they were brought to the receiver, along with a list of all claims on the public, which were discharged with the bills. The assembly appointed additional commissioners to examine the receiver's accounts weekly and to ensure the destruction of all bills redeemed by taxes.[83]

After South Carolina failed to take St. Augustine in 1702, its Yamasee, Creek (Muscogee), and Cherokee allies went on to destroy numerous Spanish missions in the Apalachee province. As historian Alan Gallay explains, "the Carolinians had learned that they could make greater profits by attacking and enslaving a European foe's allies than by assaulting the Europeans directly."[84] Following the St. Augustine fiasco, James Moore led an army of Creek soldiers into Florida, and over the next six years the English trapped fifteen thousand Spanish-allied Apalachee people in the web of Indigenous slavery. Had South Carolina not coopted Native soldiers for imperial purposes, the demands on the public purse would have been much greater. It made more financial sense to attack the Spanish by proxy than head on.[85]

Like Massachusetts, South Carolina depended on Native men in wartime, but for a different reason: the colony needed able-bodied Europeans on the home front to police its growing population of enslaved Africans. Even as European settlers sought to extract greater profits from the trade in Indigenous captives, the growing importance of plantation agriculture made enslaved African laborers valuable assets requiring protection. The colonial government was soon using bills of credit as a means to fortify the province against external and internal threats, earmarking public funds for the construction of moats and drawbridges; establishing a salaried night watch in Charles Town to surveil poor and enslaved people; and enlisting drummers to beat the "tattoo and reveille" every evening. Each of the watchmen received a twenty-pound salary, to be financed by a quarterly tax on the townspeople. The percussionists were almost always enslaved men granted one pound per month, a sum their enslavers likely took the liberty of taking.[86]

If South Carolina depended on its Native allies to attack the Spanish and their Native allies, however, the colony needed enslaved people to help repel Spaniards and free Africans to the south and resistant Native peoples to the west. The assembly routinely drafted enslaved men in wartime, including during the Tuscarora and Yamasee (1715–17) wars. Subsequent militia acts provided for enlisting enslaved men and arming them out of the public stores in case of an alarm and for paying them ten pounds "at the charge of the publick" for every enemy captured or killed.[87] While a few Black soldiers were freed for their service, the English never formally integrated Black men into the militia as the Spanish did, and the presence of enslaved soldiers on the battlefield must have disconcerted their enslavers. It was far more common for the colony to pay enslavers for the labor of their enslaved craftsmen and sailors. And indeed, the colony relied on forced labor for everything from repairing the fortifications of Charles Town in 1707 to constructing a new statehouse in 1712 to assisting the press master in an expedition "against the Pirates" in 1726.[88]

Although no records of the South Carolina public receiver (whose office was eliminated in 1721) survive, the treasurer Alexander Parris's general ledger from the second half of the 1720s suggests a strong relationship between colonial spending and militarization. As the colony's population and economy boomed, nearly half of the budget (more when major expeditions had to be financed) went toward military salaries, provisions, and supplies. For the year 1725 alone, Parris paid out £2,226 for Fort Moore in the northwestern part of the colony; £1,513 for Palachucola Fort on the Savannah River; £440 for Johnson's Fort near present-day Augusta; £1,159 for scout boats; and thirty-six pounds two shillings sixpence for expresses to and from the garrisons. The treasurer disbursed £486 for the Charles Town watch, £350 for the armorer and gunner of Charles Town, £250 for repairing Charles Town's fortifications, and £100 for colors for the Charles Town bastions. On top of his £1,000 annual salary, Parris paid himself £200 for serving as "Commissary to the Garrisons." Along with Massachusetts and New York, South Carolina allocated considerable sums for maintaining Anglo-Native diplomatic and trade ties, including £200 for a commissioner and interpreter to the powerful Creeks and nearly £140 for entertainment and presents for "Sundry Indians," possibly the equally formidable Cherokees. Among the presents were flints, guns, bullets, powder, vermilion, coats, shirts, hats, buttons, pipes, kettles, salt, corn, and peas. Property taxes, import and export duties, twenty-eight Indian trading licenses, and nineteen tavern licenses (against which the charges of the Charles Town watch were made) balanced the colony's books. That year there was even a surplus.[89]

Forged in the crucible of war, early American money was a constitutive feature of the English colonial project. King William's War and Queen Anne's War overlapped and intersected with deep-rooted regional conflicts with Indigenous peoples over trade, land, and power—namely, the Anglo-Wabanaki Wars in New England, the Tuscarora War in North Carolina, and the Yamasee War in South Carolina. Massachusetts churned out bills of credit for the Fourth Anglo-Wabanaki War, paying cash for intelligence relating to the Wabanakis or for the scalps of slain Indigenous people, or for transporting Native hostages to the Boston jail, where numerous captives succumbed to smallpox. Native people were worth more dead than they were alive: scalps fetched one hundred pounds, hostages between ten and fifty.[90] The South

Carolina bills of 1711, Lieutenant Governor William Bull would recall, were "commonly called Tusquerora bills, from the name of the Indians who made war against the people of North Carolina," a war that claimed the lives of some 600 Tuscarora men, women, and children and that shattered the society as an independent entity.[91]

As it destroyed, paper money also projected an idealized community. How it was made, who received it, and the nature of the debts it discharged delimited the borders of belonging and simultaneously reduced certain goods, labor, and people to prices. But in practice, such borders were permeable and shifting, and paper money was more inclusive than the polities that created it. In 1712, both New York and South Carolina enacted new slave codes restricting and regulating enslaved people's economic lives. They banned enslavers from giving enslaved men and women time off, barred the enslaved from holding property in most cases, and prohibited them from trading with other bondspeople and with free people.[92] Yet everywhere that they made up a significant proportion of the population, enslaved men and women began constructing complex economies based on monetary exchange. They sold surplus produce to the highest bidder, fenced stolen cloth and alcohol for cash, and hired themselves out, pocketing some of the wages. In the process, they initiated elaborate informal economies that overlapped with and cut through the colonial monetary community.[93]

For most settlers, trust in bills of credit meant trusting the people who offered such bills. Paradoxically, the bills removed the burden of trust from participants in bilateral transactions and placed it on the issuer of money, a critical third party in the process.[94] But if paper money could weaken traditional forms of social dependency based on hierarchy and deference, it also introduced new interdependencies between and among colonial governments and their constituents. Assemblies coordinated monetary circuits, issuing paper bills in payment of public debts and redeeming them for taxes. Yet for some assemblies, redeeming the bills would prove increasingly difficult, threatening to corrode the emerging interdependencies with their constituents. How assemblies made paper money shaped its value in the economy. But for the money to retain its value, it had to be able to return to the source. The next chapter reconsiders inflation in early America in light of the wars that animated it. In doing so, it returns inflation and its causes to history.

3

Accounting for Politics

"New-England is the most unhappy in its Paper-Currency of any of the Colonies, Carolina excepted," lamented Benjamin Franklin in the inaugural issue of his short-lived *General Magazine and Historical Chronicle*, published in four installments over 1741. Their bills of credit, the Philadelphia printer argued, had continually sunk in value "to the great Detriment of the Creditors of the Province," prompting "several strict Instructions from the Crown . . . to restrain the large and frequent Emissions made of those Bills."[1] What accounted for the sad state of the New England and Carolina currencies? Was the overissue of paper money to blame? Or were there other, perhaps deeper causes? A quarter-century later, Franklin thought he knew the answer. "In Times of War," he explained to the British ministry at the height of the imperial crisis, "Bills of Credit have been sometimes issued in enormous Sums . . . funded on Taxes which were to bring them in at distant Periods," which "has, in some Colonies, occasioned a real Depreciation of these Bills, tho' made a legal tender."[2] But although "the Merchants trading to those Colonies may sometimes have suffered by the sudden and unforeseen Rise of Exchange," he wrote in the *Pennsylvania Chronicle* soon after, "War is a common Calamity in all Countries, and the Merchants that deal with them cannot expect to avoid a share of the Losses it sometimes occasions by affecting Publick Credit."[3]

Just as military aims more than market demand informed whether, when, and how the colonies issued bills of credit, so too, as Franklin pointed out to both imperial and colonial audiences, did military prospects shape fiscal prospects, affecting when and whether colonial assemblies could enforce the taxes they had earmarked to redeem the bills. A few assemblies adopted fiscal policies that were suspected to depreciate the currencies and claimed by some to fuel inflationary pressures, namely, postponing or canceling those taxes. But the first debates about paper money did not set "hard-money" ideologues against "soft-money" agitators. If most hard-money partisans avowed that only silver was money according to God and nature, and most paper money advocates maintained that anything could be money with a community's consent, the first debates about paper money concerned not the money's material, per se, but how money was *made*.

These debates powerfully shaped the trajectory of provincial politics in the crucial decades following the Glorious Revolution of 1688, when the corporate body politic based on the common goal of the public good began splintering into disparate political factions.[4] Opposing interests fought over the length of time bills of credit circulated, the types of taxes that redeemed them, and the merits of making them legal tender for debts. Arguments over money and taxes accompanied rhetoric reflecting a developing class struggle over the production of money and access to credit, and the question of which class gained at whose expense—those who owned money or those who owed it—was never far from view.[5]

Queen Anne's Proclamation

All the British colonies, with a few notable exceptions, denominated their bills of credit in the shared language of pounds, shillings, and pence. But the colonial currencies did not circulate at fixed exchange rates with British sterling, nor was one colony's currency equal in value to another's. Instead of there being a single colonial currency pegged against sterling, each currency's exchange rate floated, or fluctuated, according to the interplay of the supply and demand for that currency relative to the supply and demand for sterling.[6] As a result, the actual sterling exchange rate varied both over time and from colony to colony. If a colony's bills circulated at face value (or nominal value) equal to sterling based on the official value of a Spanish piece of eight (six shillings in most cases, for an official exchange rate of £133 colonial currency for £100 sterling), then a five-shilling bill may well have fetched an actual piece of eight. Bills that circulated at face value were said to pass "current" or "on a par" with sterling. Bills that circulated below face value were depreciated or discounted relative to sterling, so that purchasing a sum in sterling would have required more than that sum in said bills. But if the bills were legal tender for debts, debtors could use them to discharge sterling debts at face value, regardless of the difference between the official exchange rate and the actual one.[7]

This was not the arrangement envisioned by Queen Anne's Proclamation on the colonial coinage. The 1704 royal proclamation, codified by Parliament in 1708, ordered all the colonies to fix the value of full-bodied pieces of eight at no more than six shillings currency beginning January 1, 1705. As the value of a piece of eight was set at four shillings sixpence sterling in England, the proclamation established an official exchange rate of £133 colonial currency for £100 sterling, the same rate Massachusetts had enacted (and the Crown approved) in the seventeenth century. In addition to pieces of eight, the proclamation established the weights and maximum values of Flemish "cross dollar" patagons, Dutch ducatoon "silver riders," French écus, Portuguese cruzados, Dutch three guilders, and German "rix dollars." It neglected to mention gold coins, so colonists could continue to overvalue Lyon dollars and other gold pieces.[8]

Queen Anne's Proclamation had been precipitated by colonial governments' practice of "crying up" the values of foreign coins in terms of their currencies and permitting the circulation of clipped, shaved, or worn coins at the inflated rates. By 1700 most of the colonies had raised the value of a piece of eight to six shillings or more and had established a legal exchange rate of at least £133 currency for £100 sterling. In some of the colonies, pieces of eight passed by custom at even higher values, from nearly seven shillings in Pennsylvania to eight shillings in Barbados. John Blackwell, Oliver Cromwell's old war treasurer who had left Boston to take up post as the Pennsylvania lieutenant governor in 1688, was especially troubled by the mishmash of light coins passing at the same values as heavy ones. He reported to the proprietor William Penn in London that "severall species of moneys are denominated that passe here: some whereof are allowed by Law; & others passe customarily in trading." English coins circulated at "one fowerth part more in denomination than in England," Spanish dollars at six shillings, and rarely did either "conteyne the weight at which they are coyned." Through clipping, shaving, and wearing, Blackwell surmised, "all the current money of this Province is advanced in denomination to double its intrinsique value."[9] Fifteen years later, Penn estimated that cut silver dollars "want 1/3 at least of the intrinsick vallue they goe at; a great abuse."[10]

In 1700, Penn had taken it upon himself to implore the Crown to standardize the colonial coinage, drawing up a set of recommendations to that effect. Then in Pennsylvania, he explained that a piece of eight passed for six shillings in Massachusetts, six shillings ninepence in New Jersey and Pennsylvania, seven shillings eightpence in Maryland, four shillings sixpence in Virginia, and five shillings in South Carolina. "It would be more convenient," he reasoned, if "there would be but one standard of coin or that mony were of the same value" throughout the colonies.[11] In 1703 Penn complained again about "the advance upon Coyne in America, and the Inequality of it," and "wish[ed] that all were at a par; that an ounce of silver should be an ounce of silver in all the Dominions of the Crown." He nevertheless predicted that if the Crown was to implement such a policy, colonists would send all their coins to England "for want of returns" and the assemblies would "take very ill" and refuse to enforce it unless the royal government offered "paper Credit, in lieu of [coin]." For his part, he was not opposed to the idea of a paper currency, having previously sent Blackwell a proposal for a bank by Edward Roberts, Cromwell's old auditor general. The measure of the bank's success, Penn remarked, would be in "laying the foundation of trade and in the increase of corn, cattle, whale oil, skins, etc."[12]

Throughout the spring and summer of 1703, the Board of Trade solicited reports on the coinage from colonial officials, and it quickly became apparent that not everyone agreed with Penn's thinking. The Maryland assembly, on the one hand, supported standardizing the values of coins in the colonies, attesting that the overvaluation of coins in the neighboring colonies had been "the occasion of drawing their coin from them."[13] But on the other hand, the agent for English Antigua, where light pieces of eight passed for six shillings and heavy for six shillings sixpence, objected to restrictions on coins in the colonies, explaining that "the people of that Island found that" their overvaluing coins relative to other colonies "had brought in money amongst them." After a year of legal wrangling over whether Anne even had the power to regulate the colonial coinage "by her Royal Prerogative," she issued her proclamation.[14]

Queen Anne's Proclamation theoretically should have extended England's new monetary system to the colonies. In the 1690s, the English "financial revolution" had established a hierarchy of financial promises. The new Bank of England, chartered in 1694, lent money to the state and produced banknotes underpinned by two promises: the promise of the state to repay the bank, and the promise of convertibility to silver coins. But clipping and counterfeiting had so eroded the coinage that coins no longer passed at face value, and the nation faced a monetary crisis. The recoinage debate divided the English ruling class. Many officials supported decoupling money's value from its commodity content, and some Tory politicians favored the establishment of a national land bank. Yet the philosopher John Locke charged that the debasement of the sovereign's coin was a breach of the promise of convertibility to coins that underpinned Bank of England banknotes and convinced the Whig government to remint the coinage at the official weight. The argument that the stability of the monetary system depended on the integrity of the coinage ultimately won out.[15]

If England's "Great Recoinage" of 1696 had established a "strong" monetary system supported by a fixed metallic standard, Queen Anne's Proclamation was administered quite unevenly across the Atlantic. Some colonies ignored it completely. Barbados and New York took advantage of the proclamation's omission of gold coins and overvalued gold pieces. Pennsylvania waited until 1709 to implement the proclamation, while South Carolina took more than a decade to enforce it. Colonies that enforced the so-called "proclamation rate" or "proclamation money" faced money scarcity, leading some of them to adopt paper currencies, which, like gold coins, the proclamation failed to mention. Meanwhile, colonists with relatively greater access to coin worked the policy to their advantage. When news of the proclamation reached Barbados in August 1704, "the monied men" of that colony gathered up as much coin as they could in order to profitably export it to "the neighbouring colonys and Plantations [that] had not paid that strict observance to her said Majesty's Proclamation as had been done in this Island," leaving small merchants and planters in the lurch.[16] The proclamation's effects were a major factor in the Barbados assembly's decision to establish a loan office and issue £65,000 in bills of credit the following year.[17]

A Political Theory of Value

Despite not being pegged against sterling, let alone backed by it, most colonies' bills of credit passed on a par with or better than coin for the duration of Queen Anne's War (1702–13). "We have no Instance" of creditors refusing to take bills, South Carolina merchant and politician Thomas Nairne boasted in *A Letter from South Carolina*, published in London in 1710, "the Funds upon which they are made being so good"—the funds being the tax revenues marked to redeem them—"that they pass in all Payments without any Demur or Dissatisfaction." He attested that Carolina bills "have never fallen lower than the intrinsic value, nor can they well do so, upon those Principles whereon they are established."[18] The anonymous author of *An Essay on Currency*, published in Charles Town in 1734, confirmed that the currency had "pass'd currant, as Silver, so that I remember in 1711, or 1712 I had a Piece of Eight for a Crown-Bill."[19] Massachusetts bills could claim the same sterling reputation. "Our province chequer notes are of that Currency and honor," Governor Joseph Dudley informed the Board of Trade in 1710, "that we buy all merchandize, goods, ships, houses, estates of land, or whatever else with those bills preferable to money."[20] A few years later, he reiterated that "The Perfect want of money was such, that the bills became currant in all trade with merchants and countrymen, with that honour that I never heard of any abatement in payment, either in trade, or market, or any dealing whatsoever."[21] The board did not even object when, in 1712, the Massachusetts assembly made the bills legal tender for debts.[22]

But as the war ended, depreciation set in. In South Carolina and Massachusetts in particular, the currency's value began to fall in terms of sterling. Nineteenth-century historians writing in the context of debates over "free silver" (which they opposed) and the gold standard (which they supported) liked to attribute the depreciation to the overissue of paper money: if too many paper notes circulate, the argument went, then the currency depreciates and prices rise.[23] The French jurist Jean Bodin first put forth the "quantity theory of money" in the sixteenth century as a way to explain rising prices in Europe following the Spanish conquest of the Americas. According to Bodin, the great influx of gold and silver from Mexico and Peru was devaluing the European currencies, resulting in a great inflation. No matter that most of the precious metals went straight to India and China to purchase luxury goods, the quantity theory became economic orthodoxy in English decision-making circles, informing and justifying punishingly deflationary policies such as Locke's recoinage.[24]

But depreciation, and the inflation that could accompany it, was never just a matter of quantity. Massachusetts and South Carolina bills of credit depreciated in the second decade of the eighteenth century not because they were issued in excess, but because they were issued in excess of *taxes*—in other words, politics, not mere quantity, determined their value. Historians and economists have recently highlighted the role of politics, policy, and the law in shaping money and prices throughout history.[25] The economist Farley Grubb illustrates how the British American colonies engaged in "extensive efforts to legislate the structure of money" and maintains that the success or lack thereof of these efforts explains changes in currency values when and where quantity cannot. In early America, paper money's real value was thus grounded in its "fiscal value," or its future expected value in paying taxes. Under ordinary circumstances, this structural feature imparted what Grubb calls "a time-discounting dimension" to bills of credit, whereby a bill's "present value" was not depreciated per se, but discounted according to how much time remained until it could be redeemed in payment of taxes.[26] The discount could be negated, however, as the legal scholar Christine Desan elaborates, if the money also carried a "cash premium" or "liquidity premium," that is, "if people recognized as valuable its services as cash in the interim."[27]

Prominent eighteenth-century writers observed the same phenomenon. In the 1760s, Benjamin Franklin described the time-discount factor to the British ministry, explaining that "a Bill promising Payment at Distant Periods of Time" and depending entirely "on such distant Payment for its Value" cannot possibly circulate at face value equal to sterling, "but must suffer a Discount in Proportion to the Time." A paper bill of credit payable in a year was therefore more valuable than one scheduled to remain in circulation for another decade. "Hence the Discount will be greatest soon after the Bills are issued," Franklin continued, "and, as the Term of Payment approaches, the Discount will gradually become less till it amounts to nothing worth Notice."[28] Founding father of economics Adam Smith expressed more skepticism, later arguing that the colonial currencies circulated at a discount because they were not convertible to coin, they bore no interest, and redemption periods were long and uncertain. He concluded, nonetheless, that depreciation was not inevitable and that it typically occurred when the currencies were issued over and above taxes.[29]

If these observations rang true under conditions of peace and prosperity, English colonial settlers were continually at war with other European colonists, with Indigenous peoples, and with enslaved persons, and there were no two colonies more bellicose than Massachusetts and South Carolina. A better explanation for why their bills of credit depreciated relative to sterling, then, was the risk of not redeeming them. That is, the bills' values depended less on *when* they would be redeemed than on *whether* they would be redeemed at all. Military outlooks and outcomes affected redemption prospects, as well as fiscal policy choices related to military contingencies. Fiscal policies that lessened the likelihood of redemption, such as postponing the taxes marked for such redemption or canceling those taxes altogether, diminished public confidence that the bills would be redeemed and consequently lowered their value in exchange.[30]

Borrowing against the Future

When Massachusetts delayed the redemption of bills of credit by postponing taxes, it was not merely buying more time to pay the public debts. It was also offering tax relief and some liquidity in hard times. From 1702 to 1708, the colonial assembly issued, redeemed, and reissued paper bills according to sixteen separate acts; the redemption periods were short, and the bills were redeemed on schedule. But between 1708 and 1714, the assembly authorized five new currency emissions totaling £150,000, a threefold increase in the nominal value of paper money in circulation. This spending spree was catalyzed by a series of military misadventures originating in New England and New York late in Queen Anne's War, including additional unsuccessful attempts to conquer French Canada. Although the bills were acceptable at the treasury, the assembly began postponing the direct taxes it had originally earmarked to redeem them, extending redemption periods from three years for bills issued in 1707 to four years after the 1709 emission, five years following the 1710 emission, and six years for all bills issued from 1711 to 1714. While the policy was popular among cash-strapped colonial settlers, political scientist Alvin Rabushka explains, delaying taxes nevertheless resulted in "a gradual loss of confidence in the stated value of bills as their growth outpaced the guarantee of redemption." The bills depreciated relative to sterling, and Boston merchants began discounting them in payments, demanding that customers pay a higher price in bills to account for the difference.[31]

Alarmed by the rise in prices of goods, and subsequently in the price of silver, hard-money men who wanted to do away with paper currency and "return" to silver payments cried that the colony's monetary experiment had gone too far. They accused the assembly of degrading the local currency beyond restitution, rendering province bills of credit worthless and fueling inflationary pressures. Prices indeed rose. The cost of silver went from seven shillings per ounce during the war to twelve shillings per ounce and rising by 1720. Imported commodities more than doubled in price, forcing local farmers to raise the cost of their produce. Before the war, a commentator wrote in 1719, a pound of butter worth sixpence per pound could purchase two pounds of sugar, whereas "if we now have Nine pence a Pound for Butter, that Nine pence will buy but One Pound of Sugar."[32] But contemporaries were divided on whether depreciation was to blame for the inflation: while hard-money men viewed higher prices as the inevitable byproduct of a depreciating currency, paper money supporters attributed the rising cost of living to money scarcity and greedy merchants.

From 1719 to 1721, prominent Massachusetts colonists debated the money question in printed essays. Historians studying these essays have tended to focus on the authors' proposals for different currencies and banks while overlooking their incisive arguments about taxes and fiscal policy.[33] Contrary to the opinion of late nineteenth-century historians, moreover, colonial hard-money advocates did not espouse a quantity theory of money per se. When they denounced the assembly's practice of postponing taxes marked to redeem paper money as a violation of "public faith," they were pointing the finger not at some abstract law of supply and demand but rather at provincial politics. "Postponing the drawing in of Bills," observed one essayist in 1719, "does sink the Credit or esteem of them, and so raise the Price of Commodities Imported and Produced here."[34] Harvard professor and hard-money defender Edward Wigglesworth, who proposed establishing a silver bank, agreed that putting off taxes depreciated the currency, and additionally lamented that "*Now as the Value of Paper hath sunk in comparison with Silver, so the Merchants have advanced upon their Goods in some proportion, and so the Price of the Country's produce hath been gradually rising also.*"[35]

Hard-money men therefore fully recognized the role of tax redemption mechanisms in anchoring the colonial currencies. For them, it was precisely paper money's fiscal nature—the fact that it was not a precious resource like gold or silver but merely a credit against some future tax—that helped explain the depreciation. "A *Note* or *Bill of Credit* is not *Money*," one held, drawing a hard-and-fast distinction, "but rather a Security that Payment shall be made in such a time."[36] If a debtor delayed paying a debt, both the value of the debt and the debtor's reputation would suffer. Likewise, if the representatives in the assembly postponed redeeming a bill, "does not this lessen the value of the bill? Do's it not give them an handle to argue; that if the fulfilling of one Publick promise be postponed, so it may be with another, and what will publick Faith (or ingagement) signifie after this rate?"[37] As Wigglesworth put it in his 1720 essay *A Letter from One in the Country to his Friend in Boston*, paper bills had value "because we know that we must all pay Taxes, and these Bills will enable us to pay these Taxes as well or better than any thing else." His reasoning was not all that different from that of Cotton Mather and John Blackwell writing in 1691. Thus "if these Taxes had never been postponed, the demand the Bills would have been in for paying Taxes, would have made us esteem them at a higher rate than we do now." Postponing taxes lowered expectations of redemption, diminishing confidence in the bills the taxes were marked to redeem. Should the assembly suspend tax payments altogether, the bills "would at once lose all their value, and be worth no more to them that have them in their keeping, than so many bits of Blank Paper."[38]

Paper money advocates who favored supplementing wartime bills with money issued through a private bank of credit or a public loan office saw things rather differently. If politics was driving prices up, it was the colonial government's failure to provide a sufficient currency relative to demand, not its habit of postponing taxes, that was to blame. And outstanding bills of credit were being redeemed, if gradually. The Boston merchant John Colman, who led the charge to establish a bank of credit like the one Blackwell had proposed in 1686, blamed the rising cost of living not on an abundance of bills but on a scarcity, "for though the bills grow scarcer," he maintained, "yet Goods of all sorts keep up their Prices." He believed that money scarcity allowed lenders to charge usurious interest rates and encouraged merchants to create artificial scarcity of necessities, enabling them to boost their profits by raising prices.[39]

Some paper money supporters rejected the premise that depreciation caused inflation altogether. Hard-money men had it all backward: the source of *inflation* was not *depreciation* based on the policy choices of assemblies; the source of *depreciation* was *inflation* based on the price-setting of private actors. Ipswich minister John Wise, who endorsed a loan office, pointed out that inflationary pressures had preceded the currency's fall in value relative to sterling. In his 1721 essay *A Word of Comfort to a Melancholy Country*, he reasoned that the arrival of the British naval fleet during the war in 1709 had been "some Means of Raising the Price of our live Stock," there being so many more mouths to feed than usual. More recently, merchants had taken advantage of the colony's "considerable scarcity of salt Provisions" by raising the cost of fish and pork.[40] Colman's friend, the Boston physician Oliver Noyes, accused Boston-based Atlantic merchants of depreciating the currency when they used bills of credit to buy up all of the available silver to ship to Britain. There is "a Sett of Men among us" who bid up the price of bills of exchange and gold and silver coins, raising the sterling exchange rate and fueling inflation, Noyes warned, "and these are the Men who Import the fineries . . . who indeed serve more to hurt us than to help us."[41]

Paper money partisans agreed, however, that both public spending and private consumption could affect money and prices. When the assembly levied goods and labor from colonists in exchange for bills of credit redeemable in payment of taxes, it put a price on the goods and labor and thus set the value of the bills in which taxes were to be paid. But in the company of private buyers and sellers, the assembly's control over money and prices was incomplete. Even in wartime, the colonial government was not the sole procurer of goods and labor. Wise explained that it competed with British officers and private merchants (including "Foreign Ships of Trade") offering higher prices for provisions, which caused inflation and, in turn, depreciation. Noyes similarly decried import merchants for using paper bills to purchase silver at exorbitant rates, depreciating the currency relative to sterling and raising overall prices.[42]

Moreover, when the assembly curtailed public spending after Queen Anne's War, colonists became the primary purchasers of goods and labor, including imported European goods. With private consumption part of the picture, then, colonists sought bills of credit not only for paying taxes, but also for buying things. They sold their produce at the highest price someone was willing to pay in order to get bills for buying things, instead of simply selling it to the assembly at the assembly's price to get bills for paying taxes. In this context, John Colman maintained, money scarcity and high prices went hand in hand, "for there being not a Medium to pay with, the Seller, if he must take other things in Exchange for his Commodities will make his Price accordingly & then the Shops, when they come to answer the Merchants Notes, are obliged to advance according to the Prices they give; and by this means the burden is laid on the poor Trades-men." In other words, the shopkeepers raised their prices so they could pay back the merchants, the farmers raised their prices so they could pay back the shopkeepers, and the tradesmen could barely keep up.[43]

Colman observed yet another factor contributing to inflation: Massachusetts's worsening trade and payments balance with Britain. If hard-money men attributed the trade deficit to the scarcity of silver for making returns, paper money advocates retorted that silver was scarce because of the deficit, since whatever silver entered the colony was quickly purchased by merchants and sent abroad to make payments. And the deficit grew apace not because there was insufficient silver to make up the balance. Rather, the colony was unable to improve its payments balance with the metropole because its import merchants were driving up the cost of local produce, making it difficult to market the produce in Newfoundland and other locales. Noyes saw this as a vicious cycle: the high prices of local provisions made it impossible for the colony to offload its produce, decreasing the colony's output and worsening its terms of trade with Britain, which increased the cost of "European Goods" and helped "to keep up their Prizes [prices]."[44] Even Wigglesworth conceded that "there is hardly any thing fit to be exported, that will turn to any account in other Countries."[45]

Supporters of paper money wondered how the poorest among them would get by if hard-money men had their way and all outstanding bills of credit were redeemed without something to replace them. As it was, people were struggling to buy food to eat. In a 1720 essay that got him arrested for disturbing the peace, John Colman lamented that "there are so few Bills Circulating . . . that People are distressed to a very great degree, to get Bills to procure the Necessaries of Life," even "to purchase their daily Food." He denounced creditors for taking advantage of the growing scarcity of money, crushing their debtors by demanding payment in precious silver when much of Boston "can hardly get Bread to satisfie Nature," let alone get their hands on such silver, and accused the "Gentlemen who are against Emitting more Bills" of hoarding them and exacerbating the scarcity. But he reserved his toughest criticism for the assembly, which he accused of abdicating its responsibility to the people "to take care they are not Oppressed or distressed."[46] In another essay published that year, Oliver Noyes lauded Colman for illuminating "the Poverty and Oppression which is breaking in like a Flood upon us," and branded Edward Wigglesworth as a liar whose writings were "mostly Evasions, Misrepresentation and Amusements, and perhaps some Mistakes." He concluded that while it might be "prudent" for the public to pay its debts, it was just "as prudent to look forward and consider how we shall Live when the

Bills are all in. There will not be then a Farthing of Money to Buy a morsel of Bread for this great Multitude."[47]

While most paper money advocates believed it was the colonial government's duty to provide a sufficient circulating currency, Colman raised the stakes of the money debate when he suggested using public spending to stabilize prices. If the assembly refused to endorse his scheme for a bank of credit, he imagined that nothing would be better than for the government "to go on some great & Expensive Work, & Emit Bills to carry it on." For one, he proposed using province bills for "Fortifying our exposed Settlements," encouraging people "to sit down, & till the Earth, and raise Hemp and Flax and so bring down the Prices of Linen and Canvas, as well as Provisions." Colman also recommended appropriating £50,000 in public funds to build a toll bridge "over Charles River." The bridge would supply a steady stream of public revenue and "help us by imploying the Poor." As such, "the circulation of the Bills would be a great service to every Body."[48] If hard-money men urged financial prudence, paper money supporters advocated fiscal stimulus. After decades of continual war, they envisioned paper bills of credit as a means of encouraging internal and external trade, increasing employment, funding public improvements, and even stabilizing prices. Perhaps the value of money was to be found in its productive capacities as much as in its destructive ones.

During the first half of the 1720s, increases in public spending and lending indeed mitigated depreciation and inflation. How the government spent money mattered a great deal. Mobilization for the Fourth Anglo-Wabanaki War (1722–25) and internal improvements pumped bills of credit into local markets, increasing the demand for goods and labor on the home front. The assembly had long used public funds to aid import substitute industries, and in 1722 it instituted a five-year bounty for linen made in the colony. For the year 1725, the treasurer paid out £134 3s. 4d. "for 19 pieces Linnen & for 38 pieces Duck," up from the previous year's £43 5s. payout.[49] In addition, before it was taken off in 1725, New England merchants received a bounty from the Royal Navy on all pitch and tar exported to Britain, most of it transshipped from South Carolina. An econometric study of monetization and growth in colonial New England found that the benefits of paper money issued to finance public spending outweighed the costs of inflation. Meanwhile, the extension of public loans to towns and individuals (discussed in the next chapter) expanded the colonial monetary community, providing a source of income for localities while promoting inland trade and development.[50]

But the relief that Colman and other paper money supporters advocated was as temporary as the bills of credit themselves were. The experience of one colonial merchant illustrates how the flush times could end as quickly as they began. In 1719, Thomas Amory moved from Charles Town to Boston, where he made a living importing rice, pitch, tar, rum, and molasses from South Carolina, reexporting the rice and naval stores and selling the rum and molasses wholesale to country retailers. He routinely accepted paper bills in payment of debts, including the "Twentyone Pounds in Bills of Credit" he received from John and Samuel Wainwright on January 29, 1722 and, after some pressing, the "Bills of Credit Twenty Nine Pounds" they paid him on March 12 of that year. He collected sixty-seven pounds eightpence "in Province Bills" on Martha Logan's account on November 12, 1723, and fifty-eight pounds "in Paper Bills from Captn Nickols" on April 19, 1725.[51] By the spring of 1722, Amory had made enough money to purchase a plot of land and was in the process of setting up a rum distillery. He hoped to have it up and running by the following winter but still needed to purchase molasses. Having invested all his profits in the distillery, however, he soon found himself at the mercy of his debtors.[52]

By the time money scarcity revisited the colony in 1726, Amory was struggling to make ends meet. He tried his hand at the European trade after the bounty on naval stores expired, renting a warehouse by the wharf where he planned to sell foreign goods wholesale. On July 21 he reached out to Nicholas Oursel, a French merchant he had met several years earlier in London, proposing that they could turn a hefty profit "on Good European Goods . . . with which I could easily turn into Money to procure fish Logwood or Any thing the Country affords."[53] But when the public loans matured and the bills of credit issued to pay the costs of the Fourth Anglo-Wabanaki War returned to the treasury, local business screeched to a halt. Amory could not sell any of the goods he had imported from London to shopkeepers for under six months' credit, let alone purchase local provisions to ship abroad.[54] By the fall of 1727, he was pleading with his British creditors for more time to pay his debts, lamenting to one of "ye. Great Scarcity of Money the like was never known," which impeded the collection of his own debts and made bills of exchange prohibitively expensive.[55]

More depreciation and inflation would follow. In November 1727, however, hard-money men in the assembly seized the opportunity to introduce legislation for measuring the extent of past depreciation and for setting the value of future currency accordingly. Massachusetts's bills of credit, the act's preamble read, "have been found to vary and alter in their value from time to time since the year 1710, and may hereafter be lyable so to do, whereby the Creditor has been and may be prejudiced in his just dues and demands and the Debtor lyable to Great Oppression." Had it passed, the act would have provided that all debts contracted in paper money since 1710 that were still due would be payable "when demanded or suit brought therefor by any Creditor" according to an inflation schedule indicating the rate in silver: eight shillings per ounce in 1710; eight shillings sixpence per ounce in 1712; nine shillings per ounce in 1714; and all the way up to sixteen shillings per ounce in 1727. In other words, for debts contracted in paper bills between 1710 and 1727, debtors would have had to pay an additional sum to make up for the bills' depreciation between the time the debt was contracted and when it was due.[56]

The act would have changed the nature of debtor-creditor relations in the colony. Ever since the 1712 legal tender act, a 1742 or 1743 memorial to the governor's council recounted, it had been the courts' practice to issue judgments in paper money at face value. Thus, debtors and creditors who had borrowed and lent money expected "to pay and be paid the same nominal sum in bills of credit again and to run the risque of their rising and falling in value."[57] Although both parties to contracts knew the risks involved, the act would have mainly benefited creditors, since the bills had only ever fallen in value and were expected to continue to do so. When the measure failed to pass, one chronicler of the colony's currency wrote in 1901, "the hard-money men began a struggle for the resumption of specie payments" that would end in "defeat" a decade later, though the so-called defeat would ultimately prove more of a temporary setback.[58]

Paper money supporters, meanwhile, would continue to insist that the advantages of a sufficient circulating currency, even a depreciated one, far outweighed the costs to an already wealthy and powerful creditor class. Postponing taxes in hard times delivered direct relief to taxpayers, and if depreciation happened to follow, well then, it benefited struggling debtors by reducing the real value of what they owed. Since the assembly contracted debts in money of its own creation, moreover, depreciation also lessened the real value of the public debts, making them more manageable, the discount akin to a seigniorage fee. But while the wealthy certainly had the most to lose from depreciation, unabated inflation would prove to be especially devastating for laboring people and those on fixed incomes.

Debt Forgiveness and Depreciation

In South Carolina, fiscal policy choices were inseparable from considerations for settler safety and welfare. Of the £6,000 in bills of credit issued to pay for the 1702 siege of St. Augustine, £4,000 had been redeemable by direct taxes, £2,000 by duties. In late 1704, however, the assembly discovered that the public receiver, George Logan, had not canceled redeemed bills but had redirected them to other purposes, including overpaying himself six pounds seven shillings threepence and attributing tax payments to colonists who had not actually paid their taxes. William Bull, Carolina's lieutenant governor between 1738 and 1755, later explained to the British ministry that "the receiver was indemnified and acquitted, as fully as if he had duly applied the same to the uses appointed by the Acts first recited." What Logan did with the bills and why he was exonerated for apparently embezzling public funds remain unclear. Whatever the reason, the assembly paid for his indiscretion by issuing £4,000 in new bills "to pay and cancel" those outstanding.[59] In the spring of 1706, moreover, it appointed five auditors "to Inspect into the Receivrs accot: ffrom time to time as they shal think ffitt" and to oversee and announce the cancellation of bills in the future.[60] Yet the same year, the assembly postponed the taxes it had earmarked to redeem the new bills, proclaiming that it would not be levying the taxes and duties "which had been established as a fund for sinking the bills . . . to the payment of the public debts." Instead, "all the bills of credit outstanding and uncancelled were continued and made current."[61] Borrowing a page from Logan's own playbook, the assembly continued the bills in circulation—"uncancelled" them, as it were—rather than retiring them to be burnt as the law required.

Contemporaries observed that South Carolina's bills of credit circulated on a par with coin through at least 1711. If these observations were correct, then the bills retained their value despite the assembly having repeatedly delayed their redemption. In fact, however, the assembly had found a loophole: it would effectively refinance the public debt by redeeming old bills for newly printed ones, a policy it institutionalized following the unsuccessful Franco-Spanish invasion of Charles Town in 1706. Twice in 1707 and again in 1710, the representatives authorized new currency emissions with portions of each emission—£8,000, £2,000, and £1,000, respectively—marked to redeem outstanding bills.[62] Around the same time, they shifted part of the tax burden from planters to merchants. Thomas Nairne estimated in 1710 that export duties on deerskins and import duties on wines, spirits, sugar, molasses, flour, dry goods, and African captives netted the province £4,500 a year, £3,500 of which went to pay the salaries of all ten Anglican ministers, several officers and other military personnel, and the governor, as well as expenses for repairing the garrisons and building new fortifications; the remaining £1,000 went toward redeeming outstanding bills. Nairne explained, however, that the budget was always subject to change "either by unexpected Demands upon the Public, or by the Increase of Trade, and consequently of the Revenue."[63] Five years later he fell in the Yamasee War (1715–17), which nearly destroyed the province and wreaked utter havoc on its currency.

While data on prices and exchange rates in South Carolina are sparse for the first decade of the eighteenth century, the colonial government later determined that although the "Price of Produce" rose considerably between 1709 and 1711, it was not from "the multiplying the Paper-Bills" but from an increase in imports. And despite the rise in commodity prices, "the Exchange or Rates between Paper and [sterling] were at or near Par."[64] At least one disgruntled public servant disagreed. Francis Le Jau arrived in Charles Town in 1706, where he served as a missionary for the Society for the Propagation of the Gospel for more than a decade. He wrote frequently to his superiors in London, lamenting how difficult it was to live on his annual salary of fifty pounds, which was "paid in Bills as other payments are; which has occasion'd every thing to raise to a price I am asham'd to speak of."[65] In 1708 he reported that fifty pounds currency "will not come to 25 £ Sterling," the following year less than "18 £."[66] By 1714, on the eve of the Yamasee War, he complained that "what we could purchase 9 years ago for half a crown should be now at 7 s 6 d or more," a 200 percent increase.[67] For Le Jau, it was the overissue of paper money, not an increase in imports, that drove up prices and diminished the purchasing power of his fixed salary.

When the value of the South Carolina currency finally did collapse during the Yamasee War, it was because the English nearly lost. Like other Indigenous societies, the Yamasee had eagerly sought trade connections with the English. And like other societies, they had grown increasingly exasperated by English traders' abusive tactics. Entangled in a never-ending cycle of trade and war, they owed the traders the equivalent of 100,000 deerskins, and the traders had begun seizing and enslaving their wives and children for repayment. In April 1715 the Yamasees launched a pan-Indigenous insurgency against the English, killing 400 settlers, destroying houses and cattle, and forcing the remaining colonists to flee or seek refuge in Charles Town. That August, the assembly prepared for war by issuing £30,000 in bills of credit redeemable by direct taxes within two years, enabling them to raise an army of 1,200 planters, servants, enslaved men, and volunteers from neighboring colonies. But Yamasee guerilla tactics were extremely effective, and the English outlook remained grim until the colony secured an alliance with the large and powerful Cherokee people in late 1715.[68]

Soon it became apparent not only that there would be no taxes, but that more money was needed to continue the fight. In March 1716, the assembly printed off another £5,000 in bills of credit. Rather than make the bills redeemable in payment of taxes, however, the assembly merely made them legal tender for debts. In June 1716 it issued an additional £15,000 "for payment of the soldiers and other charges of the war," bringing the total cost of the war to £50,000. About that time, William Bull later recalled, "by reason of the late troubles and confusions occasioned by the Indian war, and for that diverse of the estates and effects of the inhabitants lying on the frontiers and being exposed to dangers," the assembly repealed the direct tax marked for redeeming the 1715 emission. The bills "could not be suddenly sunk, without laying too great and insupportable a tax and burthen on the inhabitants," Bull explained, and "therefore, the currency of the said £30,000 and £5,000 were continued till such time as they should be called in and sunk by Act of Assembly."[69] In a grand irony, the Yamasee War—a war provoked by the predatory lending practices of English traders—was itself financed by debt, debt that the colony could pay at the time and in the manner of its choosing, if it paid at all.

Even before its redemption was called off, the 1715 currency was a sore spot between the colony's planters, most of whom were debtors, and its merchants, the planters' creditors. In August of that year, Francis Le Jau wrote home predicting that the emission would "cause the price of everything to raise," by which "We salary men suffer cruelly . . . as well as the merchts," while "the Planters alone grow rich by it." A few months earlier he had reported that several families were "absolutely ruin'd" and worried that "our honest Merchts of London & Bristol will be great Sufferers."[70] News of the war soon spread to Britain, where those who had business interests in the colony feared losing their property and profits. The merchants were so distraught, colonial agent Francis Yonge narrated in a 1726 essay published in London, "that they writ to their Correspondents, to make them Returns at any Rate, for fear of losing the Whole." The "sudden demand for returns," together with "the Money being Notional, having no Intrinsick Value," raised prices "to such a height" that a twenty-shilling bill of credit could not fetch two shillings sterling worth of rice. But since the bills were legal tender for debts, Carolina creditors had to accept them at face value, so "those who had Money owing them on Bond or otherwise before the War . . . lost Seven Eighths of their Money: These Losses fell chiefly on the Merchants and such of the Inhabitants of Charles Town as were Money'd Men, and, on the contrary, the Planters, who were their Debtors, were the Gainers."[71] Boston merchant Thomas Amory was relieved that he "did not want money at C[arolina]" during the war, explaining in a June 16, 1720, letter to his uncle that "several Merchts. of London have been great Loosers on their riseing of their money wch is all paper not receiving 1/5 of their due."[72] Amory had debts in South Carolina too, but refused to be paid "as money goes now in Carolina," reckoning that it was "abt. 100 p ct. worse than" Massachusetts currency.[73]

The economic historian Bruce Smith calculated that the colony's exchange rate rose from £300 currency for £100 sterling in 1715 to £575 currency for £100 sterling in 1717. The increased demand for silver, produce, and bills of exchange for making returns to Britain swelled prices and depreciated the currency relative to sterling in turn.[74] According to the colonists themselves, however, the inflation was inextricable from the war. Many men had fled the colony, one contemporary later recounted, while those who had stayed and fought sent their wives and children to the northern colonies, paying any price in bills of credit for silver or rice "to send with their Families to provide for them ... By this means our Bills were so much depreciated in their Value, that they were not worth above the one fourth part of what they had been."[75] Likewise, the assembly later attributed the inflation more "to the Fears Men were generally under" and their willingness "to secure something" rather than lose everything, "than to the natural Consequences attending the Emission of Paper-Money." In short, "the most obvious and natural Causes" of the rise in prices "were the Calamities of the *Indian* War and its Effects."[76] A half-century on, Benjamin Franklin explained to the British ministry that while the British merchants trading to Carolina had perhaps suffered some losses, it was not due to paper money, but because "the Colony was thought in danger of being destroy'd by the Indians and Spaniards." The merchants called for remittances and the colonists "gave any Price in Paper Money" for produce, bills of exchange, "or other Effects fit for Exportation." By this means, the currency "was suddenly and greatly depreciated."[77]

Once the province was out of immediate danger, the British merchants sought redress from the proprietors, demanding the redemption of all outstanding South Carolina bills of credit. They accused the planter-dominated assembly of defrauding local creditors by continuing the bills in circulation past their redemption dates, causing them to depreciate in terms of sterling, and then forcing the creditors to accept them at face value. In a September 1718 petition to the proprietors, the merchants warned that Carolina's representatives were scheming either to postpone more taxes "in Breach of the publick ffaith, or to stamp more Bills of Credit," which the proprietors acknowledged by instructing Governor Robert Johnson to veto any act that would postpone taxes or issue new bills.[78] Although there were no plans as yet to make more currency, the assembly had indeed repealed a 1717 tax act that would have redeemed all bills issued since the start of the Yamasee War. "However, this action cannot be viewed as a breach of public faith, when the financial burden the colonists had placed upon themselves is realized," historian Richard Jellison noted. "They can hardly be criticized for granting themselves more time to discharge the indebtedness brought about by the war."[79]

When the assembly repealed the tax act, it was effectively forgiving a portion of the public debt. Still, canceling taxes necessarily diminished confidence in the bills of credit those taxes were marked to redeem, causing the colonial currency to further depreciate. Consequently, like Edward Wigglesworth and others in Massachusetts, hard-money advocates in South Carolina argued that the assembly's fiscal policy choices unjustly benefited debtors, who could pay their sterling debts in depreciated paper bills, while unfairly costing creditors, who had to accept the bills at face value or forfeit everything. "To proffer any Payment with them is a Tender in Law," Thomas Nairne explained in 1710, "so that if the Creditor refuse to take them, he loseth his Money, and the Debtor is discharg'd from the Minute of the Refusal."[80] The colony's legal tender law, like that of Massachusetts, was in any case consistent with nominalism in England, where creditors had to accept the sovereign's coin as payment for debts regardless of changes in the silver content. English rulers knew, of course, that nominalism could create losses for particular interest groups.[81] In the colonies, legal tender laws produced spirited debates over the nature of money, the balance between public good and private gain, and the balance of power between those who owned money and those who owed it.[82]

Under the auspices of Francis Nicholson, the first South Carolina governor under royal rule, the sterling exchange rate stabilized. Rice prices recovered, reversing the *deflation* of the previous five years when economic growth had outpaced the currency supply. Writing in 1732, the author of *An Essay on Currency* reflected that "our Money has kept near the same Value, for these Ten or Twelve Years last past . . . altho' there has been of late as much more added to it," and he was certain that "the Prices of our Commodities are not advanced" by the addition.[83] Benjamin Franklin likewise remarked that since "the Colony has been in the Hands of the Crown, their Currency became fixed, and has so remain'd to this day."[84] In addition, the 1720s saw tremendous growth of the colony: the European population doubled, rice exports trebled, and the importation of enslaved laborers accelerated. As rice production expanded, aided by African knowledge, so did the African population. Charles Town became the largest transatlantic slave market in mainland North America, most of the enslaved arriving directly from Africa on ships owned by Bristol, London, and Boston merchants. From 1720 to 1730, some 11,600 African captives disembarked in Carolina who would do the backbreaking, deadly work of clearing fields and sowing, threshing, and winnowing the rice. By 1730, Charles Town was exporting nearly 17 million pounds of rice annually.[85]

South Carolina's growth contrasted with Massachusetts's stagnation. Throughout the colonies, commentators attributed the former's capacity to send crops and coins to Britain to its paper money. "If there was not Paper-Money in South-Carolina," Philadelphia merchant Francis Rawle marveled in a 1721 essay, "how could the Trade of that Country be so readily dispatched as it is?"⁸⁶ Two years later, New Jersey governor William Keith wrote to the Board of Trade estimating that "by means of their Paper only," Carolina settlers "carry on three times the Business, which they ever did before, or indeed could possibly do now without it."⁸⁷ As long as South Carolina produced enough "Pitch, Tar and Rice" to make returns for British "Cloths, Iron and Linens," another commentator retorted, "what need [the British merchant] care, what we make Use of as a Medium for our Trade? . . . Paper-Money in America will always make England the Center of all the Silver that is brought into the British Dominions in America, and it will not only center in England," he added for good measure, "but abide there."⁸⁸

"Making Good the Publick Credit"

Unlike Boston, which bore the brunt of the imperial conflicts, or Charles Town, which faced the continual threat of a Spanish or French naval invasion, New York City was rarely exposed to any actual fighting. Its merchants had turned King William's War (1688–97) to their advantage, supplying colonial hinterlands with British and Dutch goods, and shipping food, clothing, and provisions to Caribbean plantations in exchange for sugar and specie. The colonial assembly taxed products shipped from Boston and other colonial ports, fostering New York City's commercial autonomy, while skilled craftsmen flocked to the colony to set up shop in the city, where they employed a growing number of enslaved African laborers. But as the economy of New York expanded in size, complexity, and opportunity in the first decade of the eighteenth century, most of the gold and silver coins that entered the colony were set aside to ship to England. The demise of beaver skins as currency by the late seventeenth century and the demonetization of wampum in 1701 made matters worse. Without a reliable medium of exchange, the colony's laboring classes were compensated in money substitutes, from tobacco and liquor to cloth and grain, while merchants and tradesmen relied on promissory notes, bills of exchange, and bonds. By 1708, the colony faced a currency crisis.⁸⁹

The introduction of bills of credit during Queen Anne's War oiled the works for a more agile local market and paved the way for New York's ascendance in the Atlantic system. As the historian Michael Kammen noted, the bills "increased the amount of money in circulation and thereby added fluidity to the commercial life of New York," and "contributed mightily to economic recovery and growth" after the war. They may even have shielded New York from the depression that ricocheted across the Atlantic after the bursting of the South Sea Bubble in 1720.⁹⁰

While historians have stressed the importance of both private credit and paper money to New York's growing economy, less attention has been paid to how the money was made and how that process changed over time. Like the early bills of credit of Massachusetts and South Carolina, the New York bills of 1709 and 1711 were short-term notes redeemable in payment of direct taxes. But between 1712 and 1714, the colony's leading merchants, landholders, and slaveowners sought to consolidate the assembly's power of the purse as a counterweight against truculent governors and rebellious bondspeople. As early as 1711, Governor Robert Hunter grumbled of "ye Assemblye's claiming all ye privileges of a House of Commons and stretching them even beyond what they were ever imagined to be there."[91] The following year the assembly appointed David Provoost, Robert Watts, John Cruger, Abraham Wendall, and Philip Schuyler as a committee to receive, examine, and report claims on the government since King William's War.[92] In 1714 they concluded that due to the "Misapplication" and "Extravagant Spending of the Revenue" by "former Governours," the province was deeply in debt and needed to act quickly to restore the public credit. Hundreds of claims for goods and services were yet unpaid, which if not expeditiously settled "will be the utter Ruin and Undoing of many of the said Claimants, and prove a great and irreparable Loss to most of them." The assembly's ability to appropriate public funds in the future depended on its willingness to fulfill promises past due.[93]

Under the auspices of Governor Hunter, that September the assembly passed an act for issuing £27,680 in new bills of credit and for satisfying all outstanding claims on the colony. Each of the hundreds of claimants in the act had to sign a receipt before witnesses and swear an oath to the treasurer that they had not already been paid, and any claimant who refused to accept bills in payment forfeited their due. Once settled, all claims originating before June 1714 would be null and void. In addition to indicating how the bills were to be disbursed, the act detailed the process for redeeming them. The bills were not redeemable by direct taxes as before, but rather by a liquor excise enacted the previous year. The redemption period was twenty-one years, hence the nickname, the "First Long Bills." Finally, the bills were denominated in ounces of silver plate or in Dutch ducatoons, known as Lyon dollars, with one Lyon dollar equal to five shillings sixpence currency or thirteen pennyweight eighteen grain silver.[94] By levying taxes and appropriating funds in ounces of plate or Lyon dollars rather than in pieces of eight, the assembly evaded Queen Anne's Proclamation of 1704. While the proclamation required the colonies to set the value of full-bodied Spanish dollars at six shillings per piece, it made no mention of either uncoined silver or Lyon dollars, allowing the assembly to set an effective par of exchange of £155 currency to £100 sterling. By approving the emission, the Crown inadvertently exempted the province from the proclamation.[95]

A subsequent act, however, drew fire from a group of prominent New York City merchants. In December 1717, after the assembly discovered numerous additional claims on the public, it issued another £16,607 or 15,000 ounces of plate redeemable by the liquor excise, known as the "Second Long Bills."[96] A grand jury found that the emission lacked sufficient security, but Governor Hunter rebuffed the charge, supposing that it was politically motivated, and the pro-Hunter assembly followed suit. Consequently, the merchants prevailed on their friends in London to petition the Board of Trade to stop the act, declaring that it threatened the trade and credit of the province.[97] When the board asked Hunter for an explanation, he countered that both the 1714 and 1717 bills of credit had not only retained their value owing to "so good and solid a fond [fund] as that of the Excise," but had also "vastly increas'd" commerce, adding that any attempt to recall the latest emission would only bring chaos. He surmised that "whatsoever the pretended" reason for the opposition, "men of private views piques and interests" disliked the emissions because they enabled "the many to venture their stocks in trade to the prejudice of the few who had so long monopoliz'd it." The board was satisfied, and the bills were allowed to continue in circulation.[98]

As New York grew more enmeshed in Britain's capitalist empire, contemporaries remarked on the superiority of the province's bills of credit over those of other colonies and even British money. A London essayist marveled in 1720 that "the Bills are established on a secure Fund, and of a certain fixed Value, and made current in all Payments whatsoever," making them as valuable "as any other the Current Coin of the Kingdom."[99] Neither a fiat currency nor a mere tax credit, the writer concluded, "this New Species is Money itself."[100] In December 1723 Governor William Burnet exclaimed that the bills were not only "as great value at New York, as the Coin of Great Britain is at London," but also "much securer than Bankers Bills in London," for "they carry on business among themselves and send home all the Gold and Silver to Great Britain as it comes in to them by trade, which I apprehend to be an advantage which Great Britain would not have so much of, if there was not paper money among us."[101] A year later, he reiterated "how well the Bills of New York keep up their Credit, and . . . have not fall'n in value, as those of Carolina and New England."[102] As a nineteenth-century historian summed up: "The currency being based on so solid a fund as that of the excise, trade and navigation were favorably affected."[103]

Compared to the currencies of Massachusetts and South Carolina, New York bills of credit hardly budged in terms of sterling, and prices and wages remained stable through the outbreak of war with Spain in 1739, despite an economic recession in the 1730s. The price of silver increased from eight shillings per ounce in 1716 to only nine shillings per ounce in 1739, while the exchange rate rose from £155 currency for £100 sterling in 1714 to barely £167 currency for £100 sterling in 1739. Over a quarter-century, the bills depreciated by a relatively trivial 7.6 percent.[104] When contemporaries praised the currency's fund, they were referring to the indirect taxes marked to redeem it: the duties on goods imported from other colonies; the duties on wine, liquors, beer, cider, cocoa, salt, and molasses; the tonnage duty; and the duties on enslaved African persons. These taxes were not designed to restrict imports of unwanted commodities, but to raise revenue from a thriving Atlantic commerce.[105]

Fueled by the Atlantic trade, the period saw remarkable commercial and physical growth. Though Philadelphia would eventually overtake New York City as the British empire's premier North American port, early eighteenth-century New York flourished. More than sixty vessels cleared the Port of New York between 1714 and 1717, more than 200 by 1721. Yet underlying the expansion was the trade in African captives that brought hundreds of captives to the colony every year in the decades following Queen Anne's War. By 1731 nearly a fifth of New York City's population was enslaved, allowing free men and women to avoid the most unsavory work and contributing to the prosperity that attracted European laborers. In the two decades after 1720, the urban population grew by 73 percent.[106]

If markets are often creatures of money, the relationship between currency and growth in early America was more of a two-way street. As Boston lost its leverage in the Atlantic economy, its commerce irreversibly harmed by imperial conflicts and its population stagnant, the Massachusetts currency depreciated, reflecting and reinforcing the colony's decline. By contrast, coin, currency, and credit were fundamental to the expansion of New York, and vice versa. Paper money helped stimulate local business, including activities that supported Atlantic shipping and marketing. In addition to sending provisions to Massachusetts, Rhode Island, and South Carolina, New York City merchants sold flour, pork, and butter to Caribbean planters in exchange for rum, molasses, sugar, cocoa, pieces of eight, and bills of exchange. In 1723, New York official Cadwallader Colden thus reported to the British ministry that the trade was so great that "we have money frequently remitted from thence or Bills of Exchange for England." All of the money imported from the Caribbean "seldom continues six months in this Province, before it is remitted for England The Current Cash being wholly in the Paper Bills of This Province & a few Lyon Dollars." No wonder a prolonged recession rippled through New York in the early 1730s, a decade when no new bills of credit were issued.[107]

Colonial settlers were discovering that in a booming economy, the value of paper money derived as much from the productive capacity of the society that used it as from the politics of taxation. The depreciation of the Massachusetts currency mirrored the colony's marginal productivity, while New York's commercial growth exerted a stabilizing force on its paper money. South Carolina suffered shattering depreciation and inflation during the Yamasee War, but the expansion of rice production and slavery stopped depreciation dead in its tracks. It seemed that in the growing world of trade and markets, the value of a colony's currency hinged as much on economic output as on the promise of redemption.

Bills of credit entailed public faith, but public faith did not preclude private property. As a medium of exchange, paper money had the potential to undermine traditional forms of social and economic dependency based on hierarchy and deference. To some, its supposedly leveling tendencies were disconcerting. But the political community that coalesced in early America can hardly be described as egalitarian. For when the wars ended and public spending contracted, colonial governments responded to renewed demands for a currency by making liquid the one thing European settlers claimed in abundance: land. The next chapter examines the loan office system that lent paper bills at interest to colonists against land mortgages. On the one hand, anyone could use the bills once they were in circulation, from landless tenants and poor widows to itinerant sailors and enslaved Black laborers, while interest from the loans redounded to the public. But on the other hand, by restricting loans to individuals who claimed property in lands, assemblies prioritized modes of production based on landownership, invested the public in the profits of slavery, and ultimately legitimated new forms of hierarchy and dependency in the name of "improvement."

4

Coined Land

In a letter to the Board of Trade dated December 18, 1722, Pennsylvania lieutenant governor William Keith reported "that the people of this place are just now in a very great Ferment" due to the "want of a sufficient currency of cash amongst themselves." He continued that "Under these Circumstances, The Clamor is universall for Paper Money," and anticipated that the assembly would soon emit "such a quantity" of currency "as will serve to Transact the necessary Business" between "Merchant and Farmer." The following year the representatives passed an act for issuing £45,000 in bills of credit and established a loan office to lend the bills at 5 percent interest. Loans were secured by lands at double the value of the loan or by houses at triple, to be repaid in annual installments over twelve years. In the meantime, the bills circulated as a local currency that anyone could use. "Thus by pledgeing our Lands for a Security to one another," boasted Keith to the board, "we convert a third part of their value into an imaginary specie, which fully answers the End of a permanent Currency & common measure of Trade amongst our selves."[1]

As demand for paper money outstripped its fiscal core, early Americans came up with new ways of supplementing the bills of credit that spending and taxing created. One of these was the loan office system that Keith described in 1723. Rather than limit money creation to public expenditures, colonial assemblies augmented the currency by chartering loan offices that lent bills to colonists at interest against mortgages of lands. If treasuries made money by *spending* money, loan offices did so by *lending* it. Barbados issued the first paper bills on loan in 1705, followed by South Carolina (1712), Massachusetts (1714), Rhode Island (1715), Pennsylvania, Delaware, New Jersey (all in 1723), North Carolina (1729), Connecticut (1732), Maryland (1733), New York (1737), and Georgia (1755). Although colonists had to pay money to borrow money, effectively bearing the costs of making money, they were willing to "buy" bills because they transformed illiquid land into liquid currency. The loan office system was a good deal for borrowers if interest rates were below prevailing market rates, and it was a good deal for assemblies because it provided them with steady streams of revenue.[2]

This chapter considers how public lending markets helped shape the conditions of economic life in British North America. While there is some truth to one historian's claim that loan offices worked "in an egalitarian way, sustaining small producers on their land by providing mortgages to them," they more often replicated social hierarchies than eroded them.[3] First, by gearing loans toward landholders, loan offices reinforced the stature of property in lands—and in some colonies, enslaved human beings—and prioritized agricultural modes of production. In doing so, they bolstered colonial private property, jurisdiction, and wealth. Second, if loan offices sustained some farmers on their lands, they gave others the means to profit from the growing world of trade and markets, and others still the wherewithal to pay old debts and incur new ones. Currencies that public lending created circulated widely among colonial settlers, from small farmers to import merchants to day laborers to women shopkeepers. Loan offices ultimately reproduced unequal power relations, even as those relationships were increasingly understood more in monetary terms and less in terms of dependency and obligation.

Such an outcome was not inevitable. In Massachusetts and Pennsylvania, the two colonies at the center of this chapter, the monetary systems that coalesced in the 1730s were the products of fierce struggles over currency creation and access to credit. These contests animated colonial politics in the 1720s, deepening the divisions between popular and court parties, between new merchants and old, and between debtors and creditors. Paper money politics took place in the assemblies, where pro–paper money representatives clashed with hard-money men on governor's councils; in the printed public sphere, where, the historian Perry Miller observed, "the paper money argument . . . contained the threat of revolution"; and for the first time in the streets of colonial cities, where the politics of money intersected with a rising politics "out-of-doors."[4] Alternatives from all sides of the currency debate abounded and sometimes prevailed. In both colonies, the circulation of new and arresting ideas about money as a productive force shifted the debate away from questions about what money was and how it was made, and toward arguments for what it could *do*.

Coined Debts

In a 1729 pamphlet touting paper money's benefits, Philadelphia printer Benjamin Franklin memorably referred to the bills of credit issued by the

Pennsylvania loan office as "coined land."[5] But as he and his contemporaries well knew, the bills were actually coined debts. While the colonial loan office system has long interested historians, the legal and institutional structures that transformed private debts into public currencies within colonial spaces are not well known. At least two preconditions made the transformation possible. First was the transferability of debts, which would allow the debts to circulate as money among strangers. The rule of transferability was introduced from England, where it was established over the seventeenth and eighteenth centuries in custom and law. The second precondition was the alienability of property in land, which enabled borrowers to mortgage their farms as security for loans. The ideas behind both were English, not American, in origin.

As the sociologist Geoffrey Ingham has detailed, the establishment of transferability in medieval and early modern Europe was a "long-term historical process" whereby "the promises of banks and states to pay gradually became currency."[6] Although, as Ingham notes, the English state would not codify transferability until the early eighteenth century, proposals for making debts transferable had been percolating in Puritan reform circles since the 1640s.[7] In 1651, English social reformer William Potter urged the Rump Parliament to improvise a credit currency by converting all promissory notes and domestic bills of exchange into "bills of credit." Then the bills could "passe from hand to hand" as if they were "so much money," and "there would be as many Bills dispersed at once throughout the land, as the debts of all the men in the Nation do amount to."[8] According to Potter, money and debt were one and the same: "security for obtaining some other Commodity of like or greater value" given "as an Evidence or Testimony (that is as it were a Token or Ticket) to signifie how far forth, other men are indebted for, and ingaged to recompence the fruits of their Labors or possessions by Commodities of some other kind."[9]

In 1650, Potter wrote *The Key of Wealth*, a proposal for a bank that would raise credit by mortgages of land instead of by deposits of coin. He lamented that trading on "words and credits" alone—what the historian Craig Muldrew has called "the currency of reputation"—led to "mens losses by desperate debts." But if all debts "might be made as sure and firm" as those "of the Chamber of London, Bank of Amsterdam, or any Bills of Exchange," though secured by land rather than gold, they would be preferable to the finest coin.[10] Potter's comrade and fellow reformer Samuel Hartlib, for whom the era's most important reform group was named, boasted that such a bank would eliminate "all Counterfeiting; (as in case of Copper-money) all danger of surprize (as lately in Holland) there being (by Law of the Bank) no money to rest there;

all hazard to them, that shall be (from time to time) Owners of all the credit in the Bank, because there is no credit in the Bank, but what is sufficiently secured in the same manners as money, that is now borrowed upon Land."[11] And while banks of deposit merely transmitted ownership of existing money (and thus did not produce "any new Medium of Commerce"), through the alchemical-like process of turning nature into currency, land banks would create new money.[12] Hartlib confidently estimated that they would "multiply Money" to the tune of "four fifths" or more "of the value of the Lands of the Nation, which can amount to little lesse than a hundred millions Sterling."[13]

There was, however, a catch: lands given as collateral for a mortgage would be liable to seizure by creditors. That is, if a borrower defaulted on their loan, the mortgaged lands would be "forfeited without redemption" and "divided, among the Owners of the Credit in Bank," Hartlib explained.[14] If anything seemed possible in the radical milieu of the English Commonwealth, in hindsight the land bank was a long shot because the very notion of land as divisible, let alone alienable, flew in the face of the English legal system's long-standing distinction between real property, on the one hand, and personal or chattel property, on the other. As the eighteenth-century English jurist William Blackstone would expound, "Things *real* are such as are permanent, fixed, and immoveable, which cannot be carried out of their place; as lands and tenements: things *personal* are goods, money, and all other moveables; which may attend the owner's person wherever he thinks proper to go."[15] The law of real property aimed to protect the inheritance of landed estates across generations and to maintain their cohesiveness and integrity by preventing creditors from seizing the land in payment of unsecured debts.[16] Despite their growing popularity, English proposals for credit currencies and land banks faltered against the inviolability of "real" property.

Yet the same proposals resonated in the colonies, where early laws recognized land as freely alienable and merchants treated nearly all property as personal property. At the start of the 1660s, Hartlib corresponded with Connecticut governor John Winthrop Jr. about alchemy and the tincture of philosophers, the oppression of the poor, and William Potter's proposal for a land bank, which Hartlib avowed was "better than the philosopher's stone." Regretful that the English "hath not been at leisure hitherto to accept" the scheme, he hoped "that it might be begun and practiced in a plantation for their greatest good."[17] While Winthrop agreed that a land bank "would greatly advance commerce and other public concernments for the benefit of the poor and rich," he failed to obtain the necessary political support, and seems to have abandoned the idea by the end of the decade.[18] Then in 1682, the Massachusetts minister John Woodbridge, who had apparently met Potter in London some years prior, published a proposal for "a Fund of Land . . . in the style of a Money-Bank . . . to pass Credit upon, by Book-Entries; or Bils of Exchange, for great Payments: and Change-bills for running cash." While gold and silver were liable to be "covetously hoarded up" by greedy merchants and "subject to *wear adultering*, (*fires, robberies, mistakes*, & the like contingencies[)]," Woodbridge argued, "payments in this *Bank*, or bills issued thence, are free from: having a *Fund*, or Deposit in *Land*; real, dureable, & of secure value."[19]

Colonial supporters of credit money and land banks even moved to codify the transferability of debts—a full decade before Parliament did. Philadelphia merchant Thomas Budd's 1685 proposal for "a *Bank* of *Monies* and *Credit*" stipulated that all bills and bonds "by Act of Assembly be made transferable by Assignments . . . in the Nature of *Bills of Exchange* . . . and so one Bond or Bill would go through twenty hands, and thereby be as ready Monies, and do much to the Benefit of Trade." The plan provided for borrowers to "tender a particular of our Lands and Houses" to lenders, facilitated through the "Bank," and so "Mortgage our Land & Houses."[20]

When Benjamin Franklin described paper money as "coined land," he was implying that a parcel of real property backed every bill of credit. "As Bills issued upon Money Security are Money, so Bills issued upon Land, are in Effect *Coined Land*," he expounded.[21] But the metaphor sat poorly with the Philadelphia lawyer and Franklin's onetime rival in the editing business, John Webbe. Unlike European banks of deposit that received gold and silver in exchange for bank notes, Webbe pointed out in a 1742 or 1743 essay, a colonial loan office "does not borrow but *lend* money, and therefore *takes* security from the borrowers for the repayment at the times stipulated." Banks of deposit and loan offices were therefore "*essentially* opposite." Whereas bank notes "have the same power as the silver promised by 'em," the notes being convertible on demand, "those of *Pennsylvania* cannot, for a like reason, nor for any reason, be considered as land; for tho' they be lent upon land, yet the possessors have no *right* to demand from any man, or any body of men, any land for 'em."[22] Loan offices bore more resemblance to modern financial institutions that create money in the form of interest-bearing debt or to nineteenth-century commercial banks that served as intermediaries between savers and borrowers than to early modern European banks of deposit. They neither received money on deposit nor discounted drafts, but, as William Potter, Samuel Hartlib, and their colonial correspondents envisioned decades earlier, lent paper bills on mortgages of land.[23]

Abstraction and Improvement

The land bank idea took hold in British North America because affordable specie was often hard to come by, and because the colonies already recognized land as freely alienable. In 1833, US Supreme Court Justice Joseph Story reflected on "the strong tendency of the colonies to make lands liable to the payment of debts . . . a natural result of the condition of the people in a new country, who possessed little monied capital; whose wants were numerous; and whose desire of credit was correspondingly great." In the 1670s, colonial assemblies broke with English precedent and began passing acts making lands liable for unsecured debts to facilitate borrowing and credit extension among European settlers. The consequence, Story explained, "was to make land, in some degrees, a substitute for money, by giving it all the facilities of transfer, and all the prompt applicability of personal property."[24] The acts commodified land, facilitating the creation of a capital market in which land and chattel alike circulated as fungible assets. In turn, land could be offered as security for payment of debts, or "coined," to borrow from Franklin, entailing a reconceptualization of land as liquid, or land as a money equivalent.

But in order to commodify and coin land, colonists first had to acquire and privatize it. As the legal scholar K-Sue Park, drawing on the anthropologist Karl Polanyi, powerfully illustrates, decades before assemblies began making lands liable for unsecured debts, European settlers were using predatory lending and mortgage foreclosure as tools of Indigenous dispossession, offering food and supplies to Native leaders on mortgages of lands and then seizing said lands when they were unable to pay their debts.[25] The earliest Virginia colonists documented the practice. John Rolfe noted, for example, that several minor chiefs had mortgaged their lands to the colony in exchange for wheat, while Sir Thomas Dale lent 500 bushels of corn to Native persons "for Repayment whereof the next Year, he took a Mortgage of their whole Countries."[26]

Indigenous land deeds may have been used to capitalize Massachusetts's first bank of credit. In 1686, John Blackwell secured permission from the Dominion of New England to establish a bank in Boston that would lend "Bank-bills of Credit" to borrowers against "Lands or Reall estates mortgaged."[27] The bank went nowhere because Governor Edmund Andros would shortly invalidate all land titles. Much of the land had been "purchased" from Native communities following Metacom's War (1675–76). Such was the case of the "Million Purchase," a large tract along the Merrimack River that Blackwell and fifteen other land speculators—including three of the bank's four assessors—"purchased of the undoubted Indian Princes and Posessors" in 1685.[28]

In fact, the tract was more of a patchwork of Native deeds that the speculators had pieced together. Some of the deeds came from Native individuals who had sold ancestral lands in order to get out of debt. In January 1684, Paagushen alias Joseph Trask, a Wamesit or Pawtucket man, sold one of the Million Purchase proprietors a piece of property near the Merrimack in exchange for forgiveness of "Several Pounds due by Book."[29] Other deeds made concessions to Indigenous authority. The same year, for instance, an agreement between some Wabanaki sagamores and another proprietor confirmed the Wabanakis' sale of the Pejebscot lands to the English and simultaneously preserved their "hereditary rights & ancient traditions & customs," including fishing and hunting rights and "liberty of . . . improvement of our Ancient planting grounds."[30] Whether the proprietor planned to mortgage the Pejebscot claim to the bank and how this would have worked given the preservation of customary use rights is unclear, but regardless, Governor Andros later rejected the claim as having derived from an "invalid" transfer "from certain Indians." Of another, unrelated land title, Andros determined that it had been "extorted by a troop of horse from Massachusetts, and that the debt was fictitious." (In contrast, he accepted a claim based on a 1660 grant from several Narragansett sachems "on condition of release from a debt of six hundred fathoms of wampumpeage.")[31] Then in 1688, Andros reverted all land titles to the Crown; to reclaim them, landowners had to petition the governor to survey their land and confirm the title. The policy, as the bank associate and Massachusetts judge Samuel Sewall complained to a friend in England, had "greatly defamed and undervalued" the titles, leaving "the Owners of very little Credit."[32]

Although Blackwell's bank failed, acquiring Indigenous lands in order to commodify and coin them remained an important colonization strategy for Massachusetts following the arrival of the royal charter in 1692. But in addition to confirming land sales (whether consensual or coercive), the colony was soon sponsoring murderous violence against Native peoples that was itself monetized in the form of bounties for dead Indigenous men, women, and children. The colonial government paid out the scalp bounties in the lands of slain Native people or in the same paper currency that financed the colonial wars. Captain John Lovell, the hero of Governor Dummer's War (1722–25) and namesake of Lovell, Maine, returned home with "Eleven Indian Scalps & one Indian Prisoner," for which the treasurer awarded him £1150.[33] In the 1730s, veterans of the Anglo-Wabanaki Wars received grants of "vacated" Native lands as rewards for prior service, which some would mortgage to the Land Bank of 1739–41 (discussed in chapter 7).[34]

Serving to rationalize and facilitate Native dispossession was the public title recording system, which erased preexisting claims to the land through the imposition of colonial property law and creation of racial value. By the eighteenth century, most of the colonies had passed acts allowing colonists to record land deeds for modest fees with local registers, who maintained publicly searchable registries of deeds, sales, and mortgages in their towns or counties. Local title recording authenticated English settlers' claims to property and helped enforce credit agreements. Public registries recorded forms of property that could serve as collateral for loans, increasing transparency in both land and lending markets. In certain colonies, colonial and county registers would file mortgages to loan office trustees alongside land titles, land sales, and private mortgages, making registries unique windows onto the legal alchemy that turned private debts into public currencies.[35]

Land title recording reflected a new logic of property as alienable and fungible, a suitable basis for money and mortgages. As the legal scholar Brenda Bhandar argues, moreover, the new conception of property unfolded in conjunction with the fabrication of racial difference, producing what she calls "racial regimes of ownership" that underlay the historical development of capitalism. While Bhandar's research focuses on title by registration as a legal strategy of dispossession and ownership in nineteenth-century South Australia, land title recording in colonial North America played out in a similar fashion, replacing Indigenous systems of land tenure with a legal structure based on individual private property ownership secured by the state and "rationalized through the bureaucratic function of the registry."[36]

Public registries did more than just provide colonists with more secure titles. Title recording, Bhandar maintains, "renders prior ownership interests irrelevant; that which is recorded on the document archived in the state registry becomes the proof of ownership, not the historical memory, social use, kinship ties, or other relations that were bound up with land use and ownership for centuries prior to becoming more fully commodified."[37] Like the treasurers' records that transformed colonists' sufferings and sacrifices into numeric values examined in chapter 2, registries reduced Native homelands to paper and gave expression to a more abstract conception of property. Further, through the creation of private property, the registries bolstered a nascent colonial territorial jurisdiction and helped it flourish.[38] That jurisdiction supported colonial monetary experiments and authority over monetary transactions in turn.

Amid the widespread adoption of public registries in the early eighteenth century across British North America, colonial leaders embraced a definition of landownership and an ideology of improvement that justified seizing lands from racialized populations that failed to settle and cultivate the land for profit.[39] Proponents of paper money and land banks saw no contradiction between commodifying and coining land, on the one hand, and settling and cultivating it, on the other. Mortgaging land for loans was warranted, they argued, if the money was used to develop the land for capitalist agriculture. In doing so, they drew on the work of the early political economist and English surveyor William Petty, who had created new methods to quantify the value of Irish land and Irish people based on economic productivity; and English philosopher John Locke, who had situated historically Petty's abstract logic in his moral and legal case for Indigenous dispossession and notion of "wasteland."[40] Consider the Ipswich, Massachusetts, minister and paper money advocate John Wise, who drew a line from dispossession to land banks to improvement when he advocated both the use of bills of credit to "Subdue and Settle those Desolate Lands" now home to "a Naked Skulking Enemy" and the establishment of a loan office that would issue paper money to industrious colonists on mortgages of the conquered territory.[41]

The anonymous author of two pamphlets published in Boston, possibly Connecticut minister Joseph Morgan, made a similar proposition. Envisioning "*a Province Bank of 2 or 3 hundred Thousand Pounds*" to be let out to "any subject upon Improved Lands," he estimated that the bank would "raise the value of Improved Lands 20 to 30 per Cent. which consideration will Encourage Farmers to Improve more Lands."[42] Borrowing a page from Locke, the writer contended that "the *Indians*" had no more right to "the Property" of America, "*save the Land they have subdued and improved*"—which, he added, barely exceeded "*one hundred thousand part thereof*"—than the speculators who monopolized "great quantities of Dormant Lands" in the New England wilderness. Comparing colonial land speculation to the Lockean fantasy of Indigenous wasteland, he imagined a society of English farmers, husbandmen, and artisans replenishing, improving, and defending the continent in the name of "the Crown and Nation of *Great Britain*."[43] In this vision, money and banks, improvement, and conquest transformed property and dominion in North America.

The Massachusetts Loan Money

The Massachusetts loan money issued between 1714 and 1728 sought to braid together the binding principles of abstraction and improvement. As the colony worked to gradually redeem the bills of credit issued to finance Queen Anne's War (1702–14), two rival plans to supplement the currency with "coined land" battled for dominance, one public and one private. Private scheme partisans, led by prominent Boston residents John Colman, Elisha Cooke Jr., Oliver Noyes, and Samuel Lynde, seized the opportunity to resurrect John

Blackwell's 1686 proposal for a bank of credit, reprinting it for circulation around Boston. Then in February 1714 the land bankers, now backed by an emerging "popular party," submitted their own prospectus for a bank to the assembly and advertised their plans in the *Boston News-Letter*. The private bank would take subscriptions of £250 to £4,000 from persons pledging "Real Estate" to the bank's trustees, for a total capitalization of £300,000.[44] The "subscribers" (investors, really) would choose seven directors for appraising mortgaged lands, a treasurer for giving out "Bank Bills," and a clerk for managing the bank's books, including "a perfect Register" of all mortgages, pawns, assignments, and releases.[45] Each subscriber would take out at least 25 percent of the value of his subscription in bills, and the bank would lend the remainder at 4 percent interest to nonsubscribers against land or personal property. All of the profits would return to the subscribers "in proportion to their respective Subscriptions," but if the Boston town meeting voted to accept the bills in payment of town taxes, the bankers would pledge a portion of their earnings to public schools, hospitals, and charities.[46]

Governor Joseph Dudley and his allies opposed the land bankers, though not the coining of land in principle, and countered with their own proposal for issuing a more modest sum of money through a public loan office. Colman's bank was a "Company," the governor's son and Attorney General Paul Dudley exclaimed in a 1714 essay, and all companies had to be created "either by *Charter* from the *Crown*, or by Act of *Parliament*."[47] Free from public oversight, the bank would become a kingdom unto itself, "which like a Fire in the Bowels, will up and Consume the whole Body," and "'twill be a vain thing any longer to talk of Government, a Power of making Laws, Regulating Trade, *&c.* For they that can make at one Dash, the Sum beforementioned, and as much more when they please, will quickly Govern the Trading part, and by degrees get the Land of the Country Mortgaged to them, and so at length bear down the Government it self, *and nothing be restrained from them.*"[48] Dudley also questioned the ethics of the subscribers having all the profits, enabling them to redeem "their own Mortgages" in a few short years. Meanwhile, "the *Bubbled Borrowers* pay Interest for their own Estates . . . when their Estates are the only remaining Fund."[49] No, if there was going to be any lending, it had better be "done by the Publick" than by "this Private Projection."[50]

As Thomas Hutchinson later chronicled in his two-volume history of Massachusetts, the Dudley party's proposal for a loan office struck a balance of interests between the land bankers, on the one hand, and those who "were for drawing in the paper bills and depending on silver and gold currency," on the other. Hard-money men eventually backed the public plan, thinking it "the least of the two evils . . . and, after that, the country was divided between the public and private bank." According to Hutchinson, "the controversy, had an universal spread, and divided towns, parishes, and particular families."[51] In the end, however, the loan office party triumphed in the assembly. In May 1714, the colony passed an act for lending £50,000 in bills of credit at 5 percent interest for five years to persons pledging "good, real security." One-fifth of the principal plus interest would be due annually, the interest earmarked for "Defraying the Publick Charges of the Province." Five trustees, including Andrew Belcher and Thomas and Edward Hutchinson, would oversee the money's allocation.[52]

But the public loan's small size and strict terms only increased the land bankers' zeal, setting off a year-long struggle between the two factions that climaxed in the bankers' arrest. On August 20, 1714, evidently at Paul Dudley's behest, the governor and his council issued an order barring Colman and his partners from publishing their plans or printing any bills *"until they have laid their Proposals before the General Assembly."*[53] Nothing in the order, the land bankers would later protest, prevented them from completing their subscriptions and perfecting their proposal, "so as it might be fit to lay before the General Assembly . . . which they did at their last *October* Sessions; hoping for their Countenance and Authority."[54] When Dudley detained them for "openly carrying on their Bank with utmost Vigour and Expedition," they not only denied the charges but insisted that the governor had promised to "Write Home in their favour" and advised them to seek Secretary Isaac Addington's counsel.[55] And indeed, Addington seemed "of the Opinion that the Government would not Raise Money or Bills to Let out upon Loan" without usurping the royal prerogative to mint money, clearing the way, or so the bankers thought, for the private scheme.[56]

The controversy finally subsided when Governor Dudley's successor, Samuel Shute, signed off on a second, more generous loan in December 1716, this time with the popular party's blessing. In order "that there be some relief under these present difficulties, and that the husbandry, fishery and other trade and commerce of the province be encouraged and promoted" following "a long and expensive war," the act's preamble declared, loan commissioners would allocate £100,000 in bills of credit to the counties "according to their last tax." Then county trustees would "let out the said bills to such of the inhabitants as desire it" at 5 percent interest for ten years "on a good real security" at double the loan's value. The trustees would collect principal and interest payments, and return the bills to the commissioners so "that they may be burnt to ashes." Finally, the act contained a right of redemption clause: if a borrower defaulted on his loan and lost the mortgaged property, he could exercise a right of redemption by paying what he owed within three years, and reclaim the collateral.⁵⁷ With the stroke of a pen, Governor Shute fused together private property, public money, and colonial power.

But the relief—and the calm—was temporary. When the 1714 loan came due in 1719, it was clear that there was no money to be had, either paper or silver, for paying the principal, igniting a new flurry of writings on money, trade, and government, and widening the rift between hard-money men and paper money proponents. John Colman, Elisha Cooke, and Oliver Noyes revived their proposal for a private bank and formed a new political club, the "Boston Caucus," to disseminate pamphlets and mobilize voters. Colonists were being dragged to the courts by the hundreds for want of money to settle their debts and then forced to "Sell their Houses at half Value," lamented Colman in his 1720 essay *The Distressed State of the Town of Boston Considered*, while lawyers and officials grew rich off their suffering. Meanwhile, a "great part of the Town can hardly get Bread to satisfie Nature," let alone pay taxes in support of "Church and State."⁵⁸ Time, indeed, showed that "it was a very wrong step to Crush the Private Bank, and set up this Publick Bank in its place, for the farther we go on in this way, the worse our Case will be, for as we used to say, Pay Day will come, but when it doth come there will be nothing wherewith to Pay."⁵⁹ The private scheme would have circulated rather than retired the interest money so that "the Stock would neither have increased nor decreased, but remained the same," and now "such a Bank . . . is the only Remedy which can be proposed to extricate us out of our Difficulties" and "give us a quick Relief by setting the Wheels a going."⁶⁰

For Harvard theologian Edward Wigglesworth, who had emerged as the land bankers' biggest critic, it was a distinction without a difference. "Must publick & private Banks be established, that so when People have spent all they have earnt, they may know where to go and borrow more, to lay out for things they have no need of?" he wondered. "And must the Lands of the Country groan under Taxes and Mortgages to uphold these Fooleries?"⁶¹ John Wise of Ipswich, who had championed the public loans, came under fire from an anonymous critic who lambasted him in the *Boston Gazette* for not yet paying the principal of the £1,000 he and his sons had borrowed in 1716.⁶² As prices crept upward in the second decade of the eighteenth century, Wigglesworth, Thomas Hutchinson, and other hard-money men saw an opportunity to broaden their base. Cotton Mather and Samuel Sewall, who had previously endorsed paper bills as a means of war finance, supported them to an extent. As merchants, judges, and clergymen, they may have feared that an inflationary currency would diminish their profits and salaries, even as their public pronouncements lamented the deranging effects of easy credit and "needless Commodities" on workers and the plight of ministers, widows, and others on fixed incomes.⁶³ One paper money critic worried that speculators would try to mortgage uncolonized lands when the assembly really ought to be taxing such "Waste Lands" and making "the Owners themselves Improve 'em, or Sell 'em to those that would."⁶⁴

Once again, the compromise position prevailed. In 1721 the assembly approved a third public loan of £50,000 for ten years, followed in 1728 by a fourth loan of £60,000 for ten years. The third and fourth loans differed significantly from their predecessors. Whereas the 1714 and 1716 loans were administered by appointed colony or county trustees, the 1721 and 1728 loans were apportioned to the towns according to their last tax. Freeholders would designate town trustees to give bonds for repayment to the town treasurer; determine how to divide the town's money between expenses and loans; and decide the minimum and maximum loan levels, what security to accept, and the form and rate of interest.⁶⁵ Most towns settled on a 5 percent interest rate and issued loans against land in amounts ranging from five to twenty pounds. The five-pound minimum many towns established was much lower than the twenty-five- and fifty-pound minimums the 1714 and 1716 loan acts had stipulated. For their part, Dedham townspeople battled over a proposal to offer loans to landless servants against personal property. Several towns wanted borrowers to give security with a reliable surety, a person to assume responsibility for the debt in case of default (like a modern-day cosigner). The loans were to be repaid to the provincial treasury by an annual poll tax collected from the towns between 1726 and 1730 and between 1734 and 1738, respectively.⁶⁶

The 1721 and 1728 loans gave towns more latitude over their economic affairs and more influence over provincial economic policy, while the property claims that secured the loans bolstered territorial sovereignty at the colonial level. Town treasurers issued bills of credit to town creditors, and town constables accepted the bills in payment of town taxes. Towns petitioned the assembly for new currency emissions and instructed their representatives on how to vote on money bills.⁶⁷ With more autonomy came greater responsibility. The Ipswich freeholders voted on how to dispense their £1,429 portion of the £50,000 loan in October 1721. They chose Simon Epps, John Denison, and John Wainwright as trustees for lending the money to individuals "who will give good security, but no one person shall borrow or hire more than fifty pounds."⁶⁸ In April 1728, the Braintree freeholders gathered to decide on the provisions of their £552 portion of the £60,000 loan. They determined that ten pounds would "be the lowest sum lent out," forty pounds the highest. They chose five trustees to give bonds for repayment and lend the money to borrowers (who also gave bonds for repayment, making the trustees guarantors of sorts). Interest from the loans went toward building roads and schools, paying schoolmasters and ministers, and supporting the poor and disabled. Schoolmaster Jonathan Neal drew an annual salary of thirty pounds, while William Taunt, who had broken his leg and was unable to work, received "the loan of five Pounds for a year . . . out of the Town's Treasury, for his relief not to be Repaid." Among the town's creditors was an African man or woman held in bondage by the Jamaican-born sugar baron, Leonard Vassall. The enslaved individual received two shillings ninepence on March 5, 1732, though for what we do not know.[69]

Problems of Enforcement

How the Massachusetts loan money was distributed and in what amounts, how the loans were secured and whether they were repaid, and their impact on the colonial economy have not received much scholarly attention.[70] Certainly, repayment was not consistently enforced. When the 1714 loan matured in 1719, less than half of the principal had been paid. Subsequent loan acts deferred payments on the principal for five years so that when the loans matured, borrowers were often unable to pay the balance.[71] But rather than compel the loans' trustees to foreclose on the mortgages, the assembly granted blanket extensions to all borrowers. For example, £100,000 total from the 1714 and 1716 loans, the latter set to mature in 1726, was continued in circulation until 1731. The assembly also canceled portions of loans on a case-by-case basis. One borrower who had come upon hard times after his barn burned down successfully petitioned the assembly to forgive three years' interest on a £250 loan and discharge his mortgage—seven years after the loan had matured.[72] As late as 1738, the assembly advised the surviving trustees of the 1716 loan to "comply with their duty" and "settle their respective accounts of the said loan and pay the Ballance remaining into their hands unto the Treasurer."[73] In January 1739 it reported that "a considerable part of the Bills" of the 1728 loan were outstanding, "although the whole thereof . . . ought by Law to have been paid into the Treasury" the previous spring.[74]

The manner of securing the loans may have made enforcing payments difficult at the province level. The trustees of the 1714 and 1716 loan money had recorded loans secured by land mortgages with the proper county registers of deeds—the existing system for recording land sales and mortgages—which contain detailed information on borrowers and collateral, including the borrowers' and any sureties' occupations, as well as the size and location of the mortgaged property. But the 1721 and 1728 loans were administered through dozens of different towns, and it remains unclear what proportion was even secured by mortgages, as the loan acts authorized the towns to lend "on good real estates, or personal security." The Boston trustees recorded loans secured by mortgages, at least, with the Suffolk County register.[75] A Billerica historian later found many of the mortgages to the trustees of the 1728 loan "on record at the Middlesex Registry."[76] And in Ipswich, 1721 loans were issued on "good & landed security" and "Provision was made for inspection of the mortgages to see that the titles were free and clear."[77] The title recording system that authenticated private property ownership facilitated the coining of land, but it exposed the loan money to the whims of local officials and relationships.

Records of loans for small amounts on personal security, moreover, apparently remained under the auspices of the towns. The available evidence of these loans is fragmentary. Braintree treasurer Benjamin Webb recorded information on borrowers and loan amounts, but not forms of collateral or payment. An account dated March 1732 indicates that the town had £230 outstanding on twenty loans "of the money belonging to the town at Interest," nine of them more than a decade old. John Adams, the father of the future president, owed twenty pounds on a bond dated March 26, 1729. Presumably the trustees held the bonds.[78] In some cases only the bonds survive. In 1728, the Billerica trustees lent twenty pounds to Jeremiah Hunt, a farmer and ferry operator on the Concord and Merrimack Rivers, who gave bond with surety for repayment. His surety was Enoch Kidder Jr., his kinsman through marriage. Although Hunt made payments on the principal in 1734, 1735, and 1736 (all recorded on the backside of his bond), his death in 1737 delayed the final payment until 1740.[79]

How, then, did colonial settlers use their loans? As paper money advocates expressed optimism that borrowers would mark them for productive ventures, and hard-money men lamented the debauching influence of easy credit on the laboring classes, money was so scarce at the start of the 1720s that many borrowers likely used their loans for paying personal or business debts or for living expenses. Two Ipswich ministers received special loans of £100 apiece on mortgages of houses and lands, one declaring that his salary "has not been made good to me in vallue, however it might be in Sum" due to depreciation, compelling him to mortgage a sizeable portion of his estate. Even the wealthy pastor John Wise used his loan partly to pay his "former money obligations."[80] In 1720, a year when thousands of writs of attachment for debt were filed in the courts, John Colman renewed his campaign for a bank of credit, arguing that it would give debtors the means to satisfy their creditors without further delay.[81] Oliver Noyes predicted that "if a Private Bank or some other Medium be not Brought on to support us, we shall ere we are aware, be plunged into the most dire Circumstances that ever poor People

Province of the Massachusetts Bay. **K**NOW all Men by these presents, *That we* *Jeremiah Hunt Principle and Enoch Kidder just Surety both of Billerica in the County of Middx In his Majesties Province of the Massachusets Bay In New England Husbandmen*

are Holden and stand firmly Bound and Obliged unto *William Patten, Benjamin Tompson and Joshua Abbott*

Trustees, Chosen and Appointed by the Town of *Billerica* Pursuant to an Act of the Great and General Court of the aforesaid Province, Intituled, An Act, *For Raising & Settling a Publick Revenue, for and towards Defraying the necessary Charges of this Government, by an Emission of Sixty Thousand Pounds in Bills of Credit on this Province:* Made and Passed at a Session of the said Court at *Boston*, the 22d of *November* last past, in the full and just Sum of *twenty pounds*

Lawful Money of *of this Province* to be paid unto the said *William Patten, Benjamin Tompson and Joshua Abbott*

or their Successors in said Trust: To which Payment well and truly to be made, We Bind our Selves, our Heirs, Executors and Administrators, firmly by these Presents. Sealed with our Seals. Dated the *Eleventh* Day, of *April* Anno Domini, 172*8 In the first year of the reign of our sovereign Lord George of Great Britain France and Ireland King &c*

THE *Condition* of this present Obligation is such, That if the above Bounden *Jeremiah Hunt or Enoch Kidder just*

their Heirs, Executors, Administrators, or any of them, shall and do well and truly pay, or cause to be paid unto the said *William Patten Benjamin Tompson and Joshua Abbott*

Trustees or their Successors in said Trust, the Sum of *ten pounds* in Bills of Credit, on the aforesaid Province, with Six *per Cent.* Interest for the same, on or before the *Eleventh* Day of *April next* which will be in the Year of our Lord, One Thousand Seven Hundred and *twenty nine* without Fraud, Coven or further Delay: Then the above-written Obligation to be Void and of none Effect, or else to abide and Remain in full Force and Virtue.

Signed, Sealed and Delivered *Jeremiah Hunt* in Presence of

John Pollard *Enoch Kidder junr* *Isaac Abbott*

FIGURE 4.1 AND FIGURE 4.2. Jeremiah Hunt's obligation bond to the trustees of Billerica, April 11, 1728. Collection of the Massachusetts Historical Society.

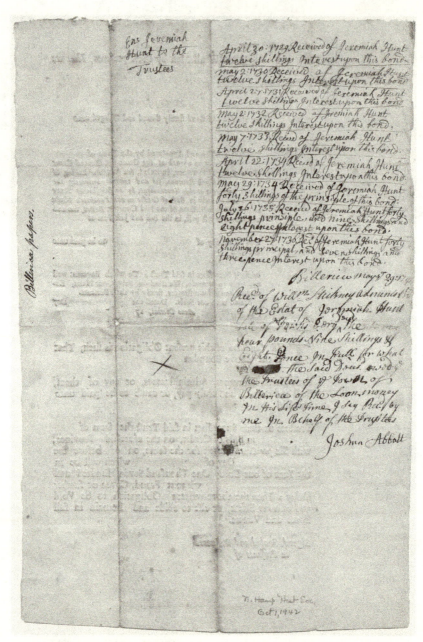

FIGURE 4.1 AND FIGURE 4.2. (*continued*)

were in," adding that "I am as uneasy as others at the thoughts of Intailing a Debt on my Posterity, but better be in Debt than Dye."[82]

The 1721 and 1728 loans must have created expectations of increased liquidity that fueled borrowing and credit extension among colonists. Farmers, artisans, and traders contracted debts in currency rather than sterling and issued bonds and promissory notes payable in bills of credit.[83] For example, in August 1724, the Ipswich joiner John Dennis received a bond for twenty-two pounds "current money of province" of the blacksmith Joseph Arnel and the farmer Richard Belcher, both of Charlestown, to be repaid in "[passable] bills of the said provence" the following April.[84] Daniel Safford likewise made out a promissory note to Thomas Dennis for "Thirteen Shillings in Bills of Credit" dated January 31, 1730. And that spring, Braintree cordwainer Amos Stetson secured an obligation to the blacksmith Richard Thayer, also of Braintree, for the payment of £145 "in Good Bills of Credit on the Province of the Massachusetts Bay" the following December.[85] Other members of the Thayer family received loans from Braintree's portion of the province loan money; John Thayer served as a trustee.[86] Their access to public loans restricted, women nevertheless played indispensable roles in the credit economy as borrowers and lenders alike. In the process, as historian Sara Damiano demonstrates, they honed financial and legal skills, elevated their visibility in public spaces, and "cultivated an authority available to them in only a few other forums."[87]

Throughout the colonies, men and women additionally used bills of credit when they purchased goods from peddlers or settled up with shopkeepers, accelerating the consumer revolution the historian T. H. Breen has documented.[88] In the 1720s, a New York or New England colonist bought rum, molasses, and allspice from a "Mr Fitch" with "a [promissory] note fifteen shillings" and "bills 5 shillings & 6 [pence]." In March 1728, the colonist settled their account with a "James McJorew" with "12 shillings in Bills of Credit," the same day McJorew left them "two yards of Calico" worth six shillings per yard.[89] Between 1725 and 1727, the Boston shopkeeper Ann Greene, whose customers included the merchants Andrew Belcher, Peter Faneuil, and James Bowdoin, did a brisk retail trade in molasses, sugar, raisins, salt, cocoa, silk, muslin, linen, and other goods, purchasing the items from wholesalers on short credit and paying them later in cash, presumably some of which was paper.[90]

By the second half of the 1720s, sluggish demand for goods and labor had made the Massachusetts loan money a crucial source of liquidity. While the proportion of borrowers who used their loans to improve their farms or invest in land or manufactures is unknown, surely the money was more valuable to more people for paying debts, extending credit, and participating in the growing world of goods. As currency created through loans circulated among friends and strangers, it integrated farmers, artisans, shopkeepers, and merchants into the colonial monetary community, reinforcing old bonds of obligation and interdependence and creating new ones. Consider the case of the aspiring entrepreneur Thomas Amory. Amory moved to Massachusetts from South Carolina in 1719, importing rice, pitch, and tar from Charles Town and wine from the Azores before setting up a rum distillery and entering the European trade. In Boston, he sold rum and molasses wholesale to country retailers on short credit and (often after some pressing) received paper money in payments. He turned a good profit on tar until the removal of the naval bounty in 1725, when the price fell from a high of thirty shillings per barrel before the bounty was taken off to twenty-four shillings per barrel and falling in the summer of 1725.[91]

Then the crash came. In 1726, a credit crisis in Britain induced creditors to call in their debts in New England. That year the 1716 loan matured, threatening a sudden contraction of the currency, and petitions from town meetings for extending the loan flooded the assembly.[92] Amory was in a bind, unable to sell his imported calicoes, linens, and other fabrics for under six months' credit, "every body causious of Buying till they see wt. ye Assembly doe."[93] With merchandise piling up in warehouses, traders competed for "good Bills of Exchange," and as demand for bills to remit to Britain intensified, the exchange rate reached "190 to 200 p ct.," or £290 to £300 currency for £100 sterling.[94] The uncertainty produced restrictions on trade, leading to declines in output, price deflation, and mass insolvency. Debt actions and writs of attachment for debt surged to 1720 levels. Money was so scarce that the assembly permitted colonists to pay their taxes for 1727 in pork, barley, rye, corn, hemp, peas, butter, leather, cod, whale bone, wax, and other products at set prices.[95]

Local business reached a nadir that summer. The Dorchester merchant Samuel Royall went out of business and had to pay his creditors in store goods at the rate of seventeen shillings sixpence in the pound sterling. Amory, pressured to pay his own debts, faced the difficult task of calling in debts he had previously been pleased to leave out. Ann Hutchinson, a shopkeeper who owed him thirty-three pounds, closed her doors until her creditors agreed to give some forbearance in the form of an additional twelve months to pay her debts. Many debtors and creditors (most of whom were themselves debtors) dealt with each other "in the shadow of the law" rather than go through the trouble and expense of litigation, as the legal historian Bruce Mann explains, for "even a final judgement for the creditor . . . often yielded little or nothing."[96] Of course, when one creditor showed forbearance, he often risked his own reputation. In November 1727, Amory described to one of his London creditors the "Great Scarcity of Money the like was never known . . . And the shop keepers by their bad pay will occasion the Factors to have a bad Name."⁹⁷ To Amory's great relief, news broke the following spring that the assembly had voted to continue £100,000 in outstanding bills of credit in circulation for another three years and to authorize a £60,000 loan, to be repaid between 1734 and 1738. "Next weeke our New Money will be distributed," he wrote to his friend Samuel Everleigh in South Carolina on April, 4, 1728, "& shortly Please God we hope to have a briske trade."⁹⁸

The currency expansion did not forestall a rare food riot from erupting in Boston in July 1729 when, one diarist recorded, "a mob rose . . . to hinder the merchants from sending away ye corn as they attempted," prompting the governor to install a night watch.⁹⁹ While the size and composition of the crowd is unknown, it likely included women, propertyless men, unfree laborers, and children. "Against those who transported foodstuffs," writes the historian Barbara Clark Smith, food rioters "acted as agents of location." Whether they were drawing on traditions of the "moral economy" and a plebeian culture with longstanding precedents, or whether more immediate needs motivated them, the Boston rioters made claims on local products that defied the logic of capitalist commodification.¹⁰⁰

The loan money was probably not much consolation, then, for landless laborers who struggled in a period of rising prices and stagnating wages. In 1728, the Boston newspapers printed a series of articles calculating the average middling family's living expenses. They determined that even if a laboring man worked five days a week throughout the year making five shillings a day, typical for tradesmen, artisans, and some sailors, his weekly earnings would be insufficient to feed, clothe, and shelter a family of six. Food costs alone were calculated at six shillings tenpence per day, plus another four shillings per day for clothing, washing, and candles. Rent and firewood added another fifteen shillings per week, for a total weekly budget of nearly seventy-three shillings. Yet few laborers had steady employment, and most working men made only thirty-five to sixty pounds per year. Laboring women earned a fraction of that, with maids bringing home ten or eleven pounds per year at the rate of seven pence a day and washerwomen making three to five shillings per month at two pence a day. As the newspapers made plain, wages were not keeping pace with inflation.¹⁰¹

Boston merchant and paper money advocate Hugh Vans later owned that unanticipated currency emissions like the 1728 loan could cause a temporary uptick in prices if they followed a period of acute money scarcity when "Trade . . . laboured, Debts were postpon'd &c." For "what could be the Consequence upon a sudden Emission," he reasoned, "but that People receiving their Debts in a much greater Proportion, and purchasing more Returns, than usual, the Silver and other Returns should remarkably *rise*." The solution was to issue bills "in a *regular Progressive* Way so as not hurt the Trade by a sudden Flood" or, he might have added, retrenchment.[102]

By the 1730s, inflation had become a persistent feature of the Massachusetts economy. As the historian Gary Nash explained, prices rose in this period due to "the excess of imports over exports" combined with "flagging confidence in New England bills of credit and the scrambling of merchants for ways to make returns to Britain, which drove up the sterling exchange rate"—in short, because of Vans's "balance of debt." But depreciation and inflation were themselves symptoms of a more fundamental problem: Massachusetts's increasingly marginal productivity.[103] Social and economic dislocation wrought by war, declining agricultural output, and fluctuations in external demand limited the colony's ability to compete in the Atlantic economy. Boston, once the chief provisioner of the plantation colonies, was undercut by New York and Philadelphia, which had richer hinterlands and shorter travel times to the Caribbean. Thin soils and a prolonged depression of sugar prices after 1720 contributed to the problem of underproduction and the difficulty of making returns to Britain.[104] Lacking commodity exports, the colony's trade and payments balance suffered, increasing competition for bills of exchange to pay British merchants and fueling the high sterling exchange rate they complained diminished their property and profits. In the 1730s, these structural problems would be exacerbated by the actions of a home government intent on restoring a proper balance of power between governors and assemblies, and between creditors and debtors.

The Best Poor Man's Country?

Though no less politically contentious, Pennsylvania's experience in coining land differed rather significantly from Massachusetts's. Unlike Massachusetts, Pennsylvania had not adopted bills of credit as a means of war finance because it had not contributed to the imperial wars. Nor had it attempted to mint its own coin. Participants in William Penn's "Holy Experiment" had been complaining about money scarcity virtually since the colony's 1681 founding. On February 7, 1689, a group of prominent colonists presented "their design for setting up a bank of money" to Lieutenant Governor John Blackwell.[105] One of them was Thomas Budd, who had published a proposal for a bank of credit four years earlier.[106] Fresh off his own attempt to establish a bank in Boston, Blackwell wrote to Penn straightaway, informing him of the group's plans and attaching "a small treatise I dedicated to your self touching a Bank of Credit proposed to have been Erected in New England."¹⁰⁷ The proposals came to nothing, partly because the colony's Quaker elite despised the Puritan Blackwell and resisted his leadership, and partly because economic conditions improved after King William's War (1688–97) broke out.

But the complaints of money scarcity returned following Queen Anne's War. Although Pennsylvania had grown rapidly during the war, geographically insulated from the French and the Spanish, and spared military expenditures, Philadelphia grain suppliers soon found themselves competing with New York City merchants for Caribbean customers, and the colony's commercial advantage over New York slipped. The recent enforcement of Queen Anne's Proclamation of 1704, moreover, was causing Pennsylvania to lose much of its circulating coin to New York. In early 1718, 200 colonial settlers petitioned the assembly to ignore the proclamation and raise the value of a piece of eight. They attributed the "want of running Cash" to the colony's "late Complyance in reducing our own coyn . . . and our neighbouring Colonies retaining their former Currency," which was "the reason they daily drain us of our money and . . . our silver is in a manner wholly Exhausted thereby."¹⁰⁸ When the assembly passed an act for establishing a loan office five years later, the popular lieutenant governor William Keith justified the legislation to the Board of Trade by explaining that Pennsylvania was "the only colony which has strictly observ'd Her late Majesty Queen Ann's Proclamation," creating a scarcity of coin to "answer the Ends of a Currency in our Home Trade or Product Manufactured."¹⁰⁹

The expansion of global commerce contributed to the money scarcity in Pennsylvania. Steered by imperial officials and British merchants, Atlantic trade brought new economic opportunities to colonists, including the opportunity to purchase imported goods on generous credit terms. Coin became more valuable as a commodity than as a medium of exchange, so traders bought up whatever specie entered the colonies to remit to their British creditors, diminishing the local supply. As silver and gold "are in Demand in most Countries," the Philadelphia merchant Francis Rawle surmised in a 1721 essay in support of a loan office, they "cannot be so certainly confined" to the colonies "as some other Things in Use may."¹¹⁰ Four years later, a pseudonymous farmer Roger Plowman swore that he "would never argue for Paper" money if the colony could attract and retain coins, "but that we cannot; and without some Currency to pass among our Selves, it will inevitably destroy all manner of Trade amongst us."¹¹¹

It took a serious recession, however, to convince the local business community to support the establishment of a public loan office. The experiences of two Philadelphia merchants, one established and one up-and-coming, tell the story of how the gambling tables turned in hard times. Jamaican-born merchant Jonathan Dickinson was one of the colony's richest men. By the time the warning signs of a slump appeared in 1715, he had amassed a small fortune trafficking in dry goods and enslaved people, served a term as the mayor of Philadelphia, and become a member of the governor's council. Yet he was not immune to the vagaries of the Atlantic economy. On April 28 he complained to John Harriot in Jamaica that money scarcity and low flour prices "Stagger the people who complain greatly."[112] Falling wheat prices diminished farmers' profits, jeopardizing artisans' and seamen's livelihoods in turn. For men like Dickinson, it meant higher prices for bills of exchange and a glut of consumer goods.[113] In August 1715, he confessed to the Bristol trader Richard Champion that he and other merchants would rather "shun the Credit given" by London merchants "until the country can raise a Bank of Credit" than be stuck with unsold stock.[114] Among the items he struggled to offload were haberdashery, pepper and spice, printed paper, and fabrics of "flaming coulers." As prices fell, surpluses of fruit, cider, wine, rum, and molasses clogged the local market.[115]

The demand for wheat had yet to recover by 1718, the year twenty-nine-year-old Thomas Lawrence came to Philadelphia to set up shop as a wholesale merchant. On April 22, 1719, Lawrence reported to Samuel Storke, one of his London suppliers, that he "found bills [of exchange] very scarce."[116] Making matters worse, he was forced to "give at Least 6 months" for retail credit "and then plagued to get in the money."[117] When the economy slipped into a depression at the start of 1720, Lawrence had to beg Storke to stop sending him goods until he was sure he could sell them.[118] Although the downturn coincided with the South Sea Bubble, the crisis had less to do with the international credit crunch that followed the bursting of the bubble than with the collapse of wheat prices in a saturated Caribbean market. Between 1715 and 1721, another bumper crop year, the price of wheat fell from four shillings to three shillings per bushel. By 1723 it had sunk to two shillings eightpence per bushel.[119]

Contemporaries could not help but draw connections between "jobbing," the decline of grain prices, and money scarcity. In the spring of 1721, Dickinson, whose brother had purchased South Sea stock, complained to family members that since "the deplorable calamity that has happened by South Sea stocke . . . all the Product of America is sunk extreamly low and that thing called money never was scarcer."[120] Bills of exchange returned protested (meaning the drawee could not or would not honor them), and "all the mony we have goes for returns & now we are ready to pull one another to pieces for money."[121] He later lamented that "South Sea & Mississippi has ruined all the trade in America."[122] Meanwhile, Dickinson's friends in Jamaica had reported that the island was "in such Distress" and money was so scarce "that its thought the Country will make paper to pass as mony," to which he replied that Pennsylvania, too, would likely settle soon on "some Expedient to make something to pass . . . paper or Country produce."[123]

While Dickinson's wealth insulated him from the worst effects of the depression, Thomas Lawrence was less fortunate. In a letter to Samuel Storke dated June 1, 1721, he speculated that "it seems your Bubbles in Europe have an Effect on These Countrys for Sundry persons here have made slips," including the Philadelphia retailer Benjamin Mayne, who was rumored to be £3,000 in debt. Lawrence concluded that "the scarcity of money makes every thing veri dull."[124] That October he reported to Storke that "the currant cash of this place is so clean gone that many people find it Difficult to buy there dayly provisions," adding that "so many [customers] Break & run that I dare not venture to let any goods go out of my store before paid for."[125] Trade was at a standstill the following year. There were work stoppages on the docks, and people were fleeing the colony to escape their debts, leaving almost a quarter of all the houses in Philadelphia empty. Lawrence had nearly £2,000 lent out, mostly for goods sold two years earlier, but could not command fifty pounds from all of his debtors.[126]

Lawrence eventually recovered and even went on to become the mayor of Philadelphia, just like Dickinson. But colonists of lesser means experienced the depression through unemployment, hunger, and penury. "How deplorable are the Lives of the common People!" Francis Rawle cried in his 1721 essay *Some Remedies Proposed, for the Restoring the Sunk Credit of the Province of Pennsylvania*. "Their Trades and Callings discouraged and valued at nought . . . The common Necessaries for Families brought to the Market are not to be bought because Change (as *Silver* and *Copper* is commonly called) is not to be had."[127] For want of money, William Keith reported to the Board of Trade on December 18, 1722, farmers could not sell their produce, "the Ship Builder & Carpenter starve for want of Employment . . . and the usurer grinds the Face of The poor so that Law suits multiply, our Gaols are full." If something was going to be done to alleviate their distress, and Keith was "of the opinion" that that something ought to be making a paper currency, it had better be done "now than afterwards."[128]

The Pennsylvania General Loan Office

In 1721, Francis Rawle and William Keith joined forces with the "antiproprietary party" leader David Lloyd to endorse a bill for establishing a loan office, which the conservative assembly promptly rejected. Popular support for the creation of a local currency surged, and colonists from both Philadelphia and the countryside flooded the assembly with petitions. "The Clamor is universall for Paper Money," Keith reported to the Board of Trade late the following year.[129] In the October 1722 assembly elections, five merchants, including Jonathan Dickinson, were swept from office and replaced by a slate of paper money advocates. By Christmas there were proposals for a loan office, debt relief, a hemp bounty, and a flour inspection act. "We are now reduced to the greatest straits through the Decay of Trade & for want of Money," Penn family agent James Logan informed a friend on November 22, 1722, "& therefore 'tis believed the Assembly which is to sitt shortly will attempt a Currency by Bills of Credit."[130]

Between 1723 and 1724, the assembly authorized £45,000 total in bills of credit to be lent through a "General Loan Office" to qualifying individuals at 5 percent interest for eight years on mortgages of lands and houses. The 1723 loan office act appointed four "gentlemen" trustees, or commissioners, to oversee the disbursal of the loans, each of whom gave a £500 bond with surety. The trustees would additionally "provide good large books of royal or other large paper, and well covered, wherein shall be recorded and enrolled all the deeds of mortgages to be taken for bills of credit to be let out upon loan . . . in a fair, legible hand." Francis Rawle and three others were named signers of the bills. The maximum loan amount was £100, the minimum twelve pounds ten shillings. Principal and interest were payable to the trustees, and the bills were legal tender at the loan office and the provincial and county treasuries.[131]

Contemporaries rejoiced. On November 1, 1724, Thomas Lawrence was pleased to inform a friend that "att present Our Trade . . . is so powerfully Carried on that all our Builders are imployed & many people waiting in order to put Vessells on the Stocks."[132] He allowed that although the bills may have been responsible for a small uptick in the sterling exchange rate, the increase mainly affected import merchants like himself, and he was "truly of the opinion that a private intrest should give way to a publick one." Lawrence concluded that the emissions had been "absolutely necessary, for the people were in a deplorable Condition for want of a Currency to supply there Common necessetys."[133] In 1725 Francis Rawle likewise observed that the currency "has been conducive to restore Credit, relieve the Exigencies of diverse Freeholders and Inhabitants of this Province, and revive the languishing State of Trade."[134] Public loans freed colonists from depending on private lenders, which lowered the costs of doing business and participating in markets.[135] Lieutenant Governor Keith later reflected that the loan office had benefited middling people with some land or a house, who had borrowed bills to pay "their usurious Creditors." He went on to note that widespread access to low-interest loans reduced the overall interest rate, drawing settlers to Philadelphia and increasing "Business all over the Province . . . at a great rate."[136]

Merchants embraced the loan office because it was good for business. The Philadelphia widow Beulah Coates, who had taken over her husband Samuel's High Street trading house following his death in 1719, started using bills of credit to settle her outstanding accounts. In October 1723, she paid "Twenty one pounds Ten Shillings in paper money" to the wealthy merchant Israel Pemberton, with whom she frequently did business. The following June she gave "the sum of twenty one pounds Currt: Money," presumably paper, "in full of all accts" to a Robert Dawes. In September 1724, Coates paid a total of eleven pounds six shillings sixpence in Pennsylvania and Delaware bills to one Christopher Smith.[137] While some merchants mortgaged their property to the loan office, most encountered paper money in the course of their ordinary business dealings. Through examining the mortgages recorded in some of the loan office registers, historian Mary Schweitzer determined that the majority of borrowers identified as yeomen. Among these, the average loan amount was about sixty-five pounds. Widows, weavers, blacksmiths, carpenters, and cordwainers also received loans in significant numbers.[138]

Despite its broad appeal, the Pennsylvania loan office was the subject of a years-long controversy between paper money advocates and their critics, namely, James Logan, Andrew Hamilton (himself a loan office trustee), and other Penn family agents. In 1726 the Penns replaced Lieutenant Governor Keith with Patrick Gordon, who was under strict orders not to approve any additional money acts without a suspending clause. Voters subsequently sent Keith to the assembly, where he antagonized the new governor and pursued his vision of a moral economy. He championed legislation to lower interest rates, reduce legal fees, and relieve debtors. Keith organized the "Leather Apron Club" for artisans, courted the growing population of German settlers, and held outdoor rallies and parades where everyone was welcome.[139] In 1725 and 1726, a flurry of new pamphlets in favor of paper money appeared in print.[140] The assembly even debated a measure that would broaden access to loans to include long-term tenants. Under popular pressure to increase the currency and the threat of not receiving his salary, Lieutenant Governor Gordon declared himself a friend of the paper medium. In 1726 he approved an act for reissuing old bills of credit against new mortgages, minus the provision allowing leaseholds as collateral.[141]

By the time depression revisited Pennsylvania in 1728, Keith had built a large support base in the assembly and out-of-doors that could push for a new round of loans, putting the proprietor's friends on the defensive. "Faction prevails amongst the People," James Logan lamented to John Penn on October 8 of that year, "nor is it Easie to determine what the factions really propose to themselves further than that they raise loud Cries for more Paper money."[142] A few weeks later, the assembly speaker Andrew Hamilton lamented that "if that Spirit raised among the people for paper money by Sir William did not constantly perplex us, his Doctrine of reducing all to a levell, suits mighty well with the inclinations of the poorer Sort." In addition to accusing Keith of inflaming the passions of poor people, he chastised the Philadelphia factors who "cry as loud as any for paper money" against the interests of their Bristol employers. Hamilton and Logan thought it was only a matter of time before Gordon caved to popular pressure.[143]

Violence nearly erupted in the spring of 1729, the same year a food riot broke out in Boston. Following the assembly's passage of an act for issuing £50,000 in new bills of credit, Gordon announced that he would support a bill for, at most, £30,000. Word spread that "about 200 Countrey men" were planning to go to Philadelphia and join with urban dissidents "to apply first to the Assembly & then storm the Governor."[144] Their "Insults" were thwarted, however, when Hamilton convinced his colleagues to enforce Parliament's riot act. Not long after, the lieutenant governor sent the compromise bill to Britain for approval.[145] In a letter to the proprietors justifying his actions, he explained that "The Cry for an addition to our Currency was so generall that all rankes and degrees of people join'd in it, so as it became absolutely necessary to give in to some measures for granting these, which was best for me to doe."[146] The civil unrest soon subsided. On October 30, 1729, Gordon reported to John Penn that the entire province "seems to be very well satisfied and in perfect peace and quiet which is Chiefly owing to that late addition to our Currency."[147]

Logan was less certain about the appropriateness of Gordon's actions. Contrary to the popular view that "while the security is good the Money cannot fall," he wrote to William Penn on November 17, paper money's value was, in point of fact, "kept up, by not exceeding its quantity." He worried that "the popular frenzy that now reigns will never stop till we are as bad with it as they are in N. England," where the cost of silver had risen to twenty shillings per ounce.[148] Twenty-three-year-old Benjamin Franklin rejected this logic. It was pointless, he said, "to object [to] the wretched Fall of the Bills in New-England and South-Carolina unless it might be made evident that their Currency was emitted with the same Prudence, and on such good Security as ours is; and it certainly was not."[149] The only way for Pennsylvania's currency to depreciate, Franklin maintained, was if land values declined, but as the colony's population was rising, and would continue to rise "by the Help of a large Addition to our Currency ... Land in consequence is continually rising."[150] In the 1730s the colony began a period of prolonged prosperity that intensified the demand for labor and meant full employment for the maritime and building trades. Buoyed by a growing settler population, rising land prices, and a steady wage-price ratio, Pennsylvania bills of credit retained their value in exchange and enjoyed a high level of public trust.[151]

In Franklin's mind, the transformation of land into money was tied to an early labor theory of value that the English tax assessor William Petty had articulated in the previous century. Just as Petty had sought to quantify Irish land and people in order to justify the colonization of Ireland, so Franklin sought to reduce colonized land and unfree labor to monetary units in order to rationalize commodification in the New World.[152] "Silver itself is of no certain permanent Value," Franklin set forth in his 1729 essay, *A Modest Enquiry into the Nature and Necessity of a Paper-Currency*, and "therefore it seems requisite to fix upon Something else, more proper to be made a Measure of Values, and this I take to be Labor."[153] As labor gave value to silver and other commodities, "thus the Riches of a Country are to be valued by the Quantity of Labor its inhabitants are able to purchase, and not by the Quantity of Silver and Gold they possess."[154] Francis Rawle had anticipated Franklin's remarks by four years, writing in *Ways and Means for the Inhabitants of Delaware to Become Rich* that although paper money might make America "nominally" wealthy, what made the colonists "really rich" was "the Value of the Farmers Labor; for by the Value of the Produce, Land will rise, and be more valuable."[155] In this formulation, paper money was a means to an end, a way to mobilize labor and turn it into "real" wealth.

For Franklin and Rawle, confidence in the currency thus derived less from its fiscal basis (and even less from the land itself) than from faith that the fictitious value advanced in the form of paper bills would be actualized by the future value produced by labor under colonial capital's command. Despite his humble origins, Franklin was no champion of the laboring classes. He held Black men and women in bondage and published slave advertisements and runaway notices in his *Pennsylvania Gazette* long before becoming a leading figure in the antislavery movement. As Karl Marx pointed out in his gloss of Franklin, the Philadelphia printer may even have conceptualized paper money as the embodiment of abstracted or alienated (indeed "coined") labor.[156] Franklin, of course, had a personal stake in the loan office: in 1729, the Pennsylvania assembly hired him to design and print the bonds (also known as loan office certificates), mortgage forms (or indentures), and bills of credit.

Through 1747 he produced an estimated 800,000 individual bills for Pennsylvania, Delaware, and New Jersey, for which the colonial governments handsomely rewarded him.[157]

While the loan office transformed the province's monetary system, it did not change the underlying fiscal structure. Unlike the early paper monies of Massachusetts, South Carolina, and New York, forged in the crucible of war, the Pennsylvania loan office was designed mainly to promote agricultural development and generate revenue. If the Massachusetts loans of 1721

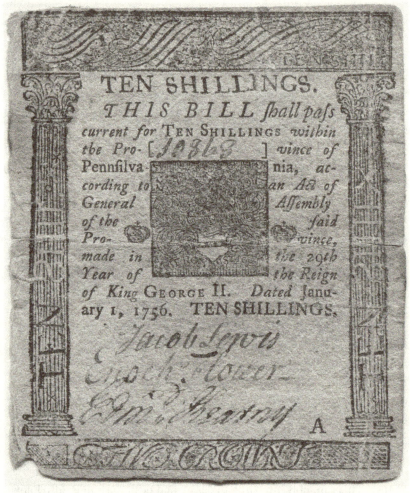

FIGURE 4.3 AND FIGURE 4.4. Province of Pennsylvania paper ten-shilling bill of credit, printed by Benjamin Franklin and David Hall, 1756. The reverse has a leaf print and a warning against counterfeiting. 0000.999.29328. Courtesy American Numismatic Society. http://numismatics.org/collection/0000.999.29328.

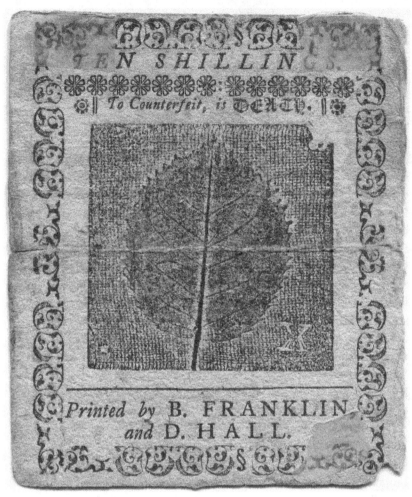

FIGURE 4.3 AND FIGURE 4.4. (*continued*)

and 1728 gave the towns more latitude over their economic affairs, reversing the colony's consolidation of fiscal power in wartime, the Pennsylvania emissions of 1723–24 and 1729 reflected an existing distribution of political power that favored the countryside and would remain that way for another quarter-century. From the 1710s on, Mary Schweitzer observed, rural settlers thus "actively sought laws to increase the money supply," and "pressure from the legislature's constituents led to the enactment of all of the laws authorizing paper money."[158] While the assembly drew virtually all of its revenue from liquor duties and loan interest, the four counties—Philadelphia, Chester, Bucks, and

Lancaster—levied the only direct taxes, to be collected by the towns. They earmarked the revenues for building roads and bridges, financing poor relief, and paying back loan money they had borrowed to put toward the construction of courthouses and workhouses.[159]

In this way, the provincial government ran relatively smoothly until the 1750s. Antiproprietary sentiment occasionally flared up around the money question, as in the late 1730s, when William Penn's son Thomas arrived in the colony and protested receiving quitrents in bills of credit, and during the War of the Austrian Succession (1740–48), or King George's War in America, when the Penn family demanded control over the appropriation of the interest money. The war itself was a subject of contention among the Quakers who dominated the assembly, more so when they discovered that the new lieutenant governor, George Thomas, had permitted their servants to enlist in the army. In 1754, the Seven Years' War (known as the French and Indian War in the colonies) broke out in Pennsylvania's backyard, giving the proprietors an opening to renew their attack on the assembly's authority to appropriate public monies. For the first time the assembly would vote supplies for the king, to be raised by direct taxes on the population, effecting a redistribution of political power from the counties to the provincial government and laying the groundwork for a colonial state unprecedented in size and scope.[160]

Early proponents of credit currency and land banks in the colonies focused less on what money was and how it was made, and more on what it could do, from facilitating trade to raising land values to increasing employment. John Woodbridge maintained that "Money, *if enough to mete Trade with* . . . inciteth to the purchasing of Land, and heighteneth its value; forwards the Improvement both of real, and personal Estates," and "encourage[s] heartless Idlers, to Work."[161] In his proposal for "a *Bank* of *Monies* and *Credit*," Thomas Budd envisioned himself and other property owners pooling their assets for a loan to build a "Linnen Manufacture . . . to the great benefit and advantage of some hundreds of People that we set to work, and to the supplying of the Inhabitants with Cloth made of Flax, grown, drest, spun and wove in our own Provinces."[162] John Blackwell argued that with a bank of credit, "the Trade and Wealth of any Countrey is establish'd upon it's own Foundation; and upon a *Medium* or Ballance arising within it self, *viz*. The Lands and Products of such Country."[163]

But farming was not the only way to wealth. Eighteenth-century proponents of land banks and loan offices wanted to use paper money to finance public projects that would put women, children, and unfree laborers to work. Francis Rawle proposed a linen manufactory because it was "lighter Work fit for Women and Children, either Negroes or White." John Wise envisaged a spinning school "for poor Women & children," a paper mill, and "a Hospital for poor Boys as in London."[164] And John Colman proposed an iron works, a wool works, and a toll bridge over the Charles River.[165] Framed in terms of improvement, paper money was not just a medium of exchange but an instrument for realizing the productive potential of British North America and of the laborers, free and unfree, who toiled there.[166]

The loan office system animated a political economy focused on the virtues of the internal economy and a model of colonial growth. At the same time, proponents of paper money argued that by energizing and diversifying internal economies, bills of credit indirectly fueled the expansion of external trade to the benefit of the British empire.[167] "If there was not Paper-Money in South-Carolina," Rawle remarked in 1721, "how could the Trade of that Country be so readily dispatched as it is?"[168] Thirteen years later a New England commentator concurred that paper money had "facilitated their own commerce among themselves at Home ... and that is forever the true way to have a large and gainful trade abroad."[169] He pointed out that "the Rope-walks, Ship-yards, still-houses, Sugar-houses, and the other Trades Depending upon these, the Number of Ships and Vessels ... and many other Things not to be numbr'd" were daily increasing. "I am far from ascribing all these Alterations to Paper money," he admitted, "but can you seriously think we shou'd have grown faster if we had none at all?"[170]

The question of paper money's production thus existed symbiotically with its function. The acquisition and privatization of Native lands necessary for their commodification and coining in turn collapsed the distinction between real and personal property, and laid the groundwork for an economy based on credit creation and agricultural modes of production. But just as land mortgages required Indigenous dispossession and stimulated colonial expansion, so too, as the next chapter details, would slave mortgages stimulate slavery's expansion. Mortgages of property in expropriated lands and enslaved human beings facilitated the circulation and growth of commodities and credit that were central to colonial territorial and economic expansion. Colonists worked Native lands and enslaved laborers both physically and financially, increasing colonial productivity and profits, and propelling the development of the early American economy within Britain's capitalist empire.[171]

5

Money and Blood

South Carolina in the 1730s was a con man's paradise. In February or March of 1730, "a Stranger" arrived in Charles Town masquerading as a Scottish baronet and promising to "do wonderful Things" for the colony. "He began his Game by issuing out Promisory Notes," reported the *Pennsylvania Gazette* later that year, "and by his punctual Payment of them in Gold or Silver upon Sight, in a little Time they acquir'd a Credit and Currency equal with Money." Then he opened "a Loan-Office of his own, sign'd great Quantities of his Notes, and emitted them upon Loan at 10 per Cent. Interest; the Borrowers mortgaging their Estates to him for Security." Once the colony "fill'd with his Notes," he used "as many as he pleased himself" to purchase gold, silver, and produce, with which he "bought several large Plantations, and built a Stone House" for a "Treasury." After several months, "having drawn Bills of Exchange to a considerable Sum" and sold them for cash, he returned to Britain. Nothing seemed amiss until three weeks later, when his bills began to come back protested. His promissory notes "immediately lost all their Credit, and sunk in the Hands of the Possessors, being now worth no more than Waste-Paper." Some angry customers broke into his treasury but found nothing "but some empty Boxes, old Iron, and other Rubbish." If there was any consolation "for the Loss of our Money," the *Gazette* teased, it was "that no Man can laugh at his Neighbour; or rather, that every Man may laugh at all his Neighbours."[1]

The financial games did not end there. In the winter of 1735, the colonial assembly learned that the treasurer had secretly reissued nearly £33,000 in paper money instead of burning it as the law required.[2] Later that year the colony discovered counterfeit bills of credit.[3] And over the next two years, a wave of forgeries of bills of exchange, warrants for payment, promissory notes, receipts, and mortgages prompted the assembly to enforce, in 1737, a British statute making forging any debt instrument a felony offense punishable by death.[4] The preponderance of cons and counterfeits suited a blood-drenched economic system based on stolen lives and stolen labor. Twenty-five slave ships had entered Charles Town the previous year alone, each carrying hundreds of African captives who, after enduring the trauma of sale, would be forced to work in rice fields producing the British Empire's most valuable commodity after sugar.[5] If physical violence fueled the plantation machine, financial fraud greased its wheels.

The two dovetailed in the slave mortgage market. As in the other paper money colonies, the South Carolina currency comprised a hodgepodge of official and informal monies, not all of them circulating, from bills of credit, to shop notes, to book credit, to interest-bearing debts. Unlike in the other colonies, the bulk of the liquid wealth came into existence by way of private mortgages of property in human beings. The slave mortgage market had emerged in the late seventeenth century and quickly became Carolina colonists' primary method of raising cash and credit. It laid the groundwork for the rice boom and expansion of slavery in the 1720s and fueled the overproduction of rice and feverish accumulation of property in people in the 1730s. And it made private lenders—many of them also speculators in enslaved lives—the primary issuers of currency. In South Carolina, the commodification of people and the dematerialization of money were two sides of the same coin.

What set the colony apart was not just the scale of its commodity production, or the gross commodification of its enslaved workers, or the innovative task system that rice cultivation entailed, but the way in which its capitalist class mobilized bondspeople simultaneously as laborers and as collateral so that "their workforce doubled as a means of securing credit."[6] The paradoxical approach created, to borrow historian Calvin Schermerhorn's definition of capitalism in the early American republic, "a highly structured system characterized by debt obligations, which were durable, mobile, and ultimately transferable, the basis of paper money."[7] This description bears comparison with colonial South Carolina, where currency and credit secured by property in people were the key to developing Lowcountry plantations, and where merchant capitalists' speculative investments in the slave market created the business for Charles Town's shopkeepers, tavernkeepers, doctors, and lawyers.[8]

Since the slave mortgage market formed the foundation of plantation enterprise and the slave trade, any effort to constrain private lending, rice cultivation, or human trafficking met with opposition from various overlapping interest groups. In the 1730s, competing programs of capitalist development pitted the planters who controlled the assembly against the wealthy merchant-planters and Charles Town slave traders who dominated local capital and credit markets. Fearful of Black rebelliousness and monopoly power alike, the assembly sought to restrain slavery-based commodity production. To that end, it taxed slave imports and reserved townships and money for "poor Protestants"—European refugees and yeomen farmers who would form a white buffer on the southern frontier.[9] More threateningly, the assembly passed an act for a public loan office that would issue paper money to smallholders against land mortgages. The merchant-capitalists challenged these policies not just because the policies threatened their profits from rice cultivation and slave sales, but because they struck at the power that derived from their monopoly on making money.

Mortgaging People

South Carolina pioneered the custom of mortgaging human beings and laid the foundation for its codification. European settlers had been offering property in enslaved Africans as collateral for credit since at least 1698, when the assembly passed an act to prevent colonists from taking out multiple mortgages on "Lands, Negroes and Chattels" by requiring all sales and mortgages of enslaved persons to be "recorded in the secretary's office in Charles-Town."[10] In contrast to Barbados and Virginia, where enslaved people were deemed real property for some purposes, a South Carolina act of 1690 defining bondspeople as real property was disallowed by the Crown, rendering the Carolina enslaved as chattel property in most cases. Though whether an enslaved person was defined as real or chattel property made no difference to their legal status, the early alienability of property in enslaved Carolinians and the registration system established by the 1698 act facilitated the practice of mortgaging people and encouraged the creation of a capital market that carried cash and credit from Charles Town to the Lowcountry.[11] Chattel slavery, itself premised on the appropriation of Native homelands, was thus rationalized by a registration system that mirrored the recording of land titles discussed in the previous chapter. And just as title recording replaced Indigenous ways of relating to the land with a legal structure based on colonial private property, so the recording of slave mortgages turned racialized subjects into objects, numerically abstracted into currency and credit.[12]

For a decade or so after the 1698 act, a portion of the enslaved people offered as collateral for a mortgage were usually transferred from the borrower to the lender, presumably because the real interest rate exceeded the legal interest ceiling during the first half-century of the colony's development.[13] The mortgages recorded in the secretary's office chronicle the conduct of enslaver-borrowers like the widow Ann Crosby, who in the spring of 1704 "did Deliver to Mr. John Haile . . . possession of ye. negroe woman named

Nann," one of three people Crosby used as collateral for a £140 loan from Haile. The other two, a boy and a girl, remained with the widow. Perhaps Nann had arrived in the colony on the same ship as the children; perhaps she was even their mother. When and if Crosby reclaimed Nann and whether she still held the two children in bondage at the time is unknown.[14]

Transfers like this one became less common in the 1720s and 1730s, as the mortgage market grew in size and sophistication and the real interest rate fell, when usually the only thing handed over was the written instrument itself. By then, enslaved people were the dominant form of collateral. Nevertheless, as the historian Bonnie Martin illustrates, the slave mortgage system was both an engine of economic growth and a tool that increased the likelihood of family separation. A mortgage itself could cause a separation if only some members of an enslaved family used as collateral were transferred to a lender, while mortgaged men, women, and children who remained in the borrower's possession were liable to seizure and sale in case of default.[15]

If the practice of mortgaging people was prevalent in early America, spreading to Virginia and French Louisiana by the early eighteenth century, the extent to which the English colonies accepted enslaved people as collateral for public loans is murkier. The first two colonial loan offices, established in Barbados and South Carolina in 1706 and 1712, respectively, were short-lived, and the latter left few records. Still, it is clear that both promised to accept property in lands and human beings alike as collateral for mortgages. In June 1706, the Barbados assembly, considering "the great Want of Money in the Island" caused by Queen Anne's Proclamation of 1704, passed an act for issuing £65,000 in bills of "Paper Credit" and empowered the provincial treasurer to "lend them to the Planters, on Security of Land and Negroes."[16] The "Paper Act" designated the treasurer as the manager of the loan office and charged him with signing and sealing the bills and lending them to borrowers at 8 percent interest for one year (renewable for up to five) against property at four times the value of the loan. The bills were legal tender for debts, including old debts contracted in sterling, and anyone who refused to accept them in payments forfeited their due.[17]

Passed by a single vote, the Paper Act divided the great planter class and provoked the ire of the London merchants trading to Barbados—members of the powerful sugar lobby—who convinced the Crown to repeal it.[18] They argued that the act would raise the price of imported provisions, driving up the price of local produce and the cost of living, and reducing sugar output. The merchants were especially alarmed that the loan office accepted property in enslaved people as collateral, since people were "the only Reall Estate some persons have, [and] are subject to so many contingencys as render them a very slender security, and not fit to be forced upon any man."[19] Landownership for sugar cultivation was concentrated at the top of the social hierarchy, so borrowers with "only" property in people to mortgage were likely among the two-thirds of European settlers with no reputation or prospects. The merchants stopped short of explaining either that the colony's growing enslaved population depended on continual imports of African captives, or that enslavers worked their laborers to death faster than they could reproduce.

After hearing the London merchants' complaints, the Board of Trade took petitions and testimony from the Royal African Company and other interested groups. In late 1706 the board recommended the royal veto, registering its first formal response to colonial paper money. The board primarily took issue not with the types of security the loan office accepted but with the currency's legal tender. Although the legal tender provision carried no force outside the colony, English creditors stood to lose if they had agents on the island with power of attorney to settle their accounts. In such cases, debts originally payable in England could be legally discharged in bills of credit at face value. Then as later, the board was inclined to protect English debts from the depreciation of local currencies.[20]

Evidently undeterred by the Crown's disallowance of the Paper Act, South Carolina, where many struggling Barbadians ultimately resettled, moved to create a public loan office. In 1712, the assembly passed the "Bank Act" to "give a farther encouragement to trade and commerce."[21] The act provided for the emission of £52,000 in paper bills of credit and established a loan office that would lend £32,000 of the bills at 12.5 percent interest for twelve years against property in land or enslaved people at twice the loan's value.[22] Maryland later followed suit. In 1733 the province on the Chesapeake Bay issued £20,000 in paper bills to "be lent on Real or personall Security" at 4 percent interest for fifteen years.[23] In 1747, the year before the loan matured, the assembly passed an act permitting the commissioners of the "Paper Currency Office" to sue for the recovery of money lent to colonists and denying the borrowers the protection of any statute of limitations. Eight years later, the assembly directed commissioners to call in the interest and principal due on bonds.[24] But if colonists defaulted on their loans or failed to pay interest on them, the commissioners put the borrowers' bonds in suit; seized their property in land, houses, and enslaved people; and advertised the assets for sale in the *Maryland Gazette*.[25] Like the private mortgage system, the loan office increased the risk of enslaved families being separated, with traumatic consequences for the enslaved.

While there are scant firsthand sources documenting how South Carolina administered the Bank Act, it left at least one contemporary with an unfavorable impression. After learning of the act's passage, Anglican missionary Francis Le Jau worried that the loan office would accelerate inflation and reduce his fixed income's purchasing power. "They are making Countrey Bills for 50000 £," he wrote to the secretary of the Society for the Propagation of the Gospel in London on August 30, 1712, "which raise the price of every thing we want, and reduce our Salaries to a Small matter." Le Jau, who lamented Carolina enslavers' sadistic punishment practices but ultimately condoned slavery, was barely scraping by as it was.[26] But other colonists praised the loan office, arguing that it gave a boost to the economy in the years leading up to the Yamasee War (1715-17). Writing in 1732, the anonymous author of *An Essay on Currency* recalled that the Bank Act had been "of vast Advantage to many Men, and of great Use to the Country."[27]

The assembly later reported to the British government that the loan office had been responsible for raising prices only insofar as it stimulated local trade and increased the demand for enslaved laborers, which the Charles Town merchants who would later oppose such lending schemes expeditiously met. Arrivals of African captives quintupled between 1712 and 1714, to which the assembly attributed the concurrent rise in exchange and produce, "and not to the making Paper-Money." It went on to note that the loan office had been properly managed, and attested that "it was never objected that the Bank-Bills were not duly sunk by the Commissioners for the first 3 or 4 Years at least," or until the outbreak of war with the Yamasee sent the colonial economy into a tailspin.[28]

Mid-twentieth-century historians, preoccupied with questions of money and inflation, debated whether the Bank Act was to blame for the rise in prices during the eighteenth century's tumultuous second decade. On the one hand, the historian Richard Jellison maintained that "the large increase in the money which resulted from the Bank Act brought about serious depreciation," but disputed that either the expansion or the depreciation was harmful to trade. Rather, "the Indian War seriously interfered with and was chiefly responsible for the decrease in trade."[29] Historian Maurice Crouse, pointing out that most of the loans were promptly repaid, suggested instead that the "Bank Bills" depreciated because subsequent emissions of bills of credit during the Yamasee War, their redemptions postponed or canceled, caused all outstanding bills to depreciate.[30] The expansion of trade in the three years before the war broke out had certainly placed the sterling exchange rate on an upward trajectory, as local merchants competed for a dwindling supply of silver and bills of exchange to send to Britain. But the values of the outstanding bills plummeted during, not before, the war. Clearly, the currency depreciated not just because the assembly postponed and canceled the emissions' redemptions, but because the Yamasee Confederacy almost overpowered the colony. Near defeat rendered the bills nearly worthless.

The overthrow of the proprietary government in 1719 and political strife between the assembly and the governor's council in the second half of the 1720s pushed paper money politics into the public sphere of print and protest. In 1723, when most of the outstanding loan money had been redeemed, Governor Francis Nicholson approved an act for emitting £120,000 in bills of credit redeemable in payment of taxes. Twenty-eight irate Charles Town merchants responded with a petition claiming that the act was fraudulent and demanding its repeal, which the assembly countered by having the petitioners arrested, fined, and forced into public apology. The royal government disallowed the act after several British merchants trading to the colony complained about it, but by then the bills were already in circulation. Nicholson's acquiescence to the representatives aggravated the merchants who dominated the council so much that he was forced to return home to defend his actions, leaving the president of the council, Arthur Middleton, in charge.[31]

Civil disorder broke out soon thereafter. Following the 1723 emission, the assembly made numerous attempts to revive the loan office. Then in early 1725, a year after the Bank Act had expired and just before Nicholson departed for London, complaints about money scarcity spread. In December 1726 the representatives passed a bill for issuing £86,100 "to the Inhabitants of this Province on good security," but the council unanimously rejected it.[32] The following spring, some representatives and their allies held several meetings in the countryside to protest the council's action and oppose a new tax, proclaiming "that it is very difficult for them to pay the tax" with no money.[33] That May 250 armed men rode to Charles Town with a petition for Middleton "containing insolent invectives against the government, accompanied with threats, unless relieved."[34] Middleton proclaimed the assembly unlawful, interceded with the protesters, and persuaded them to return home, but subsequently ordered the arrest of one of the group's leaders, Landgrave Thomas Smith. Officials violently removed Smith from his home and held him without habeas corpus, further emboldening the protestors and inspiring a company of militia to join the growing tax rebellion.[35]

Tempers were just starting to cool when in August 1727 news arrived that violence had broken out near the southern border between Europeans and Creeks (Muscogees) and Yamasees. Knowing a political opportunity when it saw one, the assembly offered to divert bills of credit from the 1723 emission to the defense of the province. The council was forced to comply. The assembly reissued £55,000 toward "defraying the Charges" of two expeditions, one "clearing our Coast from the Pirates" and the other "scouring the Southern

Frontiers, and beating the Enemy to the very Gates of St. *Augustine*."³⁶ From late 1727 to early 1729, however, the representatives refused to grant supplies unless permitted to reissue more bills marked for redemption. Middleton declined to endorse any supply act that lacked a suspending clause, maintaining that "those Bills doe greatly affect Trade, and the Property of his Majestyes Subjects, both in Great Britain and here."³⁷ By the end of 1728, the assembly had received numerous petitions praying "that the uncertain state of the present currency may be regulated," including one signed by eighty-seven residents of St. Paul and St. Bartholomew parishes, and reports were circulating of "desertion of the garrisons through want of pay."³⁸

The impasse finally ended when several prominent Charles Town merchants, tired of Middleton's intransigence, conceded the necessity of a local medium for trade and the defense of the province. They threw their support behind Nicholson in London and helped persuade the Board of Trade to back a properly regulated currency.³⁹ They meant bills of credit redeemable by taxes, *not* another emission on loan. For indeed, the Bank Act had already laid the groundwork for the local lending market, which the economic historians Russel Menard and David Hancock have studied.⁴⁰ As colonists settled their accounts with the loan office, Charles Town merchants cornered the mortgage market, extending credit to planters who gave enslaved people as collateral and using their political clout to prevent a revival of the loan office. In the mid-1730s, the chaos of commodity production, growing social distance among the colony's free white minority, and the simmering threat of collaboration between Africans and Spaniards would renew popular demand for an emission of paper money on loan. But by then, the brisk mortgage market would have matured, as it happened, controlled by a handful of wealthy colonists with influence in Britain. The merchant capitalists spun a web of private credit, anchored by slave mortgages and paper money, that greased the plantation machine.

Paper Money and the Slave Duty

In the mid-1730s, the Charles Town merchants lent their support to another cause: the repeal of the slave duty. In early 1734, a group of self-declared "Merchants of London & Bristol, who Trade to South Carolina," petitioned the Board of Trade complaining of the colony's 1731 act for issuing £104,725 in interest-bearing "public orders" that circulated as money. Governor Robert Johnson had apparently promised the same merchants that no more than £100,000 in new currency would be issued under his command, an amount that all parties had agreed "was sufficient to carry on the Trade of that

Province." Contrary to Johnson's "own proposal" and his royal instructions, however, he had consented to not one but two currency emissions totaling £211,275—more than double the approved amount—and he had been neither "passive or permissive," but "instrumental [in] promoting" them.[41]

Thomas Pelham-Holles, the Duke of Newcastle, sided with the petitioners. The same year as the public orders act, Governor Johnson had approved the re-emission of £106,500 in old bills of credit "with a Design," Newcastle alleged, "to encrease the Quantity of Paper Credit." Recalling the inflation of the Yamasee War years, Newcastle feared that the unauthorized increase would depreciate the currency and raise the sterling exchange rate, rendering British property and profits "precarious, and uncertain" and threatening the livelihoods of "many honest and industrious Trading Familys, as well in this Kingdom, as in the said Province."[42] For their part, the petitioners were less concerned about inflation than about the tax earmarked for redeeming the public orders: a ten-pound duty on African captives, first enacted in 1723 and renewed by the 1731 act. They charged that the revenues arising from the duty would be insufficient to redeem all the orders before 1741, three years after the duty was scheduled to expire, and feared that the deficiency would be supplied by continuing the hated tax, to the detriment of British trade and manufactures.[43]

As for Newcastle's prediction that increasing the currency would endanger British investments in the colony, recent history showed otherwise. While some merchants had incurred losses during the Yamasee War, the exchange rate between South Carolina and Britain had stabilized at £700 currency for £100 sterling by the early 1720s—despite the emission of £120,000 in new bills of credit in 1723—and remained unaffected by the 1731 additions. The assembly later pointed out that despite the colony's failing to properly redeem the 1723 bills, no "Evil or mischievous Consequence, either to the Trade or Interest of the Community in general, or to any private Person concerned therein in particular, hath from thence arisen . . . notwithstanding all the insinuations to the contrary."[44]

The period saw extraordinary growth, in fact. Over the previous decade and a half, London's Carolina lobby had worked hard to ensure the free movement of commodities and captives across the Atlantic, getting rice removed from the list of "enumerated goods" and campaigning against a monopoly of the British slave trade. In 1730 Parliament passed the Rice Act allowing rice to be shipped from South Carolina directly to southern European ports, provided it was transported in British ships, though Charles Town merchants continued to circumvent British trade regulations by sales to the Caribbean and other parts.[45] Continuing the "free" trade in enslaved Africans was especially important to the Carolina lobby. Before 1696, the Royal African

Company had enjoyed a monopoly on the African trade. But as soon as the trade was deregulated, "independent traders" in port cities throughout the English Atlantic world began sending ships to the African coast. In a 1729 essay, the British mercantilist theorist Joshua Gee described the "Trade with *Africa*" as "very profitable to the Nation in general," but warned that "if this Trade should fall into the Hands of the Company ... our Improvements in the Plantations, which is carried on by the Labour of Negroes, would soon decline." Turning to the rice question, Gee estimated that South Carolina merchants would save "at least 50 per Cent" on freight and other charges if they shipped their produce directly to Portugal instead of through Britain, savings that could be applied to the purchase of British goods.[46]

Yet how the colony's paper money economy fit into the Carolina lobby's vision remained to be seen. Thanks to Francis Nicholson's and Robert Johnson's efforts, most London merchants had come to appreciate that a local currency was necessary for colonial trade and defense. As the British writer Fayr Hall argued in a 1731 essay, a circulating medium would ensure that whatever specie and bills of exchange Charles Town merchants received through the Atlantic trade would be remitted to Britain.[47] The merchants' cause was bolstered by Samuel Wragg, London's leading exporter of goods and trafficker of Africans to South Carolina, who obtained signatures from twenty-one others requesting that "a paper Currency might be continued there under proper Limitations."[48] When in the spring of 1730 news reached the colony that Governor Johnson had struck a deal with the merchants and Board of Trade for a re-emission of old bills of credit, the assembly addressed the king, acknowledging his "Royal bounty, and goodness ... for that unspeakable benefit and liberty of enlargeing our Currency in proportion to our Trade."[49] The following year Johnson reported to Newcastle that the passage of the reprinting act had given "great Satisfaction to the People in General, the want of Currency being very great in this Province."[50]

Which was why, a few years later, the assembly was "surprized to hear" of a petition from a handful of British merchants containing "very unfairly stated" allegations against them. Posing as the defenders of poor Protestants arriving in South Carolina from Europe, the petitioners were accusing the assembly of misusing public funds. They argued that the revenues arising from the duty on bondspeople were for helping European refugees, not for supporting an unauthorized expansion of the currency. In an address to the king, the assembly responded to the allegations insisting that the duty was being put to good use, with a substantial portion reserved for settling "poor Protestant families" in new townships and the remainder earmarked for paying the public debts—many of which, it reminded His Majesty, had been incurred in defending the province against French and Spanish rivals and Native resisters. Far from threatening slave traders' profits, the duty was a means of building, settling, and protecting their fastest growing market. And while the duty was payable in public orders, the orders were not legal tender for debts, so they were not money per se. Nevertheless, if the petitioners got their way and the duty was repealed, the orders would be destroyed, which "wou'd at this time prove an irreparable loss to many British merchants trading to this Province," since their Carolina factors held most of the orders then circulating. The assembly suspected that the petitioners were being directed by a few Charles Town slave dealers "who have several debts of that paper credit, now outstanding, upon mortgages, judgments, and other good securitys." Destroy the currency, and the lenders would soon possess "the greatest part of the estates real and personal in this Province."[51]

The assembly's suspicions were not far-fetched. Many small and middling rural planters and some artisans had received credit from the local lending market, borrowing from Charles Town merchants on mortgages of land and enslaved people, and repaying the loans in rice or paper money. By the 1730s there were ten times the number of mortgages written as in the 1710s. At the peak in the mid-1730s, local lenders advanced some £140,000 annually. But if planters had debts too large to be cleared by the next crop and the currency was suddenly recalled, they would be left without a medium to settle their accounts and their mortgaged property would be liable to seizure by creditors.[52]

The 1734 petition appeared to the assembly to come out of nowhere because most of the petitioners, including all the Bristol merchants, were newcomers to Britain's trade with the colony. They had not, it turned out, been part of the agreement with Governor Johnson, as the merchants' agent William Wood, a British merchant and lobbyist, explained in a July 4, 1735, letter to William Popple of the Board of Trade, "tho' ten times more interested in trade every year to Carolina, in negroes, than those which [were]."[53] By 1730 Bristol overtook London as Britain's leading slaving port, but its ascendancy was short-lived, partly because it struggled to compete with Liverpool in expanding markets like South Carolina, where demand for African captives skyrocketed in the mid-1730s. Transporting the captives to North America was expensive, unpredictable, and dangerous, and the annual rate of return on investments was small—about 10 percent on average for the more successful Liverpool slave traders. Profits accruing to Bristol merchants were irregular, with slaving voyages routinely producing financial losses on initial outlays. Such voyages required heavy expenditure not only on provisions and special equipment for supporting large crews and enslaved cargoes, but also on growing quantities of consumer goods for sale in West Africa. Many vessels left the trade after only one or two ventures. Less than a quarter of those involved accounted for nearly half of Bristol's total slaving voyages, and vessels that sailed regularly were supported by a core group of large investors. In addition to the financial risk, rebellion at sea was an ever-present danger.[54]

By the late 1720s, Bristol's principal slave traders were agitating for the disallowance of any colonial act that imposed duties on enslaved lives. They hired Wood to argue that the South Carolina duty discouraged not just the slave trade but colonial settlement as well, defeating its supposed purpose of helping poor Protestants.[55] In September 1734, Wood suggested to Popple that if the assembly truly wished "to settle the province and increase its trade, the most effectual means will be, not to impose additional duties on negroes ... or create new paper currency, but to make provision for discharging all the old paper currency."[56] The following July he reiterated that all slave duties, "whether paid by the importer or purchaser, are very great discouragements to the better settling of the Province, as well as to the trade of this Kingdom."[57] Unlike Virginia's duty, enacted several years earlier to discourage slave importation and limit tobacco production, the South Carolina duty was designed to raise revenue from the growing trade in captives. That the former was repealed and the latter allowed reflected contrasting structural conditions in the tobacco and rice industries in the second quarter of the eighteenth century.[58]

The Board of Trade upheld the 1731 public orders act in July 1735. The board agreed with the assembly that repealing the slave duty would cause inconvenience "both to the merchant and the planter," but warned that the act would be disallowed if the assembly failed to apply the revenues to assisting the elusive poor Protestants.[59] By the time news of the decision arrived in the colony that fall, the assembly had already passed an act for appropriating all future revenues arising from the duty to "the use of purchasing tools, provisions and other necessarys for poor Protestants lately arrived in this Province." The duty would still be payable in public orders, but since it would be insufficient to redeem all the orders before it expired in 1738, the act provided for an additional annual tax on property holders for redeeming the balance.[60] By earmarking the duty for European settlement and levying a new tax for redeeming the remaining orders, the assembly preserved the duty for another three years and saved the orders from destruction.

But the Bristol merchants were incensed, having hoped for an outright repeal of the slave duty. Wood warned Popple that its continuation would be "so great a discouragement to the trade of this kingdom, and the better settlement of the Province itself," and urged the Board of Trade to take the 1735 appropriation act "into their immediate consideration." A colonist who opposed the act predicted that it "will be so injurious to trade, and will lay the factors here under such severe difficulties."⁶¹ But the duty neither affected the insatiable demand for, nor disrupted the sale of, African captives. Fueled by the expansion of rice cultivation, slave importation into Charles Town reached record heights, averaging more than two thousand annually in the 1730s. By 1740, Africans made up 70 percent of the colonial population.⁶²

While the duty did not discourage the slave trade, it may have contributed to its consolidation. Between 1730 and 1733, nine of the forty-five slave ships that entered South Carolina came from Bristol, five from London, and eight from Boston. But from 1734 to 1738, 17 of the 106 slavers that entered the colony were registered in Bristol, more than the previous four years but far fewer than the 28 originating in London and less, even, than the 22 hailing from Boston.⁶³ If the duty hurt Bristol merchants' ability to compete in the slave trade, the Charles Town dealers who had supported its repeal came out on top. Among them was Joseph Wragg, who handled twenty-two of the sixty-seven enslaved cargoes advertised in the *South-Carolina Gazette* between 1733 and 1740. His brother Samuel Wragg, the London merchant who had helped convince the Board of Trade that a colonial currency was necessary, supplied most of the cargoes on ships he owned or part-owned. With the Carolina lobby controlling nearly all of Britain's rice imports from South Carolina and most of its consumer exports to the colony, the Bristol slave traders may never have stood a chance.⁶⁴ As for the poor Protestants, collecting the duty from the slave traders proved arduous, leading to "many unsuccessful calls . . . made thereupon [to] the great disappointment of such Poor Protestants."⁶⁵

Yet South Carolina had compelling reasons to restrict the slave trade. The colony's proximity to Spanish Florida—even with the 1733 establishment of Georgia—was a particular source of trepidation. In 1693, the Spanish king had offered freedom to any enslaved African who escaped from British soil, creating a steady stream of refugees heading southward to St. Augustine, whom the Spanish armed and set on their former enslavers. Several slave conspiracies nearly came to pass in South Carolina in the 1720s and 1730s, by which time Africans formed a crucial component of the Spanish militia.⁶⁶ Shortly after the merchant Thomas Amory relocated from Charles Town to Boston in late 1719, he recalled that "all the time I was there they were under Arms" in anticipation of a Spanish invasion, an Indigenous uprising, or "the Negroes Riseing wch they did just before I came from there but they suppressed."⁶⁷ On February 13, 1720, following the attempted uprising, the assembly passed an act for drafting "trusty male slaves" in case of a Spanish, French, or Native invasion. The African soldiers were to be armed "with a good lance and hatchet or gun" and paid ten pounds for every enemy combatant imprisoned or killed.⁶⁸ But the deficiencies of legislative remedies betrayed the colony's weaknesses. A 1726 act required every plantation to employ "two white men" for every twenty Black men.⁶⁹ And in 1734 the assembly passed a new patrol act requiring patrols to search enslaved people's homes for weapons or stolen goods, pursue and punish freedom seekers, and search unlicensed taverns for enslaved people suspected to be drinking alcohol.⁷⁰

Concerns about the growing African population were not limited to South Carolina. Throughout the British colonies, commentators bemoaned the employment of enslaved persons in the skilled trades, arguing that it would deprive white colonists of good jobs and discourage further European settlement.⁷¹ At the same time, advertisements in colonial newspapers touting the talents of bondspeople for sale or hire reflected rising demand for cheap skilled labor. Carolina enslavers sought cooks, seamstresses, carpenters, bricklayers, painters, butchers, and boatmen. The *South-Carolina Gazette* in its February 22, 1734, issue advertised the sales of several enslaved men, one "used to a Boat, and something experienc'd in the Butcher's trade," another "a very good Sailor, and used for 5 years to row in Boats."⁷²

But slavery "reforms" such as European settlement schemes could neither quell the lurking threat of collaboration between Africans and Spaniards nor stanch the flow of African captives to South Carolina's shores. Complaints of enslaved people being "train'd up to be handicraft tradesmen, to the great discouragement of your Majesty's white subjects," papered over the centrality of enslaved Africans in the growing world of trade and markets—not just as field hands but as cattle herders, fishermen, boatmen, carpenters, coopers, and peddlers—and, in the process, obscured a pair of inconvenient truths: Africans' labor was too valuable to restrict, and enslaved people were the linchpins of the enslavers' economy. In September 1739, the Stono Rebellion would demonstrate the inescapable fact that stronger measures, both physical and economic, would have to be devised to control the colony's most formidable—and indispensable—enemy.⁷³

The Loan Office Act of 1736

In 1730, seventeen Charles Town merchants and seven Great Planters formed a partnership and lent £50,000 in interest-bearing notes of hand to borrowers pledging sufficient security. A few years later the assembly reported that the scarcity of money at the time was such that the notes "obtained a Currency throughout the Province ... tho' not enforced by any Law."⁷⁴ On the face of each note was a "drowning Man imploring Assistance," perhaps a reference to the fact that South Carolina had not issued any new currency since 1723.⁷⁵

For the anonymous author of *An Essay on Currency*, published in Charles Town in 1734, the notes set a dangerous precedent: if the colonial assembly failed to supply a sufficient currency, then someone else would.[76] At a time of rapid commercial development, the author pointed out, money scarcity disproportionately burdened farmers and laborers. It created openings for greedy merchants to extend credit at high interest rates while hoarding bills of credit and public orders, "any one or two of whom can put that sum into their Chest whenever they please."[77] Meanwhile, country storekeepers underpaid planters for their crop and forced the wage worker who received store credit instead of cash to "take perhaps what he doth not want." The stores ruined "many families" by seizing their enslaved laborers in payment of debts, reducing the families' output and income, and discounted the white laborer's earnings "as will almost starve him."[78] Two decades earlier, Francis Le Jau had likewise lamented "our Shopkeepers having contrived to make certain Tickets pass for current Coyn ... so that 100 £ of those tickets is hardly equal to 20 £ Sterling."[79] Such apprehensions focused not on the swelling ranks and increasing poverty of the enslaved majority, but on growing social distance among the free minority.

The expansion of the rice industry was soon creating new problems. By the mid-1730s, colonial production had surpassed European demand. Population growth, transportation improvements, and technical advancements all contributed to the supply shift. Encouraged by rising demand and the liberalization of Atlantic trade, explains one historian, the colony's commitment to monocrop agriculture "created overproduction and cyclical swings in the economy."[80] After trending slightly upward for most of the 1720s, the price of rice dipped in 1729 and continued to decline through the 1730s and into the 1740s. Within the same period, however, year-to-year price fluctuations were common. Rice plummeted to thirty shillings per hundredweight (cwt., or 112 pounds) in 1719 during a currency contraction, to which the assembly responded by accepting it in payment of taxes for several years at market prices. It peaked at four pounds cwt. in 1738 before collapsing to forty shillings in 1739 after output doubled from about 16 million pounds in 1738 to more than 32 million pounds in 1739. It fell further to thirty-five shillings cwt. in early 1740 when the outbreak of the War of Jenkins' Ear interrupted trade between South Carolina and the Spanish colonies.[81]

Roused into action by the unruly expansion of rice cultivation, the progressive redemption of the public orders, and the imminent expiration of the slave duty, South Carolina colonists batted around proposals for a new medium of exchange. From 1733 to 1736 they debated the merits of paper versus silver, public versus private, and spending versus lending. Most commentators agreed that the £106,500 in bills of credit that would remain in circulation after all the orders were redeemed was inadequate. Many supported the establishment of a loan office that would lend bills to individuals at interest against land mortgages. They argued that a loan office would reestablish the currency on a more secure foundation and create a permanent stream of government revenue, generated through local economic activity rather than dependent on the slave trade. The author of *An Essay on Currency* suggested that a loan office would allay the ill consequences of rapid economic growth on the colonial economy. In addition to serving as a source of credit for planters, by establishing a new stream of revenue, it would decrease the assembly's need to levy direct taxes. A loan office that issued £300,000 at 10 percent interest would draw an annual revenue of £30,000—"enough sufficiently to defray the ordinary Charges of the Government . . . without taxing the People."[82]

The money question reemerged in the mid-1730s as a source of friction between merchant-creditors who wanted to return to specie payments and planter-debtors who favored a more flexible currency. In the spring of 1733, the *South-Carolina Gazette* printed a series of articles proposing a bank that would lend £50,000 in "proclamation bills" at 10 percent interest at an exchange rate of £133 currency for £100 sterling. The interest would be payable in silver and gold, a provision the authors argued would attract coins to the colony and pave the way to resume payments in specie.[83] Critics panned the proposal as totally unrealistic. Philadelphia printer Benjamin Franklin rebutted it in his *Pennsylvania Gazette*, pointing out that making the interest payable in silver and gold would force planters to compete with merchants for a limited supply of specie, driving up the cost, and would that "not lessen the Value of their Bills, compar'd with Silver and Gold?" he asked. Franklin envisioned an inflationary spiral: merchants would increase their prices to procure specie to send to Britain, "and the Planter being still oblig'd to have it" to pay interest to the bank, "will not he be still forced to give more Paper for it," further raising the sterling exchange rate and, in turn, depreciating the currency?[84] The author of *An Essay on Currency* concurred, reflecting that whatever silver and gold came into the colony was typically sent immediately to Britain to answer "the Ballance of our Trade." Attempting to retain coins would never work because "the Trader will always carry away our Money . . . and leave our Produce to perish on our Hands, to the great Detriment both of *England* and this *Province*."[85]

Proponents of a loan office envisioned paper money as a tool for tempering the economic chaos the rice boom and the expansion of slavery had brought about. In two decades, the province had transformed from a colonial outpost centered on the Indigenous deerskin trade and cultivation of provisions for the Caribbean into a slave society based on commodity production. Paired with rapid economic growth, money scarcity stirred fears of monopoly power and the concentration of wealth. The author of *An Essay on Currency* cautioned that money scarcity "doth tend to lodge the greatest part of the Riches of a Province in a few Hands." Monopoly control of land and labor proscribed access to the means of production, making the rich richer and the poor poorer, so that "one fiftieth Man of them, will not be fit for a Helmet... And I think it much concerns the Interest of this Province, to keep up the Spirits of the lowe sort of People, for we have much reason to expect great Use of them e're long."[86] It was not the prospect of a Bacon's Rebellion–style revolt that worried him, but that of a war with the French or Spanish or an uprising of the enslaved majority. A loan office would not only draw sufficient income to repair the colony's fortifications, cannons, and firearms in the event of a foreign invasion. It would also stimulate the kind of generalized prosperity—driven by the democratization of money and slaveholding—needed to sustain a robust tax base in case of unforeseen public expenses and to unite colonists against external and internal enemies.

By the time the assembly turned to the money question in early 1736, fluctuations in rice prices due to overproduction had become a major area of concern. The colony had passed no laws limiting commodity production, as Virginia and Maryland had. And besides a 1733 article in the *South-Carolina Gazette* remarking that lessening "the Quantity of *Rice*" would "of course make that Commodity more valuable," commentators did not seriously consider restricting cultivation to raise prices before 1739.[87] Nor was there any sustained interest in shifting the burden of the slave duty from importers to purchasers to discourage planters from expanding production. Instead, commentators promoted policies that would stabilize the price of rice through stimulating demand.

On March 26, 1736, the *Gazette* printed a proposal for a loan office that would help prevent uncertainties in rice sales that could create supply gluts, and in turn maintain rice and currency values. The loan office would issue £200,000 in bills of credit at 8 percent interest, payable in the bills. The assembly would appropriate half the interest money for purchasing rice from planters, effectively turning itself into the buyer of last resort. Then commissioners would sell the rice in Britain and use the proceeds to establish "a Capital Fund there" for redeeming the bills for sterling after twenty-five years. In doing so, the loan office would raise the price of rice while creating an escape valve for the commodity in case of slow markets at home or abroad. It ultimately would give colonists more control over their economic futures. "This Method of sending home Commodities to raise a Capital Fund in *England* for our Paper Credit," maintained the proposal's author, "will put it in our Power, to take so much of our own Commodities off our own hands, and must raise consequently the Value of the Residue."[88]

The *Gazette* published a harsh rejoinder the following week from one "PAYWELL," who sarcastically praised the plan. Likening it to "the Philosopher's Stone," he lauded it as "A most excellent Project to ballance Accounts with *England!*"[89] Paywell surmised that the provision for making the colonial government the buyer of last resort was less about mitigating variabilities in international demand than about enabling planters to produce without regard to the limits of the market by artificially raising prices, or by creating fictitious demand. Planters would know that "if ever their produce were of dull Sale, or likely to fall in price, it's only employing the Commissioners to buy, and in case they should be out of Cash, there's no difficulty to have more, so long as a rowling or printing Press is to be had."[90] As Karl Marx put it more than a century later, creating "*demand for payment*" out of thin air may well transform "commodities into money." But without pegging demand to new production, printing money can fuel inflation and reduce real incomes.[91]

The public debate paved the way for the loan office act of 1736. That May, following six months of deliberation, the assembly passed an act for issuing £210,000 in bills of credit and establishing a loan office to lend the bills to individuals on mortgages of land. Lieutenant Governor William Bull sent the act to Britain with a thirty-six-page report justifying it and awaited Crown approval. A compromise between merchants' demands to resume specie payments and planters' preference for a more flexible currency, the act would establish a loan office modeled on that of Pennsylvania, complete with trustees for registering mortgages out of a Charles Town storefront. The loan office would issue bills at the current exchange rate of £700 currency for £100 sterling, £110,000 for lending at 8 percent interest against lands at double the value of the loan and £100,000 for exchanging all old bills. The interest would be payable in "Spanish or English silver coin" at one pound seventeen shillings sixpence per ounce or in gold at twenty-seven pounds per ounce. To attract and retain specie, the treasurer would accept silver and gold in payment of duties at a 10 percent discount. Five-eighths of the interest money would be reissued until the loan office drew sufficient income to exchange the old bills. Then the entire currency would be "on one and the same foundation of a public loan ... and the interest constantly paid, in silver and gold ... by means whereof the mutation or depreciating in value of the bills of credit to be issued ... will be effectually prevented, and the evil heretofore complained of, happily remedied." The remaining three-eighths of the interest would be appropriated "for the further subsisting poor Protestants who shall arrive in this Province and settle in the new townships." Depending on the availability of specie, the bills would be redeemable for gold and silver at the treasury.[92]

The same day, the assembly passed acts for regulating the markets in Charles Town to prevent the forestalling and engrossing of goods; relieving and employing the town's poor; building roads and churches and repairing old fortifications; providing subsidies out of the treasury for colonists who produced hemp, flax, and silk; and encouraging trade with Native peoples.[93] Together with the loan office act, these measures reflected a shift in the assembly's priorities away from slavery-based commodity production and toward a more risk-averse approach to economic development.

The Private Mortgage Market

Joseph Wragg, the colony's leading importer of African captives, spearheaded the effort to repeal the loan office act. In a June 1736 letter to Isaac Hobhouse, Bristol's foremost slave trader, he conveyed the hope that every British merchant with debts in the colony would join with "the trading interest here . . . to oppose the confirmation of this pernicious act." Invoking the colony's previous experience of inflation, Wragg warned of the "pernicious effects of this act (if confirm'd) . . . as has been sufficiently experienced in this province on former emissions of much smaller sums." He noted that the sterling exchange rate was rising for the first time in two decades, so that "if this act, takes effect, no man can be sure of fifteen shillings in the pound, if he lyes twelve months, out of his money."[94] Casting inflation as a monetary phenomenon, he buried the real roots of the rising exchange rate: the chaotic accumulation and sale of captives, from which he made his living.

By creating a public market in low-interest land mortgages, the loan office act promised to slow the overproduction of rice and expansion of slavery. While property in enslaved people fueled the private lending market, the loan office would issue currency on the security of "lands, houses, tenements or hereditaments," but not goods or chattels. Five years earlier, the assembly had established an independent public registry in Charles Town for recording land deeds that with the loan office would provide the basis for a market in land and land mortgages. The Quit Rent Act of 1731 required landowners to pay twenty pounds and enter "memorials" authenticating their claims to occupation and ownership or be liable for unpaid quitrents.[95] As the historian S. Max Edelson explains, the process benefited the colony insofar as it "rationalized a land system thrown into disarray" by the Tuscarora and Yamasee Wars in the 1710s and the transfer of the government from the proprietors to the Crown in the 1720s.⁹⁶ And just as land title recording in Massachusetts had replaced Indigenous land tenure with colonial private property, South Carolina's public registry obscured "turbulent land histories" and "put forth messages of occupation" that gave planters "a measure of social legitimacy."⁹⁷ Yet by threatening to displace the private mortgage market with a public market in land mortgages, the loan office and the public registry endangered the profits of Wragg and others who specialized in slave mortgages and sales.⁹⁸

The architects of the loan office act rebuffed Wragg's line of attack. In its report, the assembly maintained that "the general Increase of the Trade of the Province" over the previous two decades, not the expansion of the currency, had tilted "the Balance of Trade against us" and raised the sterling exchange rate.⁹⁹ It insisted that the only way bills of credit could depreciate relative to sterling was if "private Money-Lenders" manipulated the interest rate "by lending at lower Rates" than the loan office. But even if "a Set of Men wod actually lend out Money in this Province at 6 l. per Cent.," lower than the 8 percent rate the loan office promised to offer, "what wod be the Consequence?" Loan office customers "would borrow from those private Lenders" and use the money to "pay off the publick Principal and Interest, the Principal in the Bills and the Interest in Gold and Silver at the Rates and Prices fixed by the Act: Who then would be injured by this? Not any Body."¹⁰⁰ But private lenders' earnings depended on the brisk capital market in enslaved people and the rice monoculture that fueled it. Together, the land registry, the loan office, subsidies for hemp and flax, and aid for poor Protestants could push the local economy in new directions and diminish slave importers' profits and power.

Left unmentioned in the 1737 report was the increasing rebelliousness of the colony's enslaved workforce. Less than three months after the act's passage, South Carolina was on edge following the discovery of a conspiracy by the "entire Negro population" to attack Charles Town, seize the city's munitions, and massacre its white inhabitants.¹⁰¹ Nor did the report indicate how the evolving mortgage market was affecting enslaved communities and families. In contrast to the 1700s and 1710s, when some of the enslaved men, women, or children used as collateral for a mortgage were usually transferred from the borrower to the lender, in the 1720s and early 1730s, most mortgaged people remained in their enslavers' possession. Although enslaved people knew that any one of their friends or family members could be mortgaged at any time, they seldom knew when or who became collateral and to whom.

Beginning in the mid-1730s, however, lenders were again demanding that part of the security for redeeming mortgages be transferred to them, making the financial engine of the economy more visible and increasing the likelihood of family separation.[102] Each mortgage contains a dual narrative: a transaction between a lender and a borrower, and the implicit story, the reluctantly told counter-history, of the people who were mortgaged.[103] On August 17, 1736, Charles Hart of Berkeley County borrowed £650 from Thomas Ellery of Charles Town on a mortgage of four people, one of whom—a boy named Dick—Hart brought to Ellery as security for repayment. What the boy did in service of Ellery and whether he was accorded the same autonomy as some enslaved urban dwellers is unknown.[104] In August the following year, Hugh Tomson borrowed £140 from William Field on a mortgage of a Phillis, whom Tomson sent to Field. Perhaps Phillis left behind friends and family members, perhaps her own children.[105] And in the fall of 1737, Paul Marion of Berkley County borrowed ninety-eight pounds from Isaac Holmes on a mortgage of a woman named Lucey and a boy named Jacob, possibly Lucey's son; Marion transported only Jacob to Holmes.[106] The traumas of such forcible separations compounded the horrors of forced transatlantic dislocation. And most of those who were mortgaged in the 1730s would have experienced both.

Joseph Wragg and his business partner Richard Lambton alone held mortgages of hundreds of enslaved men, women, boys, and girls between 1735 and 1739. They sold African captives and lent money on the security of bondspeople to artisans and to planters big and small. Some of the borrowers received loans on the security of a single person. In the spring of 1738, Benjamin Pinder of Stono borrowed £141 on a mortgage of Diana, whom Pinder transferred to Wragg and Lambton.[107] In December 1739, George Coker, an Edisto Island carpenter, borrowed £140 "Lawfull Currt Money of South Carolina" on a mortgage of a woman named Venus.[108] Though most borrowers mortgaged people they already held in bondage, some used the same captives they were purchasing as collateral for loans. Just before Christmas in 1739, the carpenter Thomas Hogg borrowed £600 for three months—shorter than the typical term of six months or one year—on a mortgage of four men "sold him this Day" (presumably by Wragg), a woman named Eve, and "one girl named Dina," of whom Hogg left one of the men with the lenders.[109]

Mortgaging people was a gender-inclusive pursuit, but virtually all of the women borrowers in the second half of the 1730s whose mortgages were publicly recorded got their loans from Wragg and Lambton. In March 1735, "Spinster" Mary Stanyarne borrowed £720 12s. 3d. "Lawfull money of South Carolina" on a mortgage of five men and women, as well as all her stock of "Cattle and Hoggs" and "all other any Worldly goods," delivering one Peter to Wragg and Lambton as security for repayment.[110] On April 7, 1737, the widow Joan Upham borrowed £801 12s. 6d. on a mortgage of four men, three women, and a boy named Tony, sending the "man named Devenshire" to the lenders.[111] And in November 1739, Mary Satur of Charles Town borrowed £212 19s. from Wragg and Lambton on a mortgage of Rose.[112] Women, mostly widows, also invested in the mortgage market, lending money to neighbors and living off the interest. Profits for lenders, liquidity for enslavers, and independence for white women went together with personal insecurity for the men, women, and children who were mortgaged.[113]

By the time the Board of Trade met to consider the loan office act in the summer of 1738, dozens of Bristol, London, and Charles Town merchants had registered their disapproval. The board took testimony from a number of opponents of the act, including former council president Arthur Middleton, Scots-born merchant-planter and council member James Kinloch, and Joseph Wragg. A summary of their depositions concluded that increasing the currency would "necessarily raise" the price of bills of exchange, "or in other words diminish the value of such bills of credit to the general loss."[114] In early 1738, news reached Britain that the assembly was contemplating renewing the slave duty. In a February 7 letter, William Wood implored the board to oppose the loan office and the duty. Echoing the merchants' concerns about the rising exchange rate, he pointed out that a bill of exchange for £100 sterling had recently sold in the colony for £850 currency, giving merchants on both sides of the Atlantic pause "till they knew what they had to depend upon."[115]

But the Board of Trade again dismissed the merchants' worries, raising just two objections to the loan office act: first, the clause allowing a discount on duties paid in silver or gold at the current exchange rate, which they held contravened Queen Anne's Proclamation, and second, the lack of a provision requiring borrowers to repay any part of the principal of their loans. Otherwise, it conformed to Governor Thomas Broughton's instructions and contained "many good clauses and provisos." In June 1739 the board drew up instructions for the new governor, James Glen, in whose place Lieutenant Governor William Bull was to act until Glen arrived in the colony. The instructions reaffirmed the Carolina lobby's position that some paper money was needed for colonial trade and defense, and directed the governor to recommend to the assembly the passage of another act "for the same purpose not Lyable" to the above objections.[116] When the Bristol slave traders found out "that other reasons against the said Act were expected from them than those they had before given against paper money in general and this Act in particular," they were apparently surprised. They believed they had "shown the fatal effects which the issuing of paper bills of credit and the imposing of duties on negroes are to the trade of this kingdom."[117]

Rice Boom and Bust

The sterling exchange rate indeed rose, from 700 percent in 1735 to 750 percent in 1737. It reached 800 percent in 1740. In turn, the currency depreciated relative to sterling, accompanied by a slight overall rise in prices. The assembly maintained that neither was caused by an increase in the money stock or by its failure to secure the currency. On the contrary, "it is almost impossible that" an increase in currency "should have been the cause of" depreciation and inflation, it reported, "for none has been made among us of any Sort whatever, private or publick, since the Year 31."[118] From 1730 to 1749 the per capita money stock *declined* 40 percent, and for the five years from 1735 to 1739 the slave duty for redeeming the public orders drew £110,860.[119]

Falling colonial income due to the instability of rice prices, together with the acceleration of slave importation, had likely raised the exchange rate. The assembly blamed the slave importers.[120] Profits from human trafficking were "so very great"—an estimated £840,000 from 1734 to 1736—that dealers like Joseph Wragg could "well afford to give larger Prices for the Country Produce and higher Rates for Bills of Exchange, than any other Set of Traders whatever, and still be Gainers by their Trade." By offering higher prices for rice and bills of exchange, the importers pushed out the smaller merchants and drove up the sterling exchange rate. If they were truly concerned about the exchange rate, they would stop importing captives "for the Space of 5 or 7 Years at most, and in that Time the Balance of Trade will turn in Favour of the Province; and should the Legislature afterwards emit a Million in Paper-Money," it would not "affect the Exchange, as long as the Balance of Trade continues in Favour of the Province."[121]

Though South Carolina maintained an overall positive balance of trade and payments throughout the decade, erratic British profit margins reflect the anarchy of capitalist commodity production. In 1731, one commentator boasted that Britain made around £80,000 sterling annually by its trade with the colony, a substantial haul.[122] But for the ten years from 1733 to 1742, British merchants drew £107,379 sterling in 1733, £20,807 in 1734, £27,511 in 1735, £112,936 in 1736, £128,771 in 1737, £53,326 in 1738, £141,747 in 1739, £84,738 in 1740, £32,060 in 1741, and £27,544 in 1742.[123]

The rapid development of rice cultivation increased the demand for enslaved laborers, which the slave dealers happily met. Arrivals of African captives in South Carolina doubled in the 1730s, contributing to the growth of the enslaved population from about 20,000 in 1730 to nearly 40,000 a decade later.[124] The importation of captives peaked from 1734 to 1736, with thirty-one slave ships entering the colony in 1734 alone.[125] Demand for bondspeople was so high that when Charles Town merchant Samuel Everleigh received a slaver from Angola with 318 captives aboard in May 1735, he sold virtually all of them within two days.[126] News of arriving ships drew buyers from remote areas, many of whom trekked to Charles Town for the sole purpose of purchasing captives.[127] On June 30, 1736, Joseph Wragg reported to Isaac Hobhouse in Bristol that enslaved laborers "are much wanted, as most of our people, over plant themselves, in expectation of purchaseing slaves to assist in hoeing."[128] Then again, too many planters went into debt purchasing more captives than they could afford. "How many under the Notion of 18 Months Credit, have been tempted to buy more Negroes than they could possibly expect to pay [for] in 3 Years!" cried an anonymous writer in the March 2, 1738, issue of the *South-Carolina Gazette*.[129]

The rice bubble burst in 1739. Lured by dreams of wealth, an abundance of spurious debt instruments, and a seemingly limitless supply of enslaved laborers whose value as "real" property supported the abstract property of those instruments, small and middling planters had mortgaged their futures to compete in a race to the bottom. When the price of rice collapsed in 1739, they were unable to recoup their investments in enslaved property and service the debts they had incurred during the expansion.[130] Slave dealers competed with planters for a dwindling supply of paper money to pay the slave duty, struggled to recover planters' debts arising from purchases of bondspeople, and fought to procure gold and silver or bills of exchange to send to Britain.

Money scarcity amplified these trends, rendering small producers and wage laborers unable to access cash for purchasing necessities and paying debts, and contributing to higher interest rates on loans, a higher cost of living, and a rising sterling exchange rate. The Crown's tabling of the loan office act may have helped seal the colony's transition to large-scale monocrop agriculture and fuel the concentration of wealth in land, people, and money, as the biggest planters were the best positioned to take advantage of the crisis. While most property holders held at least a few people in bondage, slave wealth was increasingly concentrated at the top; in the decade after 1736, large planters acquired enslaved men, women, and children at a much faster rate than property holders overall. A partial tax list for St. James Parish from 1745 reveals that more than a quarter of the 2,537 bondspeople were enslaved by just three of the fifty-nine households. One of them was James Kinloch, the merchant-planter who had testified against the loan office act; another was Sara Middleton, Arthur Middleton's wealthy widow.[131]

The same period saw a significant increase in the number of Charles Town's poor white inhabitants. Poor relief expenses tripled in the years between 1732 and 1738, culminating in the establishment of the city's first workhouse, while surviving vestry records from rural parishes indicate that poverty was a growing problem throughout the colony, with perhaps a fifth of the white population just scraping by. Yet poor relief was more generous, more readily available, and less punitive in both urban and rural South Carolina than elsewhere in British North America, reflecting a concerted effort among a coalescing merchant-planter elite to ensure the unity of the white population in a society increasingly divided by race and class.[132]

Meanwhile, a small handful of Charles Town merchants came to dominate the import-export trade. They wielded their growing influence in Britain, shaping efforts to disallow the loan office act and get the burden of the slave duty shifted from importers to purchasers. No individual better exemplifies this than Joseph Wragg, whose firm Joseph Wragg & Co. imported more than 6,000 African captives during the 1730s and who alone paid nearly £40,000 in duties on twenty enslaved cargoes between 1735 and 1739. Including Wragg, eleven merchants or companies were responsible for nearly all the revenues arising from sales of captives in the period. More than half of the revenue came from just three merchants or companies: Wragg, Benjamin Savage, and the firm of Hill & Guerrard.[133] After the Stono Rebellion and the outbreak of the War of Jenkins' Ear in 1739, they used the fortunes they amassed in the 1730s to withstand the sluggish years of the 1740s, benefiting from the expansion of government spending, diversifying their investments, and laying the groundwork for the next generation.

Political Economy and the Stono Rebellion

In the 1730s, planters attempted to overcome the barriers of rice production through the frenzied accumulation of property in human beings and exploitation of Black labor. As labor demands in rice fields intensified, enslaved people were worked longer and harder, and subjected to increasing "managerial violence," contributing to rising mortality rates and declining birth rates; Charles Town merchants responded to the demographic disaster by importing more African captives.[134] Despite the persistence of customary labor and pay arrangements since the late seventeenth century, the intensification of rice production gave enslaved field hands less time to produce their own provisions and enforced what one historian has described as "a new standard of poverty" on enslaved households.[135] This was a marked shift from earlier decades, when enslaved field hands worked alongside servants and freemen growing food for export to the Caribbean and had relative autonomy and freedom of movement. They tended their own crops, peddled goods, hired themselves out for wages, and carried guns for hunting.[136]

The assembly used the threat of a Spanish invasion to justify new restrictions on Black life in 1737. That February it passed a new patrol act appointing commissioners to enlist freeholders for local slave patrols. The act empowered patrol men to search slave homes for weapons and ammunition, torture enslaved people found off enslavers' estates without a pass, and execute enslaved men and women resisting arrest. It also authorized militia officers to summon their men to forcefully disperse slave gatherings.[137] But not all the patrol men took their duties seriously, eliciting accusations a few years later of the Charles Town night watch "entertaining seamen and Negroes at unseasonable Hours." By the 1750s, some parishes had gone years without mustering patrols.[138] Turning to the Spanish threat, the assembly enabled Governor Thomas Broughton to impress any vessels, sailors, laborers, horses, guns, and ammunition; imposed stricter discipline on unruly soldiers posted in colonial forts and garrisons; and made it illegal for tavernkeepers to lodge, entertain, or sell alcohol to troops on duty.[139] Efforts to regulate soldiers' behavior reflected fears of fraternization or, worse yet, cooperation between enslaved persons and free poor people.

The assembly additionally issued £35,010 in new public orders, redeemable for taxes in five years, for supplying the soldiers and sailors, and for repairing the fortifications in Charles Town.[140] While many representatives held out hope that the Crown would approve the 1736 loan office act, critics of the act, including James Kinloch and Joseph Wragg, welcomed the public orders.[141] In their view, the Spanish threat to their property and profits more than justified a small addition to the currency. Moreover, money issued to pay for public expenses directly enriched the wealthy merchants and planters the assembly called upon to contribute money, goods, and services to the colony. In return for their largesse, the assembly earmarked public funds for projects that benefited the public creditors. For example, in 1738, the assembly spent thousands of pounds on a silk works, including £900 for the purchase of six enslaved laborers from Wragg.[142]

Everything came to a head in 1739. The economy crashed, enslaved people rebelled, and Britain went to war with Spain. Yellow fever raged through Charles Town that summer, killing hundreds of people. Philadelphia merchant Richard Hockley arrived that fall to find the city in total disarray. There to sell flour, he quickly realized that because of the bumper crop and collapse of rice prices, there was nowhere for him to store his produce, "the Wharfs being taken up with Rice."[143] Making matters worse, the city was filled with all sorts of provisions, lowering prices. In addition to the loss of Spanish markets, Hockley reckoned that the colony itself had "no occasion for the supply as formerly," because "by a moderate calculation they lost eight hundred white People in the last Sickness."[144] Just before Christmas he managed to sell 300 barrels of flour to the city's "principal Bakers." Nevertheless, he spent most of his days sitting around not selling "a single Barrel of any thing."[145] In February 1740, "quite tired out with so indolent alife," he reported to Thomas Penn in Philadelphia that the arrival of the "Men of Warr" was imminent and expressed the hope, doubtless shared by other merchants, that he could offload his stock to the British navy.[146]

The financial collapse, rumors of a war with Spain, and the epidemic all contributed to the timing of the Stono Rebellion, the largest and costliest uprising of enslaved people in British American colonial history. The rebellion erupted on Sunday, September 9, 1739. The day itself may have held significance for those of the rebels who had practiced Catholicism in the African kingdom of Kongo, the origin of many of the Carolina enslaved: September 8 was the day of the Nativity of the Virgin Mary. The previous year, moreover, the governor of Florida had established Fort Mose, a free Black settlement, two miles north of St. Augustine. It was a window of opportunity for enslaved Africans to take advantage of the Spanish king's promise of sanctuary for all freedom-seekers who professed their faith and enlisted in the Florida militia. Led by a Kongolese or Angolan man named Jemmy, a core group of rebels seized a store of arms and marched southward with drums and banners, drafting recruits, burning plantations, and engaging South Carolina troops in several pitched battles along the way. In the end, about twenty-five colonists and as many as fifty rebels were slain. A few made it to St. Augustine where they joined the free Black community; the rest were tortured and executed or transported to the Caribbean.[147]

The Stono Rebellion was not a one-off but the culmination of a surge of rebellious activity, from poisonings to barn burnings to armed escapes, precipitated by the increasing burdens of field work and the brutal measures used to force enslaved people to perform the labor. In January 1735, for example, "a great Number" of bondspeople had "run away into the Woods, where about a Hundred of them combin'd in Body, with Arms and Ammunition, for some villainous Attempt," the *Boston News-Letter* reported at the time.[148] Such resistance, S. Max Edelson argues, might be seen as "a reaction to the strains placed on slave households by the shift toward commodity production," as escalating labor demands rendered enslaved husbands and fathers less able to provide food and clothing for their families.[149]

The assembly addressed the twin threat of treacherous Spaniards and rebellious Africans in November 1739. It proclaimed that the sanctuary the Spanish gave to freedom-seekers in Florida had encouraged the enslaved "to rise in Rebellion; and that the Demolition of that Place would, in a very great

Measure, tend to free us from the like Danger for the future." Declaring the expulsion of the Spanish from Florida as their top priority, the representatives threw their support behind Georgia governor James Oglethorpe's proposed "Siege against Augustine."[150] Oglethorpe, who had helped establish Georgia as a white colony six years earlier, identified another factor motivating South Carolina colonists: the preservation of their enslaved property. On April 1, 1740, he wrote to the Duke of Newcastle that the existence of Florida "renders all their Estates precarious," so the Carolinians were eager to assist him.[151] According to Lieutenant Governor William Bull, moreover, the colonists were less worried about their laborers "rising in rebellion" than about their defecting to the Spanish, who for decades "openly received protected & set at liberty many slaves who deserted from this Province which encouraged many attempts of the like Nature." Britain's declaration of war with Spain was a convenient excuse for "the People of this Province" to "get rid of a dangerous Neighbour" and an opportunity to recapture those whom they had enslaved.[152]

The conflict with Spain came at an opportune moment in the currency debate as well, because it encouraged the colony to re-embrace paper money as a means of war finance. In the spring of 1740, the assembly earmarked £120,000 total for the Oglethorpe expedition, to be financed partly by borrowing sterling money from merchants. Of that, £40,000 worth of provisions would be bought on credit, while other expenses would be purchased with paper money, which, Richard Hockley reported to Thomas Penn, was "to be the Cash" in circulation. That April the assembly issued £25,000 in new public orders, redeemable by taxes in four years, and in September an additional £11,508.[153] Oglethorpe himself advanced £2,000 sterling "upon the Credit of their future taxes," Parliament provided some funds, and the assembly approved a £250 bounty "for every one kill'd in the Expedition." The force included both British regulars and South Carolina and Georgia militia. As with previous ventures, the assembly solicited Indigenous allies' help and encouraged every white volunteer "to carry as many trusty negroes as he pleases."[154] And as with previous ventures, the expedition failed miserably. On reaching Florida in June, the British captured Fort Mose and blockaded St. Augustine, but the Spanish successfully counterattacked, destroying the fort with minimal losses and cutting through the naval blockade. The siege collapsed in early July and the war moved south, with major battles occurring in and around Panama, Colombia, and Cuba.

By then the assembly had begun deliberations on how to prevent another insurrection. The initial response to the Stono Rebellion focused on rewarding informants and conspirators who turned king's evidence. But enslaved people were not a unified monolith of resistance. Giving money to enslaved persons who helped suppress slave uprisings was one of many strategies that colonial leaders used to try to divide the Black population, and those in South Carolina were no exception. Between the fall of 1739 and the summer of 1740, thirty-one enslaved people received rewards for opposing the Stono rebels. A few won their freedom, including July, who protected his enslaver's family from the rebels, killing one. Several others received payments in amounts ranging from five pounds to twenty pounds. Quash received "the sum of £10 in Cash" for seizing a rebel.[155] Several months later, another enslaved man received ten pounds "for apprehending one of the Slaves who was concerned in the Insurrection of Stono," while Peter received "a Suit of Cloths, Hat, Shoes and Stockings and £20 in Cash" for discovering a separate but related plot in St. John Parish. The assembly summoned both men to Charles Town to collect their rewards.[156]

The assembly next moved to strengthen the 1737 patrol act and overhaul the slave code. If some aspects of the 1740 slave code act concerned the regulation and surveillance of enslaved people as conquered subjects, other provisions regarded enslaved men and women as laborers, consumers, and trading partners. First, the new slave code prohibited managers and overseers from making enslaved people work more than fifteen hours a day from April to September and more than fourteen hours a day from October to March. Enslaved laborers were required to have Sundays off, and enslavers were ordered to provide "sufficient cloathing, covering [and] food." Additional provisions aimed to limit enslaved people's ability to hire themselves out, raise cattle and hogs, and buy and sell "goods or commodities," which the representatives proclaimed provided them with opportunities "of receiving and concealing stolen good[s]" and "to plot and confederate together, and form conspiracies." Any enslaved person suspected of marketing stolen goods was to have the goods and profits confiscated, and both they and their enslaver would be held responsible.[157] Accompanying the act was a prohibitive duty that effectively halted slave importation from 1740 to 1744.[158] Shifting the burden of the duty from importers to purchasers and raising the amount caused demand for African captives to plummet, accelerating Bristol's downfall as a leader in the slave trade.

The fifteen-hour workday was not a concession to the enslaved but a cession to the market. Throughout the 1730s the assembly had tried, but failed, to tame the lawlessness of commodity production. They proposed monetary and fiscal policies that promised to stimulate demand, stabilize prices, and diversify the economy. Planters instead chased elusive profits by purchasing more enslaved Africans on credit, supplying more rice, and working enslaved persons harder and without regard to either the constraints of the market or the needs of individual laborers. By limiting the number of hours that enslaved people could work in rice fields each day and by increasing the cost of slave labor, consequently restricting rice production, the assembly steadied the colonial economy and locked in the gains of the wealthiest planters and merchants during the expansion, ushering in an age of greater financial stability and social extremes.

The political winds shifted in the aftermath of the Stono Rebellion and the Oglethorpe expedition. In the assembly, proponents of a loan office were replaced by Atlantic elites sympathetic to big planters, local merchants and creditors, and British commercial interests. The new assembly snubbed Georgia's pleas for military assistance and ignored colonists' petitions for debt relief. The financial crisis compelled many small and middling planters to sell or mortgage their remaining property or amass heavy debts; some picked up and moved to Georgia. In turn, Charles Town creditors pursued their debtors relentlessly, seizing enslaved people for the repayment of debts and selling them to Spanish traders, who paid in silver.[159] Many British-born merchants returned home in the 1740s, where they reentered the South Carolina trade in London and represented the colony's interests in various capacities, lobbying Parliament for military aid and securing an indigo bounty in the late 1740s. The bounty "[has] had so good an effect" on the trade of the province, some of the merchants later testified, that a loan office was no longer needed.[160]

The rice boom had come and gone. Rice output dropped during the War of Jenkins' Ear and War of the Austrian Succession (1739–48), dampened by the prohibitive slave duty and rising freight and insurance rates during the wars. Rice and slave prices fell after 1739 but improved with the return of peace in 1748 as rice output recovered, slave importation resumed, and experiments in indigo cultivation bore fruit.[161] The sterling exchange rate returned to 700 percent, where it would remain until the American Revolution. It was a muted recovery. And as the economy chugged along, subsequent efforts to establish a loan office failed. By 1746, when—thanks to the election of several pro–paper money representatives from the southern parishes—the assembly finally passed another act for establishing a loan office "not liable to the objections made to the last," Parliament was already in the process of framing a coherent colonial currency policy and the Board of Trade had walked back its previous position that some money was necessary for local trade.[162] The loan office act of 1746, as one historian wryly put it, "obviously . . . did not fit into the imperial scheme of things."[163]

But just because efforts to establish a loan office failed did not mean that monetary exchange backslid to barter. In 1748 the assembly issued £106,500 in new bills of credit for redeeming all old bills. The new bills were legal tender for debts and would serve as a permanent local medium for the next three decades, with the assembly regularly replacing worn bills with freshly printed ones. There was nothing else like it in British America. The assembly additionally issued public orders annually to pay for public expenses and, after the outbreak of the French and Indian War in 1754, military costs. Like the orders of the 1730s, they were not legal tender for debts but instead merely redeemable in payment of taxes by specific dates.[164]

By far, however, private lenders like Joseph Wragg and Richard Lambton made the majority of the colony's money in the form of mortgage-backed loans. Most colonial settlers would continue to receive credit from the Charles Town lending market, and the proportion of enslaved property used as collateral in mortgages soared—to 88 percent in the quarter-century after 1748, according to David Hancock. (In contrast, land appeared in only 5 percent of the 3,252 publicly recorded loans totaling approximately £3.4M currency.)[165] This made the lenders more akin to modern financial dealers or bankers that issue currency in the form of interest-bearing debt than to early modern lenders that merely moved money around. As major financial intermediaries, they had the power of the purse in all but name.[166]

6

Money on the Margins

November 1735. Some thieves broke into a Philadelphia home "and stole some Paper Money" and a bag of "Flower'd Caps." They left "Several Drops of Blood," presumably their own, near where "the Money was taken, whence 'tis probable that the Money also may be bloodied," speculated the local press. *Summer 1736.* John Blakely of South Carolina knocked down a peddler "with a Club, and took from him his pack, hat, handkerchief and Pocket-book with about 60 odd Pounds of Money." He was later apprehended and committed to the local jail. *November 1736.* A man with a cane met two Boston gentlemen on King Street and asked "to borrow three or four Pounds," threatening to shoot them if they refused. Just then someone approached with a lantern, and the man ran off. *October 1737.* A highwayman accosted a New Jersey peddler and "ask'd him if he had any Money." When the peddler answered no, the robber took out a sharp knife "and cut his Leg, stab'd him in the Breast, and other places, cut open his Pack, wherein was ten Pound in Paper Money, which he took and made off, leaving the Man in his Blood."[1]

Whether it was hunger, greed, or something else that drove these men to violence, poverty was on the rise in 1730s British North America. While contemporaries defined the poor as those receiving public assistance or private charity—the so-called "worthy poor"—historians have broadened this definition to include the laboring poor, from the hired fishermen of maritime New England, to the indentured servants of rural Pennsylvania, to the enslaved artisans of New York City. The imperial wars were to blame, of course, but so was the uneven growth of the trade and markets that the colonies fought those wars to secure. In Boston, recurrent wars swelled the ranks of the poor and disabled, and created a new class of war widows and children reliant on public support.[2] New York City, insulated from the fighting, nevertheless endured a significant depression in the 1730s, driving up poor taxes and leading to the establishment of a workhouse in 1738. In all of the urban seaports, merchant capitalists began to abandon the semi-patriarchal system in which masters and workers partook in a "complex social relationship ... with duties on both sides." They stopped offering payment-in-kind with job security and began drawing their workforce from the unattached propertyless, who sold their labor for cash wages.[3] But even when the work was regular, which it seldom was, the wages rarely matched the cost of living, and most laborers were only an accident or personal crisis away from destitution.[4]

It is all the more remarkable, then, that wage laborers and enslaved people, servants and convicts, and widowed and abandoned women eked out a living. Through creativity and cunning, those on the margins of colonial society exploited the social and economic transformations of the mid-eighteenth century to their material benefit, not by any single means but, as the 1730s crime reporting demonstrates, by any means necessary. Some were able to live quite comfortably as a result. Historians have documented the role of consumer goods in leveling social distinctions and fueling "informal" economies in early America, and money could have similar implications. Impoverished did not mean moneyless. Like consumer goods, coin and currency penetrated deep into the social order. And like the chipped dishes and decorative buttons that retained more psychological significance than cash value, money had different meanings in different contexts.

This chapter shows how marginalized persons used colonial North America's increasingly chaotic monetary landscape to their advantage. Through "stealing" and counterfeiting, in particular, poor and enslaved people gained access to money and markets, and undermined economic relationships based on hierarchy and deference, even as they contributed—wittingly or otherwise—to the expansion of Atlantic commerce and consolidation of Britain's capitalist empire. They may even have understood their activities as a form of resistance to the cash nexus and the logic of commodification. Certainly not all who stole were poor, and those who were rarely rose above their stations in the process. They stole as a means of survival and, in so doing, enlarged their social and material worlds within the rigid confines of poverty and slavery.

Poverty and Slavery

Scholarly accounts of poverty in early America traditionally focused on the white poor: the tenants, wage laborers, servants, convicts, widows, orphans, and other dependents of European lineage. The experiences of these groups varied widely, from the severe brutality suffered by convicts, to the hand-to-mouth existence of widows, to the harsh but often temporary poverty of servants, to the relative privilege of tenants. But the majority, and the poorest, of early America's poor were enslaved Africans and their descendants, who generally had shabbier clothing, smaller quarters, higher mortality, and more monotonous, if not necessarily more meager, diets than their white counterparts.[5]

By the second quarter of the eighteenth century, nearly every British colony had codified chattel slavery as a lifelong, heritable condition based on maternal African ancestry and had passed laws making free Black people's status more like that of enslaved persons and making it more difficult for enslavers to manumit their laborers. These laws not only gave race legal and social meaning, but also made class.[6] The codification of slavery thus coincided with a huge leap in numbers of bondspeople not just in the Chesapeake and Lowcountry but in New England and the middle colonies as well, where enslaved laborers could be found in every economic sector and slave labor was central to colonial prosperity.[7] The Black population of Boston grew from 400 in 1704 to more than 1,500 in 1752, nearly a tenth of the town's inhabitants. In Rhode Island, enslaved Africans and their descendants numbered well over three thousand to make up 10 percent of the population by 1750, a more than sixfold increase from 1720. The province of New York had the largest Black population north of Maryland at just over 19,000 by the mid-eighteenth century, while the enslaved community of Philadelphia peaked at 1,400 in a city of 18,600 in 1767.[8]

Even as slavery's institutionalization created a deterioration in overall living standards for Black men and women, the concomitant expansion of trade, markets, and money created new opportunities for enslaved people to enlarge their social and material worlds—with or without enslavers' consent. Despite growing restrictions on unfree laborers' commercial dealings, the enslaved still found ways to obtain cash and credit through "legitimate" if not strictly legal channels, from participating in local lending markets to hiring themselves out for wages. Several bondspeople received loans from Boston storekeeper Ann Greene in 1728, including "John Budrey's Negro" (nine shillings), "John Budrey's . . . Negro Bristo" (nine shillings sixpence), "Edwd Durants negro Will" (five shillings sixpence), and "Mrs Frosts negro" (ten shillings).[9] Caesar Lyndon of Newport worked as his enslaver's business agent in the mid-eighteenth century and had his own lending practice that served Black and white borrowers alike, eventually earning him enough money to purchase his freedom.[10]

Recent research in probate records indicates that enslaved men, women, and children received small sums of money from enslavers' or community members' bequests, either as gifts or as payments for services.[11] Historian Christy Clark-Pujara cautions that such "gifts" are better described as bribes, however. "Rhode Island slaveholders had to find ways to coerce and convince enslaved people to work," explains Clark-Pujara. "Such compulsion could not rely solely on threats, verbal abuse, and physical punishments; consequently, slaveholders were compelled to also use inducements in their attempts to control their human property."[12] For example, in July 1725, Captain Peter Green of Warwick died and left Hager, a woman he held in bondage, ten shillings to "induce her to be kinde to my Wife." He willed her children five shillings each.[13]

Enslaved laborers in Boston, Newport, New York, and Philadelphia were also regularly "rented out," though much of their pay would have gone to their enslavers.[14] Yet as the historian Ira Berlin pointed out: "Many—building upon the ongoing system of slave hiring—jobbed independently, sometimes compensating their owners for the right to control a portion of their own time and sometimes just pocketing their earnings. While their property accumulations remained small, they were recognized in practice and sometimes in law."[15] Venture Smith, a young African man enslaved on Long Island, managed to save a handful of foreign coins and two thousand coppers—nearly twenty-one pounds New York currency—"by cleaning gentlemen's shoes and drawing boots, by catching musk-rats and minks, raising potatoes and carrots, &c. and by fishing in the night, and at odd spells."[16] Like Caesar Lyndon, Smith eventually amassed enough money—seventy-one pounds two shillings—to buy his freedom, despite being cheated, robbed, sued, and savagely beaten along the way.

Colonial assemblies drew the line at enslaved persons living on their own, a practice that had nevertheless become so prevalent in Philadelphia by the mid-eighteenth century that Benjamin Franklin took it upon himself to reprint Pennsylvania's entire 1726 slave code in his *Pennsylvania Gazette*. He prefaced the code with an explanation that "frequent complaints have been lately made" of enslaved people traveling freely, "seek[ing] their own employment," and renting rooms or houses, "where great Disorders often happen, especially in the Night time." Enslavers permitted their laborers to do all these things with the understanding that the laborers would pay them "certain Sums of Money," much to the complainants' frustration.[17]

Among enslaved men who secured permission to hire themselves out, many sought jobs on ships as sailors and cooks, where they could earn similar wages to their white counterparts. The sea was an avenue, if not of liberation, then of some personal freedom, and many enslaved men negotiated the right to hire themselves out for a voyage even knowing that their enslavers would pocket the earnings on their return. Such was the case of Briton Hammon of Marshfield, Massachusetts, who shipped from Plymouth on a sloop bound for Jamaica in December 1747. Others took their maritime skills and ran, offering their services to short-staffed captains who would not question their backgrounds.[18]

Like their South Carolina and New York counterparts during the first quarter of the eighteenth century discussed in chapter 2, the Massachusetts enslaved had limited opportunities to make money in military contexts. Since the militia laws are ambiguous on the matter, it is likely that many enslaved men participated in local alarms or as servants to colonial captains. Consider one Cuffee, who served at his enslaver's behest at Castle William on Boston Harbor and appears on the muster rolls from 1734 to at least 1741. For the year 1735, Cuffee was due thirteen pounds ten shillings for twenty-seven weeks, the same rate as a common soldier, though we do not know what portion, if any, he would have pocketed.[19] Jeffrey York, a free Black servant of the victualer of Castle William, on the other hand, received special permission to enlist in the muster roll at the "Same Pay" as a white sentinel of three pounds per month.[20] Instances of the colony hiring enslaved laborers for military jobs appear sporadically in the treasurer's accounts, though we can assume that those wages would have gone to their enslavers.[21] More Black men, free and enslaved, would fight in the siege of Louisburg in French Canada in 1745 and claim the cash bounty. The imperial wars were simultaneously a source of death and suffering and of singular opportunity for those on colonial society's lowest rungs.

Informal Economies

Poverty and slavery came together in the urban seaports, where enslaved men and women commingled with servants, apprentices, journeymen, sailors, widows, and other marginalized persons in informal economies that blurred the line between legitimate and "criminal" activity. Historians have emphasized the importance of the informal economy to the growth of colonial and even transatlantic trade networks and its connection to more legitimate commerce. While colonial elites may have interpreted activities within the informal economy as illicit, even immoral, for the participants, the historian Serena Zabin underscores, "this particular commercial world was a creative and legitimate—if not necessarily legal—part of the world of goods."[22]

Stolen and secondhand clothing was the lifeblood of the informal economy, and enslaved people played an important role in taking pieces from enslavers and pawning them to poor white women, who fenced them in turn. Indeed, clothing, Zabin explains, "frequently served as currency among shopkeepers, tavern owners, and customers . . . that could be traded for liquor

[and] rent ... [or] sold for hard currency."[23] Newspaper advertisements for stolen goods featured not only coats, breeches, gowns, hats, wigs, shoes, and pieces of linen and calico, but also silk stockings and handkerchiefs; gold buttons and lockets; silver spoons, buckles, watches, whistles, tankards, and porringers; and jewels, even diamonds—surely items that were intended for resale rather than for personal use. Some subscribers asked for the public's assistance in stopping the thieves from pawning or selling their belongings.[24] Other bandits made off with paper money, pieces of eight, shillings, pistoles, or "bullion."[25]

Certainly, stealing clothing, food, or livestock could be a means of survival for poor and enslaved people. Mercy, a free Black woman of Newport, was sentenced to receive ten lashes on her bare back for pilfering two wool blankets, items she may have planned to use to keep warm at night.[26] But the abundant reports of stolen goods with little practical use, from silk stockings to silver spoons to powdered wigs—items symbolizing elite status—reveal that theft was also a ticket to the world of consumer goods and social advancement. Robbin, a man held in bondage by John Jenkins of Boston, allegedly broke into merchant Samuel Greenwood's home and stole eight pounds in bills of credit. According to witness testimony, Robbin used the bills to purchase luxury goods for family members from women shopkeepers who could not afford to turn away his business. For Robbin and others on the margins of colonial society, participation in the informal economy offered a means of resisting the degradation of poverty and slavery. But although such participation may have momentarily subverted traditional hierarchies of race and status, the stakes were high, as those who were convicted of stealing were subject to public whippings and large fines, and the highest prize, true freedom, remained out of reach for all but a few.[27]

In addition to turning stolen money into consumer goods, enslaved men and women took cash and clothing to unlicensed taverns—dubbed "disorderly houses" or "tippling houses" by officials—and exchanged them for drink. The practice was at least as widespread as the platform; New York City authorities accused more than 200 tavernkeepers, many of them poor white women, of keeping disorderly houses in the first three-quarters of the eighteenth century.[28] Although not all of the accusations were true, many of these women would have entertained servants and enslaved people, received and fenced stolen goods, and handled counterfeit currency. Among the accused was Elizabeth Anderson, indicted for keeping "a common disordered house of Bawdry and Tipling," where she entertained "Negro Slaves and divers other persons of Idle and suspected Character."[29] Some men and women faced the more serious charge of receiving stolen goods or money from enslaved persons, as was the case of Anne White, accused of "receiving stolen goods" from Peter Mathews's laborer, and of Mary Smith, accused of accepting stolen cash from an enslaved man named Somerset.[30] Often just a room in the back of a house, illegal taverns were not only important sites of interracial theft but of interracial socializing as well, spaces where laboring men and women who toiled side by side during the day could gather after hours to gossip, drink, and gamble beyond enslavers' and employers' prying eyes.[31]

These activities hardly went unnoticed. Colonial lawmakers recognized the connection between interracial socializing and interracial theft in various acts barring white colonists from entertaining servants and enslaved people. In 1730, the New York assembly acknowledged that "notwithstanding Sundry Laws passed heretofore . . . several evil disposed Persons having nothing in View but their private gain do Clandestinely trade and traffic with Slaves." The assembly reiterated that it was unlawful to "sell any rum or other strong Liquor to any Negro Indian or Mulato Slave or Slaves or [to] buy or take in pawn from them any wares Merchandises apparel Tools Instruments or any other Kind of Goods whatever."[32] Eleven years later, when a difficult winter, simmering class tensions, and war with Spain fueled tales of a conspiracy against New York City's elite resulting in trials and executions, a group of concerned citizens blamed interracial gatherings at disorderly houses for the alleged conspirators' "Diabolical Vilanies."[33] The Rhode Island authorities likewise conceded the ineffectiveness of previous laws when they passed an act in 1750 forbidding colonists to "sell, give, truck, barter or exchange . . . any strong Beer, Ale, Cyder, Wine, Rum, Brandy, or other strong liquor to any Indian, Mulatto or Negro Servant or Slave." According to the assembly, alcohol consumption among the laboring classes was driving unfree workers to rob their enslavers and masters.[34]

Additional laws targeted gambling and gaming. In 1728 the Boston town meeting bemoaned the "Sundry Inconveniences and Disorders" caused "By young People, Servants, and Negroes Playing in the Streets with money" and moved to ban all gambling in public spaces.[35] The nine o'clock curfew was an especial point of contention, with some colonists lamenting slaveholders' permissiveness in failing to enforce it. On April 14, 1738, the *Boston News-Letter* reprinted the entire curfew act in the hope that "all Masters or Owners of any Indian, Negro or Molatto Servants . . . take effectual Care that such their Servants may not be unnecessarily abroad after Nine a Clock."[36] The entreaty was evidently unsuccessful, as two years later the *Boston Evening-Post* reported on a recent gathering of a dozen Black men and women at a Roxbury tavern, where they danced, played music, and drank wine and punch "past Nine o'Clock." The *Post* wondered how the partygoers were able to afford "these Nocturnal Frolicks, which must needs be very expensive," and asked "Whether it be convenient that publick Houses shouldn't give Entertainment to our Slaves, at all, but especially at the Time of Night above-mentioned."[37]

Other complaints fixated on the lower orders' growing power, real or imagined, over prices and markets. When inflation hit Massachusetts in 1728, the Boston freeholders pointed the finger at resourceful servants and enslaved people. That summer the town meeting ordered that no Black or Native person "be suffered to Buy any Sort of Provisions" from country farmers and retailers, "It being found by Experience" that such persons "Buying of Provisions in the Market Place or Else where has Inhanced the Price of Provisions." As for the farmers, they traveled to Boston and walked through the streets hawking produce to whoever was willing to buy it, at whatever price they were willing to pay.[38] Town markets offered additional cover for enslaved people from rural areas peddling stolen goods or selling goods on their enslavers' behalf and pocketing a share of the proceeds; some slaveholders might even encourage their laborers to steal from other households in return for a cut of the profits.[39] Enslaved New Yorkers evidently monopolized the trade in oysters, prompting the assembly to pass an act prohibiting enslaved persons from harvesting and selling them, since it "Deprive[d] the good Inhabitants of this Colony . . . from getting and fetching oysters for them Selves and their Familys."[40]

Although interracial crime was common, enslaved people had to tread carefully, since race and power could influence the outcome. A man enslaved in New Jersey, for example, had been "entic'd" by two strangers "to runaway and steal what he could from his Master; accordingly he broke open two Locks of a Writing-Desk, and stole from thence about *Nine Pounds* in Gold and gave it to them at Philadelphia, who receiv'd the said Money, and then runaway, leaving the Negro hid in a Barrack of Hay, who is since taken and put in the Work-House of *Philadelphia*."[41] In another case, Venture Smith, who had run away from his Long Island enslaver in the company of three servants, was robbed by one his white companions, who made off with the group's clothing.[42]

Marginalized persons in possession of money had to guard against charges of theft and impropriety, and were vulnerable to scapegoating; not all of the charges were true. In May 1727 a Bristol County, Massachusetts, jury indicted Silas Elisha, an Indigenous boy from Dartmouth, for breaking into Samuel Hull's house and stealing a pocketbook containing "twenty pounds of public Bills of Credit."[43] Later that summer jurors found Elisha, along with his friend Tobie Jefery, guilty of entering John Russel's property and stealing "three pieces of Woolen Cloth." The court ordered Elisha and Jefery to three and nine years of servitude, respectively.[44] Whether Elisha had pilfered the money and cloth, and how he planned to dispose of it, or whether he was used as an example to the local nonwhite population to police their economic and social activity, is uncertain. Years later, the published confession of Arthur, an enslaved Black man from nearby Taunton, focused less on the assault for which he was condemned to death than on the inventory of property crimes that had supposedly precipitated his descent, from pilfering calico, clothing, shoes, food, and drink from local shops to stealing money from enslavers to running away, at once affirming his individuality and warning those like him of the slippery slope from petty theft to violence.[45]

Whether in the formal economy or the informal one, cash was a lifeline for those who struggled to make claims to credit based on poverty, legal status, or race. Enslaved people and married women, for example, were not legally entitled to their own credit, so "cash could serve as a vital tool for purchases outside of fathers', husbands', and masters' oversight," explains historian Ellen Hartigan-O'Connor. Coin and currency likewise enabled servants, apprentices, soldiers, and sailors to "do business with those they did not know well enough to trust with credit in the form of book debt" and "in the more imperial context of mobile urban populations."[46] Newspaper advertisements for runaway laborers, moreover, reveal that a small but significant portion made off with money.

But the money, like the clothing they wore, also marked them for capture. Mary Wottson, a Maryland servant, escaped with "some English coin" as well as "her three Gold Rings."[47] If the advertisements are any indication, more laboring men than women escaped with money in their possession (or were accused of stealing money), though male servants outnumbered female servants about ten to one in the eighteenth century.[48] Such was the case of Alexander Nelson, a twenty-four-year-old Irish servant in Maryland who ran off from his master with "the old Indentures of one James Mac-Daniel" and "a Quantity of Paper Money"; John Nutty, a Philadelphia butcher's servant who made off with six pounds "in Jersey Money"; an unnamed twenty-two-year-old man enslaved in Chester County who ran away with "Several white Shirts, and some Money"; John Oliver alias Oliver Jones, who took "Thirty two Shillings of Pennsylvania Money and Five Shillings in Copper" from his Philadelphia master and fled; two Germantown servant boys who "Stole a pocket book from their master" containing "about Fifty Three Shillings of money," along with a pair of guns, before making their getaway; and Edward Demsy, an Irish convict who escaped from his Maryland master with "a considerable sum of money which probably may procure him better clothes."[49] Other freedom seekers escaped with considerable quantities of stolen goods, which they may have planned to sell for cash. Benjamin Hicks, a Pennsylvania servant, pilfered the "Horse-load of Goods" he was supposed to take and sell "to Allegheny to the Indians" on his master's behalf.[50] These unfree laborers likely had a good sense of the risks involved in their flight—made all the riskier by absconding with money. But for many on the margins, money was becoming indispensable, and it was worth the gamble.

The Slaves' Economy

In South Carolina more than in any other colony, enslaved people's independent economic activities not only benefited themselves, but also proved central to the political economy of slavery. However, what the enslavers who profited from the "slaves' economy" failed to account for—indeed, could not account for—was that enslaved people, in addition to being workers, collateral, and consumers, were also political actors.[51] Enslaved men and women ignored the laws that attempted to restrict their independent dealings, they "stole" wages and goods from enslavers, and they used the money they made in the market to improve their material conditions, enlarge their social worlds, and even seek freedom.

Across colonial North America, many urban slaveholders permitted their bondspeople to devote some of their time and energy for personal gain, and those in Charles Town were no exception.[52] But in the 1730s, objections to enslaved Carolinians' power over prices began to surface, echoing similar complaints made in Boston and New York around the same time. In March 1734, a grand jury denounced the "common Practice by several Persons in *Charles Town*, to suffer their Negroes to work out by the Week" with the understanding that they would "bring in a certain hire," contrary to the law. The jury asserted that enslaved workers used the opportunity to peddle "Corn, Pease, Fowls, &c. whereby they watch Night and Day on the several Wharfes, and buy up many Articles necessary for the support of the Inhabitants," driving up the cost of provisions and putting "an intollerable Hardship" on the white population.[53]

Thirteen years later, little had apparently changed. On February 5, 1747, a group of "poor white people" who made their livings selling pottery, produce, eggs, "& other trifling commodities" in the town market petitioned the assembly for relief on the grounds that enslaved marketers engrossed and forestalled "the Provisions &c. which come to Town for sale" and then resold them "at dear and exorbitant prices," depriving the petitioners of their livelihoods. They blamed enslavers for giving "all liberty imaginable" to their laborers "to buy sell and vend" without ever inquiring how they made their money, so long as they got their cut.⁵⁴

If the petitioners exaggerated enslaved sellers' market power, they nevertheless accurately identified the enslaved as a prominent part of the urban economy. Large numbers of Black men and women traveled from the countryside to the Charles Town market on "Sundays off," often with great difficulty and hardship, where they peddled fruits and vegetables, baked items, and dry goods. Enslaved women led the way in taking advantage of the town's opportunities for marketing, hawking oysters, peaches, milk, and cakes from street carts for cash at markups as high as 150 percent.⁵⁵ Urban enslaved women served as mediators between town and country when they sold slave-grown produce or fish their male kin had caught to urban consumers.⁵⁶

Like the poor white sellers who complained about enslaved marketers' activities, white journeymen railed against competition from their Black counterparts. But the enslaved ropemakers and shipwrights who worked on the docks and the enslaved carpenters and mechanics who kept Charles Town humming continued to dominate artisanal employment because planters, master craftsmen, and urban customers all benefited from their skills. As a result, enslaved artisans enjoyed a modicum of autonomy, working overtime and pocketing the wages or arranging for their own employment and allotting enslavers a weekly sum. Some even made enough money to live on their own and establish households.⁵⁷

Throughout the colony, enslaved persons found ways to earn cash with or without enslavers' consent. In addition to selling foodstuffs they had prepared in their "free" time and hiring themselves out for wages, enslaved men and women made money from a panoply of services, "from ferrying people across a river to directing a lost traveler, from putting out fires to refloating grounded boats, from killing a wolf to finding a lost horse, from saving on expenses to turning in a runaway, from transporting a desk to sweeping a church."⁵⁸ Historian Emma Hart determined that planter Charles Cattel's laborers took more than a hundred solo ferry trips from 1752 to 1755, and countless others must have exploited "the watery Lowcountry landscape," to buy and sell on their own account.⁵⁹

Real and imagined incidents of enslaved people "stealing" wages or selling stolen goods were common. In March 1732, Nicholas Trott placed a notice in the *South-Carolina Gazette* warning "all Persons" not to "hire or employ" the artisans he held in bondage "without first agreeing" with himself or his wife, lest they hire themselves out behind Trott's back and keep the wages.⁶⁰ In 1737, a grand jury complained about "the Practice of Negroes buying and selling Wares in the streets of *Charles-Town*, whereby stolen Goods may be concealed and afterwards vended undiscovered, as also Negroes going in Boats and Canoes up the Country trading with Negroes in a clandestine Manner."[61] Seven years later, another grand jury accused Black women of using stolen money to buy themselves fine clothing.[62] And in 1747, a group of white residents of Charles Town accused enslaved people of marketing goods "which they often acquired by many indirect methods."[63] Enslaved women's business acumen put them in direct competition with poor white women, making them particularly vulnerable to accusations of theft.[64]

Yet enslaved Carolinians may well have regarded such theft not only as harmless but also, as the historian Roderick McDonald observed of those enslaved in Jamaica and Louisiana, "as resistance to slavery, and as the appropriation and redistribution of illicitly accrued wealth."[65] Historian Alex Lichtenstein cast slave theft in the antebellum South in a similar light, arguing that it was not simply the negation of hegemonic values but "a crucial pressure point of class-conflict" over food to eat as well as over "goods for exchange beyond the bounds of the plantation." Indeed, it was when the enslaved moved outside the moral economy to the market economy that "they more directly challenged the class relations of the South and their masters' hegemony within those relations." More than stealing food because they were hungry, "the bolder step of stealing in order to participate in market transactions rested on a stronger consciousness of counter-morality and an inherent right to economic autonomy, and thus represented a greater threat to the slave system."[66] The politics of subsistence, in other words, proved not an end in itself for the enslaved, but rather a means to more substantial engagement in the political economy of slavery.

Certainly, even those enslavers who profited from slave self-hiring and marketing worried when access to money and markets facilitated individual resistance to slavery. In January 1732, a man named Primus ran away "having stolen money."[67] A few months later, three men and two women escaped in "a Poplar Canoe 25 Foot long."[68] On April 8 of that year, one Owen "rid away upon a bay colour'd Horse," presumably his own, "under Pretence to go and see his Wife."[69] Runaway advertisements from the 1730s and 1740s indicate that many freedom seekers had regular access to canoes, horses, guns, tools, or cash and that they lived or worked in Charles Town. Such was the case of Aaron, "who used to go about the Town with a Cart & Mule," and of Harry, a former shopkeeper's assistant.[70] Others had routine contact with the town market, where they would have encountered enslaved artisans, white laborers, sailors, and other unfree workers who shared their aspirations of freedom.[71] Some ran away *to* Charles Town, including a young woman named Franke, who it was reported was "known by most People in *Charlestown*, where she has been seen lately by several, and without doubt harbour'd by some free Negroes or Slaves," and the cooper Quamino and his wife, who were "both supposed to be harboured about Charles-Town."[72] It was uncommon, but not unheard of, for Black and white people to flee together, as when two enslaved men and two Irish servants jointly slipped their masters in the spring of 1735.[73]

Even if men and women enslaved in South Carolina did not try to escape slavery outright, they understood cash power and used it enlarge their social and material worlds, fueling concerns among white settlers about how they spent their time and money. Grand juries accused enslaved persons in Charles Town of "publickly cabaling in the Streets, and Disorders in Punch-houses," and enslaved women of "dress[ing] in Apparel quite gay and beyond their Condition."[74] Enslaved "market women," the historian Betty Wood writes in the context of colonial Georgia, "were singled out for particularly scathing criticism . . . as posing a particularly invidious threat to the social and moral fabric, as well as to the economic interests, of the white community."[75] In 1734, the same grand jury that accused Black peddlers of price gouging complained that the peddlers took their earnings to dramshops, where they drank and played at dice and other games with propertyless white folk, drawing allegations of "Idleness, Drunkenness and other Enormities."[76] Evidently, "many Retailers of strong Liquors" sold rum to enslaved people, contrary to the law, the purchasers of which carried the "Rum and other Goods, to trade with Negroes in the Country."[77] Black men and women used the money they stole from slaveholders or made in the market to socialize, divest themselves of slavery's trappings, and achieve at least a semblance of autonomy in the process.[78]

Many nonslaveholding colonists saw opportunity in the slaves' economy, including the white vendors who purchased goods from enslaved sellers in Charles Town and from there descended on remote plantations with money, merchandise, and credit for enslaved field hands who, despite the growing demands of field labor, still found time to grow and market their own crops.[79] In 1738, at the behest of established shopkeepers who complained about unfair competition from traveling salesmen and of planters who demanded first rights to their workers' produce, the assembly passed an act requiring white peddlers to pay £100 for a license to sell goods to servants and enslaved people on plantations. The persistence of shopkeepers' and planters' complaints over the eighteenth century, however, suggests that this interracial trade was not easily curtailed.[80]

Enslavers' predilection for profits created new opportunities for the slaves' economy to flourish following the Stono Rebellion of 1739. The South Carolina slaveocracy ignored complaints about slave self-hiring and marketing, stymied proposals to ban the training of enslaved people in the mechanical trades, and blocked measures to restrict the numbers of Black shipwrights, ropemakers, porters, and fishermen. Consequently, the proportion of enslaved men and women in the skilled trades grew. By the late 1740s, one colonist observed, "through all Carolina; the negroes are made to learn all the trades and are used for all kinds of business. For this reason, white people have difficulty in earning their bread there."[81] Enslaved carpenters, mechanics, seamstresses, and weavers were not limited to service within the "family" but sought additional, more remunerative opportunities on neighboring plantations and in Charles Town, where they might hire themselves out and try to pocket some of the wages. The "Handicraft Slaves" who worked for future founding father Henry Laurens, for example, received payments in sugar, rum, and cash.[82]

The task system, whereby enslaved people had "free" time to pursue their own productive activities after completing a day's tasks, had been instrumental in the evolution of the slaves' economy.[83] Enslaved field hands fought for and won the "right" to tend their own gardens, sell their own produce at their own prices, and lawfully accumulate their own property, even horses, provoking complaints about slaveholders who permitted their workers "to keep canoes, and to breed and raise horses, neat cattle and hogs, and to traffic and barter in several parts of this Province, for the particular and peculiar benefit of such slaves."[84] Enslavers recognized these rights not out of concern for enslaved persons' well-being but because they themselves profited from those economic activities on and off the plantation, not least since they were thus partly relieved of their charge to provide for their laborers' upkeep.

Yet the slaves' economy was a double-edged sword. If cash in hand gave enslaved people greater means to enlarge their social lives and improve their material conditions, it did not smooth over the rigid hierarchies of race, class, and gender that structured how Africans and their descendants experienced Charles Town and the Lowcountry. Urban spaces entrenched racial hierarchies through both lavish displays of wealth and spectacular scenes of violence.[85] Enslaved people were made to perform the most menial labor in the shabbiest clothing, and enslaved women, in particular, were under enslavers' continual surveillance and at their constant beck and call.[86] Nor did money protect enslaved people from enslavers' personal violence. On the contrary, in the second quarter of the eighteenth century slaveholders introduced new forms of compulsion based not merely on physical force but on economic pressure as well. This was especially true for men and women enslaved on isolated plantations, where compensation and coercion went fist in glove.[87] Although enslaved laborers maintained customary rights to keep gardens and raise their own provisions, planters sought to limit their commercial dealings by trading with them directly, strengthening patriarchal relations in the process. The legislative response to the Stono Rebellion discussed in the previous chapter reflected slaveholders' desire not to dismantle the slaves' economy but to redefine it on their terms.[88]

Slaveholder Elias Ball's accounts illustrate how money supplemented the threat of physical violence as an inducement to get enslaved persons "to go along with the system." For planters like Ball, explains the historian Edward Ball, "a thin system of wages was a means of buying cooperation."[89] Ball purchased provisions and livestock from his laborers, paying Abraham fifteen shillings for eighteen chickens and Maree two pounds for a pig in 1728, and Johnny seven pounds for two pigs in 1735. Two years later he paid fifty-seven pounds to twenty-two bondspeople for 152 bushels of rice for resale, including one pound three shillings for Windsor for three bushels of rice and twelve pounds fifteen shillings for Abraham for 34 bushels. In 1744, he sold six bushels of "Negro Rice" on his laborers' account.[90] To raise crops for sale, Ball's workers negotiated pieces of land close to their cabins, where they also grew vegetables and kept chickens and pigs for their subsistence. They purchased hats, clothing, blankets, pipes, and knives with the money they made, but they never earned enough to purchase their freedom, and later, when Ball suspected that his laborers' rice market gave them too much power over prices, he stopped purchasing their product.[91]

While it is important not to overstate unfree workers' bargaining position, the persistence of complaints about enslaved people's self-hiring, marketing, and theft suggests that Carolina slaveholders failed to rein in completely their laborers' independent economic activities. That different grievances rang from different quarters, moreover, implies that enslaved persons were able to exploit conflicting interests within the white community to some extent. Indeed, as Betty Wood observed, "the fact of the matter was that all whites were forced to accommodate themselves to, at the same time as they sought to channel to their own advantage, the aspirations of a black population that was far from helpless."[92] Enslaved people's commercial dealings opened a new arena of conflict with enslavers every bit as defiant as their bare life struggles on plantations. Even if their forays did not weaken the slavery system as a whole, their hard-won access to money and markets allowed them to push the bounds of economic power in the face of enslavers' constraints.

Making Money Plentier

By the second quarter of the eighteenth century, the colonial currency was already failing to keep up with the growth of trade and markets. While the expansion of Atlantic commerce, a booming settler population, and the spread of waged labor increased the demand for money, assemblies faced growing restrictions on paper currency emissions from the Crown. Desperate for cash, early Americans from all backgrounds devised clever, if not always legal, ways of multiplying their money. They sewed bills of credit that had split apart back together again or they used the pieces as small change, passing them for fractions of the original denominations. They began deliberately tearing bills, making it easier to pass counterfeited sections or to join sections of lower denomination bills to those of higher denominations. The "open and convict Villany passing in our Streets" of "tearing your Bills to pieces, and then artfully patching those of greater Value and less together" infuriated the Boston minister Benjamin Colman, as it not only cheated "the Ignorant" but also insulted "the Government" as much as "any Felonious Clipping of Coin," strong words for an offense whose British equivalent was nevertheless punishable by death.[93] The trick was apparently so common that it warranted state intervention. In 1737, acknowledging the "many frauds . . . committed by taking and joining Bills of a lower Denomination to those of a higher Denomination," the Massachusetts assembly banned the circulation of quarters and halves of bills as small change and ordered everyone with the pieces to bring them to the treasury "to be exchanged for the Value of the Parts of said Bills."[94]

Some swindlers erased the denominations on genuine bills of credit and either used matching ink to draw in higher amounts or pasted newspaper cutouts over the areas. In June 1742, Jacob Ebberman, a Germantown, Pennsylvania, butcher, was apprehended on suspicion of altering some small bills of New Jersey and Delaware into larger ones "and then passing them," only to escape from the local constable as he was being taken to the Philadelphia jail. The authorities offered five pounds as a reward to whoever took up and secured the butcher, who was wearing a linen jacket and pants, a felt hat, and a cinnamon brown wool coat when last seen.[95] Five years earlier in Massachusetts, Silas Church of Watertown, a cordwainer, was found with "one Twenty Shilling Bill . . . turned into a Five Pound Bill, tho' in a very bungling Manner, and Two counterfeit upper Quarters of a Twenty Shilling Bill on this Province, made with a Pen." The altering and patching was done "so wretched clumsily," the *Boston Evening-Post* quipped, that anyone who tried to pass them "deserves no small Punishment, [if] only for supposing there is any one so ignorant as not to discover the Cheat at the first View."[96] Like clipping coins, altering paper money was a small-scale fraud requiring little in the way of skills, resources, and collaborators, and in Massachusetts, at any rate, few were prosecuted for the act; only five of the nearly two hundred counterfeiting cases between 1734 and 1776 involved altering bills.[97]

Others got money by appealing to the colonial government to replace currency they claimed had been accidentally damaged or destroyed. In the fall of 1738, for example, the Plymouth, Massachusetts, mariner Theophilus Cotton successfully petitioned the assembly for paper money to replace a stack of cash that had supposedly met a fiery fate. According to Cotton, he forgot to remove a five-pound Rhode Island bill of credit and about six pounds in Massachusetts bills from his jacket pocket before giving the jacket to a young servant woman to be washed. He did not realize the mistake "'till by washing ye woman found something in ye Pocket wch. Upon search we found to be pieces of Bills of Credit . . . totally spoild & good for nothing." The servant, Jane Allen, told the authorities that by the time she realized there was paper in the pocket, it was "washt to pieces, which [she] flung down upon the Hearth & some of it went into the fire." She could not discern "what sort of paper it was . . . not being able to read, but heard Mr. Cotton & his Wife say that there was twelve Pence or one shilling upon one Piece of it." Three months later, Cotton received the full value of the Massachusetts bills out of the treasury; what thanks or payment Allen received for her extraordinary testimony is unknown.[98]

In every colony, men and women took matters into their own hands when they decided to enlarge the money supply in the shadow of the law. The possibilities for counterfeiting increased enormously with the spread of paper money in the first half of the eighteenth century, since the printing advancements that facilitated the mass production of bills of credit also made them easier to copy. Most counterfeiters printed bills from engraved copper plates they had procured from skilled metalworkers, but others adopted more primitive techniques, including, in at least one instance, drawing them entirely with a pencil.[99] Counterfeiting was thus a never-ending headache for colonial governments; some bills were so widely copied that assemblies had to recall and replace entire emissions. The forty-shilling and five-pound denominations of the Rhode Island bills of 1715 were recalled in 1726 and 1727, as were several denominations of the Pennsylvania emissions of 1723–24 due to British-made counterfeits. South Carolina reprinted £120,000 in paper bills in 1722 because "many had been counterfeited," while a Connecticut act of 1735 ordered the calling in and replacing of all prior emissions due to extensive counterfeiting.[100]

That genuine bills of credit were themselves often clumsily designed or sloppily printed complicated the discovery of false pieces. And the signatures that marked every bill, which were supposed to *deter* counterfeiting, were not always readily verifiable when the bills in question passed outside the issuing colony. When in 1724 the Massachusetts authorities suspected that the five-pound Connecticut bills in circulation were counterfeits, they sent a sample to Connecticut governor Gurdon Saltonstall. After the signers of the original bills examined the suspected counterfeit and were "not able to say anything as to the signing," there being not one true bill "either in the Treasury, or in the keeping of the signers," Saltonstall decided to send the printer, Timothy Green, to Boston with the plate. The governor was confident that a comparison between the suspected counterfeits and the plate would reveal them to be fakes, but "If need be, Mr Green is instructed to [print off] one or two Bills of the five pound plate, for better comparing the fals Bills with the true."[101] It is telling that not even the original bills' signers could discern a counterfeit without an authentic bill on hand. In 1729, New Jersey governor John Montgomerie wrote to the Board of Trade about a discrepancy between the government's expenditures and income, explaining that "by cancelling counterfeits in place of true Bills" accidentally, some genuine bills remained in circulation. Surely other colonies made the same mistake.[102] True bills were also readily worn, torn, and defaced, requiring officials to occasionally recall and exchange the tattered notes for new ones. As Montgomerie's predecessor, William Burnet, had written to the board justifying a new currency emission: "The constant use of these Bills in the Market, and among common People, had destroyed so many of them, that it was necessary in common Justice to find a way to exchange them when they were no longer fit to pass."[103]

South Carolina discovered counterfeit bills of credit in 1735, before apprehending one of the counterfeiters in Savannah, Georgia, along with "a Gang of Men of very vile Characters" the following year. The "gang," which included the counterfeiter's mother and other family members, had also been hiding stolen goods.[104] The spread of false bills forced Charles Town's more mercenary lenders to adopt creative approaches to payments. Joseph Wragg's firm, which held hundreds of mortgages of enslaved people, announced in the *South-Carolina Gazette* that "For the Ease of their Debtors, and to avoid [the firm's] being imposed on by counterfeit Money," he was "willing to take good Rice in Payment at the Market Price."[105] James Crockatt, a prosperous merchant who sold cloth, tea, sugar, and fine china from his Broad Street shop and had a reputation as a merciless creditor, promised to accept "Rice or Pitch at the Market price in payment at all times of the Year," as well as "Rangers, or Scout boat orders, on the publick Treasury, as ready Money." The orders had been paid out to rangers and scouts the colony had recruited to help settle the province of Georgia in 1733 and since circulated as currency.[106]

At a time when mercantile credit was increasingly seen as the exclusive domain of men, counterfeiting was a gender-inclusive pursuit. Mary Peck Butterworth of Rehoboth, Massachusetts, who led a counterfeiting ring out of her kitchen for seven years without being detected and produced upward of one thousand pounds in New England counterfeits, developed a method of forging currency that was ingenious in its simplicity. Whereas most counterfeiters made reproductions from imperfectly engraved plates, she used a hot iron and cloth to transfer the ink pattern from a genuine bill onto a piece of blank paper, after which she went over the letters with a crow quill pen, throwing the cloth into the fireplace when her work was finished and destroying the evidence. Unlike poor men and women who sometimes passed counterfeits unwittingly, Butterworth was not a marginal member of colonial society. Rather, like other women successful in trade, she created claims to credit through preexisting family networks and particularly through her marriage to John Butterworth Jr., a skilled housewright. Two of his carpenters also worked for Mary selling counterfeits. She drew on her family to expand her business, enlisting her four brothers and a sister-in-law to distribute the pieces. When the authorities finally caught up with the counterfeiters in August 1723, their main defense was to destroy the credibility of one of their own, a non–family member of the ring who had turned king's witness, and eventually the gang was acquitted.[107]

"Money-makers" also evaded punishment due to poorly guarded jails and a weak colonial state. Jailbreaks were a regular occurrence. Colonial jails regularly allowed visitors, which was how John Abbott, accused of counterfeiting the five-pound Rhode Island bills of credit, managed to escape from a Connecticut jail dressed in his wife's clothes. Together they had "got off his Fetters" and switched outfits, and when Abbott "call'd to the Keeper to let out his Wife; the Door being open'd, he came out with her Apparel, and went thro' a Room where was several Persons sitting, making them the usual Complements of a Women, and pass'd off undiscovered."[108] Another reason many counterfeiters eluded justice was jurisdictional: a significant volume of counterfeits was prepared in Britain and Ireland and brought into North America by sailors. Although the importers were sometimes caught red-handed and convicted, British counterfeiters of colonial currency operated with virtual impunity.[109]

Two cases from the 1730s reveal the cracks in the colonial legal system that helped counterfeiting flourish. In 1735, counterfeit Connecticut bills of credit found on a Rhode Island saddler were traced to John MacDonnell of Wells, who had procured the bills in Ireland several years earlier. He then transported them to Maine, where he delivered them to the blacksmith William Patten. In the fall of 1734, MacDonnell and Patten recruited William Mortimore of Boston or York and John Davis, a Boston sloop master, to take the bills and distribute them, which was how they arrived in the saddler's hands. Davis later testified that he had not used any of the bills himself, save one he spent in Rhode Island, and "all the others he tore in pieces at Sea." Nevertheless, he witnessed Mortimore, who was picked up by the authorities in a Boston pub, spend the bills all over New England. In the summer of 1736, a York County jury declared Patten not guilty of "Advising and Assisting" in counterfeiting the bills, but found MacDonnell guilty of "procuring to be Forg'd and Counterfeited" several Connecticut and New Hampshire bills. Two other men were indicted for "uttering," or passing, them but not tried due to a lack of evidence, and Mortimore broke jail and disappeared before his court date. MacDonnell pleaded his clergy—an English legal tradition dating to medieval times that allowed defendants convicted of capital crimes to escape execution—"and was therefore Sentenced . . . to be burnt in the Hand" and imprisoned for six months.[110]

In the second case, Robert Jenkins, a sailor from Salem, New Jersey, got from his cousin Peter Long the idea to have counterfeit bills of credit made in Britain. He departed for London in August 1739 and awaited instructions from Long on how to execute the scheme. That December he approached Abraham Ilive, a Southwark printer, who after initially agreeing to produce £3,100 in Pennsylvania, New Jersey, and Delaware counterfeits in exchange for five guineas, got cold feet and informed the local authorities. According to Ilive's testimony, Jenkins planned to age the false bills by placing them in a bag with shot and riding with them until they appeared "worn & soiled as though they had been in Trade ever since their date." On determining that Jenkins could not be prosecuted in London, however, the British secretary of state instructed Ilive to finish the job as if everything was normal and made him promise to "make some private mark . . . to distinguish them by from true ones," before informing the Pennsylvania and New Jersey governors of Jenkins's activities and anticipated arrival in New York City.[111] He disembarked in June 1740 from a ship where he was serving as a cook and was promptly apprehended along with a chest of paper bills and conveyed to Delaware, where he awaited trial.[112] On August 28, Philadelphia's *American Weekly Mercury* reported that Jenkins had been sentenced to death the week before "for aiding and assisting in Counterfeiting the Paper Money of that Government," but his final fate remains unknown.[113]

Counterfeiting Networks

Those who brought counterfeit bills of credit from across the Atlantic took advantage of the growing presence of other colonies' currencies—and the lack of local laws making it illegal to copy them—to try to pass counterfeits of one colony's currency within another's jurisdiction. Although single individuals could be successful counterfeiters, the most prolific money-makers had extensive networks of passers who carried the forgeries to distant settlements and other colonies. They relied on others to supply paper and ink or to hide the materials, and they enlisted experienced metalworkers who engraved plates for printing. Historian Katherine Smoak, who identified 102 gangs operating in British North America and the Caribbean, points out that counterfeiting brought together "marginal people" and "people of substance," so that it "helped to integrate people from across the social spectrum into an increasingly monetized economy." Like fencing secondhand clothing in unlicensed taverns, counterfeiting blurred the lines between legitimate and criminal activity, while forging important links between the growing Atlantic economy with its center in London and the "economy of makeshifts" that stretched into colonial hinterlands.[114]

Rhode Island bills of credit were some of the most extensively copied, and both genuine and counterfeit Rhode Island bills were widely accepted in Massachusetts, where the two colonies' currencies circulated on a par. In 1731, "*a Lover of his Country*" wrote in *Money the Sinews of Trade* that the times were so tough in Massachusetts "that for want of a sufficient Medium of our own to buy with, [Rhode Island's] is become as currant as ours, & will buy any thing on equal terms with our Province Bills."[115] But exchangeability had its limits. The problem was that only Massachusetts bills could be used to discharge the Massachusetts loan money. Thus Rhode Island traders demanded precious Massachusetts bills in payments and hoarded them "in order to make a prey of us," since they knew "that nothing but our Province Bills, will answer for Bonds and Mortgages made to the Government," leaving Massachusetts borrowers with no choice but to "go to *Rhode Island*, & give those people what advance they are pleased to ask, for our Province Bills to answer those Occasions."[116]

Rhode Island bills of credit were not only useless for making public payments in Massachusetts. They were also notorious for being counterfeited there. Boston merchant John Colman lamented that "so great is the Want of Money among us [that] We receive [Rhode Island's] ragged Bills, when we have all the Reason in the World to believe many of them Counterfeits."[117] In a 1735 speech to the assembly, Massachusetts governor Jonathan Belcher offered no solutions to the problem of money scarcity but lambasted the "many evil minded Persons among us who make a Business of counterfeiting the Bills of Credit" of the New England colonies, and begged the representatives "to do something further for putting a stop to this vile Practice."[118] It would be another four years before the assembly finally began prosecuting colonists for counterfeiting other colonies' bills. After receiving information in the summer of 1739 that "a Large Quantity" of counterfeit five-pound Rhode Island bills "now lye in the hands of a number of ill minded Persons who are attempting to put them off in payment," the assembly dispatched the Suffolk County sheriff to arrest the suspects, a trio of military officers, in York County.[119]

A counterfeiting ring, possibly the one that had supplied the bills to the officers, was broken up in Essex County later that year. In September 1739, the authorities arrested a colonist "who goes by several fictitious Names" and his companion, a free Black man, who had been "strolling about the Country" passing fake Rhode Island bills. When they questioned the Black man, he revealed "a Combination of Persons at Andover, and Parts adjacent, who have been concern'd in this Affair."[120] Within a week, several men had been "apprehended, examined and committed to Gaol, it appearing, upon strong Proof, that they have been concern'd in counterfeiting, or uttering" the five-pound bills.[121] One of the ringleaders, Joseph Parker of Andover, was quickly convicted and pleaded the clergy. Over the following year, five other men who may have belonged to the gang were found in possession of the counterfeits and arrested.[122] After Rhode Island governor William Wanton announced a £200 reward for the discovery of the plates, one Cornelius Thayer, having received information that Robert Gray of Andover "had in his keeping a Counterfeit Plate," took "great Pains" and "great Expence" to obtain it from Gray. But nearly three years later, Thayer had not received his reward and had to petition the Massachusetts assembly to represent his case to the Rhode Island government.[123] In 1745, Rhode Island stopped offering rewards to "discoverers in other colonies, a lack of cooperation between provinces which did much to encourage malefactors," explained the historian of counterfeiting Kenneth Scott.[124]

Even after the Andover gang's trials had ended, Rhode Island counterfeits kept cropping up. In a few instances, the signers of the original bills of credit testified at counterfeiting trials. But unless Massachusetts's neighbor was willing to recall and exchange the counterfeit bills, much less aid in the capture of money-makers operating beyond its borders, there was little the authorities could do. And even then, counterfeiting networks were so extensive, and demand for counterfeits so great, that a handful of convictions or the discovery of plates was often of no consequence. As historian John L. Brooke explains: "the spreading of counterfeits required a sophisticated gang structure; the engraver might sell his plates to a group of printers, who in turn might take into their scheme a number of passers. And there is some evidence that counterfeiters enjoyed widespread support in backcountry regions, where they may have provided the only available paper currency."[125] The colonial government grasped at straws. The summer after the York County officers were convicted, for example, the Boston justices of the peace issued a search warrant for Captain James Woodside, who had recently returned to town from England, and it was "suspected whether he may not have brought some such counterfeit Bills with him." Sheriff Edward Winslow searched Woodside's baggage, chests, and home "in all the suspected places" but found "nothing whereby I may suspect he has any counterfit Bills or any materialls" to make them.[126]

The Rhode Island government uncovered two major counterfeiting rings in early 1742, one headed by John Potter, a prominent South Kingston Quaker who had sat on the committee for signing the 1740 bills of credit (his signature on the counterfeits must have worked wonders for their credibility). The other gang, which had connections to Potter's, having obtained plates from the same engraver (goldsmith Obadiah Morse), initially operated out of Mendon, Massachusetts. It eventually grew to include Samuel Thompson, Benjamin Vorce, Samuel Hunt, Daniel Darling, and Stephen Ellis of Mendon; Henry Bosworth of New York; Israel Phillips, Seth Arnold, Samuel Staples, Daniel Comstock Jr., and Azariah Comstock (his brother) of Smithfield; Israel Arnold of Gloucester; Jacob Boyce and Moses Bartlett of Bellingham; and Joseph Boyce (Jacob's cousin) of Salem, who supplied or distributed the counterfeits.[127]

Benjamin Boyce Jr. of Mendon, whose family relation to Jacob and Joseph Boyce is unclear, was arrested on suspicion of passing bad money and implicated Joseph Boyce and a half-dozen others in the operation. According to Benjamin Boyce's testimony, Joseph Boyce had come to his house with several bundles of three-pound and forty-shilling Rhode Island bills of credit and given him a stack totaling "about fifteen pound." When Benjamin "asked [Joseph] how he came by that money he replied he knew where he could git enough of such but did not tell me plainly that it was counterfit but by his hint I did guess it was counterfit." Over the next several days, Benjamin Boyce gave five pounds to Moses Bartlett, used some of the money to purchase a bushel of salt from David Thayer of Mendon, put off forty shillings to "Theophilus Dotys wife in Smithfield," and gave two bills to his father. Meanwhile, he learned from a George or Job Keith that the gang was in possession of some plates and that Joseph Boyce and Stephen Ellis were headed to Cape Cod to print off or pass more fake bills. William Phillips was in Salem picking up an additional £500 in unsigned counterfeits.[128]

Before long, Benjamin Boyce was entrusted with carrying fifty pounds from Joseph Boyce and Robert Neal in Salem to Bartlett in Mendon. Later he saw Stephen Ellis give Benjamin Taft of Uxbridge two three-pound counterfeits in exchange for an authentic five-pound bill and heard Ellis tell Taft "to be carefull and not to pass [the counterfeits] any where there about he Replied he would take care & pass them far enough of[f] so that they should not be found." Similar to John Davis, the Boston sloop master who claimed to have passed a single counterfeit before tearing up the rest at sea, Benjamin Boyce said that he was "sorry for what I had done" and that he burnt his remaining supply "some time after." Sincere or not, his apology apparently made an impact. The Rhode Island justice of the peace who examined him wrote to the Massachusetts secretary that "The poor fellow seems to be deeply sencible of his error," adding "to my knowledge he was always accounted an honest man." When the authorities asked Boyce about the plates, he replied that "Robert Neal told me he Got sd. Plates in Ireland & got ye money struck there & brought it over with him." Unfortunately, the record of his examination ends there and it is unclear whether he intended to mislead his interrogators into thinking the counterfeits had come from Ireland.[129]

In the spring of 1742, after a Smithfield justice of the peace announced a reward of £50 a head for the capture of the money-makers, nine of the Mendon gang were apprehended. That the authorities had to rely on large rewards to entice informers at all underscores the weakness of colonial policing. Eight were tried, convicted, and sentenced to pay large fines or to stand in the pillory and have their ears cropped (nailed to the pillory and later torn or cut off).[130] By summer the authorities had discovered "Considerable Sums" of counterfeit bills, plates, ink, and "other Things necessary for carrying on the Business" in a barn in Lynn and arrested four more men, including Joseph Boyce, who was convicted and burnt on the hand.[131] In August, Robert Neal was apprehended for passing counterfeit Rhode Island bills of credit and confessed that "the said Bills were made and sign'd in London, and that he had brought over a Number with him, which were in a Box hid in a rocky Place, at Salem." Neal led the authorities to the box, wherein they found four plates and 800 sheets of unsigned Rhode Island and Connecticut bills totaling over £2,500, a "most seasonable Discovery," reported the *Boston News-Letter* on August 26.[132] If Benjamin Boyce's testimony is to be believed and Joseph Boyce and Robert Neal were working together, we are left with an elaborate picture of colonial counterfeiting where rings overlapped and intersected, so that it was not always clear where one ended and the next began.

While a dozen convictions over a single spring and summer may sound like a lot, the amount of people actually arrested for counterfeiting must have represented only a small percentage of those who made or passed bad money. Consider that in the first three-quarters of the eighteenth century, ninety-nine people were accused of counterfeiting or passing counterfeits in New York alone. Even fewer were put on trial, since some turned king's witness to avoid prosecution and some escaped from jail. In the same period, Rhode

Island had fifty-three convictions, seventeen acquittals, thirteen cases that grand juries declined to indict, seven jailbreaks, two cases of skipping bail, two cases in which the accused got off on legal technicalities, and one extradition to another colony. In Massachusetts between 1734 and 1775, 135 people were charged with counterfeiting coin or currency.[133] And a conviction was not necessarily a career-ender, as many condemned counterfeiters simply picked up and plied their trade elsewhere.

Such was the case of Joseph Boyce, who was implicated again in August 1744, this time by an old comrade who had been caught passing counterfeits, and confined to the Salem jail along with his longtime associate, John Scias of Durham, New Hampshire.[134] On the night of September 7, the pair broke out of the jail. The *Boston Evening-Post* described them as "good looking strong able bodied Men; *Boyce* wore his own Hair, which was short and black, *Syas* wears a Wig or Cap."[135] They made their way to New York undetected, where they set up shop in the "Oblong," a contested territory along the New York–Connecticut border, with Henry Bosworth of the old Mendon gang.

By the end of the summer, the governors of New Jersey, New York, and Connecticut were in communication about the operation. The New York council acted quickly, producing depositions from a number of people in the Oblong gang's orbit between October 1744 and March 1745. The evidence initially pointed to a Daniel Hunt of Dutchess County, whom several witnesses swore was involved in passing fake twenty-shilling and forty-shilling Rhode Island bills of credit in Connecticut and New York. One deponent claimed to have received the counterfeits from either Hunt or a Joseph Plummer in payment of an enslaved Black man.[136] When the Dutchess County justice of the peace Jacobus Swartout investigated the charges against Hunt in early April, however, at least twenty-one local residents refused to implicate him, and several others retracted accusations they had previously made against him.[137]

Then New York governor George Clinton received a letter from Massachusetts governor William Shirley revealing the identities of Boyce, Scias, and Bosworth. According to Shirley, based on information from a Robert Clark of Uxbridge, the three men, who had associates in Massachusetts and New York, "some of whom are persons of note," were "deeply concerned in making false Bills of Credit of the neighbouring Governments and passing the same in great parcells for valuable Effects," including, evidently, property in enslaved human beings. Shirley explained that Boyce and Scias were convicted counterfeiters and "repeating their Crimes were again apprehended" but escaped, and were wanted in Massachusetts.[138]

On May 9, Governor Clinton's council deposed Clark, who confirmed that Boyce and Scias were living in Dutchess County and declared that Scias had told him that he had "some plates of New York and Jersey Governments." He continued that one Israel Keith of New Sherburn had told him "that a great part of the people of Dutchess County about ye Oblong were concerned in making or passing ye counterfeit money & it would be very difficult to get them all away & bring them to justice."[139] In another statement Clark implicated Joseph Verry of Salem and explained that "Verry, Scious, & Boyce & their Gang" had cheated him out of money and tried to repay him in counterfeits, before convincing him to join the operation as a passer. He reiterated that Verry, Scias, and Boyce spread their counterfeits far and wide by "constantly send[ing] out their emissaries" to distant places "purchas[ing] therewith Horses Cattle & [other] things of worth to a great Value." Whether Clark went to the authorities to escape prosecution or whether he informed on the gang out of revenge is unclear. Either way, his testimony is illustrative of the elaborate networks money-makers used to disperse bad money, in this case involving perhaps a majority of the county's settlers.[140]

Governor Clinton issued arrest warrants for Scias and Boyce, but it was Connecticut officials who surprised the gang just over the colony's border with New York "in ye Very act of using ye Counterfeit plates," in the middle of a marsh no less, and transported Boyce, his father, and one Hurlburt to the Newhaven jail.[141] After extracting a confession and the names of twenty-two collaborators from Hurlburt, Connecticut governor Jonathan Law wrote to Clinton that he was unsure whether the counterfeiters could be tried there or "whether they shall be sent for Trial in your Courts."[142] When Boyce and Hurlburt escaped from the jail sometime between mid-July and late August, Law asked the Rhode Island government to aid in their recapture by offering a reward to whoever discovered them, but the assembly dismissed the request and instead suggested that the costs of prosecuting counterfeiters ought to be defrayed by the colony where the crime took place.[143] Certainly, ambiguity around where counterfeiters could be tried and a lack of cooperation between colonies could impede colonial governments' efforts to convict counterfeiters. Community members' reluctance to implicate money-makers, and the large numbers of people involved in their operations from across the social spectrum, whether as passers or as beneficiaries of increased economic activity, suggests that counterfeiters enjoyed broad support.

To Counterfeit Is Death?

As much as a lack of secure jails, the jurisdictional patchwork of early America, and elaborate forging networks provided escape hatches for counterfeiters, money-makers evaded punishment because popular opinion was on their side. Like the pirates of the late seventeenth and early eighteenth centuries who brought gold, calico, and captives to underserved markets, counterfeiters served an indispensable economic function: providing cash in a cash-poor environment. Perhaps tens if not hundreds of thousands of counterfeit bills were produced in the first half of the eighteenth century, and more never made their way into circulation. But if colonists recognized pirates' brutal tactics, they appreciated counterfeiters' relatively bloodless, if not always victimless, efforts to alleviate money scarcity in their communities. Those who relied on the circulation of small-denomination bills of credit for their survival were especially grateful to get cash to purchase their necessities, whether it was authentic or not. Popular indifference to the illegality of counterfeiting was thus closely related to the role paper money had come to play in everyday life. At a time when personal interactions influenced market transactions, paper bills offered possibilities for more marginal members of colonial society to partake economically, improve their material conditions, and potentially alter their social status.[144]

Unlike pirates, however, accused counterfeiters were entitled to a trial by jury, and juries sitting on counterfeiting cases routinely returned verdicts of not guilty. The burden of proof was high. Hard evidence such as plates was well hidden—in barns, in caves, on boats, and in at least one case on "an Island in the Middle of a great Marsh"—and most counterfeiters used large networks of passers to put bad money into circulation.[145] Members of counterfeiting rings often made verbal or written covenants not to betray each other, so that unless one or more members of a ring turned king's witness, a conviction was unlikely. Evidence or not, juries often refused to give guilty verdicts in death penalty cases, and also when many of those tried were poor people who had sometimes passed counterfeited bills of credit unknowingly. In felony cases, juries usually withheld convictions unless there was an understanding that the defendant would be permitted to plead his clergy.[146] Recall John MacDonnell of Wells, Maine, who "prayed the Benefit of the Clergy" and escaped the death sentence.[147] Some money-makers were acquitted on legal technicalities, such as a misspelled name in an indictment, while others were charged with uttering counterfeits, which was made punishable by death in Britain but considered a lesser crime in the colonies.[148]

Punishments for counterfeiting varied from colony to colony as much as the currencies themselves. Consider that New York made counterfeiting paper money punishable by death without benefit of the clergy in 1709, whereas a Connecticut act of 1710 only required convicted counterfeiters to pay a fine and serve six months of prison time.[149] North Carolina made counterfeiting a capital crime in 1714, followed by South Carolina in 1722, Massachusetts in 1736, New Hampshire in 1738, Pennsylvania in 1739, Rhode Island in 1751, Maryland in 1754, and Virginia in 1755. But legal standardization did not translate to more executions or even more convictions. When two men confessed to counterfeiting the Massachusetts currency and were sentenced to hang, "most of the Gentlewomen" of Boston addressed the governor "with Prayers and Tears" for their lives, "whereupon his Excellency was pleased to pardon them."[150] There were no executions for counterfeiting bills of credit in Massachusetts, and no executions for counterfeiting bills until 1756 in New York and 1770 in Pennsylvania, and the New York execution had to be postponed because the authorities could not find anyone willing to serve as a hangman and then again because the gallows were cut down "by Persons unknown."[151] When New York executed another counterfeiter in 1762, Lieutenant Governor Cadwallader Colden had to summon the soldiers from Fort George to prevent a crowd from freeing the prisoner.[152]

A frequent refrain of colonial newspapers was that given juries' reluctance to convict in felony cases, counterfeiting laws were arguably less effective when the punishment was death. In October 1742, Thomas Fleet's *Boston Evening Post* reported on the recent sentencing of two Connecticut money-makers who were to be branded, cropped, and imprisoned for life. "If some *moderate* Punishment were to be inflicted on such Offenders in [Massachusetts]," the *Post* contemplated, "'tis tho't we should soon exceed any of our Neighbours in Convictions."[153] John Draper's *Boston News-Letter* reckoned that the answer lay outside the justice system altogether. Perturbed that "the Penalty of Death it self will not deter Persons from the wicked Practice," the *News-Letter* proposed changing the way bills of credit were produced, suggesting making stronger paper and using molds "with several Devices" to protect against counterfeiting.[154] If laws and punishments could not stop counterfeiters, then perhaps better technology would.

In Philadelphia, Benjamin Franklin was already working on a safeguard against copying the Pennsylvania bills of credit that he had been printing for the colonial government since 1729. With his friend, botanist and fellow member of the Junto philosophical club Joseph Breintnall, Franklin developed of method of double-casting leaves, an early experiment in stereotyping whereby a single leaf was cast to create a plaster mold that was in turn cast in metal for mass production. "The leaves were good counterfeit protection," explains the art historian Jennifer Roberts, "because the quality of line made by the venation was too soft, subtle, and variable to be made by hand with engraving tools, and the randomness built into the reticulated structure was difficult to manufacture artificially."[155]

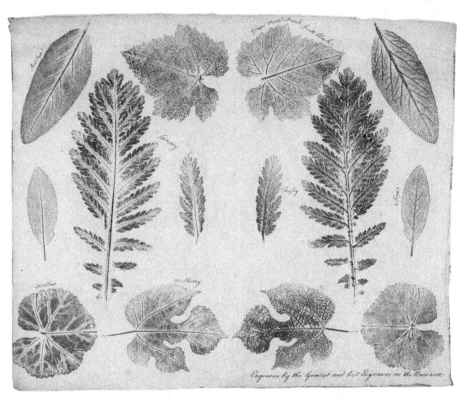

FIGURE 6.1. Joseph Breintnall, Nature prints of leaves, 1746. Courtesy Library Company of Philadelphia. https://digital.librarycompany.org/islandora/object/digitool%3A37954.

While scholars have long been interested in Franklin's leaf prints as a counterfeit detection device, recent research by scientists reveals that he incorporated a whole range of security features, including special ink made from graphite and paper with colored silk fibers and muscovite crystals.[156] Ironically, although these features would have made it easier for the authorities to detect counterfeits—and although the bills confidently bore the message "To counterfeit is Death"—Pennsylvania bills of credit were among the most copied in the colonies precisely because they enjoyed people's trust. Notices of counterfeits appeared in Franklin's own *Pennsylvania Gazette* with increasing regularity in the 1740s and 1750s, including some brought from Germany, and still the currency kept up its value.[157]

Try as they did, the authorities struggled to propagate the idea that counterfeiting bills of credit merited harsh punishment when it violated none of the principal tenets of Christian morality. Colonial governors called the

FIGURE 6.2. New Jersey twelve-shilling bill of credit, 1756 (reverse). The bill has a nature print of a leaf and a warning against counterfeiting. The printer, James Parker, worked for Benjamin Franklin before serving as the official printer of New Jersey. Franklin trained Parker and other colonial printers in nature printing techniques. 0000.999.29767. Courtesy American Numismatic Society. http://numismatics.org/collection/0000.999.29767.

practice "vile," "villainous," "wicked," and "detestable" in printed proclamations and speeches to assemblies. Pennsylvania lieutenant governor Patrick Gordon likened it "to the Poisoning the Waters of a Country; the blackest, and most detestable Practice that is known."[158] Making counterfeiting a felony without benefit of clergy seemed like a reasonable way to establish its depravity, but it was difficult to communicate to colonists that forging bills constituted a sin against God and mankind simply because the law said it was so. At a time when financial credibility increasingly pivoted on visible markers of status, such as polite behavior and fine clothing, colonial governments instead worked with newspaper printers to cultivate a negative stereotype of counterfeiters as confidence men bent on disturbing peaceful exchange and inciting public disorder.[159]

Con artists took advantage of the increasing fluidity of trade and markets to masquerade as respectable gentlemen and put off bad money. Early America's most famous swindler, Tom Bell, adopted the manners of genteel masculinity when he "pretended to be a Son of Mr. Levingston's in New-York." Bell spent several years traveling "from Colony to Colony," adopting various personas, and feigning connections with "all Persons of Note."[160] A skilled confidence man, Bell had performed gentility, built trust, and used that trust to pass false representations of value that could circulate beyond personal connections.[161]

Other counterfeiters, though, assumed more humble identities. On May 18, 1738, the *Pennsylvania Gazette* warned that "*an* Irish *Man, pretending to be a Pedlar*" had given several counterfeit five-shilling Pennsylvania bills of credit in Burlington County, New Jersey, "*in Payment for Buck-skins and other Things.*"[162] Just a few weeks later, the *Gazette* printed "A *Caution* to the *Paper-Money* Colonies To *beware of one* Joshua Dean, *who having been convicted of counterfeiting the Paper Stamps at Home, has been transported to the Plantations for Life.*" Dean had run away from his master, Alexander Spotswood of Virginia, the previous summer, and the authorities feared that he would injure the public by counterfeiting coin or paper money. The notice described him as "*a very sly artful Fellow, discourses well upon most Subjects of the Mechanicks, and is a Jack of all Trades*" and offered forty shillings sterling to whoever secured him and returned him to Virginia.[163]

The *Gazette* and other colonial newspapers made examples of the few money-makers who got caught. Punishments for counterfeiting were public in nature, exponentially so when the punishments circulated in newspapers as mutually recognizable "printed artifacts."[164] Convicted counterfeiters were often placed in a pillory and whipped; some had their ears cropped, while others were branded on the forehead or hand with a hot iron. Sometimes the culprits themselves circulated around town. On December 26, 1727, Andrew Bradford's *American Weekly Mercury* reported that David Wallace and David Wilson, two men convicted of passing counterfeit New Jersey bills of credit that Wallace had procured from an Irish money-maker, were to be "placed in a Cart" and paraded through the streets of greater New York City "with Halters about their Necks," getting lashes at stops in Brooklyn, Queens, and Westchester.[165] Anthony Adamson and William Scot, who were found guilty of counterfeiting and uttering New Jersey bills two years later, received a similar sentence in northern New Jersey, save that each man was to be carted from town to town wearing "a Paper fixed on your Back and Breast, declaring your Offence, with one of the Counterfeit Bills fixed thereto."[166] Unlike fines or jail time, convicted men getting carted and lashed about town served to maximize public awareness of the counterfeits and the wrongdoers—and to wreck the credibility of both.[167]

Money and Mentalities

At a time of growing pushback from British officials and merchants against colonial paper money practices, newspaper accounts of counterfeiters being pilloried, whipped, and cropped served to make colonial monetary authority legible to the public. As legal scholar Steven Wilf argues, law in early America was an imaginative discourse of the public sphere that included "punishment as a symbolic language." Punishments not only penalized criminals in real time but, by virtue of their often physical violence, turned punished criminals into "representational objects" that articulated political meaning.[168] According to the literary scholar Kristin Boudreau, moreover, early American criminal narratives functioned to promote law and order and to reflect and police public sensibilities; by placing counterfeiters on a par with convicted murderers and other violent persons, publishers sought to render monetary crime, like crimes against property, as commensurate with murder and assault. In doing so, by inscribing retribution onto counterfeiters' own bodies, they simultaneously reinscribed colonial governments' authority over money matters at a time when their ability to supply a sufficient currency was in doubt.[169]

But the same accounts reveal conflicting mentalities among elites and commoners. On January 4, 1733, the *Pennsylvania Gazette* published news of a "hog-seller" who had attempted to pass a "a new Twenty Shilling Bill" at the Indian Prince Tavern in Philadelphia. The tavernkeeper, "suspecting it to be a Counterfeit," immediately took the bill to loan office trustee Andrew Hamilton, who promptly apprehended the man. He claimed to have received the money in exchange for some pigs, but when the authorities searched his lodgings, they encountered his sister and "found in her Pocket" twenty-three more counterfeits. "Finding the Story of the Hogs would not answer," the man confessed that a Joseph Watt had given him the bills, having gotten them from "one *Grindal*" by way of Ireland. He continued that Watt had promised him a share of the profits, "telling him, to persuade him to it, that it was no Sin, for it would make Money plentier among Poor People." The next day colonial officials found Watt and "committed [him] to Prison, to keep company with his Friend the Pork-seller, who it seems," the *Gazette* smirked, "has *brought his Hogs to a fine Market*."[170] But when Watt "receiv'd part of his Punishment, being whipt, pilloried, and cropt" a few weeks later, "he behaved so as to touch the Compassion of the Mob, and they did not fling at him (as was expected) neither Snow-balls nor any Thing else."[171] Like the story of the Boston "gentlewomen" who pleaded with "tears" for the lives of two counterfeiters sentenced to hang, the tale of Watt touching the crowd's "compassion" must have provoked more sympathy than outrage.

According to John Brooke, borrowing from the historian Eric Hobsbawm, "'money-making' could have connotations of 'social banditry.'" While there were gentlemen counterfeiters like John Potter, and middling money-makers like Mary Butterworth, many counterfeiters and many more passers came from the margins of colonial society. Among the forty-one people accused of counterfeiting in Essex County, Massachusetts, between 1738 and 1745, one was a gentleman, two were doctors, five were farmers, nineteen were tradesmen, and six were laborers.[172] As Brooke illustrates, moreover, numerous Essex County money-makers had ties to the radical sectarianism of the English Revolution, the same milieu that had inspired the alchemical experiments and credit currency proposals of Samuel Hartlib, William Potter, and their correspondents in the colonies, discussed in chapter 4. Both the Andover and Oblong gangs had members with Quaker roots, and Quakers were among the local inhabitants of the Oblong who had vouched for Daniel Hunt. Counterfeiting was itself a kind alchemy, and "counterfeiters drew upon a wide knowledge of chemistry and metallurgy intersecting with the old alchemical tradition."[173]

Most counterfeiting gangs incorporated people from different social backgrounds, from skilled craftsmen and yeomen farmers to Irish mariners and London convicts. Such cross-class collaboration may have enhanced the counterfeits' acceptability, even authenticity. But that did not mean the profits were evenly distributed, since race and power could influence labor negotiations. An enslaved Black man named Zadock was promised his freedom for his role in breaking his enslaver, who led a Connecticut counterfeiting ring,

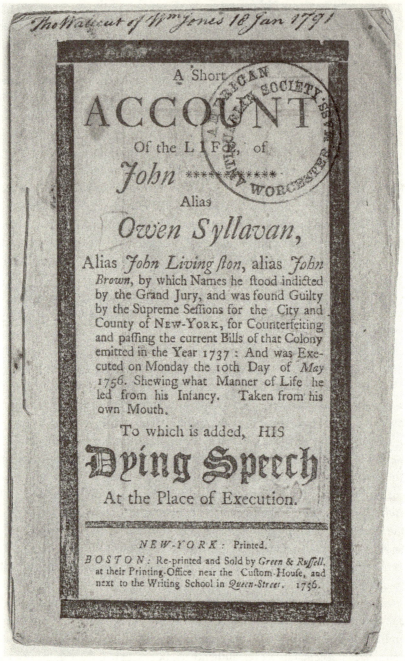

FIGURE 6.3. Title page of *A Short Account of the Life, of John ********* Alias Owen Syllavan* (Boston, 1756). John Sullivan was the first counterfeiter of paper money to be executed in New York. His execution had to be postponed several times because the authorities could not find a willing hangman. Courtesy American Antiquarian Society.

out of the New Haven jail. But when the authorities caught up with the gang, Zadock received twenty lashes and was taken away, it seems, with the rest of the counterfeiter's property.[174]

Engravers commanded the largest cost up front. Connecticut goldsmith Obadiah Mors demanded £100 in exchange for producing a plate for the Mendon gang.[175] Robert Jenkins paid London printer Abraham Ilive five guineas (a little over five pounds) for printing counterfeit Pennsylvania, New Jersey, and Delaware bills, while David Wallace paid Thomas Morough of Dublin "about Ten Pounds for his share of the Printing and Signing the said Counterfeit Bills, and was to pay him something more when he came over."[176] At least some laborers and suppliers received compensation in counterfeits, and passers a share of what they passed.[177] Wallace employed David Wilson to put off Morough's counterfeits, "for which he was to have Four or Five Shillings in the Pound."[178] Joseph Watt gave the "pork-seller" twenty-seven counterfeit twenty-shilling Pennsylvania bills, "of which he was to have a Share for himself."[179]

Women counterfeiters went to great lengths to aid and protect male comrades. Mothers, wives, and sisters passed bad money, broke their male family members out of jail, and destroyed evidence. Famed counterfeiter Owen Sullivan's organization had at least two members "of the *Fair Sex*," while moneymaker Daniel Lewis's sister, "Miss Polly," was said to have "distributed the ink upon the plates when the impression was struck."[180] Women were valuable additions to counterfeiting rings because they were rarely prosecuted. And even when they were, the authorities showed them relative leniency.[181] This was not, however, the fate of Ann Lockwood of Connecticut, convicted of altering a Rhode Island bill of credit to pay for some wool and sentenced in 1717 to three days in the pillory plus court costs, or of Catherine Johnson of New York City, tried and convicted in 1735 of passing ten-shilling New York counterfeits and punished with twenty-one lashes. Johnson's husband, the maker of the false bills, had fled to Philadelphia and disappeared, forsaking his wife and young son, whom the authorities ordered apprenticed to the printer William Bradford following Johnson's arraignment. Thereafter, Catherine may have made her living in the informal economy; she would be convicted in 1766 of stealing some cloth and again in 1773 of keeping a disorderly house.[182]

If likening counterfeiters to social bandits is overstating the case, historians of eighteenth-century Britain and the Atlantic world have shown that money-makers enjoyed widespread support at a time of growing popular enthrallment with pirates, highway robbers, and confidence men. Such was the case of the Yorkshire coiners in the 1760s and 1770s, when the region suffered an acute money shortage caused by a slump in the textile trade, and of the Rhode Island traders who sent counterfeit coins to Jamaica, where specie scarcity and malleable ideas about money made counterfeits an uncontroversial facet of everyday life.[183] In early eighteenth-century Philadelphia, support for counterfeiters reflected a "plebeian value system in which social and economic relations were viewed in both moral and utilitarian terms," argues the historian Daniel Johnson. "If governing authorities failed to provide a sufficient amount of money, local commoners seemed to believe an unofficial form of currency would have to suffice."[184] Throughout the British Atlantic world, both the failure of officials to supply a circulating medium and plebeian ideas of legality shaped general sympathy toward counterfeiting coin and currency alike.[185]

At a time of social and economic transformation, thieves and counterfeiters worked early America's chaotic monetary landscape to their advantage. While scholars have sometimes described their activities in terms of the historian E. P. Thompson's concept of a "moral economy" based on customary rights to subsistence and community consensus around marketing practices, theft and counterfeiting were constitutive of, not antithetical to, the growing world of trade and markets.[186] Nor were the moral economy and the market economy mutually exclusive. Poor and enslaved participants in theft or counterfeiting rings may have understood their actions as resistance to poverty, wage labor, slavery, and commodification. But they were also meeting a demand, using informal and illicit means to infiltrate the formal economy and enlivening it in the process. They not only resisted and challenged the market economy but, in doing so, also helped substantiate it. Like a leg of a three-legged stool, if the authorities had kicked theft and counterfeiting out completely, the whole economic structure might well have crashed to the floor. Counterfeiting was thus equal parts necessary and dangerous in terms of social control. While thieves redistributed goods and money already in existence, money-makers injected new value into the economic realm. More than merely redistributive, their activities were as generative as real money itself was.

7

From Currency to Coin

Jonathan Belcher had a money problem. Shortly after taking office in September 1730, the Massachusetts governor warned the assembly that the Crown had instructed him to limit annual currency issues to a lean £30,000 and to redeem all outstanding bills of credit—an estimated £335,000—by 1741, after which the colony was to "return" to the fixed metallic standard envisioned by Queen Anne's 1704 Proclamation. Evidently, it was punishment for "the miserable State" of the colony's bills, "how much Publick Credit has sunk, and the Value of Every Mans Estate depreciated," which had placed "the Merchants of Great-Britain trading hither under great discouragements."[1]

Belcher's dilemma was that he faced an assembly that had no intention of giving up its power to make money without a fight. Elisha Cooke Jr.'s "popular party" sprang into action, taking up the governor's instructions in addresses to the king and the Parliament. Massachusetts secretary Josiah Willard was not particularly optimistic about the outcome. "The Affairs of the next Genll. Assembly will, I suppose, be full as much embarrass'd as those of the last," he wrote on May 8, 1732, to his stepson in London. "For although we are very Sanguine about the good Success of our Address to His Majesty . . . the next Measures to be used are to apply to the Parliamt. & in the mean Time to leave the Treasury empty. 'tis not easy to tell all the ill Consequences wch. Will attend such Resolution, but no rational impartial Man can do otherwise than foresee some very pernicious Effects of it."[2] The following summer, both the Privy Council and the House of Commons informed Belcher that they would not be entertaining the representatives' "frivolous and groundless" grievances.[3] The assembly avoided a fiscal crunch by issuing £76,500 in new bills of credit that October, a sum Belcher had to justify to the Board of Trade as being for a period encompassing twenty-two months when "no bills were emitted."[4]

The British government's rebuff hardened the popular party's resolve to resist Belcher's instructions, but it reinvigorated hard-money men's struggle to resume specie payments. And for the next two decades, Massachusetts colonists faced an uncertain monetary path. While the hard-money men would ultimately prevail, with some help from the Crown and Parliament along the way, the road from currency back to coin was rocky. Not even the harshest critics of paper money wanted the colony to lose its whole circulating medium. For John Colman and the land bankers, meanwhile, the royal instructions offered an opportunity to finally get their scheme off the ground, short-lived though it was. When the last bill of credit was redeemed in 1750, for most colonists the results would be all but ruinous.

The Money Question and the Labor Question

At least Belcher appeared sympathetic. He suspected that the colony's monetary mess had more to do with its worsening trade and payments balance with Britain than with the overissue of paper currency. It was a problem of flagging productivity, in other words. If the assembly would only put its energies into producing import substitutes such as "Hemp, Flax, and other Naval Stores," then the balance would be improved, the exchange rate would stabilize, and the London merchants would be mollified.[5] But all of that would be difficult given Britain's latest efforts to regulate the New England economy. While lobbyists were successfully campaigning for the liberalization of South Carolina commerce discussed in chapter 5, policymakers advocated for mercantilist regulation of New England trade and manufacturing, resulting in the Hat Act of 1732, which imposed heavy duties on colonial products, and the Molasses Act of 1733, which sought to proscribe Massachusetts's profitable business with the French and Dutch sugar islands.[6]

These acts may have been retaliation for the assembly's refusal to fix previous governors' salaries. In the spring of 1729, English dissenting minister Daniel Neal warned Thomas Foxcroft of Boston's First Church that if the assembly continued down its defiant path, the king would "find a way, & means by his Parliament here, to touch you in the most sensible parts of your Trade and Commerce; something of which, If I am not misinformed, is already upon the Anvil."[7] Another Englishman argued that the Molasses Act was a necessary check on the colony's growing economic power, which nearly exceeded that of "her Mother Country in Navigation and the Fishery."[8]

Other commentators argued that colonial industry and free access to foreign markets benefited the metropole. Writing in 1731, British essayist Fayr Hall estimated that the New England fisheries produced 230,000 quintals (or hundredweights) of dried fish annually for a net profit of £130,000 sterling, "every Penny" of which was transmitted to Britain in exchange for finished products such as "Woollen, Iron-Work, Lead-Shot and Lead, with all Manner of wearing Apparel, Houshould-Goods, &c." New England merchants sent the fish along with "Provisions of all Sorts" to South Carolina and Barbados, and sold the rest to the French and Dutch islands in exchange for cheap molasses and rum. Restrict the trade with foreign markets, Hall cautioned, and risk suppressing colonial demand for British goods.[9]

The Massachusetts fisheries figured prominently in paper money advocates' vision of political economy based on local monetary autonomy within Britain's capitalist empire. Britain depended on the colonial fisheries, but the fisheries depended on foreign markets—and paper money. According to the author of "A Modest Apology for Paper Money," published in Boston's *Weekly Rehearsal* on March 18, 1734, "we can't carry on the Fishery and other Business without some Currency" for paying resident fishermen, salters, and shoremen and for purchasing food and supplies from local retailers. "We must without *Paper Money* have all lived poorer, and sent less Fish and other Things abroad, and *Silver* to *England*, and received less of their Woollen and other Manufactures . . . 'tis certainly their Interest to encourage us in our Plantation Trade, that we may pay them for what we can consume, and for that End to suffer or rather to necessitate us, to have chiefly a *Paper Currency* among our selves."[10]

Both the Molasses Act and the currency restrictions put the thousands of men employed in New England shipping—"a great Nursery of Seamen for his Majesty's Navy," as one author later described it—in a precarious position.[11] Massachusetts's offshore fishery had attracted hundreds of fishermen and their families to Essex County, swelling the waterfront population to nearly four thousand by 1725.[12] When the Newfoundland fishery rebounded and cod prices fell in the 1730s, moreover, colonial merchants stopped extending long-term credit with no interest to quasi-independent fishermen whose obligations had begun to outweigh their catches. Some merchants dragged their fishermen debtors to court to seek remuneration for inflation or to convert old book debts into written instruments payable in silver.[13] Merchants with sufficient capital began investing in their own vessels and redirected their energies to the offshore fishery, dispatching ships manned by servants or hired hands drawn from the colony's booming maritime population.

As fishing profits flowed to successful merchants like John Higginson and William Pickering of Salem, the average fisherman made little headway in accumulating personal wealth. He inherited his father's house or rose to be a skipper at best, and teetered on the edge of subsistence at worst, forced into class dependency and subjected to brutal ship discipline. Economic transformation spurred urbanization and simultaneously increased inequality. In Marblehead, once a humble fishing village, the richest tenth of the population controlled more than half of the wealth, while the poorest third held less than 2 percent of the wealth by 1725.[14] Many fishermen found themselves out of work in the 1730s, prompting town leaders to petition the assembly in 1734 for a tract of land for settling unemployed fishermen. Two years later, the local Anglican minister reported "that no less than 300 families have been forced to seek shelter and subsistence elsewhere."[15]

While they could have attributed local fishermen's plight to the growing consolidation of wealth or the shift from dependency to wage labor, paper money advocates fixated on the problem of money scarcity. It was no different for the fisherman than it was for the farmer or day laborer. "If Money be scarce, the Difficulty of exchanging the Produce of his Labour will keep him low and back," the author of "A Modest Apology for Paper Money" wrote, "but if there be a reasonable Plenty of any Currency . . . he could the more easily support himself by his Labour in a comfortable Manner," because there would be more work available at higher wages, paid in the circulating medium.[16] When "poor Men can get Money for their Labour," another essayist pointed out two years later, they "have it in their Power to lay it out where they can be best used."[17]

According to paper money partisans, an abundant supply of currency would ensure that all of the colony's resources were being used productively and guarantee sufficient demand for British manufactures. "If Money were Plenty," argued John Colman in his 1737 proposal for a bank of credit, "many more People" would produce import substitutes such as hemp and flax, "so that in a few Years we should raise so much of those Commodities, that we should not want any supply of them from abroad," leaving more money for British goods, "but such Things can't be carried on without money."[18] As for the propertyless laborers without their own land to till, Ipswich minister John Wise suggested that the colonial government hire them to raise schools, colleges, and other public buildings, and pay their wages in cash, since "The common or ordinary demand for Labour is not sufficient to prevent the prevailing of Idleness," and "Men will work for Money, when they won't work for other Species."[19]

Plenty of laborers had, in fact, been forced to work for "shop notes"—certificates permitting the holder to demand goods in the future—in lieu of cash. In addition to having to spend the notes on things they neither needed nor wanted, by the time the laborers brought them to the shops, the notes were often so discounted that the laborers could not purchase what they might have obtained for the same nominal amount in money.[20] As early as

1720, Colman lamented that householders were "obliged to Work for half, nay, some for two thirds Goods." And "what will they do when it comes to working for all Goods," he wondered. "Is it possible for Men to Truck for a Pound of Butter, a Pound of Candles, or a Loaf of Bread, or many other things a Family is Daily in need of. No? it is impossible."[21] William Douglass, a Boston physician and harsh critic of paper money, observed in 1740 that some retailers charged "25 per Cent. or more Advance above the Money Price" when dealing in shop notes instead of cash.[22] An inadequate medium of exchange underscored the paradox of "free" labor in a market economy: since no one in New England was self-sufficient, money scarcity created particular difficulties for the producing classes. While laborers were forced to accept notes on shops, farmers endured complex calculations to receive the full value of the produce they offered in payment for goods from the same shops.[23]

This arduous and unfair system, Boston merchant Hugh Vans warned, threatened to chase away hardworking craftsmen, laborers, and farmers to other parts of British North America, "where they have Money of one Sort or other to receive for their Labour." Since the notes had to be spent on store goods at marked-up prices, moreover, they fueled "an excessive Importation of *European* Goods," worsening the province's trade and payments balance with Britain and raising the sterling exchange rate.[24] Some critics of the practice appeared less worried about laboring lives and more concerned that the notes "exposed the inhabitants to appear in extravagant garbs," which according to the critics such laboring men and women would "gladly avoid ... were they to receive money" instead.[25] For the laborers' part, on February 19, 1741, the *Boston News-Letter* published a declaration from the town's caulkers that they had toiled for many years "amid great inconvenience and had suffered much damage, wrong and injury, in receiving pay for their work by notes on shops for money or goods; and thereby have greatly impoverished themselves and Families."[26]

Early American money was enmeshed within matrices of power in which the mere possession of it could command dependence. And when money was scarce, control over capital and credit influenced the terms of trade. Thus a large merchant with diverse stocks "is very much in his power to set the price of his Chap-mans Goods as well as his own," noted one author in 1731.[27] In times of money scarcity, another commentator observed five years later, "a few rich Men" monopolized the supply, pushing up produce prices, "until a lucky Opportunity offers it self for them to make their Market with on their poor Neighbours."[28] Vans maintained that without cash there "must be *long Credit, excessive Usury* and *Extortion*."[29] Even in relatively egalitarian Worcester County, where land was widely allocated, differential access to money and credit, one historian wrote, "formed a key source of gentry power."[30] Colonial elites nevertheless scoffed at the notion that the wealthy—or the state, for that matter—could determine prices. In May 1737, two months after 500 men and boys hacked apart the public market to supply themselves with firewood and pulled down "Several butcher's Shops" to protest the high price of meat, Benjamin Colman of Boston's Brattle Street Church complained to London merchant Samuel Holden that there was "murmuring against the Government & the rich People among us . . . as if they could (By any means within their Power, besides prayer) have prevented ye Rise [in price] of Provisions."[31]

Surely, though, Colman and his ilk could not ignore that inflationary pressures were pushing laboring lives to the brink of crisis. In the mid-1730s, for example, most of the men and women who did jobs for George Minot, a wealthy Boston merchant, made between four shillings and ten shillings depending on the task—four shillings for sweeping the chimney, four to eight shillings for a month's laundry, five shillings for fixing a pair of shoes, five shillings for gardening, and ten shillings for locksmith services. It was barely enough to feed a family for a day.[32] And real wages were not merely stagnating but declining. The average fisherman had been making between two pounds and three pounds per month since the end of Queen Anne's War in 1713, and would not see a raise until war broke out again in the 1740s. William Douglass estimated that a carpenter who made five shillings "all Cash" when bills circulated on a par with sterling in the 1710s made twelve shillings in 1740 "equal to 3 s. 4 d. of former Times."[33]

It was becoming increasingly apparent, besides, that if Governor Belcher followed his instruction to retire all outstanding bills of credit by 1741, a disaster of untold magnitude was in store. In October 1739, the assembly cautioned the governor that removing the bills from circulation "would bring on the greatest Oppression on Multitudes, Stagnation of our Trade, and the terrible Consequences of publick Confusion."[34] The following month Benjamin Colman warned the colonial agent, Francis Wilks, that "no Governor will ever be able to sit in the Chair here; nor can the safety of the Province, nor that of our Merchandize either, be provided for; unless the King pleased to ease us of his Instruction about the Emission of Moneys."[35] Money scarcity was not a problem just of the laboring classes; since paper currency was the assembly's preferred (if not sole) means of supporting and defending the province, its disappearance would resonate from the governor's seat to the Houses of Parliament and beyond.

Raising the taxes necessary to redeem the outstanding bills of credit would be a daunting task indeed. In April 1736, a full five years before the bills were to be retired, the Boston Town Meeting informed its representatives that "the Distressing Circumstances of the Province" made following the royal instructions "altogether Impracticable, if not Impossible."[36] Certainly, the 1730s slump had chipped away at the tax base and driven up poor relief expenditures. Boston's tax assessors forgave hundreds of penniless householders their tax debts in 1737 alone. Two years earlier the town had begun construction on a new workhouse to sequester and exploit the expanding ranks of the able-bodied poor, who would be put to work picking oakum.[37] Even men of means were cash poor, prompting the representatives to vote to accept hemp, flax, and other commodities in public payments in the spring of 1739.[38] A letter printed in the November 13, 1739, issue of the *New-England Weekly Journal* nonetheless predicted "terrible Consequences" unless the assembly regained the "Liberty of making such new Emissions as will render Taxes easy."[39] Two months on, the assembly drafted an address to the king maintaining that it "cannot, without greatly Distressing His Majesty's Subjects here, make any further Tax, until there be an Emission of Bills, to be laid beyond 1741."[40] Rising merchant Thomas Hutchinson later estimated that retiring the whole currency would have required more than £250,000 in taxes, "which according to the general opinion of the people it was impossible to levy."[41] Not even the fiercest paper money critics wanted the colony to lose its circulating medium—not, at least, without something to replace it.

Hard-Money Men

The money question took on a different valence in the 1730s, as more and more Boston merchants joined their London counterparts in the struggle to eradicate paper money and resume silver payments in Massachusetts. For these new hard-money men, Governor Belcher's instructions presented an opportunity to gain power and impose a new monetary regime on the struggling colony. In the assembly, a resurgent "prerogative party" endorsed Thomas Hutchinson's revaluation bill, which provided for the creation of a "New Tenor" of currency equal to silver at the rate of six shillings eightpence per ounce. The price of silver was then twenty-seven shillings per ounce. New Tenor bills of credit would be redeemable in payment of taxes at the rate of three "Old Tenor" for one New Tenor, thus "raising" the value of outstanding bills in terms of silver from twenty-seven shillings per ounce to twenty shillings per ounce. The bill passed on February 3, 1737, providing for the emission of £9,000 in New Tenor bills plus £18,000 in Old Tenor bills. The assembly authorized additional emissions totaling £29,625 New Tenor between June 1737 and January 1738. Belcher was optimistic. On September 17, 1737, he communicated to the Board of Trade that "as the Assembly . . . have got into a method of emitting Bills of a much better Value than heretofore," he believed annual government expenditures would stay under the £30,000 limit his instructions stipulated.[42] But further depreciation befell both tenors of currency, effectively negating the revaluation.

Thereafter, hard-money men coalesced around Hutchinson's bill for a public silver bank. As proposed, the bank would issue £60,000 in New Tenor bills of credit on loan, redeemable for silver in five and ten years. Although the assembly endorsed the scheme in 1739, the Board of Trade took issue with the act's lack of a suspending clause and withheld its approval. Upon consulting numerous British merchants with financial interests in Massachusetts, moreover, the board insisted that as the act compelled acceptance of the new bills at the rate of six shillings eightpence per ounce of silver, "which is at present more than equal to 20 s. of the old outstanding Bills," the value of the new bills ought to be fixed against sterling rather than free to float, "and no Person obliged to take them at a higher Rate, under several Penalties." The merchants also opposed the provision that made the bills redeemable for silver in five and ten years, as "the locking up so much Bullion for so long a Time must be detrimental to the County," and proposed making them exchangeable in three, six, and ten years instead. Finally, they wanted to make the province liable for any deficiencies arising from misfortunes befalling the borrowers, an impossible ask for a colony with no silver and no way of getting any.[43]

Paper money advocates must have been pleased with the board's decision. For them, a silver bank flew in the face of logic. In response to Hutchinson's claim that "nothing can relieve us" from depreciation and inflation except by banishing "imaginary" paper money and "introducing Silver and Gold, which the World has given a real value to," Hugh Vans retorted that a silver bank could "never answer the End of Money; *viz* to have free Circulation in trade, nor to lower the Price of Silver; but must on the one Hand greatly encourage all money'd Men, where the [silver bank] Bills are known, to purchase and keep them up, or make a *Stock-Jobbing* Affair of them."[44] John Colman likewise warned that such a bank "would, in a few Months," be emptied by merchants who "would want Silver to ship off as much as ever; and then what would those Bank Notes be worth; the Bank would be at an End, because there would be no manner of Security for them."[45]

Recent history revealed as much. Just a few years earlier, in 1733, a combination of merchants had attempted to profit from the currency chaos by lending £110,000 in "merchants' notes" to interested parties who promised to refuse Rhode Island bills of credit in payment. The loans were to be repaid not in the notes themselves but in silver over a ten-year period at the rate of nineteen shillings per ounce, the current market price, after which anyone holding the notes could convert them to precious metal. The scheme was an utter disaster. As a concerned citizen wrote to the publisher of the *New-England Weekly Journal* in early 1734, the merchants not only had caused confusion by introducing a new species of money into the economy, but had also "assum'd a Power that no ways belongs to it; it being indisputably the Government's right, and theirs only, to Emit and Regulate the Money."[46] Within a few months, moreover, the cost of silver had jumped to twenty-seven shillings per ounce. Some critics accused the merchants of intentionally eroding confidence in the currency, likening them to the counterfeiters seen in the last chapter.[47] Vans later charged the notes with being more to blame for "the late extraordinary Rise of Silver, than all other Emissions."[48]

Despite sympathizing with the hard-money cause, Benjamin Colman agreed that the merchants' notes had been ill conceived. In his opinion, the notes had failed precisely because they contained "real value," promising "so much Silver or Gold," whereas paper bills were "only received in their respective Treasuries in ye payment of Rates." Thus those who had notes in their possession "hoarded them up" in hopes of redeeming them for coin, meanwhile, "ye whole Currency, & our Exchange is risen . . . & in proportion Goods & ye necessaries of Life."[49] But Colman, who in a 1736 sermon lambasted "the Merchants" for "Sacrifice[ing] the Medium of Trade to their private gains," struggled to practice what he preached.[50] On November 12, 1735, he wrote to Samuel Holden in London confessing that the £550 currency Holden expected him to get for his order (similar to a bill of exchange) for £100 sterling was too high a price to ask. "[H]aving privately inquir'd," Colman found £530 to be "the highest for Bills [of exchange] here." Never mind that the money was for charity, to ask for twenty pounds more would cause "to[o] much hurt to the public what then that I do?" he questioned. Colman thought that he could sell the order to Boston merchant Thomas Cushing, who was apparently willing to purchase it "at the most favourable exchange," but "if he yield to the 550," Colman hoped that all parties would "keep it private & not let it be known . . . You see sir my Difficulty, that it is from the Regard I owe to the common & public Good."[51] If Colman accepted £550 currency for £100 sterling when the market price was £530, it would be he himself sacrificing the currency at the expense of the society at large. He would be no better than the hard-money men he chastised.

The Sterling Standard

Although the Board of Trade had endorsed colonial paper money secured by taxes or mortgages on numerous occasions over the previous three decades, the London merchants who pulled the board's strings were finding it increasingly difficult to tolerate colonial legal tender provisions. Of course, the colonies' legal tender laws carried no force outside their respective jurisdictions. But if British merchants had factors with power of attorney over their accounts in, say, Massachusetts, sterling debts payable in Britain could, in fact, be discharged in local bills of credit at face value. And if the bills had depreciated relative to sterling between the time a sterling debt was contracted and when it was repaid, the creditor might fail to recoup his whole investment. Depreciation, the board concluded in a 1733 report to the royal administration, "could not but tend to the Great Detriment of the Creditors of the Province, to the entailing a heavy Load on all Estates there, and to the Loss of the British Merchants trading to the *Massachusetts-Bay*."[52]

Certainly, a connection between paper money emissions and the exchange rate did exist. Between 1723 and 1728, the assembly had issued £270,000 in new bills of credit for the support and defense of the province, plus an additional £60,000 on loan. The exchange rate had climbed from £220 currency for £100 sterling in 1720 to about £340 currency for £100 sterling in 1730. The market price of silver had risen proportionally, from twelve shillings per ounce in 1720 to sixteen shillings per ounce in 1727. By 1733 the price of silver hovered between nineteen shillings and twenty-one shillings per ounce.[53] But the merchants' claim that the overissue of paper money had increased the exchange rate oversimplified a complicated relationship. For one, the quantity of Massachusetts bills per capita was *decreasing*—from 1725 to 1730, it had declined 7 percent. Per capita bill issue continued to fall following Governor Belcher's arrival, by 13 percent between 1730 and 1735 and by 16 percent between 1735 and 1740. The exchange rate nevertheless climbed from £340 currency for £100 sterling in 1730, to £360 currency for £100 sterling in 1735, to £525 currency for £100 sterling in 1740.[54]

The failure of the outstanding bills' ongoing retirement to reverse some of the decade's depreciation confirmed for at least one paper money apologist his belief that it was "in the Power of Traders to advance or depreciate any currency . . . and they always will do that which Interest directs."[55] According to the commentator, the source of depreciation was not the overissue of paper bills but the oversupply of British goods. "If it be objected, that some Merchants have lost in their Trade with us," paper money was no more to blame than silver was responsible for Spanish merchants' losses in their trade with Peru. "And if it was constantly a losing Trade, no merchant wou'd be concern'd with it." But if the home government would merely grant Massachusetts "equal Liberty of other Governments, of supplying our selves with a proper Medium of Exchange, suitable to our Necessities," it would not only encourage local and Atlantic trade, but also "prevent the ill Effects of *private Contracts* and the *groundless Objections* against our Neighbours"—namely, Rhode Island—"for using that Liberty [of making money] we shou'd rejoice to have the Advantage of."[56]

For his part, Benjamin Colman confided to Francis Wilks in November 1739, he had "hoped that the scarcity of our Bills upon our approach to forty one, would raise the Value of them, which it does not in the least." On the contrary, Massachusetts's bills of credit were continuing to depreciate "with the flood from Rhode Island." As the deadline for redeeming the bills loomed, even he recognized that "It is certainly far better for the province to have a Currency of their own, bad as it is, than to depend upon a supply from Rhode Island; & the merchants in London wil certainly in their End find it better for themselves." He maintained that the merchants had "honestly judged then that the [retirement] of the Province Bills would raise their Value; & [reverse] our sinking Exchange; But I think Time & Experience show the Contrary."[57]

But as it became increasingly clear that money *scarcity* was at least partially to blame for the rising exchange rate, the British merchants and their colonial allies doubled down on their contention that paper money rendered sterling investments in North America unsafe. In the beginning, William Douglass recounted in 1738, all the colonies had "the same" money as Britain. "But by the Iniquity of some Administrations, all of them have cheated their Creditors at Home" through reducing the real values of their currencies, some by clipping and raising coins, others by issuing inflationary paper money.[58] The cheat was especially galling in the case of Massachusetts, where, as paper bills depreciated in terms of sterling, "the Merchants at Home were from Time to Time paid a less Value than they had contracted for; thus, for a Debt contracted 25 Years ago, he now receives only 7 s. in the Pound, that is the Debtor (defrauds) retains 13 *s.* in the Pound of the Merchant's Money, and with this he builds fine Houses, makes Purchases *&c.*"[59] Depreciation trends incentivized debtors to contract long-term credit and then refuse to pay, Douglass explained two years later in an essay that commanded a wide readership in Britain, "because while Bills are continually depreciating, the longer the Debt is outstanding, they pay their Creditors with a less and less Value, than what was contracted for."[60]

But the problem of depreciation extended far beyond Massachusetts. Barbados planter and politician John Ashley highlighted the variations in sterling exchange rates among the colonies and proposed that all the currencies be reduced to a single, fixed standard. He recalled in his 1743 essay, *Memoirs and Considerations Concerning the Trade and Revenues of the British Colonies in America*, that over time, "almost every Province, as well as the Islands, varied more or less in their Currency, and consequently in their several and respective Exchanges between Great Britain, which put the whole American Trade upon a state of uncertainty, and into such Confusion that no Trader could tell how to value his Debts after they were once contracted."[61] For Ashley, the solution lay in the imposition of "an equal and fixed Price for Silver throughout all those Colonies and Plantations" in which all debts would be contracted and all payments made. It would "naturally be called Sterling Money, Proclamation Money, or new Money," while the current monies of the colonies, whatever their respective values, "will be called old Currency or old Money."[62] Every British merchant could thereafter "expect an equal Value upon the Repayment of the Money he shall credit, lend, or trade for in the Plantations, without having the Value of his Property depreciated by any Law or Custom while it is in other People's Hands."[63]

The precarity of British property loomed large in the commentary, but so did the themes of reciprocity and obligation. The anonymous author of a 1740 essay published in London lamented that a merchant who "ventured his Property abroad," by lending "considerable Sums to the Planters" for their "mutual Advantage," should be able to expect repayment "according to his Contract." Yet "as Matters now really stand . . . he is not secure, but must depend upon the Honour and Integrity of the Person he deals with," that is, at least "'till a Stop be put to the least Variation in the Coin, and to the Option of the Debtor to pay in such Currency as he thinks most advantageous to himself."[64]

Renewed imperial conflict in 1739 raised the stakes of the currency debate. When Britain declared war on Spain that year, the royal government decided that the colonial assemblies would raise soldiers for the king's service on the king's payroll, but it was unclear how they would be compensated. One option would be to pay them in their respective home currencies. The former Virginia lieutenant governor, Alexander Spotswood, who was slated to command the Anglo-American regiments in Cartagena before his untimely death in the summer of 1740, doubted that this would be feasible. As he reminded New York governor George Clarke in April of that year, there were "scarce any two provinces in this continent that agree in the value of their Currency and in every one of them the Exchange between their Currancy & Sterling is continually varying." Therefore, unless the troops' pay be placed "upon one uniform footing," when the new enlistments from the different colonies came and fought and died alongside one another, "Dissatisfactions and consequently mutinies might arise from some receiving higher pay then others." He proposed instead paying each "common soldier," whatever his home colony, "one pistole for every calendar month" and offering advances to men "desirous of leaving some subsistence money with their familys."[65]

Spotswood's replacement from Britain, Colonel William Blakeney, warned future Prime Minister Thomas Pelham-Holles, the Duke of Newcastle, that the "great Variety of Paper Currency all over the Provinces in America" would have to be resolved if Britain was going to defeat Spain. Rather than "Paying the Troops in the different Currencies where levying," Blakeney drew bills of exchange on the British government and distributed them to the soldiers' respective governors, who could sell the bills to colonial merchants for "the Paper Currency of the Province" and "pay the Troops their full Sterling Subsistence" at the local exchange rate, so that "there may be no Complaints among them" of "unequal pay." This method avoided not only the "Inconveniency" of bringing over "Pieces of Eight," but also the "Mutiny and Desertion" that would surely arise from disbursing them "at any fixt Sterling rate."[66]

Then Parliament got involved. On April 25, 1740, six months into Britain's war with Spain, the House of Commons announced that the colonial currencies "hath frustrated the good Intentions" of Queen Anne's Proclamation of 1704 to establish a fixed exchange rate between the colonies and Britain. Floating exchange rates against sterling and variations in exchange rates among the colonies "hath been a great Discouragement to the Commerce of this Kingdom, by occasioning a Confusion in Dealings, and lessening of Credit in those Parts," expounded the Commons.[67] Rumors of imminent Parliamentary intervention swirled. The following month, the *Pennsylvania Gazette* printed a letter from London warning that "Parliament are actually going to settle the Standard of Money in America, which 'tis supposed, will be Sterling; and make the present Exchange of Paper Money in all the Colonies, and all Merchandize and Provisions conform thereto."[68] On June 12, the *Gazette* reported that the Board of Trade "are making out an exact Account of the Paper Currency of America, in order to lay the same before the House of Commons."[69]

A year before, the House of Commons had asked the Board of Trade to obtain detailed reports from all of the colonial governors of gold and silver exchange rates and quantities of paper money issued since 1700.[70] But when the board solicited the governors' opinions on how best to retire the outstanding currencies on behalf of the Commons, only New York's George Clarke responded. Clarke agreed with Parliament's "thoughts of reduceing the Money in all the plantations to one uniform standard, and that to be sterling," as being "the only means to preserve the Merchants in England from being defrauded as they have Hitherto greatly been."[71] The other governors were evasive, as were the colonial agents, who refused to give their "Opinion till they have received proper Instructions on that Subject" from the assemblies. Then on January 21, 1741, the board reported that it would not be endorsing the proposal in the Commons "for the sinking and discharging of the said Bills of

Credit," as it would not fix "the Evil complained of."[72] Parliament responded by taking matters into its own hands, calling for draft bills for regulating and restricting the colonial currencies. But by the time the Commons heard "a Bill to prevent the Issuing of Paper Bills of Credit in the British Colonies and Plantations in America, to be legal Tenders in Payments for Money" on May 4, 1744, France had declared war on Britain and consideration of the bill had to be postponed indefinitely.

"The rising of the Land Bankers"

In the meantime, however, as the 1741 deadline for retiring the outstanding currency loomed, the Massachusetts assembly tried to get ahead of Parliamentary interference by inviting bids "for the furnishing a further medium of trade" on a private basis.[73] The land bankers were at the ready. On December 5, 1739, John Colman and his partners submitted to the assembly their proposal for a land bank or "manufactory company." As the historian Margaret Newell has pointed out, the land bank was not just a currency-issuing "bank" but "a collective marketing service . . . akin to the Populist subtreasury scheme of the late nineteenth century" for public warehouses for farmers to cheaply store and mortgage their goods.[74] Similar to the later subtreasury proposal but on a smaller (and colonial) scale, the land bank plan promised to increase the production of import substitutes, improve the colony's trade and payments balance with Britain, and reduce the sterling exchange rate. The land bank offered loans to "subscribers" at 3 percent interest for twenty years against land or on surety bond, with 5 percent of the principal due annually. To encourage the subscribers to use their loans productively, the bank permitted the payment of interest and principal in hemp, flax, iron, linen, copper, tanned leather, flaxseed, beeswax, nails, tallow, and lumber. Directors would then sell the items and award the subscribers dividends from the profits.[75] Thus the bank "forced the Subscriber yearly to be industrious, and he had it not in his Power to postpone" payments, explained one supporter, "which has been too frequently the case between the Publick and Borrower in former Paper Emissions"—the province loan money issued between 1714 and 1728—"to the Injury of the one, and the intire Ruin of the other."[76] Hugh Vans likewise argued that the bank would "promote Industry, and so far be of the Nature of a Bounty."[77]

The land bank roiled Massachusetts politics for more than two years. Initially the assembly forbade Colman and the original 395 subscribers from issuing any notes or bills, inspiring an influx of memorials and petitions for and against the scheme.[78] That summer, however, colonists elected several land bankers to the new assembly, which swiftly voted against barring the bank from issuing bills. Frustrated, Governor Belcher responded with a proclamation "against receiving or passing the said Notes, as tending to defraud Men of their Substance and to disturb the Peace and good Order of the People." As many as 145 Boston merchants signed on to an agreement to refuse the bank's bills and instructed their debtors to do the same, lest the debtors accept the bills "*in Expectation of our receiving them at their Hands.*" The signatories also asked masters and mistresses "to caution their Servants" against taking the bills, "as such a thing may lead to give 'em an entrance into Credit, which would prove of dangerous consequence."[79] Seventy-four Newport merchants signed and circulated a similar covenant.[80]

The land bank opened for business on September 19, 1740. Belcher used his position and patronage to try to undermine confidence in the bank and punished subscribers and those who received or passed its bills.[81] On November 5, he warned commissioned officers against "signing or giving any Countenance or Encouragement to the Passing of the sd. Notes," prompting land bank supporters William Stoddard, Robert Hale, Samuel Adams, and John Choate to immediately tender their resignations.[82] Other officers followed. "Whole troops, nay almost whole Regiments," one colonist informed a British merchant in early 1741, "either resigned or told their Colonels, who examined them, that they would resign, rather than not encourage the bills," and those who refused to resign were removed from their posts.[83] Belcher additionally instructed officials to withhold licenses from "Taverners, Retailers & Common Victualers" who passed or encouraged "the said Bills."[84]

In Suffolk County alone, 121 men and one woman received loans from the land bank in the fall of 1740. According to the deeds they filed at the county registry, they were lawyers, doctors, harbormasters, bricklayers, carpenters, brewers, clothmakers, farmers, gentlemen, weavers, tanners, wheelwrights, potters, blacksmiths, wigmakers, shipwrights, innkeepers, joiners, merchants, traders, and shoemakers. Fifty-eight identified as yeomen. The lone woman—the Boston widow Rebecca Collins—registered a mortgage on October 15.[85] Middlesex, Essex, and Worcester Counties were early land bank strongholds, with 118, 115, and 164 subscribers, respectively, by December 1740.[86]

The land bankers grew in number and were politicized in the new year. Town meetings petitioned the assembly in support of the land bank, voted to accept the bank's money in payment of town taxes, or both.[87] On February 19, 1741, the *Boston News-Letter* published a declaration of local caulkers pledging to only receive land bank bills, bills of credit, merchants' notes, or specific products at set values "in Pay for their Work," and encouraged "other Artificers and Tradesmen" to follow their example.[88] Belcher's efforts to defeat the land bank soon inspired the establishment of sister banks. In April, residents of Scituate and the neighboring towns resolved to issue notes on land. The Ipswich freeholders organized a bank and began issuing small denomination notes the following month.[89]

Meanwhile, the land bankers may even have conspired to march on Boston and force the town's merchants to accept their money "on pretence of getting Corn for their Families." While "the rising of the Land Bankers" never materialized, the governor and his council gathered enough evidence of a plot to arrest and charge four men. A Weymouth man informed "that he heard a report in that Town of a Confederacy in the Countrey of about 5000 Men who design'd to come to Boston to know the reason why there was not a Currency for the Land Bank Money."[90] Additional affidavits revealed that the conspirators had posted notices on meetinghouses and taverns, openly threatened merchants who refused to sell corn for bank bills, and gathered signatures from hundreds of supporters in Hingham, Weymouth, Stoughton, Abington, Plymouth, and Bridgewater.[91] Witnesses reported "disorderly Meetings," and a Hingham man swore he had heard that twenty thousand people would rise in the country and "come to Boston, & if Corn was there & the Merchants would not let them have it they would throw them into the Dock."[92] Whether a real conspiracy to force Boston's merchants to turn over their corn to the people was afoot, or whether Belcher and his allies invented it, such colorful testimony evoked a deep-rooted moral economy based on the right to eat as well as the authorities' intolerance of collective violence in confrontation with the economic order.

Thomas Hutchinson later wrote of the land bank that "Perhaps the major part, in number, of the inhabitants of the Province openly or secretly were well wishers to it."[93] By 1741, there were 1,253 subscribers hailing from 123 towns, accounting for five-sixths of the total towns. Some borrowers were town proprietors with considerable holdings or wealthy speculators with no intention of settling their mortgaged properties. Others were military veterans who pledged expropriated Indigenous homelands. Some were converts from a rival silver bank. The vast majority identified as yeomen, but there were also shopkeepers, artisans, mariners, and journeymen.[94] Historians have additionally identified links between the land bank and the Great Awakening, observing that many of the subscribers worshipped at evangelical churches and arguing that the movements shared a popular, even class-specific, element.[95] At least three Worcester County subscribers, including Henry Bosworth, Benjamin Boyce Jr., and Benjamin Taft, were later implicated in the Mendon counterfeiting gang discussed in the previous chapter.

FIGURE 7.1. Two-shilling "Bank Bill" from Ipswich, Massachusetts, 1741. The signers are Robert Choate, Jonathan Hale, John Brown, and Edward Eveleth. National Numismatic Collection, Smithsonian Institution.

The land bankers helped double the turnout for the May 1741 assembly elections and won a sweeping majority. After the representatives purged sixteen hard-money men from the council and tried to replace them with land bank supporters, however, Belcher dissolved the assembly in a huff and called for new elections. By the time the next house met, news of his removal from the governor's chair—and of a Parliamentary statute suppressing the bank—had reached Boston.[96] Belcher knew that it would take Parliamentary intervention to defeat the land bank. "Never was so vile a scheme set on foot," he had fumed to his brother-in-law, Richard Partridge, who also happened to be one of the bank's agents, in November 1740. "Yet what is done about it will not be sufficient without an Act of Parliament."[97] As it happened, private banks were legal in the colonies: only six years earlier, the Privy Council had annulled Belcher's disallowance of a group of New Hampshire traders' "merchants' notes" on the grounds that private currencies posed no threat to the royal prerogative to mint money. Two years after that the British attorney general had ruled that the Bubble Act—passed in 1720 after the collapse of the South Sea Company—did not apply to private banks in the colonies.[98]

When a group of London merchants petitioned Parliament in February 1741 to amend the Bubble Act to include colonial banks, the House of Commons jumped at the opportunity to put the rebellious colony in its place.[99] According to one of Massachusetts's agents in London, Christopher Kilby, Parliament viewed the land bank "as a design to defeat and Evade" its efforts to reform the colonial currencies.[100] Two years earlier, a land bank critic had declared that the bank was such an affront to British rule as to appear to have been designed by "Enemies to all Paper Money," and predicted that it would "raise *the Indignation of the Parliament* against all Paper Currencies in the Plantations."[101] News of the Bubble Act's extension to the colonies arrived around the time of the July 1741 assembly elections. A chronicler of the land bank controversy later maintained that the land bankers had "perswaded themselves that the Act of Parliament could not be carried into Execution, and had even bid Defiance by their Threats."[102] In the opinion of future founding father John Adams, "the act to destroy the Land Bank scheme raised a greater ferment in this province than the Stamp Act did."[103]

But Governor William Shirley was a much better politician than his predecessor. Armed with orders to dismantle the land bank, he made friendly overtures to the land bankers in the assembly, restored subscribers to their government posts, and gave the directors an opportunity to close the bank on their own terms. In September 1741, the subscribers voted by a slim majority to dissolve the bank, and the directors began redeeming the bills and discharging the mortgages. Within a month, £37,000 of the £49,250 in circulation was called in and destroyed, leading Shirley to report that "the malignant Spirit raised by the Land Bank Scheme . . . is now vanished."[104] The following spring, the assembly appointed a committee for inspecting outstanding accounts and reporting delinquent subscribers. A final measure, authorized in 1743, empowered commissioners to prosecute the delinquents and released from liability borrowers who had already paid their debts. Though it would take another twenty-seven years for the commissioners to wrap up the bank's business, the remaining claims represented a small fraction of subscribers. Within a few years of Shirley's appointment, much of the uproar over the bank had dissipated.[105]

Securing Creditors' Debts

But the time had come for redeeming the outstanding bills of credit, and not even the sharpest paper money critics wanted Massachusetts to lose most of its circulating cash. With Britain and Spain at arms and war with France looming, the stakes were too high: "the Province must necessarily be thrown into the utmost Disorder and Confusion; the Government be without any Support; the Forts and Garrisons remain in a defenceless Condition, and wholly unprovided with War-like Stores; and the Province be unable to equip suitable Vessels of War to guard their Coasts; and their Trade and Commerce be ruined and undone," Francis Wilks and Christopher Kilby warned Parliament.[106]

So Governor Shirley and the assembly reached a compromise. In exchange for the assembly's support of an act enabling judges to adjust debts for depreciation, Shirley would approve a supply bill for the emission of a "Second New Tenor" of currency redeemable for taxes at the rate of four Old Tenor for one Second New Tenor.[107] But first he had to convince the Board of Trade to drop the suspending clause requirement, and to do that he needed the support of the London merchants who pulled the strings. This was where the act for securing creditors' debts came in. In a letter dated October 17, 1741, Shirley solicited Boston slave trader Charles Apthorpe, in London on business, to gather the merchants "one Evining [for] a Glass Wine . . . & assur 'em from me that the Province bills shall never be a Tender, whilst I am in the Chair, without securing the full Value of every man's debt to him."[108] The act, Shirley later boasted to the board, "[secured] to creditors the full value of their outstanding debts for the future, by making an allowance for the depreciation of the bills between the time of contracting the debt and the time of payment."[109]

The "Act for Ascertaining the Value of Money and of the Bills of Credit," passed on January 15, 1742, was not designed to reverse past depreciation or to prevent it in the future. It was intended, rather, to insulate creditors from its distributive effects by enabling the courts to render judgments if the real value of Shirley's Second New Tenor bills should fall below the six shillings eightpence per ounce of silver legislated. The act stipulated that creditors no longer had to accept depreciated paper bills in payment of debts at face value equal to sterling but could instead appeal to a judge to have sums owed on running contracts adjusted upward to account for the bills' decline relative to silver. This sudden policy change, some remarked, "was not only quite new in the Province, but unpopular," and "contrary to the inclinations" of those who had voted for it.[110]

The act provided that an inflation schedule be recalculated every six months by the representatives, by a committee of the council, or by a committee of five "able and sufficient men" appointed by the Superior Court.[111] If they determined "that the Bills are depreciated since the Debt was contracted," explained Shirley to the Board of Trade on March 19, "then the Judges are bound to make up Judgment for the true value of the Debt in Silver, or in want thereof for the nominal value of the Debt in Province Bills with an Addition of so much more in those Bills as will make the Creditor amends for the depreciation."[112] The assembly may well have entrusted judges with determining the measure of depreciation as a counter to democratic demands. Yet "the popular cry was [so much] against" the act, Thomas Hutchinson later chronicled, that most judges made relatively small allowances. They "never had firmness enough in any instance to make a full allowance, but when silver and exchange had rose 20 per cent. or more, an addition was made of 4 or 5 only." And the representatives were not above retaliation for unpopular judgments. When Bristol County judge and council member Nathaniel Hubbard sought to give a larger allowance than had been made in previous years, they ousted him from the council in the next election.[113] Not until August 17, 1744, moreover, did the assembly approve a silver rating higher than six shillings eightpence per ounce, and this was after it had authorized yet another tenor of currency (the "last new tenor"), equal to silver at the rate of seven shillings sixpence per ounce, the same as the August 17 rating.[114]

According to legal historian Claire Priest, the act's main consequence was to alter litigation trends, with debtors becoming more inclined to resolve financial disputes out of court than to delay payment in the hope that the currency would continue to depreciate in the time it took creditors to settle suits against them, as they had theretofore been inclined to do.[115] As one contemporary put it, the act had "a strong Tendency to correct that Spirit of Dishonesty, which had before too much prevailed in the Province by Debtors neglecting to pay plain, indisputable Debts without being compell'd to it by Judgments at Law and Executions, for the Sake of the Advantages that were before gained by them upon the Depreciating of the Bills."[116] It eliminated, in other words, the incentive that depreciation gave debtors, complained about by William Douglass, to refuse to pay their debts when due. An act for raising court fees, passed around the same time, however, also reduced creditors' incentives to sue. Since debts could not be adjusted without a suit, Hutchinson lamented, "demand was not ordinarily made for depreciation," nor did the act "prevent the loss from the depreciation of the bills in those persons hands through which they were continually passing."[117] In the estimation of one early twentieth-century economist, "the law failed to secure all that had been hoped from it."[118]

The Death of Old Tenor

The outbreak of war in the spring of 1744 forced Parliament to postpone its review of the colonial currencies, as the New England colonies joined in issuing large sums of bills of credit to finance military expenses. In Massachusetts, Governor Shirley had already extended the deadline for redeeming the outstanding bills from 1741 to 1742, and the new deadline had come and gone. On September 25, 1744, the Boston town meeting cautioned its representatives that it would be "Oppressive ... to Increase the Burden ... by laying Any of the Extraordinary Charge of the War On [the next] Two years." If, instead, the assembly could "[lay] the funds on some future unencumbered years," then "the Great & Expensive Charge of War may be defrayed & paid in the Days of peace when the people are at leisure to Till the Ground ... and not make Grim and Savage War look yet more Terrible."[119]

The colonial war machine hummed again. Between 1744 and 1749, Massachusetts alone emitted £2,135,300 Old Tenor in bills of credit, with taxes to retire the bills scheduled through 1760. Connecticut, Rhode Island, and New Hampshire followed suit. Rhode Island issued £440,000 on loan between 1740 and 1750. In New Hampshire, the face value of bills in circulation rose to £471,896 by 1746.[120] These emissions wreaked havoc on the Massachusetts currency before war had even broken out. As early as February 1744, Governor Shirley grumbled that the sterling exchange rate had risen from "450 to 485 per Cent." or from £550 to £585 sterling for £100 currency—a £25,000 loss—over the previous nine months, thanks to the influx of Rhode Island and Connecticut bills "now current among us."[121] And this was just the beginning. Shirley predicted that in the coming years "five Sixths" of all Rhode Island bills and more than half of all Connecticut bills would flood the province, generating more damage, and "every Person must share in it more or less," especially the debtors "who are subject by the late Province Law to make an Allowance to their Creditors for the depreciating of the Bills." If the neighboring colonies continued to make such "immoderate Quantities" of money "without any Prospect of Redemption," then all of Massachusetts's efforts to regulate "its own Bills"—the multiple revaluations, the resolution of the land bank controversy, the act for securing creditors' debts—would be for naught. And "in Case of a Parliamentary Inquiry," the governor warned, the colony would face certain "Censure and Condemnation."[122]

War, as always, had its advantages for the laboring classes. While gunsmiths, sailmakers, and caulkers found work refitting merchant ships for war, poorer men picked up jobs on privateers, where wages were more than double the prewar rate, or enlisted in the army. But although thousands did so voluntarily, many more were pressed into service in the royal navy, and most never returned home. As much as 20 percent of the colony's able-bodied men perished in the campaigns against the French and the Spanish, leaving behind penniless widows and children and swelling the poor relief rolls. Meanwhile, up-and-coming merchants had seized the opportunity to supply military campaigns; military contracts meant hefty profits for Boston firms and made the merchant Thomas Hancock one of the richest men in town. Coupled with the unprecedented loss of life, rising food costs, and shattering depreciation, the end of the fighting brought dislocation and suffering for all but the wealthy few.[123]

Then in 1748, the Crown recognized Massachusetts's right to be reimbursed for some of the costs of King George's War (1744–48). Direct Parliamentary reimbursements to provincial treasurers, known as "free gifts," became a significant component of British spending in the colonies following the war, constituting nearly 25 percent for the period from 1749 to 1755. Between 1749 and 1750 Parliament earmarked £467,000 sterling for compensating the colonies for their services relating to the defense of Nova Scotia in 1744, the siege and garrisoning of Louisburg in 1745–46, and the failed assault on Canada in 1746–47. On September 19, 1749, the *Mermaid* man-of-war arrived in Boston carrying £179,160 sterling in Spanish milled silver—about what the colony had expended "in Taking, Repairing and Securing Louisbourg."[124]

News of the Parliamentary reimbursement ignited a bitter public debate over how to apply the grant. Hard-money men consolidated around a plan endorsed by Governor Shirley for using the silver to immediately redeem all outstanding currency and return the colony to a fixed metallic standard once and for all. For them, the Parliamentary grant involved a question of righteousness. Thus the Harvard theologian Nathaniel Appleton longed to do away with "such a declining Medium, that has caused so much Oppression" of soldiers, widows, ministers, and creditors.[125] A letter to the editor of the *Independent Advertiser* published in its March 28, 1748, issue argued that using the grant for anything other than immediate redemption would "be misapplying it" and disagreeable to "Justice and Righteousness."[126] Another author hoped that redemption would "restore the Trade to the State it was before the Paper Currency commenced ... so that Fraud, Injustice, and Oppression, which for thirty Years past have reigned triumphant among us, may be banished for ever."[127] One commentator went so far as to represent paper money as "an Abomination to the righteous GOD."[128]

But their opponents, too, considered the grant a matter of justice and equity. One essayist, posing as a Frenchman, urged Canada to encourage "the rich Merchants" design "to have a final Stop put to Paper Money," which would "weaken and impoverish" New England "and advance ourselves upon their ruin."[129] Writing in 1748, a "Mylo Freeman" accused hard-money men of lamenting "the Badness of the [paper] Money" while "hoarding of it up to make it scarce ... in order soon to have *them* all redeemed for *Silver Money*."[130] Once having "Scrabled, Graspt, and Collected this D—d Paper Money into their own Possession" and exchanged it for silver, "Vincent Centinel" likewise warned, these "violent Promoters of a Silver Medium" would "Import all Sorts of Goods to get us into their Debts, then we must sell our Lands to pay them; then go, and work upon their Farms, or Starve, or go to Sea as their Slaves, or go to—Jail." In lieu of immediate redemption, Centinel proposed gradually retiring the outstanding currency and keeping the silver "still in the Treasury" as "a Fund, or Bank" for the good of the province.[131] Others proposed investing it in interest-bearing Bank of England bonds.

At the end of 1748, following five weeks of deliberation, Thomas Hutchinson rammed through the assembly a bill for immediate redemption and sent it to Britain, where it awaited Parliamentary approval. The act would take effect as soon as the grant arrived, Shirley informed the Duke of Bedford on January 31, 1749. Colonists would have until March 31, 1750, to exchange their bills of credit for "Lawful Money," a new currency that would be backed by and pegged against silver at the rate of six shillings for a piece of eight, or six shillings eightpence for an ounce of silver. Ten pounds Old Tenor would fetch one pound Lawful Money (or forty-five shillings Old Tenor for a piece of eight).[132] The remaining bills would be redeemed by taxes by the end of 1750, after which Shirley hoped that "the whole Paper Currency of new England" would be put on the same footing "by the Interposition of the Parliament."[133] Parliament approved the act, but not without considerable opposition from the neighboring colonies' agents and intense debate in the House of Commons.[134]

The redemption act was the outcome of "complex political jockeying among a range of competing interests," and had it not been for "the fortuitous

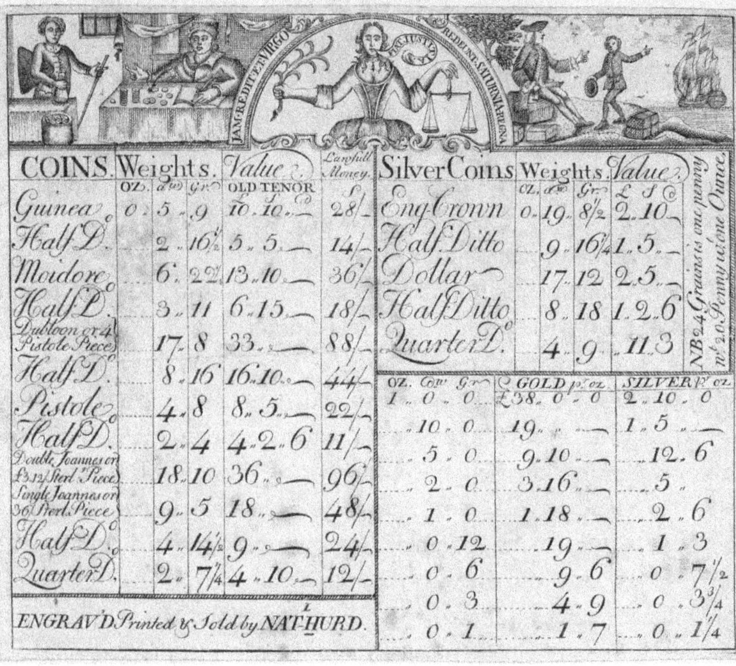

FIGURE 7.2. Currency conversion table, engraved, printed, and sold by Nathaniel Hurd (Boston, 1765). The table gives Old Tenor and Lawful Money values of various coins. Courtesy American Antiquarian Society.

specie grant from England," Margaret Newell speculates, "the paper money forces might have prevailed."[135] As Thomas Hutchinson later detailed in his *History of Massachusetts*, two major agreements had to be reached before the bill could pass in the assembly: between those for redeeming the outstanding bills of credit at the exchange rate when they were issued of thirty shillings per ounce of silver and those for redeeming them at the prevailing exchange rate of sixty shillings per ounce (they settled on fifty shillings per ounce); and between the act's sponsors and the land bank directors (Governor Shirley bought the latter's support with military bounties and a release from financial liability for the bank). The bill was bolstered, moreover, by the unexpected backing of two representatives "in favor of paper," as well as by the fortuitous absence of several popular party leaders during the vote for its passage.[136]

The arrival of the silver, the *Independent Advertiser* reported on September 25, 1749, was met with "various Speculations, as People are differently affected towards our late Act for altering the Currency." Hard-money men feared that the redemption act would raise the value of Massachusetts bills of credit in Rhode Island and Connecticut colonists' hands and depreciate the neighboring colonies' bills that Massachusetts colonists held. Although the act prohibited neighboring colonists from redeeming Massachusetts bills for silver, the *Advertiser* anticipated that "it will be very easy for them... to part with those Bills to good Advantage, as if they were allowed to exchange them for specie," while Massachusetts holders of other colonies' bills "will meet with great Loss ... till an Act of Parliament shall oblige them to redeem theirs in like Manner."[137] Another commentator likewise argued that for immediate redemption to be effective, the neighboring colonies had to redeem their outstanding bills so that "all the neigbouring Provinces are brought upon the same Footing, in relation to their Currency, and Paper-Currency intirely destroyed."[138]

Those who had opposed immediate redemption seemed more concerned about the Massachusetts merchants who would profit from past depreciation and the toll it would take on laboring lives. Paper money advocates had already voted Thomas Hutchinson and his allies out of office in May 1749. When the silver arrived, crowds roamed Boston's streets and threatened Hutchinson (whose house had mysteriously burned down the previous spring), forcing him to flee the town. But the rich only got richer and the poor, who had served disproportionately in the war, would get none of the bounty.[139] In the summer of 1750, a humorist published a ballad lamenting "the sad and deplorable death of Mr. Old Tenor; who after a long confinement by a deep and mortal wound which he received above twelve months before, expired on the 31st of March 1750."[140] After sixty years, the colony's paper money experiment had arrived at an unhappy end.

But Mr. Tenor lived on in name. With the help of various tables printed for popular consumption that year "shewing the Value of *Old Tenor* Bills" in terms of "*Lawful Money*," merchants, farmers, and artisans would record book debts, local transactions, and household inventory in both currencies for years, even decades, after the redemption.[141] Consider, for example, the Boston merchant Samuel Abbot. In 1758, Abbot took "an Accott. Of Stock" determining his "Worth in—Old Tenor" as £6,750, or £900 "in Law. Money." An invoice for combs, needles, and other imported goods he purchased on short credit listed totals in sterling, Old Tenor, and Lawful Money. Only one-off or final payments were documented just in Lawful Money.[142] Wrentham carpenter Nathaniel Wragg likewise translated some of his running book debts into Lawful Money but not others, while Daniel Noyes and Nathan Wheeler of Newbury continued to record debt payments in Old Tenor.[143] In February 1752, Thomas Dennis of Boston purchased hardware from Mary Jackson totaling five pounds six shillings eightpence Old Tenor, or fourteen shillings twopence "Reduced to Lawfull money." His itemized receipt listed prices only in Old Tenor.[144] Boston landlord and physician John Clarke continued to record payments from tenants whose leases predated redemption in Old Tenor well into the 1750s, but documented payments on leases beginning after 1750 in Lawful Money.[145]

While Massachusetts settlers were mourning Old Tenor's death, news arrived that Parliament had resumed its inquiry into the colonial currencies and would soon pass a bill restricting colonial paper money. In the spring of 1749, several colonies had dispatched their agents, including Connecticut's Eliakim Palmer and Pennsylvania's and Rhode Island's Richard Partridge, to protest the bill, with mixed success.[146] Although earlier versions of the bill would have applied to all of the colonies, the Currency Act of 1751 restricted only the New England assemblies' ability to issue bills of credit. And since Massachusetts had already returned to silver payments voluntarily (and Connecticut planned to do so by 1754), the act mainly affected Rhode Island and New Hampshire. The Currency Act banned the four colonies from postponing the redemption of outstanding bills, reissuing old currency, and creating new bills except in cases of "Emergencies of Government." Future emissions were to be redeemed within two years and could be legal tender for taxes but not debts. Any governor found not enforcing the act would be dismissed from office. Endorsed by merchants in London, Boston, and Newport, the act was a victory for capitalist creditors on both sides of the Atlantic and paved the way, or so many thought, for all the colonies to return to a fixed metallic standard.[147]

When the Seven Years' War broke out in 1754, Massachusetts would finance military expenses out of a generous loan from the colony's wealthiest merchants, but six years of conflict and casualties atop a crippling interwar recession devastated the province. Taxes to pay the war debt soared, but without any money to pay them, most of the levies went uncollected. Outside New England, meanwhile, Virginia issued bills of credit for the first time, igniting a controversy between British merchants and the colony over the payment of sterling debts. Following decades of Quaker governance, the Pennsylvania assembly seized the war as an opportunity to expand its fiscal capacity and extend its reach into new areas of colonial life. And in North Carolina, a postwar depression gave rise to the popular movement for debt relief and paper money known as the Regulator Rebellion. Across early America, news that Parliament was preparing a general bill for restricting the colonial currencies drew fear and confusion from all quarters and, after the bill passed, the liberty to create money became the rallying cry that made the slogan "no taxation without representation" not only popular but meaningful.

EPILOGUE

The Currency Act Crisis

In 1744, a Pennsylvania writer expressed alarm at a Parliamentary bill intending "to put an End to the Use of Paper-Money, and to take away Liberty."[1] Twenty-three years later, colonial agents in London were instructed to tread carefully "while there was the least Danger that the Assemblies in America must be deprived of the Liberty of issuing the Bills," which would "affect their most valuable Rights and Privileges."[2] And in its 1774 "Declaration and Resolves," the First Continental Congress listed the Currency Act of 1764 as a violation of colonial settler rights.[3] In the traditional narrative of the American Revolution, the colonists rebelled against Britain because Parliament taxed them without their consent.[4] The Currency Act, in this telling, is secondary to the Stamp Act, even though the Stamp Act was never enforced and was repealed less than a year after its passage, while the Currency Act was in force for seven years before it was even amended. It was hated every bit as much as the infamous Stamp Act, but its effects were delayed and the opposition was often tangled up with other grievances, making the breadth of its dissent somewhat harder to follow in the historical record.

If patriots viewed the Currency Act as an infringement of colonial rights, the act did not signal a sharp break with imperial policy. Since 1720, royal officials had insisted that all paper money acts contain a suspending clause, though the instruction was often ignored, especially in wartime. Then in 1751, Parliament passed the first Currency Act restricting paper money emissions in the New England colonies, after which those colonies adopted a fixed metallic standard.[5] Yet the Currency Act crisis brought into focus the economic transformations and internal divisions that helped undermine British control in North America. Different groups experienced and responded to the crisis in different ways, igniting new political rifts and further straining traditional bonds of dependency and obligation in the crucial decade before the revolution. While the imperial crisis leading to the revolution may not have pivoted wholly on the money question, the accrued social and economic frictions of decades of monetary policy and controversy suffused virtually every aspect of the settler revolt.

Money, Debt, and the Seven Years' War

When war broke out between Britain and France in 1754, all the colonies joined in issuing large sums of paper money to finance military operations, including—for the first time in its colonial history—Virginia. As Governor Robert Dinwiddie wrote to the Board of Trade in 1756, justifying the colony's turn to bills of credit, "the great Scarcity of Silver and Gold, and the present Emergency of our Affairs made it absolutely necessary . . . and I assure you without the above Currency we cou'd do nothing in support of the Expedition," referring to General Edward Braddock's attempt to capture French Fort Duquesne in present-day Pittsburgh the previous summer.[6] Though the expedition happened to fail, the failure of future expeditions was all but assured without the support of paper bills.

The 1764 Currency Act, like its 1751 predecessor, was Parliament's response to British merchant groups' demands for the protection of sterling debts in North America against rising exchange rates, which the merchants blamed on the overissue of paper money. While earlier complaints had focused on South Carolina and Massachusetts, the latest protests singled out Virginia, where the sterling exchange rate rose to new and great heights in 1762—not because of paper money, but from a complex interplay of factors, which the historian Joseph Ernst identified as a growing trade deficit, a depressed tobacco market, and the retrenchment of British credit.[7] The war was yet another factor. As a New York merchant explained a few years later, the depreciation of the Virginia currency relative to sterling "was honestly acquired, by the Governments exerting itself" against the French enemy. "We have no resources upon an Emergency," he pointed out, echoing Dinwiddie, "but in Paper Money."[8]

British merchants trading to Virginia were less concerned about why the exchange rate was rising than about how the colony's newfound liberty to make money could affect their future profits. In 1762, a group of London, Liverpool, and Glasgow slave and tobacco dealers petitioned the Board of Trade requesting that sterling debts in the colony contracted before the war be payable only in sterling money.[9] The assembly responded with a bankruptcy law to protect tobacco growers and accused the merchants of conspiring to strip Great Planters of their estates. The merchants knew full well that most colonists lacked the specie to settle their accounts, the representatives charged, and without another legal tender to pay their debts, the planters would be forced to liquidate their property for pennies on the pound.[10] The assembly's stubbornness, together with rising concern over the depreciation of the North Carolina currency, convinced the Board of Trade to put the matter to Parliament, and it was decided that the regulation of paper money would be extended to all of the colonies south of New England.[11]

The Currency Act of 1764 banned the colonies from issuing new legal tender bills of credit and from postponing the redemption of old tender.[12] But since the act was passed when most of the colonies still had plenty of paper money circulating from wartime issues, and when more objectionable features of Prime Minister George Grenville's legislative agenda took precedent, the initial opposition was muted—except, perhaps, in Pennsylvania, where, Benjamin Franklin reported to the colony's London agent, Richard Jackson, that summer, "It occasions much Talk."[13]

The Seven Years' War (1754–63), or French and Indian War, had been a boon to Philadelphia merchants thanks to British military spending. All that spending stimulated consumer demand, so that even traders who were not military contractors or privateers benefited from the influx of troops and money. Full employment for mechanics, mariners, and construction workers, moreover, meant higher wages and greater purchasing power. But as soon as the war began to wind down, the inflow of specie dried up, credit contracted, and a depression gripped the town of 19,000. Customers could not settle their accounts with shopkeepers, shopkeepers could not pay their debts to merchants, and merchants could not make their remittances to Britain. While the wealthiest colonists were insulated from the shock, some retailers began declaring bankruptcy as early as 1761. The hardest hit were laboring men and women, including the hundreds of householders who, no longer able to pay property taxes, lost their homes to foreclosure, as well as the growing ranks of the desperately poor. Among them were more than six hundred families that received public support in the bone-chilling winter of 1761–62.[14]

The trading community knew from past experience that a currency emission could help kick-start the economy, prompting a group of Philadelphia merchants to solicit their London counterparts for help. "Unless we can have Liberty for emitting a sufficient quantity of paper currency as a medium of Trade," leading merchant and civic leader James Pemberton informed English physician and fellow Quaker John Fothergill on February 17, 1765, "our Commerce with Great Britain must certainly diminish, and in time utterly drop."[15] The following year the assembly petitioned Parliament for redress and dispatched Franklin to Britain with instructions to use all of his influence "to obtain Repeal of the Act of Parliament prohibiting the making Bills of Credit lawful Tender in the Colony Debts." The representatives were confident that he would "be joined in this Measure by every Merchant in London trading to America; as without [bills] their Exportation must be greatly diminished, and the People here compelled to go into Manufactures, which otherwise they might never attempt." Without a local medium to facilitate trade and debt payments, Atlantic commerce would suffer. The colonists might even have to start making their own goods.[16]

As money grew scarce in the city of brotherly love, a handful of local traders sought to take advantage of the crisis by jointly issuing promissory notes bearing 5 percent interest for nine months, which "they intend to pass upon the public in lieu of Money." Despite being emitted by "Reputable Merchants," the notes caused enough of a stir for at least 217 individuals and firms to publicly renounce them. In one agreement to refuse the notes, the signatories expressed concern that some of the notes "have already passed in Lieu of Money," even though "the Practice has been by Experience found in other Provinces to be prejudicial to Trade"—perhaps alluding to the Massachusetts merchants' notes of 1733—"and we conceive has a Tendency to depreciate our paper money." Another agreement cautioned "all who have regard to the good or safety of the Community not to receive them or countenance the Circulation of them." The covenantors included such prominent Philadelphians as Pemberton, William Fishbourne, Thomas Paschall, Charles Meredith, Thomas Wharton, and Isaac Bartram.[17]

Meanwhile, local newspapers across the colonies warned that the Currency Act would compound the ill consequences stemming from the flight of coin to pay colonial debts in Britain. A writer in the *Pennsylvania Journal* estimated that 1.8 million Spanish dollars had been exported in 1763 and 1764 from Pennsylvania alone.[18] The *Newborn Gazette* reported "vast quantities of Spanish mill'd dollars having been exported from Charlestown since the peace."[19] Making matters worse, the British government had switched from a policy of reimbursing the colonies out of taxes collected in Britain to demanding that part of the cost of defending the continent be paid by the colonists themselves—and in silver, a currency few early Americans possessed. The royal navy's crackdown on smuggling and the Sugar Act of 1764 restricting the colonies' rum trade cut colonists off from the Caribbean, an important market for colonial produce and their one reliable source of silver. "Can we do without paper?" one commentator cried in the *Virginia Gazette*. "Our foreign trade is extinguished, so that we may bid farewell to the pieces of eight." With no paper money and no silver coming in, what would colonists use for a medium of exchange? And without silver, how would they settle their accounts in Britain, let alone pay the hated stamp tax?[20]

Before long the effects of the Currency Act began to register with the general population—about the time that news of the Stamp Act arrived. Thus "a Gentleman at Virginia" declared that the latter was "ill-timed, their Trade with the West-Indies being ruined, the Act preventing their making and issuing any more Paper Currency, enforced so, that you cannot conceive the dismal Situation the Provinces are in for Want of Money of every Kind."[21] The situation there was especially dire, the Great Planters falling deeper into debt to the British merchants who purchased their tobacco on consignment. In 1766, the same year the colony's longtime treasurer, John Robinson, was discovered to have embezzled £100,000 from the public purse for making illegal loans to his gentry friends rather than burning the money as the law required, enslaver and future founding father Richard Henry Lee proposed another debtor protection law that would have been in violation of Parliament's 1732 Debt Recovery Act, which allowed British creditors to claim colonial debtors' lands, houses, and enslaved property.[22]

The Great Planters were worried not just about their own debts but about how smaller debtors' dependence on Scottish factors was eroding traditional bonds of deference and obligation. As fearful of being replaced as they were of losing their own independence, the gentry viewed the stores with suspicion, reflected in the concern they voiced for their poorer neighbors. If the planters felt betrayed by their British friends calling in their debts, they would not let the same fate befall their social inferiors.[23] "If it should be remarked that an increase of paper currency would do little good towards discharging sterling debts," one "Philautos" wrote, "I own that I have chiefly in view the VIRGINIA currency debtors, as being supposed to be the most indigent, and stand in the greatest need of relief."[24] Public displays of gentry largesse notwithstanding, indebted tenants and smallholders began directing their resentment at their creditors, who started carrying guns into the backcountry to collect old balances, and at local sheriffs, who could seize the debtors' property or persons. In some counties, farmers made pacts to shield one another from officers of the law, further alarming the gentry who controlled the court system.[25]

Virginia governor Francis Fauquier, who had succeeded Robert Dinwiddie in 1758, underscored the compounding effects of the Currency Act and the Stamp Act in a June 14, 1765, letter to the Earl of Halifax. As Fauquier explained of the current situation, "Circulating Currency is grown very scarce so that people are realy distressed for money of any kind to satisfy their Creditors: and this Evil is daily encreasing; for the Treasury notes are annually diminish'd by the burning and sinking all that are received for Taxes." He went on to note that "this private Distress which every man feels, increases the general Dissatisfaction at the Duties laid by the late Stamp Act, which breaks out and shews itself on every trifling occasion."[26] The author of *A Letter from a Merchant in Philadelphia, to his Correspondent in London* likewise lamented that "our paper currency will soon be done, and in a short time all the hard money on the Continent will not suffice to pay the taxes laid upon us. Bankruptcies are daily following bankruptcies. Suits are multiplying to an immense degree. Numberless plantations exposed to sale, and few or no buyers." He added that "In Virginia ... a great part of the moveable property (especially in the back counties) is under execution to pay the taxes already laid by their own laws," including, presumably, property in enslaved people, so "how then will it be when the Stamps take place?"[27] Such breathless accounts of the Stamp Act's wide-ranging consequences at once attest to the urgency of the money question as well as its radical potential for uniting broad segments of colonial society.

The Currency Act Repeal Movement

A transatlantic movement to repeal the Currency Act was steadily gathering steam in Britain. The movement included a core group of colonial agents and a significant subset of London merchants, those who helped get the Stamp Act repealed in 1766. Their arguments were more economic than constitutional, Joseph Ernst argued, "rooted in the needs and demands of [colonial] merchants, planters, and farmers," and, indeed, the needs and demands of British businessmen.[28] As the merchants and manufacturers of Manchester put it in a November 1765 memorial to the Lords of the Treasury, "the extreme Want of current Cash" in North America was making it impossible for their colonial correspondents, "though of the greatest Property, and highest Credit," to offload their goods, and consequently "very scanty Remittances have been made in Return for their Manufactures exported last Year." From the colonies' misfortune, the trade of Manchester "suffered a great and sudden Diminution."[29] In October 1765, "A MERCHANT" wrote to the editor of London's *Public Ledger* opposing the previous year's Sugar Act and stated that, "concerning the Paper-currency Act, I think plainly shews, that our national interests must require [the Currency Act's] being new modelled, if not entirely repealed."[30]

The repeal movement kicked into high gear in the spring of 1766. First Benjamin Franklin, who was in London representing several colonies, drafted a bill for eliminating the Currency Act's legal tender provision. His principal aim was winning over the British traders who opposed paper money, including those who claimed to have "suffer'd in Virginia by Depreciation of the Currency there in which their Debts were paid." To that end, Franklin incorporated a clause allowing judges to adjust for depreciation sterling debts payable in paper money, a practice several colonies, including Massachusetts and Virginia itself, had already adopted by law or custom.[31] The following year, the London merchants for repeal presented to the Board of Trade the case for restoring the colonial currencies' legal tender status, while Franklin circulated his own objections to the Currency Act around London. Although the merchants were mostly in agreement with the agents, the merchants wanted the repeal bill to include more precise language protecting British debts in America.[32] After many meetings over many months, Franklin reported in June 1767, "the Ministry had agreed to the Repeal."[33]

But the agents and merchants were suddenly forced to withdraw their support when it became possible that the Currency Act could be replaced by something far worse. That something worse was a scheme for a "continental currency," proposed by none other than Franklin himself to Lord Grenville two years earlier as a revenue-raising alternative to the Stamp Act, whereby the Bank of England would issue interest-bearing paper money for the use of the colonies, the interest payable to "the Crown . . . as a general Tax on the Colonies."[34] At that point even Franklin was reluctant to press on with repeal, "afraid an ill Use will be made of" his plan by politicians eager to exploit "our Necessities for Paper Money, to draw a Revenue from that Article whenever they grant us the Liberty we want of making it a legal Tender."[35] Besides, surely the assemblies would never agree to a scheme that usurped their authority, formal or otherwise, over the appropriation of public funds.

The year 1768 brought a new challenge. The new secretary of state for the colonies Wills Hill, the Earl of Hillsborough, had pushed for the Currency Act and was firmly against its repeal. On February 2, North Carolina governor William Tryon endorsed the assembly's petition to the king laying out "the Inconveniences" the colonists suffered "for want of a greater Medium of Trade," including having their "Effects" seized by tax collectors and creditors.[36] Hillsborough responded by reminding Tryon not only that the king lacked the authority to intervene in the money question, but also that "this Matter has already received so full a Discussion at the Board of Trade, at the Privy Council and in each House of Parliament; & so strong and unanimous a Determination that Paper Currency with a Legal Tender is big with Frauds, & full of mischief to the Colonies, & to commerce in general, that I apprehend no consideration of a possible local Inconvenience will induce a deviation from the sound Principles of the Act of Parliament relative thereto."[37] He made similar remarks to the governor of New York, the only other colony as persistent as North Carolina in its resolve to make paper money legal tender following the French and Indian War.[38]

The Currency Act crisis was about more than just a lack of cash for paying taxes or participating in the world of goods. From New York to Georgia, the land dispossession and debt bondage that money scarcity portended haunted tenants, farmers, and planters alike. "What greater pain can a man feel," one commentator wrote to the printers of the *Pennsylvania Gazette* in January 1768, "than the apprehension of having his goods and estate taken from him by execution, and perhaps himself shut up in prison, thus rendered incapable of providing himself and family with a morsel of bread? Alarming thought! enough to make a careful, thinking man, shudder; and the more so, when he reflects, it is not for want of industry and assiduity in him, but for want of a currency, which it is impossible for him to reach."[39] A writer in the *Pennsylvania Chronicle* warned that "in a short time the remainder of our paper money will be sunk, whence must follow barter, trust, declension of trade, and of course bankruptcies, poverty, and want."[40] And the *Virginia Gazette* reported on April 28 that lawsuits would soon begin "against the principal estates in the country, which must be sold; and though they go at half the expected price, where is the money to pay for them?"[41] Another author found the Currency Act to be "a very strange one." He agreed that making paper money legal tender for sterling debts "was wrong," but saw no reason why it should not be so for currency debts. "[W]as there no remedy for this without destroying all our currencies?" he asked. "Would a surgeon be entitled to the praise of either skill or humanity who should amputate a limb before trying milder applications, because a sore appeared upon some part of it?"[42]

The Currency Act crisis was felt keenly in the back counties of North Carolina, where in 1766 farmers had complained to the governor and assembly that there was no money for paying local taxes and debts. Debt cases in the county courts and forced sales surged, and some debtors had to work off the debts they owed. An act for granting £15,000 to Governor Tryon for a new house was the final straw before the Regulator Rebellion burst onto the scene.[43] In the spring of 1768, 500 Regulators closed the Anson County courthouse to stop debt suits before moving on a village in Orange County, where they broke out of jail one of their members who was accused of insulting an officer of the court. When Tryon relayed the event to Hillsborough, he tried to explain that "these Regulators declare [that] they are not satisfied with the Public & County Taxes and that it is not in their Power to procure Specie or Currency from its scarcity to discharge them. Under such Circumstances they have associated themselves together by solemn Oath to prevent the sheriffs levying on their Goods & Chattels." But "if His Majesty in His Wisdom should grant the Address of this Colony for a Currency I persuade myself the Public Taxes would be collected without any Obstruction."[44] The

Pennsylvania Gazette likewise attributed the "great disturbances in that province" to the Currency Act.[45]

The Regulators struck again that September, refusing to pay any local taxes until the act for granting a sum for the governor's mansion was repealed and shutting down the courts to prevent the execution of debts. The *Virginia Gazette* reported that the Regulators' greatest grievance "is the want of a paper currency, or some medium to answer the trade of the country."[46] Similar actions unfolded in Worcester, Massachusetts, where a crowd of farmers closed the courts from November 1765 to April 1766 to protest money scarcity and high taxes, and in New Jersey, where settlers closed the courts in 1769 and 1770 to stop debt lawsuits.[47] While the colonial elites who dominated the North Carolina assembly also wanted to expand the currency so they could finally receive their salaries, their hands were tied. The assembly thought it could get away with a new emission if the money was earmarked, ironically, for paying the troops who had opposed the Regulators in Orange County. But the best it could do was issue non–legal tender "treasury certificates." Hardly anything was done to rectify debt-related hardships, all but ensuring that the Regulators would continue to seek redress.[48]

Colony after colony petitioned the Crown and Parliament complaining of money scarcity and asking for permission to issue additional sums of legal tender. New Jersey "requested Liberty for the Emission of a Paper Currency" for the encouragement of "Trade and Commerce."[49] Virginia lamented that money scarcity was obstructing trade, deflating commodity prices, and subjecting "the Poor . . . to dangerous Oppressions."[50] South Carolina gave the king a glowing account of its bills of credit and cautioned that their discontinuation would subject every debtor to imprisonment and his estate to seizure and sale even "for the most inconsiderable Debt." Without paper currency, moreover, colonists would be forced to adopt specie as a local medium rather than export it to Britain, and then "so much the less of British Manufactures must We Import because the less able to pay for them."[51] Several colonies relented and issued small sums of short-term, non–legal tender bills to provide temporary relief. Some delayed the redemption of old bills in violation of the Currency Act, while others suspended taxes to redeem the bills altogether.[52] At all events, the disparate colonies seemed to be speaking in the same need-based dialect of the monetary language.

The Currency Act and the Loan Office System

The Currency Act threw the colonial loan office system into disarray, particularly in Pennsylvania and New Jersey. Ordinary colonists and officials alike could not fathom that their paper bills of credit were no longer legal tender for public loan payments. In 1769, when forced sales of property were at a high, perhaps thousands of freeholders in total petitioned their representatives for relief. Twenty-one inhabitants of Lancaster County in Pennsylvania professed that they were "well aware of the Act of Parliament which prohibits our Paper Money . . . being a legal Tender in the Payment of even Colony Debts," but if the assembly could merely make their money legal tender in the discharge of mortgages, that would be enough for them to gladly "take the same in Discharge of all Contracts, though it be not a legal Tender."[53] Future loyalist Joseph Galloway fumed to Benjamin Franklin in June 1770 after the Crown had rejected New York's and New Jersey's recent attempts to renew their respective loan office acts: "A Farmer Pledges his Land with the Government and takes Paper—when he comes to redeem his Pledge ought he not to return the Paper, and ought not the Government to be obliged to receive [it] in Discharge of the Land? To say that the [Currency Act is] intended to prevent this is to say it is Prohibitory of all Paper Money in America."[54]

The freeholders of Middlesex County in New Jersey were especially concerned about the lack of money for paying debts, but they, too, would settle for a currency that was legal tender at the loan office. On October 26, 1769, they petitioned the assembly about "the deplorable State of this Country and Province in general, arising, as we apprehend, partly from the excessive Scarcity of Money, and Decay of Trade," but mostly from the devastating flood of debt lawsuits, "which like an overflowing Stream have deluged the Land, and ruined Hundreds of Families, formerly in easy Circumstances, and swept away their Livings and Estates; and yet threatens the Destruction and Desolution to many more in every Part of the Province." The freeholders instructed their two representatives to do everything in their power to "lessen the Number of Law-suits, especially in Actions for Debt," as well as to "get an Emission of Paper Currency, to be lett out on Land Security."[55]

The previous year, New Jersey governor William Franklin had written to Hillsborough about the nonimportation boycott (started by Boston merchants to protest new imperial taxes on glass, paper, lead, paint, and tea imported from Britain), assuring him that as long as Jersey farmers had enough land and were "allowed a moderate Quantity of Paper Currency to be issued on Loan as formerly" against said land, they would have no reason to turn to manufactures.[56] "The People here are so anxious about this matter," he reiterated a few months later, "that they would not hesitate to take the money, and mortgage their Estates for the repayment of it with Interest tho' it should not be made a legal tender [for debts]."[57] On September 29, 1770, after the Crown vetoed the colony's loan office act because it made the currency legal tender in discharge of mortgages, Franklin ranted to Hillsborough that "it was never imagined here that so extensive a Construction would be put upon the Act of Parliament for restraining Paper Currencies in America, as that the Money should not even be a Tender to the Loan-Offices that issued it. If this had been known here," he continued, echoing Galloway's frustrations, "the Assembly would not have attempted to pass an Act for Striking Paper Money, for it would have been the Heighth of Absurdity to expect that any Persons would mortgage their Estates to the Loan Office for Money which they could not afterwards oblige the Office to receive again in Discharge of their Mortgages."[58]

A few years earlier, in 1766, the Virginia assembly had petitioned the king for permission to establish its own loan office to help small growers pay their debts and to prevent the undervaluation of debtors' property at sheriffs' sales, but the Board of Trade disapproved.[59] The paper money shortage not only decreased the purchasing power of tobacco farmers, for it was always more expensive to buy on credit, but also hurt the farmers when their debts were called in. Without money to pay their creditors, debtors had their property seized by county sheriffs—not just land but livestock, tools, household goods, and enslaved laborers as well. And because of money scarcity, the sheriffs struggled to liquidate the assets, often selling them at auction at a steep discount, forcing the sheriffs to seize and liquidate more and more assets until enough money came in to satisfy the debt. In light of the growing crisis, the assembly argued that public loans would help facilitate local debt payments and help keep up property values. To put it another way, a loan office would enable anxious Great Planters to collect their debts more easily, putting them in a better position to satisfy the debts they themselves owed to British merchants.[60]

As efforts to enlarge the Virginia currency were thwarted, public slave auctions became increasingly common in the decade before the American Revolution, with traumatic consequences for the enslaved.[61] The rise in slave rebelliousness in Virginia in the years leading to the revolution may well have been connected to the rising numbers of bondspeople being trotted to the auction block, moving legislators to pass a suite of new bills concerning slave punishment. Poisonings, barn burnings, and armed flight stoked fears of a Tacky's Rebellion in the Tidewater.[62] Doubtless many enslaved people were simply trying to make their way back to kith and kin. Take Harry, an enslaved Virginian who "was taken by execution, and sold at public sale" to satisfy his enslaver's debt to Henry Brodnax, only to "[make] his escape in a few hours," headed, the enslaver suspected, to "the neighborhood where he formerly lived." Or Curry Tuxent, a fifty-year-old carpenter who had gone after "a parcel" of enslaved people "lately purchased" at an estate sale, presumably his friends.[63] Only after failing to obtain approval for a loan office, in 1769, did the assembly try to pass an act for curbing the importation of African captives—if small planters insisted on purchasing enslaved people, the reasoning went, they had better buy them from their wealthy neighbors than from British slave dealers. The Crown's disallowance of the act worsened relations between the Virginia gentry and the British government, and informed the gentry's decision to join the nonimportation boycott. As for the small farmers, they were doing quite well by the end of the decade, thanks to a tobacco boom in the late 1760s.

By the time Virginia finally managed to issue additional sums of legal tender currency in July 1775, it was under the auspices of the Virginia convention. The emission was in defiance of Governor John Murray, the Earl of Dunmore, who had rejected a bill to pay for his war against the Shawnee and Mingo the previous summer, and it was to raise and provide "for the forces and minute-men directed to be embodied for the defence of this colony." This was after Dunmore had threatened to free and ally with patriots' enslaved property a few months earlier, a threat he made good on that October, after dozens of enslaved people had already joined his regiment of their own volition. The same patriots who approved the emission and paid their workers' wages in the new paper money were less keen on accepting it in payment of rent, setting off a Christmas rent strike in Loudon County.[64]

The New York Exception

One colony eventually received a special Parliamentary dispensation to make its bills of credit legal tender for taxes but not debts. In the summer of 1766, the recently installed New York governor Henry Moore convinced the Board of Trade to alter his instructions to allow him to approve a new paper money bill, provided it contained a suspending clause.[65] But the assembly rebuffed the concession, insisting that any paper money act not only *not* have a suspending clause, but also make the money legal tender for debts.[66] Although the assembly was dominated by conservative merchants, those merchants depended on artisans' and laborers' votes to keep them in office—and those artisans and laborers needed money. On June 3, 1767, the assembly, lamenting of "the [Jails], for Want of a circulating Medium, being filled with Debtors," refused to spend a penny more on quartering the king's troops until Parliament repealed the Currency Act.[67] Obliged by "the Clamours raised in the Country on account of the wretched state to which numbers of Families have been lately reduced," they next tried to establish a new loan office. In the summer of 1769, at the height of the nonimportation movement, Moore suggested to Hillsborough that "the emission of Paper Currency" would "make such impression on the minds of the People, as to . . . prevent their following these recent examples of opposition which can only tend to widen the Breach between Great Britain and her Colonies."[68]

A few months later the assembly reversed course and made the daring and controversial move to vote supplies for the troops. Moore's successor, Cadwallader Colden, nevertheless cautioned Hillsborough that unless the Crown approved the loan office bill, it would "be difficult to make them continue the Provision for the Soldiers quartered in their Province" in accordance with the Quartering Act of 1765.[69] The assembly's betrayal, however strategic, infuriated Son of Liberty Alexander McDougall. He warned, not unreasonably, that "every Overture for procuring the requested Aids, by promising the Emission of a Paper Currency, must be Insidious and hollow."[70] But the maneuver may have worked. Parliament agreed to a revised version of the loan office bill and, in May 1770, passed a special statute permitting passage of the act. The assembly initially snubbed the concession, refusing to pass a law that did not make paper money legal tender for debts, but eventually took the favor.[71] This feat may well have emboldened the province's merchants to abandon nonimportation that summer.[72]

The same privilege was not extended to the New Jersey assembly, whose act for a loan office was disallowed, or to the Virginia and Georgia assemblies, which both tried, and failed, to enact measures making paper money legal tender for taxes. Assemblies retaliated by refusing to comply with the Quartering Act unless relieved, governors wrote to the Board of Trade complaining about money scarcity, and newspapers documented a surge in pickpockets, counterfeits, and robberies. In the fall of 1770, South Carolina governor William Bull reported that "our internal Commerce is carried on by Credit or Barter especially between the Back Settlers and Charles Town."[73] Earlier that year William Tryon had informed Hillsborough that North Carolina "continues in extreme want of a larger Medium of Trade" and that "the Paper Currency now in Circulation [is] big with Mischiefs from Counterfeits."[74] That summer he declared victory against the Regulators, managed with only £500 in the treasury and neither arms nor ammunition in the magazines. He estimated the total cost at £40,000, "a Load the Province is absolutely incapable to Discharge unless by a new Emission of Currency, or an Aid from parliament."[75]

There was little progress on the money question until William Legge, Lord Dartmouth, replaced Hillsborough as Secretary of State. Dartmouth and the Board of Trade moved to apply a more lenient interpretation to the Currency Act. The catalyst was not colonial protest but the British credit crisis of 1772, the worst recession since the bursting of the South Sea Bubble in 1720.

British merchants who had liberally extended credit to colonial importers called in their debts, renewing economic dislocation in Virginia, where some Great Planters were forced to sell entire plantations to pay their creditors. In Philadelphia, "daily accounts of heavy failures among the Shopkeepers" were reported in the fall of 1773. Following the boom years of 1771 and 1772, merchants' shelves and warehouses overflowed with dry goods as commodity prices fell, bills of exchange to send to Britain grew scarce or were returned protested, the sterling exchange rate climbed, and real estate values collapsed. Between 1770 and 1773, counterfeit bills of credit were discovered in Pennsylvania, Connecticut, New York, New Jersey, and Virginia.[76]

Against this backdrop, Parliament passed a special statute amending the Currency Act of 1764. The statute, enacted in May 1773, permitted assemblies to designate paper money as legal tender for taxes but still not for debts or mortgages. It was thus on a par with both the Currency Act of 1751 and the New York statute of 1770.[77] The same month, Parliament bailed out the failing East India Company to the tune of £1,400,000 and granted it a tea monopoly. Undeterred by the politics of tea, Pennsylvania established a new loan office the following year. New Jersey soon followed. But not all the colonies were satisfied with the new arrangement. North Carolina and New York continued to demand the liberty to make their paper money legal tender for debts. In a 1775 petition to the king, the loyalist-leaning New York assembly denounced the Currency Act as a detriment to trade "and a violation of our legislative rights," one that "may hereafter disable your Majesty's subjects, upon proper requisition, and upon certain emergencies, from granting such aids as may be necessary for the general safety of the empire."[78] The following month the assembly delivered a remonstrance to Parliament containing several grievances, including "the act for prohibiting the legislature of this colony from passing any law for the emission of a paper currency to be a legal tender in the colony." It reiterated that "the want of this power may in future prevent his Majesty's faithful subjects here, from rectifying their loyalty and affection to our gracious Sovereign, and from granting such aids as may be necessary for the general weal and safety of the British empire."[79]

The colonies finally got their money. But the 1773 concession was too little, too late: the colonial economy was in shambles, and Parliamentary supremacy had been asserted and acknowledged.[80] By 1774, the year the Continental Congress issued its Declaration and Resolves, some assemblies were already issuing new paper money independent of governors and councils. In the spring and summer of 1775, Massachusetts and Virginia seized the opportunity to form extralegal congresses, and through those congresses issued legal

THE CURRENCY ACT CRISIS 227

tender currencies. The Currency Act crisis thus merged with the wider imperial crisis, and soon the rejection of Parliamentary meddling with the colonies' power to make money became part of the logic of the American Revolution.[81] On the eve of independence, a bill of credit appeared in Massachusetts, the birthplace of America's first paper money, proudly—and finally—"issued in defence of American liberty."

FIGURE E.1. Colony of Massachusetts Bay sixteen-shilling bill of credit, 1775. The figure is holding a sword in one hand and a copy of Magna Carta in the other. Courtesy American Antiquarian Society.

Acknowledgments

This project had its genesis in 2008 at Barnard College, when Alan Dye introduced me to the work of the economist Farley Grubb. As my interests evolved during my seven years at Boston University, Brendan McConville and Jon Roberts provided steadfast guidance and mentorship. Lou Ferleger and John Thornton showed me different ways of doing history. Christine Desan has been a generous mentor and supporter of this project since we first met at the Massachusetts Historical Society in the summer of 2015. My friends from Boston University, especially Alex Buckley, Christina Carrick, Lilly Havstad, Amy Noel Ellison, and Robert Shimp, offered emotional support and tolerated my tomfoolery. My best times were with my fellow alum from Barnard and BU, Kristin Young. I am beyond grateful for Anne Blaschke, whose friendship I cherish. Texas Tech University gave me lifelong friends in Allison Powers Useche and Patricia Pelley.

Research for this book was supported with fellowships from the Massachusetts Historical Society, the Library Company of Philadelphia's Program in Early American Economy and Society, and the Huntington Library/National Endowment for the Humanities, as well as with research funding from Boston University, Texas Tech University, and the University of California, Santa Barbara. Research assistants and staff at the American Antiquarian Society (especially Brianne Barrett), the American Philosophical Society, the Library of Congress, the New York State Archives, the Pennsylvania Historical Society, the Smithsonian Institution, and the South Carolina Department of Archives and History provided research and technical support. My eight months at the Huntington Library in 2019 and 2020 were enlivened and enriched by Dympna Callaghan, Véronica Castillo-Muñoz, Christopher Clark, and Alejandra Dubcovsky. I am especially grateful to Ann Daly for organizing the Brown University Early American Money Symposium (and its successor, the Early American Money Workshop), which brought together early American money enthusiasts virtually during the COVID-19 pandemic.

The organizers and participants of various workshops and seminars provided support and feedback at critical junctures: the USC-Huntington Early Modern Studies Institute American Origins Seminar (2019), the Global Histories of Colonialism Workshop at Queen's University (2020), the Pauline Maier Early American History Seminar at the Massachusetts Historical Society (2022), the Brown University Early American Money Workshop (2021), the Money, Power, and Print Colloquium at the University of Galway (2022), the UCSB Colloquium on History and Political Economy (2023), and the *WMQ*-EMSI Workshop on Money in Vast Early America at the Huntington Library (2023). I also had opportunities to present portions of my work at several larger conferences, including the Business History Conference Annual Meeting (2021), the Society for Historians of the Early American Republic Annual Meeting (2021), the Organization of American Historians Conference on American History (2023), and Money as a Democratic Medium 2.0 (2023). Christopher Clark, Ann Daly, Andrew Edwards, Hannah Farber, Josh Greenberg, Steve Hindle, Drew Konove, Simon Middleton, Sean Moore, Ann Murphy, Sharon Murphy, Seth Rockman, Carole Shammas, and many others to whom I am indebted provided invaluable feedback on work-in-progress.

I am especially appreciative of my comrades and colleagues in the History Department at the University of California, Santa Barbara: Véronica Castillo-Muñoz, Utathya Chattopadhyaya, Juan Cobo Betancourt, Manuel Covo, Lisa Jacobson, Stephan Miescher, Taylor Moore, Alice O'Connor, Giuliana Perrone, Ann Plane, Erika Rappaport, Sherene Seikaly, and David Stein. I am grateful to my editor, Tim Mennel, for guiding me through the publication process, and to the American Beginnings series editors—Hannah Farber, Stephen Mihm, and Mark Peterson—for their enthusiasm and support. The anonymous reviewers of my manuscript provided generous and insightful advice on ways to restructure the material and improve the narrative. Andrea Blatz at the University of Chicago Press was a huge help during the final stages of production.

This book would not have been possible without my family: my parents Dennis and Clorinda, who harbored me during the early months of the pandemic and gave me a place to think and write; my brothers Tim and Evan; and Amanda Da Silva. Evan helped me rescue many of my research and writing materials from the depths of the cloud, while he and Amanda cooked me many delicious meals and took me on adventures when I wasn't working. Dave and June Kretz welcomed me into their family. My best friend Melissa Ward got me out of my graduate school doldrums with her much anticipated

ACKNOWLEDGMENTS

visits to Boston. My partner Dale Kretz, who inspires me every day to be a better scholar and person, read every word of this book. Any mistakes are his alone. Our daughter, Florence, who was born the day after I submitted my manuscript, is my reason for being.

Portions of this book have been previously published in different forms:

> Katie A. Moore, "America's First Stimulus Package: Paper Money and the Body Politic in Colonial Pennsylvania, 1715–1730," *Pennsylvania History: A Journal of Mid-Atlantic Studies* 83, no. 4 (Autumn 2016): 529–57. © 2016 The Pennsylvania Historical Association. Reprinted with permission of Penn State University Press.
>
> Katie A. Moore, "The Blood That Nourishes the Body Politic: The Origins of Paper Money in Early America," *Early American Studies: An Interdisciplinary Journal* 17, no. 1 (Winter 2019): 1–36. © 2019 The McNeil Center for Early American Studies.
>
> Katie A. Moore, "To Counterfeit Is Death? Money, Print, and Punishment in the Early American Public Sphere," *Early American Studies: An Interdisciplinary Journal* 21, no. 2 (Spring 2023): 233–71. © 2023 The McNeil Center for Early American Studies.

Abbreviations

CCR	*Colonial Currency Reprints: 1682–1751*, ed. Andrew McFarland Davis, 4 vols. (Boston: Prince Society, 1910–11)
CLNY	*The Colonial Laws of New York from the Year 1664 to the Revolution*, ed. James B. Lyon, 5 vols. (Albany: 1894–96)
CSP	*Calendar of State Papers: Colonial, America and West Indies*, ed. W. Noel Sainsbury, J. W. Fortescue, Cecil Headlam, Arthur Percival Newton, and K. G. Davies, 45 vols. (London: His Majesty's Stationery Office, 1860–1994), digital edition by University of London and History of Parliament Trust, available at https://www.british-history.ac.uk/cal-state-papers/colonial/america-west-indies. Volume and page ranges are cited for reference.
EAS	*Early American Studies: An Interdisciplinary Journal*
Franklin Papers	*The Papers of Benjamin Franklin*, ed. Leonard W. Labaree, William B. Willcox, Claude A. Lopez, Barbara B. Oberg, Ellen R. Cohn, 43 vols. (New Haven: Yale University Press, 1953–)
HSP	Historical Society of Pennsylvania, Philadelphia
JEH	*Journal of Economic History*
JPE	*Journal of Political Economy*
LCP	Library Company of Philadelphia
LOC	Library of Congress, Washington, DC
MAC	Massachusetts Archives Collection, Massachusetts Archives, Boston, microfilm
MASS	*Acts and Resolves, Public and Private, of the Province of Massachusetts Bay*, ed. Abner C. Goodell and Ellis Ames, 21 vols. (Boston, 1869–1922)
MHS	Massachusetts Historical Society, Boston
NBER	National Bureau of Economic Research
NEQ	*New England Quarterly*
NYSA	New York State Archives, Albany
SCDAH	South Carolina Department of Archives and History, Columbia, microfilm
SLSC	*The Statutes at Large of South Carolina*, ed. Thomas Cooper and David J. McCord, 10 vols. (Columbia, 1836–41)
TNA: CO 5	The National Archives of the UK, Kew, Colonial Office 5. Department code and series number are quoted for reference.
WMQ	*William and Mary Quarterly*

Notes

Introduction

1. Sarah Kemble Knight, "The Private Journal Kept by Madam Knight, on a Journey from Boston to New-York, In the Year 1704, From the Original Manuscript," in *The Journals of Madam Knight, and Rev. Mr. Buckingham from the Original Manuscripts, Written in 1704 & 1710* (New York: Wilder & Campbell, 1825), 42–43; Mary Beth Norton, *Separated by Their Sex: Women in Public and Private in the Colonial Atlantic World* (Ithaca, NY: Cornell University Press, 2011), 105–8; John J. McCusker, *Money and Exchange in Europe and America, 1600–1775: A Handbook* (Chapel Hill: University of North Carolina Press, 1978), 117–18.

2. Knight, "The Private Journal Kept by Madam Knight," 44–45. For the view of money as a "natural product of human economy," see Carl Menger, *Principles of Economics*, trans. James Dingwall and Bert F. Hoselitz (Auburn, AL: Ludwig von Mises Institute, 2007), 262–63.

3. John Maynard Keynes, *A Treatise on Money, Vol. 1: The Pure Theory of Money* (London: Macmillan, 1930), 4–5. For the state theory of money, see Georg Friedrich Knapp, *The State Theory of Money*, abridged ed., trans. H. M. Lucas and J. Bonar (London: Macmillan, 1924).

4. W. T. Baxter, "Credit, Bills, and Bookkeeping in a Simple Economy," *Accounting Review* 21, no. 2 (April 1946): 154–66.

5. For the nineteenth-century United States, see Naomi Lamoreaux, *Insider Lending: Banks, Personal Connections, and Economic Development in Industrial New England* (New York: Cambridge University Press, 1997); Howard Bodenhorn, *A History of Banking in Antebellum America: Financial Markets and Economic Development in an Era of Nation-Building* (New York: Cambridge University Press, 2000); Stephen Mihm, *A Nation of Counterfeiters: Capitalists, Con Men, and the Making of the United States* (Cambridge, MA: Harvard University Press, 2007); Jessica Lepler, *The Many Panics of 1837: People, Politics, and the Creation of a Transatlantic Financial Crisis* (New York: Cambridge University Press, 2013); Sharon Ann Murphy, *Other People's Money: How Banking Worked in the Early American Republic* (Baltimore: Johns Hopkins University Press, 2017); Joshua R. Greenberg, *Bank Notes and Shin Plasters: The Rage for Paper Money in the Early Republic* (Philadelphia: University of Pennsylvania Press, 2020). For early modern England, see Bruce G. Carruthers, *City of Capital: Politics and Markets in the English Financial Revolution* (Princeton: Princeton University Press, 1996); Craig Muldrew, *The Economy of Obligation: The Culture of Credit and Social Relations in Early Modern England* (New York: St. Martin's Press, 1998); Margot C. Finn, *The Character of Credit: Personal Debt in English Culture, 1740–1914* (New York: Cambridge University Press, 2003); Deborah Valenze, *The Social Life of Money in the English Past* (New York: Cambridge University Press, 2006); Mary Poovey, *Genres*

of the Credit Economy: Mediating Value in Eighteenth- and Nineteenth-Century Britain (Chicago: University of Chicago Press, 2008); Carl Wennerlind, *Casualties of Credit: The English Financial Revolution, 1620–1720* (Cambridge, MA: Harvard University Press, 2011); Christine Desan, *Making Money: Coin, Currency, and the Coming of Capitalism* (New York: Oxford University Press, 2015). For Canada, see Brian Gettler, *Colonialism's Currency: Money, State, and First Nations in Canada, 1820–1950* (Montreal: McGill-Queen's University Press, 2020).

6. Daniel Johnson, "'Nothing will satisfy you but money': Debt, Freedom, and the Mid-Atlantic Culture of Money," *EAS* 19, no. 1 (Winter 2021): 135; Simon Middleton, "William Fishbourn's 'Misfortune': Public Accounting and Paper Money in Early Pennsylvania," *EAS* 19, no. 1 (Winter 2021): 68; Catherine Desbarats, "On Being Surprised: By New France's Playing Card Money, for Example," *Canadian Historical Review* 102, no. 1 (March 2021): 151.

7. Other recent works include Simon Middleton, "Runaways, Rewards, and the Social History of Money," *EAS* 15, no. 3 (Summer 2017): 617–47; Jeffrey Sklansky, *Sovereign of the Market: The Money Question in Early America* (Chicago: University of Chicago Press, 2017). For a legal approach, see Claire Priest, "Currency Policies and Legal Development in Colonial New England," *Yale Law Journal* 110, no. 8 (June 2001): 1303–1405; Christine Desan, "The Market as a Matter of Money: Denaturalizing Economic Currency in American Constitutional History," *Law & Social Inquiry* 30, no. 1 (Winter 2005): 1–60. For the revolutionary era, see Andrew David Edwards, "Grenville's Silver Hammer: The Problem of Money in the Stamp Act Crisis," *Journal of American History* 104, no. 2 (September 2017): 337–62; Justin Du Rivage, *Revolution against Empire: Taxes, Politics, and the Origins of American Independence* (New Haven: Yale University Press, 2017). The authoritative numismatic account is Eric P. Newman, *The Early Paper Money of America: An Illustrated, Historical, and Descriptive Collection of Data Relating to American Paper Currency from Its Inception in 1686 to the Year 1800* (Iola, WI: Krause Publications, 2008). Formative older works include Curtis P. Nettles, *The Money Supply of the American Colonies before 1720* (Madison, WI: Curtin Putnam, 1934); Richard A. Lester, *Monetary Experiments: Early American and Recent Scandinavian* (Princeton: Princeton University Press, 1939); E. James Ferguson, "Currency Finance: An Interpretation of Colonial Monetary Practices," *WMQ* 10, no. 2 (April 1953): 153–80; Jack P. Greene and Richard M. Jellison, "The Currency Act of 1764 in Imperial-Colonial Relations, 1764–1776," *WMQ* 18, no. 4 (October 1961): 485–518; Roger W. Weiss, "The Issue of Paper Money in the American Colonies, 1720–1774," *JEH* 30, no. 4 (December 1970): 770–84; Joseph Albert Ernst, *Money and Politics in America, 1755–1775: A Study in the Currency Act of 1764 and the Political Economy of Revolution* (Chapel Hill: University of North Carolina Press, 1973); Leslie V. Brock, *The Currency of the American Colonies, 1700–1764: A Study in Colonial Finance and Imperial Relations* (New York: Arno Press, 1975).

8. A. Mitchell Innes, "The Credit Theory of Money," *Banking Law Journal* 31 (December–January 1914): 154.

9. Geoffrey K. Ingham, *The Nature of Money* (Cambridge, UK: Polity Press, 2004), 84.

10. [John Wise], *A Word of Comfort to a Melancholy Country* [Boston, 1721], in *CCR*, 2:212.

11. [Hugh Vans], *An Inquiry into the Nature and Uses of Money* [Boston, 1740], in *CCR*, 3:369–70.

12. Michel Aglietta, *Money: 5,000 Years of Debt and Power* (New York: Verso Books, 2018), 78.

13. Aglietta and André Orleans, *La monnaie souveraine* (Paris: Odile Jacob, 1998), 24–27.

14. Stefan Eich, *The Currency of Politics: The Political Theory of Money from Aristotle to Keynes* (Princeton: Princeton University Press, 2022), 6.

15. Akinobu Kuroda, "Another History of Money Viewed from Africa and Asia," in Karin Pallaver, ed., *Monetary Transitions: Currencies, Colonialism and African Societies* (London: Palgrave Macmillan, 2022), 268–69.

16. Keith Hart, "Money in an Unequal World," *Anthropological Theory* 1, no. 3 (2001): 321.

17. For a brief overview of the "money as a neutral veil" position, see John N. Smithin, *Controversies in Monetary Economics*, rev. ed. (Northampton, MA: Edward Elgar, 2003), 2.

18. For the nineteenth century, see Walter Johnson, *River of Dark Dreams: Slavery and Empire in the Cotton Kingdom* (Cambridge, MA: Harvard University Press, 2013); Edward Baptist, *The Half Has Never Been Told: Slavery and the Making of American Capitalism* (New York: Basic Books, 2014); Calvin Schermerhorn, *The Business of Slavery and the Rise of American Capitalism, 1814–1860* (New Haven: Yale University Press, 2015); Caitlin Rosenthal, *Accounting for Slavery: Masters and Management* (Cambridge, MA: Harvard University Press, 2018); Sharon Ann Murphy, *Banking on Slavery: Financing Southern Expansion in the Antebellum United States* (Chicago: University of Chicago Press, 2023).

19. Serena R. Zabin, *Dangerous Economies: Status and Commerce in Imperial New York* (Philadelphia: University of Pennsylvania Press, 2009); Ellen Hartigan-O'Connor, *The Ties That Buy: Women and Commerce in Revolutionary America* (Philadelphia: University of Pennsylvania Press, 2009); Robert S. DuPlessis, *The Material Atlantic: Clothing, Commerce, and Colonization in the Atlantic World, 1650–1800* (New York: Cambridge University Press, 2015); Christy Clark-Pujara, *Dark Work: The Business of Slavery in Rhode Island* (New York: New York University Press, 2016); Jared Hardesty, *Unfreedom: Slavery and Dependence in Eighteenth-Century Boston* (New York: New York University Press, 2016); Katherine Smoak, "The Weight of Necessity: Counterfeit Coins in the British Atlantic World, circa 1760–1800," *WMQ* 74, no. 3 (July 2017): 467–502; Emma Hart, *Trading Spaces: The Colonial Marketplace and the Foundations of American Capitalism* (Chicago: University of Chicago Press, 2019); Justene Hill Edwards, *Unfree Markets: The Slaves' Economy and the Rise of Capitalism in South Carolina* (New York: Columbia University Press, 2021).

20. For New Left and Neo-Progressive interpretations, see Staughton Lynd, *Antifederalism in Dutchess County, New York: A Study of Democracy and Class Conflict in the Revolutionary Era* (Chicago: Loyola University Press, 1962); Jesse Lemisch, "Jack Tar in the Streets: Merchant Seamen in the Politics of Revolutionary America," *WMQ* 25, no. 3 (July 1968): 371–407; Alfred F. Young, ed., *The American Revolution: Explorations in the History of American Radicalism* (DeKalb: Northern Illinois University Press, 1976); Gary B. Nash, *The Urban Crucible: Social Change, Political Consciousness, and the Origins of the American Revolution* (Cambridge, MA: Harvard University Press, 1979); Edward Countryman, *A People in Revolution: The American Revolution and Political Society in New York, 1760–1790* (Baltimore: Johns Hopkins University Press, 1981); Woody Holton, *Forced Founders: Indians, Debtors, Slaves, and the Making of the American Revolution in Virginia* (Chapel Hill: University of North Carolina Press, 1999); Peter Linebaugh and Marcus Rediker, *The Many-Headed Hydra: Sailors, Slaves, Commoners, and the Hidden History of the Revolutionary Atlantic* (Boston: Beacon Press, 2000).

21. Stephanie Smallwood, *Saltwater Slavery: A Middle Passage from Africa to American Diaspora* (Cambridge, MA: Harvard University Press, 2007); Jennifer L. Morgan, *Reckoning with Slavery: Gender, Kinship, and Capitalism in the Early Black Atlantic* (Durham, NC: Duke University Press, 2021). A foundational text is Cedric Robinson, *Black Marxism: The Making of the Black Radical Tradition*, 3rd ed. (Chapel Hill: University of North Carolina Press, 2021). On archival violence and the erasure of enslaved voices, see Stephanie Smallwood, "The Politics of the Archive and History's Accountability to the Enslaved," *History of the Present* 6, no. 2 (2016): 117–32.

22. For works influenced by literary criticism, see Jennifer J. Baker, *Securing the Commonwealth: Debt, Speculation, and Writing in the Making of Early America* (Baltimore: Johns Hopkins University Press, 2005); Michael O'Malley, *Face Value: The Entwined Histories of Money and Race in America* (Chicago: University of Chicago Press, 2012); Marc Shell, *Wampum and the Origins of American Money* (Urbana: University of Illinois Press, 2013). For political and intellectual histories, see Mark Peterson, *The City-State of Boston: The Rise and Fall of an Atlantic Power, 1630–1865* (Princeton: Princeton University Press, 2019); Jonathan Barth, *The Currency of Empire: Money and Power in Seventeenth-Century English America* (Ithaca, NY: Cornell University Press, 2021). Older but important works include Thomas L. Purvis, *Proprietors, Patronage and Paper Money: Legislative Politics in New Jersey, 1703–1776* (New Brunswick, NJ: Rutgers University Press, 1986); Mary M. Schweitzer, *Custom and Contract: Household, Government, and the Economy in Colonial Pennsylvania* (New York: Columbia University Press, 1987); Margaret Ellen Newell, *From Dependency to Independence: Economic Revolution in Colonial New England* (Ithaca, NY: Cornell University Press, 1998).

23. Barry Eichengreen, "Financial History, Historical Analysis, and the New History of Finance Capital," *Capitalism: A Journal of History and Economics* 1, no. 1 (Fall 2019): 25.

24. The major debate among economic historians has been between "backing" theorists and "quantity" theorists. For the backing school, see Robert Craig West, "Money in the Colonial American Economy," *Economic Inquiry* 16 (January 1978): 1–15; Bruce D. Smith, "Some Colonial Evidence on Two Theories of Money: Maryland and the Carolinas," *JPE* 93, no. 6 (December 1985): 1178–1211; Elmus Wicker, "Colonial Monetary Standards Contrasted: Evidence from the Seven years' War," *JEH* 45, no. 4 (December 1985): 869–84; Charles W. Calomiris, "Institutional Failure, Monetary Scarcity, and the Depreciation of the Continental," *JEH* 48, no. 1 (March 1988): 47–68. For the quantity school, see Ronald Michener, "Fixed Exchange Rates and the Quantity Theory in Colonial America," *Carnegie-Rochester Conference Series on Public Policy* 27 (1987): 233–308; Bennett T. McCallum, "Money and Prices in Colonial America: A New Test of Competing Theories," *JPE* 100, no. 1 (February 1992): 143–61. More recently, Farley Grubb has put forth an alternative approach for explaining the value and performance of colonial paper money that considers the institutional barriers colonial assemblies faced and the legal tools they used to achieve their monetary goals. Farley Grubb, "Is Paper Money Just Paper Money? Experimentation and Variation in the Paper Monies Issued by the American Colonies from 1690 to 1775," NBER Working Paper 17997 (Cambridge, MA: National Bureau of Economic Research, April 2012); Farley Grubb, "Colonial American Paper Money and the Quantity Theory of Money: An Extension," NBER Working Paper 22192 (Cambridge, MA: National Bureau of Economic Research, April 2016).

25. As Sharon Murphy has pointed out, "Despite this modern focus on inflation, deflation has historically been the bigger problem for the economy." Murphy, *Other People's Money*, 14.

26. The sterling exchange rate in a given colony—the price of a sterling bill of exchange in terms of the local currency, essentially—turned not simply on the balance of trade between that colony and Britain, but on the balance of payments as well. While the balance of trade concerns only "visible" items, that is, goods and merchandise, the balance of payments includes "invisible" items, such as shipping and insurance costs, profits, and debts. Ernst, *Money and Politics in America*, xv, 11–12.

27. For a similar observation in the context of the French Revolution, see Rebecca L. Spang, *Stuff and Money in the Time of the French Revolution* (Cambridge, MA: Harvard University Press, 2015), 217.

28. On personal and financial credit in early American capitalism, see Zabin, *Dangerous Economies*, 1–31. On "colonial capitalism" as an analytic, see Onur Ulas Ince, *Colonial Capitalism and the Dilemmas of Liberalism* (New York: Oxford University Press, 2018), 4.

29. Keith Hart, "Heads or Tails? Two Sides of the Coin," *Man* 21, no. 4 (December 1986): 637–56; David Graeber, *Debt: The First 5,000 Years* (New York: Melville House Publishing, 2011), 73–75.

30. Viviana A. Zelizer, *The Social Meaning of Money: Pin Money, Paychecks, Poor Relief, and Other Currencies* (New York: Basic Books, 1994), 11.

31. T. H. Breen, *Tobacco Culture: The Mentality of the Great Tidewater Planters on the Eve of Revolution* (Princeton: Princeton University Press, 1985), 62–63.

32. On monetary and ritual meanings of wampum, see Gail D. MacLeitch, *Imperial Entanglements: Haudenosaunee Change and Persistence on the Frontiers of Empire* (Philadelphia: University of Pennsylvania Press, 2011), 35–36; Daniel K. Richter, *Trade, Land, Power: The Struggle for Eastern North America* (Philadelphia: University of Pennsylvania Press, 2013), 50, 56–58; Mario Schmidt, "Entangled Economies: New Netherland's Dual Currency System and Its Relation to Haudenosaunee Monetary Practice," *Ethnohistory* 62, no. 2 (April 2015): 195–216. On guns as currency, see Gregory A. Waselkov, "French Colonial Trade in Upper Creek Country," in John A. Walthall and Thomas E. Emerson, eds., *Calumet and Fleur-de-Lys: Archaeology of Indian and French Contact in the Midcontinent* (Washington, DC: Smithsonian Institution Press, 1992), 36; David Silverman, *Thundersticks: Firearms and the Violent Transformation of Native America* (Cambridge, MA: Harvard University Press, 2016), 83. On cross-cultural monetary exchange in an Atlantic African context, see Jane I. Guyer, *Marginal Gains: Monetary Transactions in Atlantic Africa* (Chicago: University of Chicago Press, 2004).

33. Karin Pallaver, "'The African native has no pocket': Monetary Practices and Currency Transitions in Early Colonial Uganda," *International Journal of African Historical Studies* 48, no. 3 (2015): 474.

34. Viviana Zelizer, "Making Multiple Monies," in Richard Swedberg, ed., *Explorations in Economic Sociology* (New York: Russell Sage Foundation, 1993), 193–212; Karl Polanyi, "The Economy as an Instituted Process," in Karl Polanyi, Conrad M. Arensberg, and Harry W. Pearson, eds., *Trade and Market in the Early Empires: Economies in History and Theory* (Glencoe, IL: Free Press and Falcon's Wing Press, 1957), 264–66.

35. Newman, *The Early Paper Money of America*, 137, 345.

36. On the "Made Beaver" as a money of account, see Ann M. Carlos and Frank D. Lewis, *Commerce by a Frozen Sea: Native Americans and the European Fur Trade* (Philadelphia: University of Pennsylvania Press, 2010), 52–58, 111, 178. On peltry as currency, see Carl L. Ekberg and Sharon K. Person, *St. Louis Rising: The French Regime of St. Louis St. Ange de Bellerive* (Urbana: University of Illinois Press, 2015), 210.

37. On silver ornaments as currency, see Marshall Joseph Becker, "The Origins of Trade Silver among the Lenape: Pewter Objects from Southeastern Pennsylvania as Possible Precursors," *Northeast Historical Archaeology* 19, no. 1 (1990): 78–98.

38. Zabin, *Dangerous Economies*, 68–69, 80.

39. Hartigan-O'Connor, *The Ties That Buy*, 110–11.

40. Geoffrey K. Ingham, "'Babylonian Madness': On the Historical and Sociological Origins of Money," in John Smithin, ed., *What Is Money?* (London: Routledge, 2000), 18.

41. David T. Flynn, "The Duration of Book Credit in Colonial New England," *Historical Methods: A Journal of Quantitative and Interdisciplinary History* 38, no. 4 (2005): 168–77; Jeremy T.

Schwartz, David T. Flynn, and Gökhan Karahan, "Merchant Account Books, Credit Sales, and Financial Development," *Accounting and Finance Research* 7, no. 3 (2018): 154–71.

42. Carl Wennerlind, "Money Talks, But What Is It Saying? Semiotics of Money and Social Control," *Journal of Economic Issues* 35, no. 3 (September 2001): 557–74; Kuroda, "Another History of Money Viewed from Africa and Asia," 267–69 (quotation). In a study comparing preindustrial Japan and China to early modern England, Akinobu Kuroda finds that societies where interpersonal credit dominated, such as England and Japan, were more likely to have a standard money of account for all transactions, whereas societies dependent on anonymous currency, such as China, tended to adopt plural monies of account. Akinobu Kuroda, "Anonymous Currencies or Named Debts? Comparison of Currencies, Local Credits and Units of Account between China, Japan, and England in the Pre-Industrial Era," *Socio-Economic Review* 11, no. 1 (January 2013): 57–80.

43. John Locke, *Two Treatises of Government* (London, 1764), 210–11, 328; Morag Barbara Arneil, "'All the world was America': John Locke and the American Indian" (PhD diss., University College London, 1992), 277–79, 292, 310. Allan Greer points out that Locke distinguished between the "legitimate" common property of European society, with its "laws" and "money," and the unenclosed "waste" land of Native America, where common land was "not collective property, but rather the antithesis of property," and so "enclosure in America requires no one's permission." No matter, Greer continues, that "common property was, in fact, a fundamental feature of landholding in both the New World and the Old in the early modern centuries." Allan Greer, "Commons and Enclosure in the Colonization of North America," *American Historical Review* 117, no. 2 (2012): 368.

44. By "inside money," I simply mean money created by colonial governments for public expenditures and local transactions. Farley Grubb, "Chronic Specie Scarcity and Efficient Barter: The Problem of Maintaining an Outside Money Supply in British Colonial America," NBER Working Paper 18099 (Cambridge, MA: National Bureau of Economic Research, May 2012; rev. November 2018).

45. Nicholas Popper, *The Specter of the Archive: Political Practice and the Information State in Early Modern Britain* (Chicago: University of Chicago Press, 2024), 1–19.

46. Ernst, *Money and Politics in America*, 25–37.

47. Adam Smith, *The Wealth of Nations*, ed. Edwin Cannan (New York: Modern Library, 2000), 531–32.

48. [Benjamin Franklin], *The General Magazine, and Historical Chronicle, for all the British Plantations in America (1741)*, 1, no. 2 (February 1741): 118–20.

49. On liberalism and British political economy, see Desan, *Making Money*, 266–94. On the Currency Acts and the imperial crisis, see Ernst, *Money and Politics in America*.

50. Christine Desan, "The Constitutional Approach to Money: Monetary Design and the Production of the Modern World," in Nina Bandelj, Frederick F. Wherry, and Viviana A. Zelizer, eds., *Money Talks: Explaining How Money Really Works* (Princeton: Princeton University Press, 2017), 109–30.

51. Eric Hinderaker and Rebecca Horn, "Territorial Crossings: Histories and Historiographies of the Early Americas," *WMQ* 67, no. 3 (July 2010): 397.

52. Michael Merrill, "Cash Is Good to Eat: Self-Sufficiency and Exchange in the Rural Economy of the United States," *Radical History Review* 3, no. 13 (1977): 42–71; Christopher Clark, "Household Economy, Market Exchange, and the Rise of Capitalism in the Connecticut Valley, 1800–1860," *Journal of Social History* 13, no. 2 (Winter 1979): 169–89; James A. Henretta, *The*

Origins of American Capitalism: Collected Essays (Boston: Northeastern University Press, 1991); Allan Kullikoff, *The Agrarian Origins of American Capitalism* (Charlottesville: University Press of Virginia, 1992).

53. Karl Marx, *Capital: A Critique of Political Economy, Vol. 1*, trans. Ben Fowkes (London: Penguin Books, 2004), chaps. 26–28. On primitive accumulation in the early modern Atlantic world as a political event, see Herman L. Bennett, *African Kings and Black Slaves: Sovereignty and Dispossession in the Early Modern Atlantic* (Philadelphia: University of Pennsylvania Press, 2019), 50–51. On primitive accumulation as racialized expropriation, see Nancy Fraser, "Expropriation and Exploitation in Racialized Capitalism: A Reply to Michael Dawson," *Critical Historical Studies* 3, no. 1 (Spring 2016): 163–78.

54. Bonnie Martin, "Slavery's Invisible Engine: Mortgaging Human Property," *Journal of Southern History* 76, no. 4 (November 2010): 817–66; K-Sue Park, "Money, Mortgages, and the Conquest of America," *Law & Social Inquiry* 41, no. 4 (Fall 2016): 1006–35; Michael Warren Murphy, "'No beggars amongst them': Primitive Accumulation, Settler Colonialism, and the Dispossession of Narragansett Land," *Humanity & Society* 42, no. 1 (February 2018): 46–67; Claire Priest, *Credit Nation: Property Laws and Institutions in Early America* (Princeton: Princeton University Press, 2021), 74–89.

55. David McNally, *Blood and Money: War, Slavery, Finance, and Empire* (Chicago: Haymarket Books, 2000), 1; Thomas Piketty, *Capital and Ideology* (Cambridge, MA: Harvard University Press, 2019), 5.

56. Barbara Young Welke, *Law and the Borders of Belonging in the Long Nineteenth Century United States* (New York: Cambridge University Press, 2010).

57. Pallaver, "The African Native Has No Pocket," 473.

58. Knight, "The Private Journal Kept by Madam Knight," 40.

59. John Maynard Keynes, *The General Theory of Employment, Interest, and Money* (1936; reprint, Cambridge, UK: Palgrave Macmillan, 2018), 263.

Chapter 1

1. "The Charter of the Province of Massachusetts-Bay" [October 7, 1691], in *MASS*, 1:8, 16.

2. Jack P. Greene, *The Quest for Power: The Lower Houses of Assembly in the Southern Royal Colonies, 1689–1776* (Chapel Hill: University of North Carolina Press, 1963), 51, 108–9.

3. Abba P. Lerner, "Money as a Creature of the State," *American Economic Review* 37, no. 2 (May 1947): 313 (quotation); Hyman Minsky, *Stabilizing an Unstable Economy* (New Haven: Yale University Press, 1986), 258n10.

4. John Maynard Keynes, *A Treatise on Money, Vol. 1: The Pure Theory of Money* (London: Macmillan, 1930), 3–5 (quotations); Geoffrey Ingham, "'Babylonian Madness': On the Historical and Sociological Origins of Money," in John Smithin, ed., *What Is Money?* (London: Routledge, 2000), 16–41; David Graeber, *Debt: The First 5,000 Years* (New York: Melville House, 2011), 38–40.

5. John J. McCusker, *Money and Exchange in Europe and America, 1600–1775: A Handbook* (Chapel Hill: University of North Carolina Press, 1978), 117, 120.

6. Hereafter, all monetary values are expressed in the local unit of account unless otherwise specified.

7. Alvin Rabushka, *Taxation in Colonial America* (Princeton: Princeton University Press, 2008), 233–34.

8. Rabushka, *Taxation in Colonial America*, 158–60.

9. Robert Chalmers, *A History of Currency in the British Colonies* (London: Her Majesty's Stationery Office, 1893), 61.

10. "An Act for making and emitting Bills of Publick Credit" [June 1709], in Charles J. Hoadly, ed., *The Public Records of the Colony of Connecticut* (Hartford, CT: Case, Lockwood & Brainard, 1870), 5:111–13.

11. Rabushka, *Taxation in Colonial America*, 6.

12. Daniel K. Richter, *Trade, Land, Power: The Struggle for Eastern North America* (Philadelphia: University of Pennsylvania Press, 2013), 56–58; Andrew Lipman, *The Saltwater Frontier: Indians and the Contest for the American Coast* (New Haven: Yale University Press, 2015), 106–11; K-Sue Park, "Money, Mortgages, and the Conquest of America," *Law & Social Inquiry* 41, no. 4 (Fall 2016): 1017–19; Lynn Ceci, "Native Wampum as a Peripheral Resource in the Seventeenth-Century World-System," in James Wherry and Laurence M. Hauptman, eds., *The Pequots in Southern New England: The Rise and Fall of an American Indian Nation* (Norman: University of Oklahoma Press, 1990), 59.

13. Ceci, "Native Wampum as a Peripheral Resource in the Seventeenth-Century World-System," 60–63; Park, "Money, Mortgages, and the Conquest of America," 1021–23.

14. Park, "Money, Mortgages, and the Conquest of America," 1029–39.

15. Jeremy T. Schwartz, David T. Flynn, and Gökhan Karahan, "Merchant Account Books, Credit Sales, and Financial Development," *Accounting and Finance Research* 7, no. 3 (2018): 154; Gary B. Nash, *The Urban Crucible: Social Change, Political Consciousness, and the Origins of the American Revolution* (Cambridge, MA: Harvard University Press, 1979), 4–5.

16. Margaret Ellen Newell, *From Dependency to Independence: Economic Revolution in Colonial New England* (Ithaca, NY: Cornell University Press, 1998), 78–80.

17. "Commission of Sir Edmund Andros, as Governor of the Territory and Dominion of New England," *Collections of the New-Hampshire Historical Society* 8 (1866): 270.

18. Rabushka, *Taxation in Colonial America*, 329.

19. Cotton Mather, *Magnalia Christi Americana, Or, The Ecclesiastical History of New-England from its First Planting in the Year 1620, Unto the Year of Our Lord 1698* (Hartford, CT, 1855), 1:176.

20. Jeffrey Sklansky, *Sovereign of the Market: The Money Question in Early America* (Chicago: University of Chicago Press, 2017), 21–29; Jenny Hale Pulsipher, *Subjects unto the Same King: Indians, English, and the Contest for Authority in Colonial New England* (Philadelphia: University of Pennsylvania Press, 2005), 253; David S. Lovejoy, *The Glorious Revolution in America* (New York: Harper & Row, 1972), 182–86. On John Wise's life and politics, see Clinton L. Rossiter, "John Wise: Colonial Democrat," *NEQ* 22, no. 1 (March 1949): 3–32.

21. [Joseph Dudley?], [1686], quoted in Frederic Austin Ogg, "Paper Money in the New England Colonies," *New England Magazine* 29, no. 1 (September 1903–March 1904): 776.

22. Stephen Saunders Webb, *1676: The End of American Independence* (Syracuse, NY: Syracuse University Press, 1984), xxv–xxvi; Margaret Ellen Newell, *Brethren by Nature: New England Indians, Colonists, and the Origins of American Slavery* (Ithaca, NY: Cornell University Press, 2015), 144.

23. Joseph B. Felt, "Statistics of Taxation in Massachusetts, Including Valuation and Population," in *Collections of the American Statistical Association*, vol. 1, pt. 3 (Boston: T. R. Martin, 1847), 263–76.

24. Rabushka, *Taxation in Colonial America*, 167.

25. [Thomas Copler?] to John Usher, May 9, 1688, Jeffries Family Papers, vol. 2 (hereafter Jeffries Papers), MHS.

26. Edward Stebbins to John Usher, May 30, 1688, Jeffries Papers, MHS.

27. Robert Chalmers, *A History of Currency in the British Colonies* (London: Her Majesty's Stationery Office, 1893), 10.

28. Mark Hanna, *Pirate Nests and the Rise of the British Empire, 1570–1740* (Chapel Hill: University of North Carolina Press, 2015), 170–71; Mark A. Peterson, *The City-State of Boston: The Rise and Fall of an Atlantic Power, 1630–1865* (Princeton: Princeton University Press, 2019), 102.

29. Carla G. Pestana, *The English Atlantic in an Age of Revolution, 1640–1661* (Cambridge, MA: Harvard University Press, 2008), 23–43.

30. Newell, *From Dependency to Independence*, 72–76; Peterson, *The City-State of Boston*, 58–60. On the rise of New England merchants in the seventeenth century, see Bernard Bailyn, *The New England Merchants in the Seventeenth Century* (Cambridge, MA: Harvard University Press, 1955).

31. Peterson, *The City-State of Boston*, 86; Jonathan Edward Barth, "'A Peculiar Stampe of Our Owne': The Massachusetts Mint and the Battle over Sovereignty, 1652–1691," *NEQ* 87, no. 3 (September 2014): 491–92.

32. Chalmers, *History of Currency*, 9; Peterson, *The City-State of Boston*, 107–10.

33. The second round of coins was approved in the fall of 1652 but may not have been minted until 1654. Additional coins featured a willow tree (1652–60), an oak tree (1660–67), and a pine tree (1667–82). All of the coins, however, were stamped with the year "1652," possibly to protect Massachusetts from charges of usurping the royal prerogative to mint money, as 1652 was eight years before the royal restoration. Louis Jordan, *John Hull: The Mint and the Economics of Massachusetts Coinage* (Hanover, NH: University Press of New England, 2002), 84–93; Barth, "'A Peculiar Stampe of Our Owne,'" 493–95, 507.

34. Jordan, *John Hull*, 11.

35. Catalina M. Vizcarra and Jane E. Knodell, "Resource Endowments, Agency Problems, and Monetary Outcomes in Two Colonial American Mints, 1600–1700," *Journal of Iberian and Latin American Economic History* (2022): 24.

36. Mark Valeri, *Heavenly Merchandize: How Religion Shaped Commerce in Puritan New England* (Princeton: Princeton University Press, 2010), 109.

37. Peterson, *The City-State of Boston*, 96.

38. Barth, "A Peculiar Stampe of Our Owne," 497–99.

39. Quoted in Jordan, *John Hull*, 34–35.

40. Jordan, *John Hull*, 35.

41. "Mr Randolph's answ'r to inquiries about New England," October 16, 1676, TNA: CO 5/903.

42. "Pet'n of the agents of Boston," 1677–78, TNA: CO 5/903.

43. Joseph B. Felt, *An Historical Account of Massachusetts Currency* (Boston: Perkins & Marvin, 1839), 41–44. On free minting, see Christine Desan, *Making Money: Coin, Currency, and the Coming of Capitalism* (New York: Oxford University Press, 2015), 70–71.

44. In 1681, for example, Joseph Dudley and John Richards petitioned the Crown to "Humbly excuse, & beg pardon for the fault of Coining." "Instructions from the Massachusetts to their messengers Joseph Dudley & John Richards Esq'r," February 15, 1681, TNA: CO 5/904.

45. Felt, *An Historical Account of Massachusetts Currency*, 44.

46. [Edward Randolph], "Report & letter concerning the government of Boston," September 15, 1680, TNA: CO 5/904; "Articles exhibited by Mr Randolph against the Massachusetts," June 12, 1683, TNA: CO 5/904.

47. "Mr Randulph's narrative of the state of New England," May 29, 1689, TNA: CO 5/855.

48. Robert N. Toppan, ed., "Council Records of Massachusetts under the Administration of President Joseph Dudley," in *Proceedings of the Massachusetts Historical Society* 13 (1899): 244–49.

49. [Edmund Andros], "Reasons for a mint in New England," 1686, TNA: CO 5/904.

50. "Report of the officers of the Mint to the commissioners of the Treasury touching a mint in New England," January 15, 1684, TNA: CO 5/904.

51. [Andros], "Reasons for a mint in New England." On the economic consequences of the "Great Recoinage," see Desan, *Making Money*, 362–67.

52. "Report of the Committee of the Mint about a mint in New England," July 15, 1686, TNA: CO 5/904; "Answer to the said reasons for a mint in New England," October 23, 1686, TNA: CO 5/904; "Order of the Council against a mint, but permitting pieces of eight to pass in New England," October 27, 1686, TNA: CO 5/904.

53. "Instructions from Governor Simon Bradstreet to Massachusetts Agents, 24 January 1690," in William H. Whitmore, ed., *The Andros Tracts: Being a Collection of Pamphlets and Official Papers Issued During the Period Between the Overthrow of the Andros Government and the Establishment of the Second Charter in Massachusetts* (Boston: John Wilson & Son, 1874), 3:60; "Proposal of Mr William Phips etc for the liberty of Coyne in New England," November 11, 1691, TNA: CO 5/856.

54. Lovejoy, *The Glorious Revolution in America*, 239–45; Pulsipher, *Subjects unto the Same King*, 255–57.

55. William Pencak, *War, Politics, and Revolution in Massachusetts* (Boston: Northeastern University Press, 1981), 16–17; Robin L. Einhorn, *American Taxation, American Slavery* (Chicago: University of Chicago Press, 2006), 70.

56. Copy of a letter from Boston, July 30, 1689, in *CSP*, 13:100–113.

57. Felt, "Statistics of Taxation in Massachusetts," 269–70.

58. Benjamin Bullivant, "Mr. Bullivant's Journall of Proceedings from the 13 Feb. to the 18th of May, 1689/90," *Proceedings of the Massachusetts Historical Society* 16 (1878): 104; Middlesex County Court, Folio Collection, September 19, 1690, fol. 131, group 3, JA, quoted in Pulsipher, *Subjects unto the Same King*, 258.

59. Bullivant, "Mr. Bullivant's Journall of Proceedings from the 13 Feb. to the 18th of May, 1689/90," 106.

60. James Phinney Baxter, ed., *Documentary History of the State of Maine*, 2nd ser. (Portland, ME: Thurston Print, 1900), 5:307–9, quoted in Pulsipher, *Subjects unto the Same King*, 259–60.

61. Samuel Sewall Papers, Account Book, 1688–92, microfilm, P-87, reel 1 (hereafter Sewall Account Book), MHS.

62. Lovejoy, *Glorious Revolution in America*, 323, 345; Sylvanus Davis, "The declaration of Sylvanus Davis, Quebec, October 1690," *Collections of the Massachusetts Historical Society* 5 (1825): 101–12. See also Samuel A. Green, ed., *Two Narratives of the Expedition against Quebec, A.D. 1690, Under Sir William Phips: The One by Rev. John Wise, of Ipswich, Mass., and the Other by an Unknown Writer* (Cambridge, MA: J. Wilson, 1901).

63. Abstract of a letter from James Lloyd, merchant, of Boston, January 8, 1691 [Boston], in *CSP*, 13:375–84.

64. Felt, "Statistics of Taxation in Massachusetts," 270.

65. Thomas Savage, *An Account of the Late Action of the New-Englanders, Under the Command of Sir William Phips, Against the French at Canada* (London, 1691), 6.

66. Abstract of a letter from Mr. Samuel Myles, Minister at Boston [December 12], in *CSP*, 13:367–75.

67. Thomas Hutchinson, *History of Massachusetts, from the First Settlement Thereof in 1628, Until the Year 1750*, 3rd ed. (Boston 1767; Salem, MA, 1795), 1:356. Citations refer to the 1795 edition.

68. Samuel Sewall to Increase Mather, December 29, 1690, in Samuel Sewall Papers, Letterbook, 1686–1737, microfilm, P-87, reel 2, MHS.

69. Abstract of a letter from James Lloyd, merchant, of Boston, January 8, 1691, [Boston], in *CSP*, 13:375–84.

70. Extract of a letter from New England to John Usher, [January?] 1691, in *CSP*, 13:375–84.

71. Extracts from several letters from Boston, February 2, 1691, in *CSP*, 13:384–93.

72. Felt, "Statistics of Taxation in Massachusetts," 271.

73. Savage, *An Account of the Late Action of the New-Englanders*, 6.

74. Hutchinson, *History of Massachusetts*, 1:357.

75. Mather, *Magnalia Christi Americana*, 190–91.

76. Jacob Melyen to Isack D. Remer, April 25, 1691, in Jacob Melyen Letter Book, American Antiquarian Society, quoted in Newell, *From Dependency to Independence*, 129.

77. Sewall Account Book, MHS.

78. Sewall Account Book, MHS.

79. Sewall Account Book, MHS.

80. Sewall Account Book, MHS. John Aquitticus was one of several Nipmucs to petition the General Court in 1685 for land for a plantation. Petition of Anookamaug, May 27, 1685, MAC, vol. 30 [Indian, 1603–1705], p. 300.

81. Sewall Account Book, MHS.

82. James Russell Trumball, *History of Northampton, Massachusetts; from its settlement in 1654* (Northampton, MA, 1898), 1:421–22.

83. Ephraim Pond's, Constable of Wrentham, Statement as to Wrentham Taxes, October 29, 1694, MAC, vol. 100 [Pecuniary, 1629–1694], pp. 512–13.

84. Petition of David Morgan as to taxes of Springfield, March 5, 1695, MAC, vol. 101 [Pecuniary, 1694–1740], pp. 20–23.

85. Receipts of taxes paid into the provincial treasury, September 19, 1690–April 5, 1693, Dennis Family Papers (hereafter Dennis Papers), MHS.

86. John Phillips [Treasurer] to the selectmen and constables of Ipswich, April 2, 1690, Dennis Papers, MHS.

87. Mather, *Magnalia Christi Americana*, 190–91 (quotation); Felt, *An Historical Account of Massachusetts Currency*, 51.

88. "An account of the monyes that [the town of] Boston gave order to Mr James Taylor town treasurer to deliver as its own from the date above" [March 26, 1692], Boston Town Records [copy], [1668–95], MHS.

89. Newell, *From Dependency to Independence*, 129; Rabushka, *Taxation in Colonial America*, 360–63.

90. Dror Goldberg, "The Massachusetts Paper Money of 1690," *JEH* 69, no. 4 (December 2009): 1093–98.

91. For the history of tallies in England, see Desan, *Making Money*, 171, 237–54. For the origins of siege money, see François R. Velde and Thomas J. Sargent, *The Big Problem of Small Change* (Princeton: Princeton University Press, 2003), 203–4.

92. Richard A. Lester, "Playing-Card Currency of French Canada," in E. P. Neufield, ed., *Money and Banking in Canada* (Toronto: McClelland & Stewart Ltd., 1964), 9–23.

93. Ann Marie Plane, *Dreams and the Invisible World in Colonial New England: Indians, Colonists, and the Seventeenth Century* (Philadelphia: University of Pennsylvania Press, 2014), xi–xiii.

94. [Cotton Mather and John Blackwell?], *Some Considerations of the Bills of Credit Now Passing in New-England, Addressed unto the Worshipful, John Philips Esq; Published for the Information of the Inhabitants* [Boston, 1691], in *CCR*, 1:194.

95. [Cotton Mather and John Blackwell?], *Some Additional Considerations Addressed unto the Worshipful Elisha Hutchinson, Esq.* [Boston, 1691], in *CCR*, 1:198–99, 204.

96. Philip S. Haffenden, *New England in the English Nation, 1689–1713* (Oxford: Clarendon Press, 1974), 38–71.

97. "An Act for Enforcing the Collecting and Paying in the Arrears of Public Assessments, &c." [June 14, 1692], in *MASS*, 1:27–29; "An Act for the Granting to their Majesties an Assessment upon Polls and Estates" [June 24, 1692], in *MASS*, 1:29–30; "An Act for Impost, Excise and Tonnage of Shipping" [June 24, 1692], in *MASS*, 1:30–34.

98. "An Act for Making the Former Bills of Credit to Pass Currant in Future Payments" [July 2, 1692], in *MASS*, 1:35–36.

99. "Committee to receive the Bills," July 1, 1692, MAC, vol. 100 [Pecuniary, 1629–94], p. 400.

100. "Committee for Adjusting of former Accounts," July 1, 1692, MAC, vol. 100 [Pecuniary, 1629–94], pp. 398–99.

101. Petition of David Edwards and John Endicott, October 12, 1692, MAC, vol. 100 [Pecuniary, 1629–94], p. 402.

102. Petition of John Gardner for pay of expenses incurred in consequence of a message from Gov. Fletcher requiring the obedience of Nantucket to New York Government, July 15, 1693, MAC, vol. 100 [Pecuniary, 1629–94], p. 449.

103. Petitions of merchants for money loaned to the province, August 2, 1693, MAC, vol. 100 [Pecuniary, 1629–94], pp. 452, 454.

104. "An Addition to the Act Entituled 'An Act for the Setting Forth of General Priviledges,'" [June 7, 1694], in *MASS*, 1:170.

105. Desan, *Making Money*, 44.

106. "An Act for the Present Supply of the Treasury" [December 11, 1693], in *MASS* 1:146; "An Act for the Reviving and Continuing of the Duties upon Goods, Impost, Excise and Tunnage of Shipping, and the Acts for Granting the Same" [June 8, 1694], in *MASS*, 1:165.

107. "An Act for Better Enabling the Treasurer to Answer Present Demands" [June 22, 1694], in *MASS*, 1:173; "An Act for the Payment of the Province Debts" [October 27, 1694], in *MASS*, 1:187–88; "An Act for Granting unto their Majesties a Tax on Polls and Estates, and Additional Duties of Impost and Tunnage of Shiping" [March 15, 1695], in *MASS*, 1:200–201.

108. Felt, *An Historical Account of Massachusetts Currency*, 56; Newell, *From Dependency to Independence*, 130.

109. Desan, *Making Money*, 328–29.

110. Sklansky, *Sovereign of the Market*, 6–7. The 1690 bills of credit prefigured the territorial currencies of the nineteenth and twentieth centuries, albeit on a much smaller and informal scale. According to Eric Helleiner, the construction of a territorial currency in the nineteenth-century United States was driven in part by policymakers' desire to "strengthen the fiscal capacity of the federal state by expanding the potential for seigniorage revenue (profits derived from production of money) and by facilitating payments to and from the federal government." Eric Helleiner, "The Macro-Social Meaning of Money: From Territorial Currencies to Global

NOTES TO PAGES 37-42

Money," in Nina Bandels, Frederick F. Wherry, and Viviana Zelizer, eds., *Money Talks: Explaining How Money Really Works* (Princeton: Princeton University Press, 2017), 146-47.

111. Thomas Nairne, *A Letter from South Carolina* (London, 1710), 22.

112. Thomas Pownall, *The Administration of the British Colonies*, 5th ed. (London, 1774), 1:82.

113. Representation by John Pynchon to the General Court as to the loss in Conn. River of peas sent for taxes of Springfield, June 14, 1693, MAC, vol. 100 [Pecuniary, 1629-94], p. 441.

114. Petition of Simon Willard, as to Salem taxes, June 19, 1694, MAC, vol. 100 [Pecuniary, 1629-94], p. 491; Petition of Cyprian Stevens, as to Taxes, at Lancaster, (list of persons removed from L.), June 4, 1694, MAC, vol. 101 [Pecuniary, 1694-1740], pp. 33-34.

115. Order as to arrears of public rates, March 8, 1695, MAC, vol. 101 [Pecuniary, 1694-1740], p. 35.

116. Petition of Andrew Sigourney as to taxes of the plantation of Oxford, a French settlement in past deserted, October 19, 1694, MAC, vol. 100 [Pecuniary, 1629-94], pp. 501-2; Petition as to Dartmouth taxes with papers, October 24, 1694, MAC, vol. 100 [Pecuniary, 1629-94], pp. 503-6.

117. Petition of David Morgan as to taxes of Springfield, March 5, 1695, MAC, vol. 101 [Pecuniary, 1694-1740]:20-23.

118. Petition of John Hoyt, a prisoner of Amesbury, relative to taxes—his house burned by Indians, June 14, 1695, MAC, vol. 101 [Pecuniary, 1694-1740], pp. 38-39.

119. Petition of Nathaniel Lovejoy and Joseph Hoyt their father of Amesbury, (a collector of taxes,) killed by the Indians at Andover, September 12, 1696, MAC, vol. 101 [Pecuniary, 1694-1740], p. 58.

120. Report of the Committee on Treasurer's accounts, May 20, 1696, MAC, vol. 101 [Pecuniary, 1694-1740], pp. 53-54; "An Act for Granting unto his Majesty a Tax upon Polls and Estates" [June 16, 1697], in *MASS*, 1:281; "An Act for Ascertaining the Value of Coyns Currant within this Province" [October 21, 1697], in *MASS*, 1:296.

121. "An Act Prohibiting the Exportation of Money and Bullion" [December 22, 1697], in *MASS*, 1:306-7.

122. Report of a committee as to value of gold and silver coin, and means for a supply of a scarcity of money, March 5, 1701, MAC, vol. 101 [Pecuniary, 1694-1740], p. 184.

123. "An Act to Impower the Treasurer to Issue Forth Bills of Credit" [April 19, 1701], in *MASS*, 1:454; "An Act for Granting unto his Majesty a Tax upon Polls and Estates" [June 30, 1701], in *MASS*, 1:486; Resolve for printing and emitting Bills of Credit, August 7, 1701, MAC, vol. 101 [Pecuniary, 1694-1740], p. 209.

124. "An Act for Granting unto her Majesty a Tax upon Polls and Estates" [June 25, 1702], in *MASS*, 1:494-97; "Order for the emission of bills of credit, February 26, 1702," MAC, vol. 101 Pecuniary, 1694-1740], p. 215.

125. Hutchinson, *History of Massachusetts*, 1:357.

Chapter 2

1. Governor Dudley to the Council of Trade and Plantations, December 1, 1713, in *CSP*, 27:253-71.

2. [John Wise], *The Freeholder's Address to the Honourable House of Representatives* (Boston, 1721), 3.

3. Governor Burnet to the Lords of Trade, November 21, 1724, TNA, CO 5/1092.

4. David Graeber, *Debt: The First 5,000 Years* (New York: Melville House, 2011), 21–41; Christine Desan, *Making Money: Coin, Currency, and the Coming of Capitalism* (New York: Oxford University Press, 2014), 23–33.

5. Desan, *Making Money*, 43–50.

6. John Childs, *Armies and Warfare in Europe, 1648–1789* (Manchester, UK: Manchester University Press, 1982), 79.

7. Accounts of James Taylor, treasurer and receiver of Massachusetts, of assessments and duties in the counties, duties on imported goods and merchandise, and excises. Also, payments made to captains and their companies employed against the French and Indians during King William's War, 1693–94, MHS.

8. Petition of John Houghton, for the Town of Lancaster, to be paid for expenses of the Garrison, December 13, 1694, MAC, vol. 100 [Pecuniary, 1629–94], p. 466.

9. Petition of Ambrose Dawes, as to his service at Pemaquid, February 16, 1694, MAC, vol. 70 [Military, 1680–1703], p. 220; Vote for a donation to Ambrose Dawes who lost one of his eyes in service, June 19, 1694, MAC, vol. 100 [Pecuniary, 1629–94], p. 490.

10. Maggie Blackhawk, "Petitioning and the Making of the Administrative State," *Yale Law Journal* 127, no. 6 (April 2018): 1538–637.

11. For an overview of pensions in the English colonies, see Robert L. Clark, Lee A. Craig, and Jack W. Wilson, *A History of Public Sector Pensions in the United States* (Philadelphia: University of Pennsylvania Press, 2003), 31–32.

12. "[T]he petision [*sic*] of Nicholas Pickett of Marblehead," in *MASS*, 7:574.

13. Jeremiah Allen [Treasurer] Account Book, 1714–16 (hereafter Allen Account Book), MHS.

14. Allen Account Book, MHS; "Resolve Allowing £15 to Hugh Pike" [November 1720], in *MASS*, 10:26–27; "Resolve Allowing £15 to Hugh Pike" [November 1721], in *MASS*, 10:125; "Resolve Allowing £10 to Hugh Pike" [June 1722], in *MASS*, 10:296; "Resolve Allowing £5 to Hugh Pike" [November 1723], 379, in *MASS*, 10:452–53; "Resolve Allowing £15 for Hugh Pike" [June 1724], in *MASS*, 10:533; "Resolve Allowing £15 to Hugh Pike" [December 1725], in *MASS*, 10:695.

15. Mary Poovey, *A History of the Modern Fact: Problems of Knowledge in the Sciences of Wealth and Society* (Chicago: University of Chicago Press, 1998), 29–91. For a similar observation in a different context, see Stephanie E. Smallwood, *Saltwater Slavery: A Middle Passage from Africa to American Diaspora* (Cambridge, MA: Harvard University Press, 2007), 98.

16. William T. Baxter, "The Account Charge and Discharge," *Accounting Historians Journal* 7, no. 1 (Spring 1980): 69; Simon Middleton, "William Fishbourn's 'misfortune': Public Accounting and Paper Money in Early Pennsylvania," *EAS* 19, no. 1 (Winter 2021): 80–83.

17. Allen Account Book, MHS. According to Samuel Adams Drake, the *Green Dragon* "goes back to 1712" as a public house, "when Richard Pullen kept it." Samuel Adams Drake, *Old Boston Taverns and Tavern Clubs* (Boston: W. A. Butterfield, 1886), 47–49 (quotation on 47).

18. Allen Account Book, MHS. On the Pawtucket Bridge, see *Pawtucket Past and Present: Being a Brief Account of the Beginning of Its Industries and a Brief Resume of the Early History of the City* (Boston: Slaton Advertising and Printing Company, 1917; printed for Slater Trust Company, Pawtucket, RI, 1917), 3.

19. Poovey, *A History of the Modern Fact*, 35.

20. John Fearing Account Books, 1692–1737, Joseph Downs Collection, Winterthur Library, Winterthur, DE. The Fearing and Wilder families were related by blood and marriage. For an analysis of credit culture that aims to bridge the divide between "individualist" and "communal" readings of the early New England economy, see Daniel Vickers, "Errors Expected: The

Culture of Credit in Rural New England, 1750–1800," *Economic History Review* 63, no. 4 (November 2010): 1032–57. On money scarcity and the use of book credit as a money "substitute," see William T. Baxter, "Observations on Money, Barter, and Bookkeeping," *Accounting Historians Journal* 31, no. 1 (2004): 129–39.

21. For 1686 and 1687, see Hingham Town Meeting Minutes, Hingham (MA) Records, 1644–1720, 1:168–71, MHS. Compare with October 9, 1709, Hingham Town Meeting Minutes, Hingham (MA) Records, 1644–1720, 3:8–9, MHS.

22. John Brown Account Book, 1718–42, Haverhill, MA (photocopy), MHS.

23. Henry Tebbets pocket ledger, 1695–1723, Records of general stores in New Hampshire and Vermont, Series I. General Stores of New Hampshire, Baker Library Special Collections, Harvard Business School, Harvard University.

24. Governor Burnet to the Lords of Trade, December 16, 1723, TNA: CO 5/1092.

25. Allen Account Book, MHS; Rachel Wheeler, *To Live upon Hope: Mohicans and Missionaries in the Eighteenth-Century Northeast* (Ithaca, NY: Cornell University Press, 2008), 18–21; George Marsen, *Jonathan Edwards: A Life* (New Haven: Yale University Press, 2008), 115.

26. Account of Jeremiah Allen, Treasurer and Receiver General, showing receipts and disbursements between May 31, 1727, and May 31, 1728, MAC, vol. 123 [Treasury, 1707–34], p. 354.

27. John Stoddard Account Book [1727], MHS.

28. On earmarking as a social practice, see Viviana A. Zelizer, *The Social Meaning of Money: Pin Money, Paychecks, Poor Relief, and Other Currencies* (New York: Basic Books, 1994), 1–35.

29. Treasurer and Receiver General, showing receipts and disbursements between May 31, 1727, and May 31, 1728, MAC, vol. 123 [Treasury, 1707–34], p. 355; F. E. Oliver, ed., *The Diaries of Benjamin Lynde and of Benjamin Lynde, Jr.* (Boston, 1880), 22, 51, 69.

30. Margaret Ellen Newell, *From Dependency to Independence: Economic Revolution in Colonial New England* (Ithaca, NY: Cornell University Press, 1998), 179.

31. Elizabeth Deering Hanscom, ed., *The Heart of the Puritan: Selections from Letters and Journals* (New York: Macmillan, 1917), 155–56.

32. K-Sue Park, "Money, Mortgages, and the Conquest of America," *Law & Social Inquiry* 41, no. 4 (Fall 2016): 1017–21.

33. Serena Merrino, "Currency and Settler Colonialism: The Palestinian Case," *Review of International Political Economy* 28, no. 6 (August 2020): 1731. For money as a "technology of settler colonialism," see Brian Gettler, *Colonialism's Currency: Money, State, and First Nations in Canada, 1820–1950* (Montreal: McGill-Queen's University Press, 2020), 31–58.

34. Catherine Desbarats, "On Being Surprised: By New France's Card Money, for Example," *Canadian Historical Review* 102, no. 1 (March 2021): 125–51.

35. David Silverman, *Thundersticks: Firearms and the Violent Transformation of Native America* (Cambridge, MA: Harvard University Press, 2016), 97. On the anthropology of gift exchange, see Marcel Mauss, *The Gift: Forms and Functions of Exchange in Archaic Societies*, trans. Ian Cunnison (London: Cohen & West Ltd, 1966); Marshall Sahlins, *Stone Age Economics* (New York: Routledge Classics, 2017).

36. Jenny Hale Pulsipher, "Gaining the Diplomatic Edge: Kinship, Trade, Ritual and Religion in Amerindian Alliances in Early North America," in Wayne E. Lee, ed., *Empires and Indigenes: Intercultural Alliance, Imperial Expansion, and Warfare in the Early Modern World* (New York: New York University Press, 2011), 31–36; Jenny Hale Pulsipher, *Subjects unto the Same King: Indians, English, and the Contest for Authority in Colonial New England* (Philadelphia: University of Pennsylvania Press, 2005), 261.

37. Ian Saxine, *Properties of Empire: Indians, Colonists, and Land Speculators on the New England Frontier* (New York: New York University Press, 2019), 35.

38. Bill for giving necessary supplies to the Eastern Indians and for regulating trade with them, July 14, 1699, MAC, vol. 30 [Indian, 1639–1705], pp. 445–46a; Account of goods delivered in Indian Trade for furs, &c, 1701, MAC, vol. 30 [Indian, 1639–1705], p. 476.

39. Report of Committee with proposals for settling the trade with the Indians at the Eastward, June 26, 1699, MAC, vol. 30 [Indian, 1639–1705], p. 444.

40. Bill for giving necessary supplies to the Eastern Indians and for regulating trade with them, July 14, 1699, MAC, vol. 30 [Indian, 1639–1705], pp. 445–46a.

41. Order expressing the dissatisfaction of the House with that clause of the treaty with the Eastern Indians which supplies them with an armourer free of charge, June 11, 1701, MAC, vol. 30 [Indian, 1639–1705], p. 473.

42. Saxine, *Properties of Empire*, especially chaps. 2 and 3. In the 1730s, some Wabanaki leaders received military commissions from the Massachusetts government, with most claiming pensions or "annuities" of about ten pounds. For examples, see Capt. Joseph Kellogg, Hampshire Co., 1735–36, MAC, vol. 91 [Muster Rolls, 1710–40], p. 280; Capt. Thomas Smith, Block House at Saco, 1736, MAC, vol. 91 [Muster Rolls, 1710–40], p. 282; Account of William Foye, Treasurer and Receiver General, showing receipts and disbursements between May 26, 1736, and May 25, 1737, MAC, vol. 124 [Treasury, 1735–57], p. 60.

43. Statement of presents for the Five Nations, etc, May 12, 1710, MAC, vol. 31 [Indian, 1705–50], pp. 63–67; Account for a dinner for Mohawks at Boston, etc, 1709, MAC, vol. 31 [Indian, 1705–50], p. 76; Sundry Bills for "entertainment" of Indian visitors, January 19, 1727/8, MAC, vol. 31 [Indian, 1705–50], pp. 161–65; Richard R. Johnson, "The Search for a Usable Indian: An Aspect of the Defense of Colonial New England," *Journal of American History* 64, no. 3 (December 1977): 637–39.

44. Account of Jeremiah Allen, Treasurer and Receiver General, showing receipts and disbursements between May 30, 1716, and May 31, 1717, MAC, vol. 123 [Treasury, 1707–34], pp. 85–86.

45. Daniel R. Mandell, *Behind the Frontier: Indians in Eighteenth-Century Eastern Massachusetts* (Lincoln: University of Nebraska Press, 1996).

46. Brian D. Carroll, "The Effect of Military Service on Indian Communities in Southern New England, 1740–1763," *EAS* 14, no. 3 (Summer 2019): 510–19; Johnson, "The Search for a Usable Indian," 641.

47. Petition of an Indian, Ben, of Scituate, May 29, 1706, MAC, vol. 31 [Indian, 1705–50], pp. 7–8; Petition of Sinkawah (Natick), an Indian soldier for aid, MAC, vol. 31 [Indian, 1705–50], pp. 13–14.

48. Petition of Wm Jeffrey, an Indian of Harwich, wounded, June 24, 1724, MAC, vol. 31 [Indian, 1705–50], p. 112; Petition of Wm Jeffrey, an Indian of Harwich, wounded at George's River, Jan. 1, 1727/8, MAC, vol. 31 [Indian, 1705–50], p. 154; Pet. for aid of Wm Jeffrey, Harwich Indian, wounded at eastward, Nov. 27, 1741, MAC, vol. 31 [Indian, 1705–50], pp. 346–47.

49. Carroll, "The Effect of Military Service on Indian Communities in Southern New England," 528–36.

50. Gary B. Nash, *The Urban Crucible: Social Change, Political Consciousness, and the Origins of the American Revolution* (Cambridge, MA: Harvard University Press, 1979), 55, 66; Simon Middleton, *From Privileges to Rights: Work and Politics in Colonial New York City* (Philadelphia: University of Pennsylvania Press, 2006), 99–100; Serena Zabin, *Dangerous Economies: Status and Commerce in Imperial New York* (Philadelphia: University of Pennsylvania Press, 2009), 12; Michael Kammen, *Colonial New York: A History* (New York: Oxford University Press, 1975), 152.

51. John B. Pine, ed., *Seal and Flag of the City of New York, 1665–1915* (New York: G. P. Putnam's Sons, 1915), 36–50.

52. "An Act for the Currency of Bills of Credit for five thousand pounds" [June 1709], in *CLNY*, 1:666–68. On the dual role of personal reputation and financial credit in assessing and establishing trustworthiness, see Zabin, *Dangerous Economies*, 1–31. For the English context, see Craig Muldrew, *The Economy of Obligation: The Culture of Credit and Social Relations in Early Modern England* (New York: Palgrave Macmillan, 1998), 2–8.

53. "An Act for Levying Four Thousand Pounds" [June 1709], in *CLNY*, 1:669–74.

54. "An Act for the Currency of Bills of Credit for Four Thousand Pounds [November 1709], in *CLNY* 1:689–92; "An Act for the Currency of Bills of Credit for Tenn Thousand Ounces of Plate or Fourteen Thousand five hundred & fourty five Lyon Dollars" [November 1709], in *CLNY*, 1:695–97; "An Act for the Treasurers Issuing Bills of Credit to Pay the present Debt of the Expedition to Canada and other Uses" [November 1709], in *CLNY*, 1:698–700 (quotation on 698).

55. "An Act for the Treasurers Issuing Bills of Credit to Pay the present Debt of the Expedition to Canada and other Uses" [November 1709], in *CLNY*, 1:698–700; "An Act for the Currency of Bills of Credit for Twenty five Thousand Ounces of Plate" [July 1711], in *CLNY*, 1:737–40.

56. "An Act for the Treasurers Issuing Bills of Credit to Pay the present Debt of the Expedition to Canada and other Uses" [November 1709], in *CLNY*, 1:700.

57. "An Act for the Treasurers paying to his Excellency a sum of money for Presents to the Five Nations of Indians and for his Expence in going to Albany to treat with them" [August 1714], in *CLNY*, 1:814.

58. Silverman, *Thundersticks*, 51–54.

59. "An Act for Paying and Discharging the Several Debts and Sums of Money claimed as Debts of this Colony, to the several Persons therein named, and to make and enforce the Currency of Bills of Credit to the Value of Twenty Seven Thousand Six Hundred and Eighty Pounds, for that Purpose; also to make void all Claims and Demands made, or pretended to be due from this Colony before the first Day of June, One Thousand Seven Hundred and Fourteen, and to prevent this Colony from being in Debt for the Future" [September 1714], in *CLNY*, 1:815–26. The full act is published in *Acts of the Assembly, Passed in the Province of New-York, from 1691, to 1718* (London: John Baskett, 1719) (hereafter *Acts of Assembly Passed in New York*), 160–95 (quotation on 161).

60. Daniel K. Richter, *Trade, Land, Power: The Struggle for Eastern North America* (Philadelphia: University of Pennsylvania Press, 2013), 56–58; David Graeber, *Toward an Anthropological Theory of Value: The False Coin of Our Own Dreams* (New York: Palgrave, 2001), 118–27.

61. *Acts of Assembly Passed in New York*, 162. For Van Olinda's activities, see Jonathan Pearson, *A History of the Schenectady Patent in the Dutch and English Times; Being Contributions Toward a History of the Lower Mohawk Valley* (Albany, NY: Joel Munsell's Sons, 1883), 275–76; Jonathan Pearson, *Contributions for the Genealogies of the First Settlers of the Ancient County of Albany from 1630 to 1800* (Albany, NY: J. Munsell, 1872), 129; *Calendar of N.Y. Colonial Manuscripts: Indorsed Land Papers; In the Office of the Secretary of State of New York, 1643–1803* (Albany, NY: Weed, Parsons & Co., 1864), 75–76; "The Letters and Papers of Cadwallader Colden, Volume VI: 1761–1764," in *Collections of the New-York Historical Society for the Year 1922* (New York: Printed for the Society, 1923), 359–60.

62. Sahlins, *Stone Age Economics*, especially chaps. 5 and 6.

63. Nancy L. Hagedorn, "Brokers of Understanding: Interpreters as Agents of Cultural Exchange in Colonial New York," *New York History* 76, no. 4 (October 1995): 380–81, 389 (quotation on 380).

64. *Acts of Assembly Passed in New York*, 161–62, 165, 183, 185.

65. *Acts of Assembly Passed in New York*, 161.

66. "An Act for Settling the Militia of this Province and the making of it usefull for the Security and Defence thereof and for Repealing all former Acts Relating to the same" [July 27, 1721], in *CLNY*, 2:84–92; "An Act for Settling and Regulateing the Militia in this Province and making the Same usefull for the Security and defence thereof and for Repealing all other Acts Relateing to the Same" [July 24, 1724], in *CLNY*, 2:187–97.

67. "An Act for Defraying the Cost and Contingent Charges of the Trading house Erected at Oswego . . ." [November 25, 1727], in *CLNY*, 2:372–404.

68. "An ACT for the more Effectuall preservation of Deer and other Game and ye Destruction of Wolves Wild Catts and other Vermin" [September 18, 1708], in *CLNY*, 1:618–20; "An Act for Destroying Wolves in the County of Orange" [July 21, 1715], in *CLNY*, 1:878–79 (quotations).

69. "An Act for Destroying Wolves & Foxes in the County of West Chester" [September 1, 1716], in *CLNY*, 1:893; "An Act for destroying Wolves in Dutchess County [June 24, 1719], in *CLNY*, 1:1027–28 (quotation on 1028); "An Act for destroying Wolves in the County of Albany Dutchess County and Orange County" [November 11, 1726], in *CLNY*, 2:346–47; "An Act to Encourage the Destroying of wolves in the County of Albany, Ulster County, Orange County, Dutchess County and County of West Chester" [October 14, 1732], in *CLNY*, 2:750–52.

70. Jon T. Coleman, *Vicious: Wolves and Men in America* (New Haven: Yale University Press, 2004), 60–61.

71. "An Act for Paying and Discharging Several Debts Due from this Colony to the Persons therein named and for Raising and Putting into the Hands of the Treasurer of this Collony Severall quantities of Plate to be apply'd to the Publick and necessary Uses of this Colony and to make Bills of Creditt to the value of fforty One Thousand ffive hundred and Seaventeene Ounces and an half of Plate for that purpose" [December 1717], in *CLNY*, 1:938–91.

72. "An Act for preventing Suppressing and punishing the Conspiracy and Insurrection of Negroes and other Slaves" [December 1712], in *CLNY*, 1:761–67.

73. Governor Hunter to the Lords of Trade, November 12, 1715, in E. B. O'Callaghan, ed., *Documents Relative to the Colonial History of the State of New York* (Albany, NY: Weed, Parsons & Co., 1855), 5:461.

74. "An Act for Paying and Discharging Several Debts Due from this Colony to the Persons therein named and for Raising and Putting into the Hands of the Treasurer of this Collony Severall quantities of Plate to be apply'd to the Publick and necessary Uses of this Colony and to make Bills of Creditt to the value of fforty One Thousand ffive hundred and Seaventeene Ounces and an half of Plate for that purpose" [December 1717], in *CLNY*, 1:938–91 (quotation on 983).

75. Silverman, *Thundersticks*, 60–68.

76. A. S. Salley Jr., ed., *Journal of the Commons House of Assembly of South Carolina for 1702* (Columbia: Printed for the Historical Commission of South Carolina, 1932), 64.

77. Salley, ed., *Journal of the Commons House of Assembly of South Carolina for 1702*, 84–85.

78. Michael Cole to William Blathwayt, December 22, 1703, in *CSP*, 21:170–87.

79. Charles W. Arnade, "The English Invasion of Spanish Florida, 1700–1706," *Florida Historical Quarterly* 41, no. 1 (1962): 29–37.

80. Michael Cole to William Blathwayt, December 22, 1703, in *CSP*, 21:170–87.

81. Nairne, *A Letter from South Carolina*, 35.

82. "An Act for Raising the sum of four thousand pounds of the reall and personall estates, and of and from the profitts and revenues of the inhabitants of this province, and establishing of

bills of credit for satisfying the debts due by the publick on account of the late expedition against St. Augustine" [May 1703], in *SLSC*, 2:206–10.

83. Nairne, *A Letter from South Carolina*, 36–37.

84. Alan Gallay, *The Indian Slave Trade: The Rise of the English Empire in the American South, 1670–1717* (New Haven: Yale University Press, 2002), 197.

85. For a similar point in the context of the French colonies, see Desbarats, "On Being Surprised," 148.

86. "An Act for keeping and Maintaining a Watch and good Orders in Charles Town" [May 8, 1703], in *SLSC*, 7:22–27; A. S. Salley Jr., ed., *Journal of the Commons House of Assembly of South Carolina, March 6, 1705/6–April 9, 1706* (Columbia: State Company for the Historical Commission of South Carolina, 1937), 57; A. S. Salley Jr., ed., *Journal of the Commons House of Assembly of South Carolina, October 22, 1707–February 12, 1707/8* (Columbia: State Company for the Historical Commission of South Carolina, 1941), 53.

87. "An Act for the Enlisting such trusty Slaves as shall be thought serviceable to this Settlement in time of alarms . . ." [February 13, 1719/20], in *SLSC*, 3:110.

88. "An Act for building a convenient State-House for the Holding of the General Assemblies, Courts of Justice, and other Publick Uses" [June 7, 1712], in *SLSC*, 2:378–79; A. S. Salley Jr., ed., *Journal of the Commons House of Assembly in South Carolina for the Session Beginning February 23, 1724/5 and Ending June 1, 1725* (Columbia: Joint Committee on Printing, General Assembly of South Carolina, 1945), 59; "An Act for repairing and expeditious finishing of the Fortifications in Charlestown" [May 15, 1707], in *SLSC*, 7:43–47; A. S. Salley Jr., ed., *Journal of the Commons House of Assembly of South Carolina, November 15, 1726–March 11, 1726/7* (Columbia: State Commercial printing Company for the Historical Commission of South Carolina, 1946), 79.

89. Records of the Public Treasurers of South Carolina, 1725–76, Ledger A, 1725–30, South Carolina Archives Microcopy Number 3, SCDAH.

90. For examples of scalp bounty payments, see Account of Jeremiah Allen, Treasurer and Receiver General, showing receipts and disbursements between May 30, 1724, and May 31, 1725, MAC, vol. 123 [Treasury, 1707–34], pp. 298–99, 314.

91. [William Bull], "An Account of the Rise and Progress of the Paper Bills of Credit in South Carolina, from the year 1700 to this present time . . ." [1739], in *SLSC*, 9:769.

92. "An Act for the better ordering and governing of Negroes and Slaves" [June 7, 1712], in *SLSC*, 2:381; "An Act for preventing Suppressing and punishing the Conspiracy and Insurrection of Negroes and other Slaves" [December 10, 1712], in *CLNY*, 1:761–67.

93. Ira Berlin, *Many Thousands Gone: The First Two Centuries of Slavery in America* (Cambridge, MA: Harvard University Press, 2000), 66–69, 156–57.

94. Geoffrey Ingham, *The Nature of Money* (Cambridge: Polity Press, 2004), 72.

Chapter 3

1. [Benjamin Franklin], *The General Magazine, and Historical Chronicle, for all the British Plantations in America (1741)* 1, no. 1 (January 1741): 10–11.

2. Benjamin Franklin, "The Legal Tender of Paper Money in America," February 13, 1767, in *Franklin Papers*, 14:32.

3. Benjamin Franklin, "Remarks and Facts Relative to the American Paper Money," March 11, 1767, in *Franklin Papers*, 14:76.

4. Gary B. Nash, *The Urban Crucible: Social Change, Political Consciousness, and the Origins of the American Revolution* (Cambridge, MA: Harvard University Press, 1979), 76.

5. Jeffrey Sklansky, *Sovereign of the Market: The Money Question in Early America* (Chicago: University of Chicago Press, 2017), 2, 7–8.

6. Joseph Albert Ernst, *Money and Politics in America, 1755–1775: A Study in the Currency Act of 1764 and the Political Economy of Revolution* (Chapel Hill: University of North Carolina Press, 1973), xviii.

7. John J. McCusker, *Money and Exchange in Europe and America, 1600–1775: A Handbook* (Chapel Hill: University of North Carolina Press, 1978), 120–21.

8. *An Act for Ascertaining the Rates of Foreign Coins in Her Majesties Plantations in America* [London, 1708]; Leslie Brock, *The Currency of the American Colonies: A Study in Colonial Finance and Imperial Relations* (New York: Arno Press, 1975), 132–34.

9. John Blackwell to William Penn, February 1688/89, John Blackwell correspondence to William Penn, 1688–99 [transcripts], HSP.

10. "William Penn to the Council of Trade and Plantations," April 21, 1703, in *CSP*, 21:369–77.

11. "Heads of several things proper for the King's plantations, and set to be recommended home to England, drawn up by Mr. Penn," 1700, TNA: CO 5/931.

12. "William Penn to the Council of Trade and Plantations," April 21, 1703, in *CSP*, 21:369–77; Joseph Dorfman, *The Economic Mind in American Civilization* (New York: Viking Press, 1946), 1:105.

13. "Letter from Mr. Penn, about coine in the Plantations," read April 21, 1703, in *CSP*, 21:349–69.

14. William Popple to Sir E. Northey, June 1, 1703, in *CSP*, 21:472–88.

15. Carl Wennerlind, *Casualties of Credit: The English Financial Revolution, 1620–1720* (Cambridge, MA: Harvard University Press, 2011), 123–55; Geoffrey Ingham, *The Nature of Money* (Cambridge: Polity, 2004), 129–30.

16. John Poyer, *The History of Barbados* (London: K. Mawman, 1808), 192 ("monied men"); Robert Chalmers, *A History of Currency in the British Colonies* (London: Her Majesty's Stationery Office, 1893), 50 ("the neighbouring colonys").

17. John Olmixon, *The British Empire in America* (London, 1708), 2:65.

18. Thomas Nairne, *A Letter from South Carolina* (London, 1710), 35, 38.

19. [Anon.], *An Essay on Currency, Written in August 1732* (Charles Town, 1734), 7–8.

20. Joseph Dudley to the Board of Trade, November 15, 1710, quoted in Brock, *The Currency of the American Colonies*, 150.

21. Governor Dudley to the Council of Trade and Plantations, December 1, 1713, in *CSP*, 27:253–71.

22. Joseph Albert Ernst, *Money and Politics in America, 1755–1775: A Study in the Currency Act of 1764 and the Political Economy of Revolution* (Chapel Hill: University of North Carolina Press, 1973), 26.

23. See, most notably, William Graham Sumner, *A History of American Currency* (New York, 1876).

24. David Graeber, *Debt: The First 5,000 Years* (New York: Melville House Publishing, 2011), 312–13. On the great recoinage, see Wennerlind, *Casualties of Credit*, 123–55.

25. Pamfili Antipa argues, for example, that fiscal prospects based on "monetary regime choices and their operations" drove inflationary pressures when Britain switched from the gold standard to a "paper pound" during the Napoleonic Wars. Pamfili M. Antipa, "How Fiscal Policy

Affects Prices: Britain's First Experience with Paper Money," *JEH* 76, no. 4 (December 2016): 1047.

26. Farley Grubb, "Is Paper Money Just Paper Money? Experimentation and Variation in the Paper Monies Issued by the American Colonies from 1690 to 1775," NBER Working Paper 17997 (Cambridge, MA: National Bureau of Economic Research, April 2012), 2, 14–20.

27. Christine Desan, *Making Money: Coin, Currency, and the Coming of Capitalism* (New York: Oxford University Press, 2014), 48.

28. Benjamin Franklin, "The Legal Tender of Paper Money in America," February 13, 1767, in *Franklin Papers*, 14:32.

29. Adam Smith, *The Wealth of Nations*, ed. Edwin Cannan (New York: Modern Library, 2000), 356–57.

30. According to the Sargent-Wallace approach, fiscal expectations may be a significant factor in determining the value of money, prices, and exchange rates. Thomas J. Sargent, "The Ends of Four Big Inflations," in Robert E. Hall, ed., *Inflation: Causes and Effects* (Chicago: University of Chicago Press, 1982), 45–46; Thomas J. Sargent and Neil Wallace, "Some Unpleasant Monetarist Arithmetic," *Federal Reserve Bank of Minneapolis Quarterly Review* 5, no. 5 (Fall 1981): 1–17. For an application of the Sargent-Wallace approach to colonial South Carolina and Maryland currency, see Bruce D. Smith, "Some Colonial Evidence on Two Theories of Money: Maryland and the Carolinas," *JPE* 93, no. 6 (December 1985): 1178–211. For the revolutionary era, see Charles W. Calomiris, "Institutional Failure, Monetary Scarcity, and the Depreciation of the Continental," *JEH* 48, no. 1 (March 1988): 47–68.

31. Alvin Rabushka, *Taxation in Colonial America* (Princeton: Princeton University Press, 2008), 472.

32. [Anon.], *The Present Melancholy Circumstances of the Province Consider'd* [Boston, 1719], in *CCR*, 1:359–60.

33. Two important exceptions are Margaret Ellen Newell, *From Dependency to Independence: Economic Revolution in Colonial New England* (Ithaca, NY: Cornell University Press, 1998); Sklansky, *Sovereign of the Market*.

34. [Anon.], *An Addition to the Present Melancholy Circumstances of the Province Considered* [Boston, 1719], in *CCR*, 1:385.

35. [Edward Wigglesworth], *A Letter from One in the Country to his Friend in Boston* [Boston, 1720], in *CCR*, 1:419.

36. [Anon.], *An Addition to the Present Melancholy Circumstances*, 380.

37. [Anon.], *An Addition to the Present Melancholy Circumstances*, 384.

38. [Wigglesworth], *A Letter from One in the Country*, 431–32.

39. [John Colman], *The Distressed State of Boston Further Considered* [Boston, 1720], in *CCR*, 2:70; Sklansky, *Sovereign of the Market*, 44–54.

40. [John Wise], *A Word of Comfort to a Melancholy Country* [Boston, 1721], in *CCR*, 2:194. "So vast a number of Mouths more than our own to feed, might well raise Provisions, and did so," he reiterated in another essay, "and ever since that Fleet have been gone, they have been falling more or less." [John Wise], *The Freeholder's Address to the Honourable House of Representatives* (Boston, 1721), 4.

41. [Oliver Noyes], *A Letter from a Gentleman, Containing some Remarks upon the Several Answers* [Boston, 1720], in *CCR*, 2:9.

42. [Wise], *A Word of Comfort*, 194; [Noyes], *A Letter from a Gentlemen*, 9; L. Randall Wray, *Understanding Modern Money: The Key to Full Employment and Price Stability* (Cheltenham, UK: Edgar Elgar, 1998), 159.

43. [Colman], *The Distressed State of the Town of Boston Further Considered*, 70; Wray, *Understanding Modern Money*, 170–74.

44. [Noyes], *A Letter from a Gentleman*, 9.

45. [Wigglesworth], *A Letter from One in the Country*, 420.

46. [John Colman], *The Distressed State of the Town of Boston Considered* [Boston, 1720], 398–402.

47. [Noyes], *A Letter from a Gentleman*, 4–5, 14.

48. [Colman], *The Distressed State of the Town of Boston Considered*, 406.

49. "An Act for Encouraging The Linen Manufacture, And The Making of Canvas Or Duck Proper For Ships' Sails, &c." [June 1722], in *MASS*, 2:241–42; Account of Jeremiah Allen, Treasurer and Receiver General, showing receipts and disbursements between May 30, 1724, and May 31, 1725, MAC, vol. 123 [Treasury, 1707–34], p. 303; Account of Jeremiah Allen, Treasurer and Receiver General, showing receipts and disbursements between May 26, 1726, and May 31, 1727, MAC, vol. 123 [Treasury, 1707–34], p. 339.

50. Peter L. Rousseau and Caleb Stroup, "Monetization and Growth in Colonial New England, 1703–1749," *Explorations in Economic History* 48 (2011): 600–613.

51. Thomas Amory to John and Samuel Wainwright, January 29, 1721/2, Thomas Amory Letterbooks, Amory Family Papers, 1697–1882, box 4 (hereafter Amory Letterbooks), LOC. Thomas Amory to John and Samuel Wainwright, March 12, 1721/2; Thomas Amory to Martha Logan, November 12, 1723; Thomas Amory to Edward Moseley, April 19, 1725; all in Amory Letterbooks, LOC.

52. Thomas Amory to John and Samuel Wainwright, March 12, 1721/2; Thomas Amory to John and Samuel Wainwright, April 9, 1722; Thomas Amory to Benjamin Godin and Benjamin De La Conseillere, April 11, 1722; Thomas Amory to John and Samuel Wainwright, July 20, 1722; all in Amory Letterbooks, LOC.

53. Thomas Amory to Nicholas Oursel, July 21, 1726, Amory Letterbooks, LOC.

54. Thomas Amory to Edward Moseley, May 16, 1727; Thomas Amory to William Jones, May 24, 1727; both in Amory Letterbooks, LOC.

55. Thomas Amory to William Jones, November 8, 1727, Amory Letterbooks, LOC.

56. "An Act Concerning the value of bills of credit," November 25, 1727, MAC, vol. 101 [Pecuniary, 1694–1740], pp. 473–75.

57. Quoted in Willard C. Fisher, "The Tabular Standard in Massachusetts History," *Quarterly Journal of Economics* 72, no. 3 (May 1913): 420n1.

58. Andrew McFarland Davis, *Currency and Baking in the Province of the Massachusetts-Bay, Part I. Currency* (New York: Macmillan, 1901), 84.

59. [William Bull], "An Account of the Rise and Progress of the Paper Bills of Credit in South Carolina, from the year 1700 to this present time . . ." [1739], in *SLSC*, 9:767.

60. A. S. Salley Jr., ed., *Journal of the Commons House of Assembly of South Carolina, March 6, 1705/6–April 9, 1706* (Columbia: State Company for the Historical Commission of South Carolina, 1937), 54–55.

61. [Bull], "An account of the rise and progress of the paper bills of credit in South Carolina," 767.

62. [Bull], "An account of the rise and progress of the paper bills of credit in South Carolina," 768.

63. Nairne, *A Letter from South Carolina*, 39.

64. "The Report of the Committee of the Commons House of Assembly of the Province of South-Carolina, on the State of the Paper-Currency of the said Province," TNA: CO 5/367, p. 20.

65. [Le Jau to the Secretary, March 13, 1708], in Frank J. Klingberg, ed., *The Carolina Chronicle of Dr. Francis Le Jau, 1706–1717* (Berkeley: University of California Press, 1956), 36.

66. [Le Jau to the Secretary, September 15, 1708], in *The Carolina Chronicle of Dr. Francis Le Jau*, 42; [Le Jau to the Secretary, August 5, 1709], in *The Carolina Chronicle of Dr. Francis Le Jau*, 58.

67. [Le Jau to the Secretary, April 20, 1714], in *The Carolina Chronicle of Dr. Francis Le Jau*, 140.

68. Alan Gallay, *The Indian Slave Trade: The Rise of the English Empire in the American South, 1670–1717* (New Haven: Yale University Press, 2002), 329–38.

69. [Bull], "An account of the rise and progress of the paper bills of credit in South Carolina," 771.

70. [Le Jau to John Chamberlain, August 22, 1715], in *The Carolina Chronicle of Dr. Francis Le Jau*, 161–62; [Le Jau to the Secretary, May 10, 1715], in *The Carolina Chronicle of Dr. Francis Le Jau*, 152.

71. Francis Yonge, *A Narrative of the Proceedings of the People of South-Carolina, in the Year 1719* (London, 1726), 8.

72. Thomas Amory to Thomas Amory Esq., June 16, 1720, Amory Letterbooks, LOC.

73. Thomas Amory to James Ramsey, June 20, 1720, Amory Letterbooks, LOC.

74. Smith, "Some Colonial Evidence on Two Theories of Money," 1190.

75. [Anon.], *An Essay on Currency*, 8–9.

76. "The Report of the Committee of the Commons House of Assembly of the Province of South-Carolina, on the State of the Paper-Currency of the said Province," TNA: CO 5/367, pp. 21–22.

77. Franklin, "Remarks and Facts Relative to the American Paper Money," 76.

78. Lords Proprietors to Robert Johnson and the Council, September 4, 1718, TNA: CO 5/290.

79. Richard M. Jellison, "Paper Currency in Colonial South Carolina: A Reappraisal," *South Carolina Historical Magazine* 62, no. 3 (July 1961): 138.

80. Nairne, *A Letter from South Carolina*, 35.

81. Desan, *Making Money*, 94, 149.

82. Christine Desan, "The Market as a Matter of Money: Denaturalizing Economic Currency in American Constitutional History," *Law & Social Inquiry* 30, no. 1 (Winter 2005): 50; Claire Priest, "Currency Policies and Legal Development in Colonial New England," *Yale Law Journal* 110, no. 8 (June 2001), 1380–91.

83. [Anon.], *An Essay on Currency*, 10–11.

84. Franklin, "Remarks and Facts Relative to the American Paper Money," 76.

85. Peter A. Coclanis, "Rice Prices in the 1720s and the Evolution of the South Carolina Economy," *Journal of Southern History* 48, no. 4 (November 1982): 531–44; Henry C. Dethloff, "The Colonial Rice Trade," *Agricultural History* 56, no. 1 (January 1982): 233–36; Daniel C. Littlefield, "The Slave Trade to Colonial South Carolina: A Profile," *South Carolina Historical Magazine* 101, no. 2 (April 2000): 114, 128.

86. [Francis Rawle], *Some Remedies Proposed, for the Restoring the Sunk Credit of the Province of Pennsylvania* (Philadelphia, 1721), 12.

87. William Keith to the Lords of Trade, December 12, 1723, TNA: CO 5/1233.

88. [Anon.], *An Essay on Currency*, 18–20, 24.

89. Serena Zabin, *Dangerous Economies: Status and Commerce in Imperial New York* (Philadelphia: University of Pennsylvania Press, 2009), 11–13; Simon Middleton, *From Privileges to*

Rights: Work and Politics in Colonial New York City (Philadelphia: University of Pennsylvania Press, 2006), 99–105; Nash, *The Urban Crucible*, 14.

90. Michael Kammen, *Colonial New York: A History* (New York: Oxford University Press, 1975), 163–64, 189. On the uniqueness of colonial New York's economy within the wider British Atlantic world, see Zabin, *Dangerous Economies*, 3–8; John J. McCusker and Russel R. Menard, *The Economy of British America, 1607–1789* (Chapel Hill: University of North Carolina Press, 1985), 189; Cathy Matson, *Merchants & Empire: Trading in Colonial New York* (Baltimore: Johns Hopkins University Press, 1998), 3.

91. Governor Hunter to Secretary St. John, September 12, 1711, in E. B. O'Callaghan, ed., *Documents Relative to the Colonial History of the State of New York* (Albany, NY: Weed, Parsons & Co., 1855) (hereafter *DRCNY*), 5:255–56.

92. "An Act to appoint Commissioners to Examine and State the several Claims alledged as Debts of the Government" [December 1712], in *CLNY*, 1:770.

93. "An Act for Paying and Discharging the Several Debts and Sums of Money claimed as Debts of this Colony, to the several Persons therein named, and to make and enforce the Currency of Bills of Credit to the Value of Twenty Seven Thousand Six Hundred and Eighty Pounds, for that Purpose; also to make void all Claims and Demands made, or pretended to be due from this Colony before the first Day of June, One Thousand Seven Hundred and Fourteen, and to prevent this Colony from being in Debt for the Future" [September 1714], in *CLNY*, 1:815–26. The full act is published in *Acts of the Assembly, Passed in the Province of New-York, from 1691, to 1718* (London: John Baskett, 1719) (hereafter *Acts of Assembly Passed in New York*), 160–95 (quotations on 160).

94. *Acts of Assembly Passed in New York*, 160–61, 187–91.

95. Rabushka, *Taxation in Colonial America*, 491; Eric P. Newman, *The Early Paper Money of America: An Illustrated, Historical, and Descriptive Collection of Data Relating to American Paper Currency from Its Inception in 1686 to the Year 1800* (Iola, WI: Krause Publications, 2008), 270–75; John H. Hickcox, *A History of the Bills of Credit or Paper Money issued by New York, from 1709 to 1789* (Albany, NY, 1866), 15–20.

96. "An Act for Paying and Discharging Several Debts Due from this Colony to the Persons therein named and for Raising and Putting into the Hands of the Treasurer of this Collony Severall quantities of Plate to be apply'd to the Publick and necessary Uses of this Colony and to make Bills of Creditt to the value of fforty One Thousand ffive hundred and Seaventeene Ounces and an half of Plate for that purpose" [December 1717], in *CLNY*, 1:938–91.

97. Ernst, *Money and Politics in America*, 29; Rabushka, *Taxation in Colonial America*, 491.

98. Governor Hunter to Mr. Popple, December 3, 1717, in *CSP*, 30:118.

99. Humphrey Mackworth, *Sir H. Mackworth's Proposal in Miniature, As It Has Been Put in Practice in New-York, in America* (London, 1720), 16.

100. Mackworth, *Sir H. Mackworth's Proposal in Miniature*, 4.

101. Governor Burnet to the Lords of Trade, December 16, 1723, TNA: CO 5/1092.

102. Governor Burnet to the Lords of Trade, November 21, 1724, TNA: CO 5/1092.

103. Hickcox, *A History of the Bills of Credit or Paper Money issued by New York*, 15–20.

104. Rabushka, *Taxation in Colonial America*, 491–92.

105. Rabushka, *Taxation in Colonial America*, 499–507.

106. Kammen, *Colonial New York*, 161–62; Nash, *Urban Crucible*, 107, 119, 124; Middleton, *From Privileges to Rights*, 99–101, 129.

107. Cadwallader Colden, "Mr. Colden's Account of the Trade of New-York" [1723], in *DRCNY*, 5:686; Zabin, *Dangerous Economies*, 11–12; Middleton, *From Privileges to Rights*, 102–7; Nash, *Urban Crucible*, 124–25.

Chapter 4

1. Letter from William Keith, with abstract [to the Lords of Trade], December 18, 1722, TNA: CO 5/1266; William Keith to the Lords of Trade, December 12, 1723, in TNA: CO 5/1233; Mary M. Schweitzer, *Custom and Contract: Household, Government, and the Economy in Colonial Pennsylvania* (New York: Columbia University Press, 1987), 116, 126–30.

2. Theodore Thayer, "The Land-Bank System in the American Colonies," *JEH* 13, no. 2 (Spring 1953): 145–59; Christine Desan, "From Blood to Profit: Making Money in the Practice and Imagery of Early America," *Journal of Policy History* 20, no. 1 (January 2008): 28–29.

3. Allan Kulikoff, *The Agrarian Origins of American Capitalism* (Charlottesville: University Press of Virginia, 1992), 108.

4. Perry Miller, *The New England Mind: From Colony to Province* (Cambridge, MA: Harvard University Press, 1953), 322.

5. [Benjamin Franklin], *A Modest Enquiry into the Nature and Necessity of a Paper-Currency* [Philadelphia, 1729], in *CCR*, 2:349.

6. Geoffrey Ingham, "Money as a Social Relation," *Review of Social Economy* 54, no. 4 (1996): 524.

7. Geoffrey Ingham, *The Nature of Money* (Cambridge, UK: Polity Press, 2004), 121–22, 129.

8. William Potter, *Humble Proposalls to the Honorable the Councell for Trade* (London, 1651), 5–6, 8.

9. William Potter, *The Key of Wealth* (London, 1650), 38.

10. Potter, *The Key of Wealth*, 39–40; Craig Muldrew, *The Economy of Obligation: The Culture of Credit and Social Relations in Early Modern England* (New York: Palgrave, 1998), 3.

11. Samuel Hartlib, *A Discoverie for Division or Setting out of Land* (London, 1653), 32.

12. Hartlib, *Discoverie for Division*, 29.

13. Hartlib, *Discoverie for Division*, 33. On the "Hartlib Circle" and the relationship between alchemy and proposals for land banks and credit money, see Carl Wennerlind, "Credit-Money as the Philosopher's Stone: Alchemy and the Coinage Problem in Seventeenth-Century England," *History of Political Economy* 35, no. 5 (2003): 234–61; Carl Wennerlind, *Casualties of Credit: The English Financial Revolution, 1620–1720* (Cambridge, MA: Harvard University Press, 2011), 44–79.

14. Hartlib, *Discoverie for Division*, 31–32.

15. William Blackstone, *Commentaries on the Laws of England*, ed. Joseph Chitty (London, 1826), 2:16.

16. Claire Priest, "Creating an American Property Law: Alienability and Its Limits in American History," *Harvard Law Review* 120, no. 2 (December 2006): 387–88.

17. Samuel Hartlib to John Winthrop Jr., March 16, 1660, in G. H. Turnbull, ed., "Some Correspondence of John Winthrop, Jr., and Samuel Hartlib," *Proceedings of the Massachusetts Historical Society* 72 (October 1957–December 1960): 48–49.

18. John Winthrop Jr. to Samuel Hartlib, January 7, 1660/61, in Turnbull, ed., "Some Correspondence of John Winthrop, Jr., and Samuel Hartlib," 65. For John Winthrop Jr. and alchemy,

see Walter Woodward, *Prospero's America: John Winthrop, Jr., Alchemy, and the Creation of New England Culture, 1606-1676* (Chapel Hill: University of North Carolina Press, 2010).

19. [John Woodbridge], *Severals relating to the Fund* [Boston, 1682], in *CCR*, 1:112, 114.

20. Thomas Budd, *Good Order Established in Pennsilvania & New-Jersey in America* (Philadelphia, 1685), 49-50.

21. [Franklin], *A Modest Enquiry*, 349.

22. John Webbe, *A Discourse Concerning Paper Money* (Philadelphia, [1742 or 1743]), 6.

23. Donald L. Kemmerer, "The Colonial Loan-Office System in New Jersey," *JPE* 47, no. 6 (December 1939): 867.

24. Joseph Story, *Commentaries on the Constitution of the United States: With a Preliminary Review of the Constitutional History of the Colonies and States, Before the Adoption of the Constitution* (Boston, 1833), 1:168.

25. K-Sue Park, "Money, Mortgages, and the Conquest of America," *Law & Social Inquiry* 41, no. 4 (Fall 2016): 1007-8, 1012. On commodification as a social process rather than as the natural outcome of market forces, see Karl Polanyi, *The Great Transformation* (New York: Ferris Printing Co., 1944), 72. On property as socially constructed, see Christine Desan, "The Market as a Matter of Money: Denaturalizing Economic Currency in American Constitutional History," *Law & Society Inquiry* 30, no. 1 (Winter 2005): 24.

26. William Stith, *The History of the First Discovery and Settlement of Virginia, Book III* (Williamsburg, VA, 1747), 140, quoted in Park, "Money, Mortgages, and the Conquest of America," 1013.

27. [John Blackwell], *A Discourse in Explanation of the Bank of Credit* [Boston, 1687], in *CCR*, 1:123-24.

28. Joseph Dudley and Samuel Shrimpton to William Blathwayt, January 18, 1685, Jeffries Family Papers, (hereafter Jeffries Papers), MHS. For a list of the original Million Purchase proprietors, see copy of a letter from Capt Leatherhead to General Nicolson, August 22, 1720, Jeffries Papers, MHS. On the relationship between Blackwell's bank and land speculation, see Daniel R. Mandell, *King Philip's War: Colonial Expansion, Native Resistance, and the End of Indian Sovereignty* (Baltimore: Johns Hopkins University Press, 2010), 119; Margaret Ellen Newell, *From Dependency to Independence: Economic Revolution in Colonial New England* (Ithaca, NY: Cornell University Press, 1998), 90; John Frederick Martin, *Profits in the Wilderness: Entrepreneurship and the Founding of New England Towns in the Seventeenth Century* (Chapel Hill: University of North Carolina Press, 1991), 87-100; Theodore B. Lewis, "Land Speculation and the Dudley Council of 1686," *WMQ* 31 (April 1974): 255-72.

29. Joseph Trask deed to Jonathan Tyng, January 3, 1683/84, Jeffries Papers, MHS.

30. Quoted in Jenny Hale Pulsipher, " 'Dark Cloud Rising from the East': Indian Sovereignty and the Coming of King William's War in New England," *NEQ* 80, no. 4 (December 2007): 596-97.

31. "Report on Mr. Richard Wharton's claim to lands at Pojebscot" and "Report of Sir Edmund Andros on the claims to the Naragansett Country," in *CSP*, 12:407-426.

32. "Diary of Samuel Sewall, 1675-1729, vol. I, 1674-1700," *Collections of the Massachusetts Historical Society* 5 (1878): 251.

33. Account of Jeremiah Allen, Treasurer and Receiver General, showing receipts and disbursements between May 30, 1724, and May 31, 1725, MAC, vol. 123 [Treasury, 1707-34], 298; David McNally, *Blood and Money: War, Slavery, Finance, and Empire* (Chicago: Haymarket Books, 2020), 180.

34. George Athan Bilias, *The Massachusetts Land Bankers of 1740* (Orono, ME: University Press, 1959), 26–27, 30–31.

35. Claire Priest, *Credit Nation: Property Laws and Legal Institutions in Early America* (Princeton: Princeton University Press, 2021), 38–56.

36. Brenna Bhandar, *Colonial Lives of Property: Law, Land, and Racial Regimes of Ownership* (Durham, NC: Duke University Press, 2018), 79–80.

37. Bhandar, *Colonial Lives of Property*, 85, 90–96 (quotation on 85).

38. K-Sue Park, "Property and Sovereignty in America: A History of Title Registries & Jurisdictional Power," *Yale Law Journal* 133, no. 5 (March 2024).

39. Ellen Meiksins Woods defines improvement—an idea that flourished in seventeenth-century England and depended on a new capitalist conception of property as private and exclusive—as "the enhancement of the land's productivity for profit." Ellen Meiksins Woods, *The Origin of Capitalism: A Longer View* (London: Verso Books, 2016), 106.

40. Bhandar, *Colonial Lives of Property*, 48.

41. [John Wise], *A Word of Comfort to a Melancholy Country* [Boston, 1721], in *CCR*, 2:188.

42. [Joseph Morgan], *Some Proposals To benefit the Province* [Boston, 1720], in *CCR*, 2:97–98, 100.

43. [Joseph Morgan], *The Original Rights of Mankind Freely to Subdue and Improve the Earth* (Boston, 1722), 7–9.

44. *A Projection for Erecting a Bank of Credit in Boston, New-England. Founded on Land Security* [Boston, 1714], in *CCR*, 1:321.

45. *A Projection for Erecting a Bank of Credit*, 325–26, 329.

46. *A Projection for Erecting a Bank of Credit*, 329.

47. [Paul Dudley], *Objections to the Bank of Credit* [Boston, 1714], in *CCR*, 1:244.

48. [Dudley], *Objections to the Bank of Credit*, 248.

49. [Dudley], *Objections to the Bank of Credit*, 249–50.

50. [Dudley], *Objections to the Bank of Credit*, 256–57.

51. Thomas Hutchinson, *The History of the Province of Massachusetts-Bay, from the Charter of King William and Queen Mary, in 1693, Until the Year 1750*, 2nd ed. (London, 1768), 2:207–8.

52. "An Act for the Making and Emitting the Sum of Fifty Thousand Pounds in Bills of Credit on this Province" [May 1714], in *MASS*, 1:751.

53. [Anon.], *A Vindication of the Bank of Credit* [Boston, 1714], in *CCR*, 1:301.

54. [Anon.], *A Vindication of the Bank of Credit*, 301–2.

55. [Anon.], *A Vindication of the Bank of Credit*, 296.

56. [Anon.], *A Vindication of the Bank of Credit*, 299.

57. "An Act for the Making and Emitting the Sum of One Hundred Thousand Pounds in Bills of Credit on this Province" [December 1716], in *MASS*, 2:61–64.

58. [John Colman], *The Distressed State of the Town of Boston Considered* [Boston, 1720], in *CCR*, 1:399.

59. [Colman], *The Distressed State of the Town of Boston Considered*, 405.

60. [Colman], *The Distressed State of the Town of Boston Considered*, 406.

61. [Edward Wigglesworth], *A Letter From One in the Country to his Friend in Boston* [Boston, 1720], in *CCR*, 1:436.

62. Thomas Franklin Waters, *Ipswich in the Massachusetts Bay Colony* (Ipswich, MA: Ipswich Historical Society, 1917), 2:144.

63. [Anon.], *The Present Melancholy Circumstances of the Province Consider'd* [Boston, 1719], in *CCR*, 1:357.

64. [Anon.], *The Present Melancholy Circumstances of the Province Consider'd*, 363.

65. "An Act for the Making and Emitting the Sum of Fifty Thousand Pounds in Bills of Credit on this Province" [March 15, 1720/21], in *MASS*, 2:189–94; "An Act for Raising and Setling a Publick Revenue, for and towards Defreying the Necessary Charges of this Government, by an Emission of Sixty Thousand Pounds in Bills of Credit on this Province" [February 1728], in *MASS*, 2:470–77.

66. Newell, *From Dependency to Independence*, 187–93.

67. Newell, *From Dependency to Independence*, 187–93.

68. Waters, *Ipswich in the Massachusetts Bay Colony*, 148–49.

69. Braintree (MA) account book, 1717–44 (hereafter Braintree account book), MHS; *Records of the Town of Braintree, 1640-1793*, ed. Samuel A. Bates (Randolph, MA: Daniel H. Huxford, 1886), 124–25, 132.

70. An important exception is Newell, *From Dependency to Independence*.

71. Thayer, "The Land-Bank System in the American Colonies," 157.

72. "Capt. Amos Turner petition, Dec. 1726," MAC, vol. 101 [Pecuniary, 1694–1740], pp. 439–40.

73. "An Act to enable and oblige the surviving trustees or commissioners of the one hundred thousand pounds loan, to comply with their duty, by law required [June 27, 1738]," MAC, vol. 101 [Pecuniary, 1694–1740], pp. 569–71.

74. "Bill for the more effective drawing in the £60,000 Loan [January 1738/9]," MAC, vol. 102 [Pecuniary, 1740–52], pp. 615–17.

75. Many of the mortgages for the 1714 and 1716 loans can be found in Suffolk, Deeds, vol. 28 [1713–14], vol. 29 [1714–15], and vol. 31 [1716–17], Suffolk County Record of Deeds, Suffolk County, Massachusetts, 1639–1920, microfilm; Middlesex, Deeds, vol. 17 [1714–16], Record Books of the Registry of Deeds, Middlesex County, Massachusetts, 1649–1900, microfilm. For examples of mortgages for the 1721 and 1728 loans, see Suffolk, Deeds, vol. 35 [1720–21] and vol. 42 [1727–28], Suffolk Country Registry of Deeds, microfilm. All land records accessed through FamilySearch.org.

76. Henry Allen Hazen, *History of Billerica, Massachusetts* (Boston: A. Williams & Co., 1883), 202.

77. Waters, *Ipswich in the Massachusetts Bay Colony*, 148–49.

78. Braintree account book, MHS.

79. Jeremiah Hunt's obligation bond to the trustees of Billerica, April 11, 1728, Broadsides Collection, MHS; W. L. G. Hunt and T. B. Wyman Jr., *Genealogy of the Name and Family of Hunt* (Boston, 1863), 23, 115.

80. Waters, *Ipswich in the Massachusetts Bay Colony*, 145, 151–52.

81. [John Colman], *The Distressed State of the Town of Boston Considered* [Boston, 1720], in *CCR*, 1:398–408. For the large numbers of writs of attachment for debt filed in the county courts in 1720, see Gary B. Nash, *The Urban Crucible: Social Change, Political Consciousness, and the Origins of the American Revolution* (Cambridge, MA: Harvard University Press, 1979), 83; Claire Priest, "Currency Policies and Legal Development in Colonial New England," *Yale Law Journal* 110, no. 8 (June 2001): 1365–67; Newell, *From Dependence to Independence*, 165.

82. [Oliver Noyes], *A Letter from a Gentleman, Containing some Remarks upon the Several Answers* [Boston, 1720], in *CCR*, 2:12.

NOTES TO PAGES 105–107

83. Massachusetts law gave parties to contracts the power to designate the form of repayment; see Priest, "Currency Policies and Legal Development in Colonial New England," 1331–32, 1347–48.

84. "Arnil and Belchers Bond," August 1, 1724, and October 30, 1724, Dennis Papers, MHS.

85. Daniel Saferd's promissory note, January 31, 1730, Dennis Papers, MHS; Amos Stetson Bond to Richard Thayer, May 8, 1730, Braintree, Miscellaneous Manuscripts, MHS.

86. Braintree Account Book, MHS.

87. Sara T. Damiano, *To Her Credit: Women, Finance, and the Law in Eighteenth-Century New England Cities* (Baltimore: Johns Hopkins University Press, 2021), 6–8 (quotation on 8).

88. T. H. Breen, *The Marketplace of Revolution: How Consumer Politics Shaped American Independence* (New York: Oxford University Press, 2004).

89. W. M. Account Book, 1713–28, New York or New England, Joseph Downs Collection, Winterthur Library, Winterthur, DE.

90. Ann Greene Account Book, 1725–1890, MHS.

91. Amory to Thomas Amory Esq., June 16, 1720, Thomas Amory Letterbooks, Amory Family Papers, 1697–1882, box 4, (hereafter Amory Letterbooks), LOC; Thomas Amory to Edward Moseley, August 12, 1725, Amory Letterbooks, LOC. In May 1727, the price of tar was nineteen shillings per barrel "& Very dull to house it." In October of that year, it sold for fifteen to eighteen shillings per barrel. Thomas Amory to Edward Moseley, May 16, 1727; Thomas Amory to Thomas Jones, October 2, 1727; both in Amory Letterbooks, LOC.

92. Priest, "Currency Policies and Legal Development," 1368; Newell, *From Dependency to Independence*, 192.

93. Thomas Amory to Edward Moseley, May 16, 1727; Thomas Amory to William Jones, May 24, 1727 (quotation); both in Amory Letterbooks, LOC.

94. Thomas Amory to Nathaniel Dukinfeild, April 5, 1726; Thomas Amory to Nathaniel Dukinfeild, June 9, 1726; both in Amory Letterbooks, LOC. Like other colonial merchants, Amory often quoted the exchange rate not as the sum of colonial currency necessary to purchase £100 sterling, but "in terms of the percentage increase in local currency necessary to buy a bill on the metropolis." John J. McCusker, *Money & Exchange in Europe & America, 1600–1775: A Handbook* (Chapel Hill: University of North Carolina Press, 1978), 120.

95. "October 5, 1727, Vote for Granting a Tax of £60000 in Bills of Credit or in Species," MAC, vol. 101 [Pecuniary, 1694–1740], pp. 459–68; Robert Craig West, "Money in the Colonial American Economy," *Economic Inquiry*, 16, no. 1 (January 1978): 6–8, 10–11.

96. Thomas Amory to Samuel Allen, June 16, 1727; Thomas Amory to William Jones, June 17, 1727; Thomas Amory to William Jones, July 25, 1727; all in Amory Letterbooks, LOC. Bruce H. Mann, *Republic of Debtors: Bankruptcy in the Age of American Independence* (Cambridge, MA: Harvard University Press, 2002), 17–18, 30–31 (quotation on 17–18).

97. Thomas Amory to William Jones, November 8, 1727, Amory Letterbooks, LOC.

98. Thomas Amory to Samuel Everleigh, April 4, 1728, Amory Letterbooks LOC.

99. C. Edwin Barrows, ed., "The Diary of John Comer," *Collections of the Rhode Island Historical Society* 8 (1893): 78.

100. Barbara Clark Smith, *The Freedoms We Lost: Consent and Resistance in Revolutionary America* (New York: New Press, 2010), 53.

101. Carl Bridenbaugh, "The High Cost of Living in Boston, 1728," *NEQ* 5, no. 4 (October 1932): 800–811; Nash, *The Urban Crucible*, 114–15.

102. [Hugh Vans], *An Inquiry into the Nature and Uses of Money* [Boston, 1740], in *CCR*, 3:444.

103. Nash, *The Urban Crucible*, 82–83. On the region's low growth rate in this period, see Terry L. Anderson, "Economic Growth in Colonial New England: 'Statistical Renaissance,'" *JEH* 39, no. 1 (March 1979): 243–57.

104. Mark Egnal, "The Economic Development of the Thirteen Continental Colonies, 1720 to 1775," *WMQ* 32, no. 2 (April 1975): 191–222; Nash, *The Urban Crucible*, 112–13.

105. "At a Councill Roome at Philadelphia," 7 February 1688/89, in Samuel Hazard, ed., *Minutes of the Provincial Council of Pennsylvania, From the Organization to the Termination of the Proprietary Government, Volume I* (Philadelphia, 1852), 236.

106. Budd, *Good Order Established in Pennsylvania and New Jersey*, 17.

107. John Blackwell to William Penn, February 1688/89, John Blackwell correspondence to William Penn, 1688–99 [transcripts], HSP.

108. "Petitions relating to the scarcity of currency cash," February 10, 1717/18, Society Miscellaneous Collections, Petitions relating to coinage/currency, 1717–1848, box 4b, folder 2, HSP.

109. William Keith to the Lords of Trade, December 12, 1723, TNA: CO 5/1233.

110. [Francis Rawle], *Some Remedies Proposed, for the Restoring the Sunk Credit of the Province of Pennsylvania* (Philadelphia, 1721), 9.

111. [Anon.], *A Dialogue between Mr. Robert Rich, and Roger Plowman* (Philadelphia, 1725), 2.

112. Jonathan Dickinson to John Harriot, April 28, 1715, Jonathan Dickinson Letterbook, 1714–1722 (hereafter Dickinson Letterbook), LCP.

113. Jonathan Dickinson to John Lynch & Co, June 28, 1715; Jonathan Dickinson to John Gale, June 18, 1715; both in Dickinson Letterbook, LCP. Nash, *The Urban Crucible*, 119.

114. Jonathan Dickinson to Richard Champion, August 17, 1715, Dickinson Letterbook, LCP.

115. Jonathan Dickinson to John Askew, September 7, 1715; Jonathan Dickinson to John Askew, October 6, 1715 (quotation); Jonathan Dickinson to Captain Barnett, December 13, 1715; Jonathan Dickinson to John Lewis, December 13, 1715; all in Dickinson Letterbook, LCP.

116. Thomas Lawrence to Samuel Storke, April 22, 1719, Thomas Lawrence Letterbook (hereafter Lawrence Letterbook), HSP.

117. Thomas Lawrence to Samuel Storke, May 10, 1719, Lawrence Letterbook, HSP.

118. Thomas Lawrence to Samuel Storke, May 25, 1720; Thomas Lawrence to Samuel Storke, July 28, 1720; both in Lawrence Letterbook, HSP.

119. Nash, *The Urban Crucible*, 119.

120. Jonathan Dickinson to his brother, May 10, 1721, Dickinson Letterbook, LCP.

121. Jonathan Dickinson to his cousin, May 11, 1721; Jonathan Dickinson to his brother, May 20, 1721 (quotation); both in Dickinson Letterbook, LCP.

122. Jonathan Dickinson to Joseph May & Co, August 28, 1721, Dickinson Letterbook, LCP.

123. Jonathan Dickinson to Samuel Bayard, August 17, 1721; Jonathan Dickinson to Joseph May & Co, August 28, 1721; Jonathan Dickinson to Richard Champion, August 28, 1721; Jonathan Dickinson to Son Joseph Dickinson, November 7, 1721; all in Dickinson Letterbook, LCP.

124. Thomas Lawrence to Samuel Storke, June 1, 1721, Lawrence Letterbook, HSP.

125. Thomas Lawrence to Samuel Storke, October 12, 1721, Lawrence Letterbook, HSP.

126. Thomas Lawrence to Samuel Storke, August 17, 1722; Thomas Lawrence to Joshua Wroe, August 20, 1722; both in Lawrence Letterbook, HSP.

127. [Rawle], *Some Remedies Proposed*, 6–7.

128. Letter from William Keith, with abstract [to the Lords of Trade], December 18, 1722, TNA: CO 5/1266.

129. Letter from William Keith, with abstract [to the Lords of Trade], December 18, 1722, TNA: CO 5/1266.

130. James Logan to Simon Clement, November 22, 1722, Penn Family Papers I. Correspondence, Official Correspondence I, 1683–1727 (hereafter Penn Papers I, Official Correspondence I), p. 119, HSP.

131. "An Act for the Emitting and Making Current Fifteen Thousand Pounds in Bills of Credit" [March 1722/23], in James T. Mitchell and Henry Flanders, eds., *The Statutes at Large of Pennsylvania from 1682 to 1801* (Philadelphia: Clarence H. Busch, State Printer, 1896), 3:324–38 (quotation on 327).

132. Thomas Lawrence to John van der Plank, November 1, 1724, Lawrence Letterbook, HSP.

133. Thomas Lawrence to Samuel Storke, April 10, 1725, Lawrence Letterbook, HSP.

134. [Francis Rawle], *Ways and Means for the Inhabitants of Delaware to Become Rich* (Philadelphia, 1725), 55.

135. Schweitzer, *Custom and Contract*, 122–23.

136. Quoted in Richard A. Lester, "Currency Issues to Overcome Depression in Pennsylvania, 1723 and 1729," *JPE* 46, no. 3 (June 1938): 339.

137. Beulah Coates Account Book, 1719–24, Coates-Horner Family Papers, Marian S. Carson Collection, box 32, folder 4, LOC.

138. Schweitzer, *Custom and Contract*, 157. The loan office trustees maintained their own registers for recording mortgages rather than rely on the existing system for registering titles and deeds (the land office and the county recorders, respectively), as was the case in Massachusetts. See James M. Duffin, *Guide to the Mortgages of the General Loan Office of the Province of Pennsylvania, 1724–1756* (Philadelphia: Genealogical Society of Pennsylvania, 1995); Keith Arbour, "Benjamin Franklin's First Government Printing: The Pennsylvania General Loan Office Mortgage Register of 1729, and Subsequent Franklin Mortgage Registers and Bonds," *Transactions of the American Philosophical Society* 89, no. 5 (1999).

139. John Smolenski, *Friends and Strangers: The Making of a Creole Culture in Colonial Pennsylvania* (Philadelphia: University of Pennsylvania Press, 2010), 255–56.

140. The pamphlets included [Anon.], *A Dialogue between Mr. Robert Rich, and Roger Plowman* (Philadelphia, 1725); [Anon.], *The Triumvirate of Pennsylvania* (Philadelphia, 1725); [James Logan], *A Dialogue shewing, what's therein to be found* (Philadelphia, 1725); [James Logan], *The ANTIDOTE. In Some REMARKS on a Paper of David Lloyd's, called A Vindication of the Legislative Power. Submitted to the Representatives of all the Freemen of Pennsylvania* [Philadelphia, 1725]; [Francis Rawle], *A just rebuke to a dialogue betwixt Simon and Timothy, shewing what's therein to be found* (Philadelphia, 1726); [Anon.], *The Observator's trip to America, in a dialogue between the observator and his country-man Roger* (Philadelphia, 1726).

141. James Logan to John Penn, December 12, 1726, Penn Papers I, Official Correspondence I, p. 233, HSP; Schweitzer, *Custom and Contract*, 164.

142. James Logan to John Penn, October 8, 1728, Logan Family Papers, 1664–1871, Collection vol. 7, James Logan Letterbook v. III, 1725–32 (hereafter Logan Letterbook), p. 274, HSP.

143. Andrew Hamilton to David Barclay, October 27, 1728, Penn Family Papers I. Correspondence, Official Correspondence II, 1728–35 (hereafter Penn Papers I, Official Correspondence II), p. 43, HSP.

144. James Logan to the Proprietors, February 30, 1728/29, Logan Letterbook, pp. 286–88, HSP.

145. Governor Gordon to the House of Representatives, May 10, 1729, Penn Papers I, Official Correspondence II, p. 65, HSP (quotation); Governor Gordon to the Proprietors, May 16, 1729, Penn Papers I, Official Correspondence II, p. 75, HSP.

146. Governor Gordon to John Penn, May 4, 1729, Penn Papers I, Official Correspondence II, p. 77, HSP.

147. Governor Gordon to John Penn, October 30, 1729, Penn Papers I, Official Correspondence II, p. 89, HSP (quotation); Governor Gordon to the Proprietors, November 15, 1729, Penn Papers I, Official Correspondence II, p. 93, HSP.

148. James Logan to John Penn, November 17, 1729, Penn Papers I, Official Correspondence II, p. 99, HSP.

149. [Franklin], *A Modest Enquiry*, 356.

150. [Franklin], *A Modest Enquiry*, 349–50.

151. Nash, *Urban Crucible*, 105–20.

152. "[The] value of Land," William Petty theorized, "depends upon the greater or lesser share of the product given for it in proportion to the simple labour bestowed to raise the said Product." William Petty, *A Treatise of Taxes and Contributions* (London, 1662), 70.

153. [Franklin], *A Modest Enquiry*, 346.

154. [Franklin], *A Modest Enquiry*, 347.

155. [Rawle], *Ways and Means*, 21–22.

156. On money as fictitious value, see Peter Linebaugh, *The London Hanged: Crime and Civil Society in the Eighteenth Century* (London: Verso Books, 2006), 51–52. On "coined" labor, see David Waldstreicher, "Capitalism, Slavery, and Benjamin Franklin's American Revolution," in Cathy Matson, ed., *The Economy of Early America: Historical Perspectives and New Directions* (University Park: Penn State University Press, 2011), 197–98; David Waldstreicher, *Runaway America: Benjamin Franklin, Slavery, and the American Revolution* (New York: Hill & Wang, 2004), 100–101.

157. James N. Green and Peter Stallybrass, *Benjamin Franklin: Writer and Printer* (New Castle, DE: Oak Knoll Press with the Library Company of Philadelphia and the British Library, 2006), 55.

158. Schweitzer, *Custom and Contract*, 17.

159. Schweitzer, *Custom and Contract*, 194–95.

160. Schweitzer, *Custom and Contract*, 195–96.

161. Woodbridge, *Severals Relating to the Fund*, in *CCR*, 1:112–13.

162. Thomas Budd, *Good Order Established in Pennsilvania & New-Jersey in America* (Philadelphia, 1685), 49–50.

163. [John Blackwell], *A Model for Erecting a Bank of Credit* [London, 1688], in *CCR*, 1:176.

164. [Rawle], *Ways and Means*, 36; [John Wise], *The Freeholder's Address to the Honourable House of Representatives* [Boston, 1721], 4–6.

165. [John Colman], *The Distressed State of the Town of Boston Considered* [Boston, 1720], 4–5, 8.

166. For writing about paper money's productive capacity, see Jennifer J. Baker, *Securing the Commonwealth: Debt, Speculation, and Writing in the Making of Early America* (Baltimore: Johns Hopkins University Press, 2005).

167. Newell, *From Dependency to Independence*, 156–80.

168. [Rawle], *Some Remedies Proposed*, 12.

169. "A Modest Apology for Paper Money, Published in the *Weekly Rehearsal*, March 18, 1734," in *CCR*, 3:93.

170. "A Modest Apology for Paper Money," 93–94.

171. Park, "Money, Mortgages, and the Conquest of America"; Bonnie Martin, "Slavery's Invisible Engine: Mortgaging Human Property," *Journal of Southern History* 76, no. 4 (November 2010): 817–66.

Chapter 5

1. *Pennsylvania Gazette*, June 19, 1730; "Cuming or Cumming, Sir Alexander," in *Dictionary of National Biography*, ed. Leslie Stephen (New York: Macmillan, 1888), 294–95.

2. Maurice A. Crouse, *The Public Treasury of Colonial South Carolina* (Columbia: University of South Carolina Press, 1977), 32–33.

3. *South-Carolina Gazette*, June 28, 1735.

4. "An Act for Putting in Force in this Province . . . Part of an Act of the Parliament of Great Britain . . ." [March 5, 1736/7], in *SLSC*, 3:468–71.

5. Daniel C. Littlefield, "The Slave Trade to Colonial South Carolina: A Profile," *South Carolina Historical Magazine* 101, no. 2 (April 2000): 121.

6. Calvin Schermerhorn, *The Business of Slavery and the Rise of American Capitalism* (New Haven: Yale University Press, 2015), 108.

7. Schermerhorn, *The Business of Slavery and the Rise of American Capitalism*, 1.

8. Gregory E. O'Malley, "Slavery's Converging Ground: Charleston's Slave Trade As the Black Heart of the Lowcountry," *WMQ* 74, no. 2 (2017): 275–77.

9. S. Max Edelman, *Plantation Enterprise in Colonial South Carolina* (Cambridge, MA: Harvard University Press, 2006), 52.

10. "An Act to prevent Deceits by Double Mortgages and Conveyences of Lands, Negroes and Chattels, &c." [October 1698], in John Fauchereaud Grimke, ed., *The Public Laws of the State of South-Carolina, from its First Establishment as a British Province down to the Year 1790* (Philadelphia, 1790), 3–4.

11. Thomas D. Morris, *Southern Slavery and the Law, 1619–1860* (Chapel Hill: University of North Carolina Press, 1996), 63–80; Russell R. Menard, "Financing the Lowcountry Export Boom: Capital and Growth in Early South Carolina," *WMQ* 51, no. 4 (October 1994): 669–70.

12. Cheryl I. Harris, "Reflections on Whiteness as Property," *Harvard Law Review Forum* 134, no. 1 (2020): 1–10; Jennifer L. Morgan, *Reckoning with Slavery: Gender, Kinship, and Capitalism in the Early Black Atlantic* (Durham, NC: Duke University Press, 2021), 8–15.

13. Menard, "Financing the Lowcountry Export Boom," 669–73.

14. Anne Crosbee mortgage to John Haile, July 1, 1705, "Grants Mortgages Bills of Sales and other Records from 1704 to 1708," Records of the Secretary of the Province and the Register of the Province of South Carolina, 1705–9, pp. 5–6, SCDAH.

15. Bonnie Martin, "Slavery's Invisible Engine: Mortgaging Human Property," *Journal of Southern History* 76, no. 4 (November 2010): 820.

16. John Olmixon, *The British Empire in America* (London, 1708), 2:65.

17. Council of Trade and Plantations to the Queen, October 17, 1706, in *CSP*, 23:262–76.

18. The Queen to the Governor of Barbados, November 8, 1706, in *CSP*, 23:286–307.

19. "Merchants trading to Barbados to the Council of Trade and Plantations," October 15, 1706, in *CSP*, 23:262–76.

20. Joseph Albert Ernst, *Money and Politics in America, 1755–1775: A Study in the Currency Act of 1764 and the Political Economy of Revolution* (Chapel Hill: University of North Carolina

Press, 1973), 24–25; Robert Chalmers, *A History of Currency in the British Colonies* (London: Her Majesty's Stationery Office, 1893), 51–52.

21. "An Act for raising the sume of fifty-two thousand pounds, by stamping and establishing new bills of credit, and putting the same out to interest, in order to call in and sink the former bills of credit, and thereby give a farther encouragement to trade and commerce" [1712], in *SLSC*, 9:759–65.

22. [William Bull], "An Account of the Rise and Progress of the Paper Bills of Credit in South Carolina, from the year 1700 to this present time . . ." [1739], in *SLCS*, 9:769–70; Crouse, *The Public Treasury of Colonial South Carolina*, 29.

23. "At a Conference held at the House of Mr Geo. Neilson in Annopolis July 29th 1732," in Bernard Christian Steiner, ed., *Proceedings and Acts of the General Assembly of Maryland* (Baltimore: Maryland Historical Society, 1917), 37:406–8 (quotation on 406).

24. "An Act directing the Commissioners of the Currency Office, speedily to call in the Interest due on Bonds and other Securities, and all Monies due on Funds payable into the said Office [March 26, 1755]," in Thomas Bacon, ed., *Laws of Maryland at Large* (Annapolis, 1765), 1755, chap. 1; Kathryn L. Behrens, *Paper Money in Maryland, 1727-1789* (Baltimore: Johns Hopkins University Press, 1923), 28.

25. *Maryland Gazette*, March 8, 1759, and September 9, 1762.

26. [Le Jau to the Secretary, August 30, 1712], in Frank J. Klingberg, ed., *The Carolina Chronicle of Dr. Francis Le Jau, 1706-1717* (Berkeley: University of California Press, 1956), 123.

27. [Anon.], *An Essay on Currency, Written in August 1732* (Charles Town, 1734), 8.

28. "The Report of the Committee of the Commons House of Assembly of the Province of South-Carolina, on the State of the Paper-Currency of the said Province" (London, 1737), TNA: CO 5/367, pp. 20–21. The report is printed in J. H. Easterby, ed., *The Journal of the Commons House of Assembly, November 10, 1736-June 7, 1739*(Columbia: Historical Commission of South Carolina, 1951), 291–320.

29. Richard M. Jellison, "Paper Currency in Colonial South Carolina: A Reappraisal," *South Carolina Historical Magazine* 62, no. 3 (July 1961): 136.

30. Crouse, *The Public Treasury of Colonial South Carolina*, 29. Farley Grubb confirms that making overlapping paper money emissions legally fungible would have stabilized the average exchange value of all emissions, so that one emission being heavily discounted could influence the value of other emissions. Farley Grubb, "Is Paper Money Just Paper Money? Experimentation and Variation in the Paper Monies Issued by the American Colonies from 1690 to 1775," NBER Working Paper 17997 (Cambridge, MA: National Bureau of Economic Research, April 2012).

31. Jellison, "Paper Currency in Colonial South Carolina," 138–40.

32. A. S. Salley, ed., *Journal of the Commons House of Assembly of South Carolina, November 15, 1726-March 11, 1726/7* (Columbia: Historical Commission of South Carolina, 1946), 32–33, 38.

33. "List of Abstract of Papers in the State Papers Office, London, relating to South-Carolina," *Collections of the South-Carolina Historical Society* 1 (1857): 291.

34. "List of Abstract of Papers in the State Papers Office, London, relating to South-Carolina," 292.

35. "List of Abstract of Papers in the State Papers Office, London, relating to South-Carolina," 293–95, 299–305.

36. "The Report of the Committee of the Commons House of Assembly of the Province of South-Carolina," 7–8.

NOTES TO PAGES 127–131

37. Mr. President [Arthur] Middleton [of South Carolina] to the Duke of Newcastle, May 17, 1728, TNA: CO 5/387.

38. "List of Abstract of Papers in the State Papers Office, London, relating to South-Carolina," 294, 299.

39. Richard M. Jellison, "Antecedents of the Currency Acts of 1736 and 1746," *WMQ* 16, no. 4 (October 1959): 557.

40. Menard, "Financing the Lowcountry Export Boom"; David Hancock, "'Capital and Credit with Approved Security': Financial Markets in Montserrat and South Carolina, 1748–1775," *Business and Economic History* 23, no. 2 (Winter 1994): 61–84.

41. "The Petition of several Merchants, and others of the City of London trading to your Majesty's Province of South Carolina," quoted in the "Remonstrance of the Governor of Council and Assembly of S. Carolina to the King," April 9, 1734, in *CSP*, 41:164–80. For the public orders act, see "An Act for Appropriating the Sum of One Hundred and Four Thousand Seven Hundred and Seventy-Five Pounds One Shilling and Three Pence Farthing, Towards the Payment of the Publick Debts" [August 20, 1731], in *SLSC*, 3:334–41.

42. "A General Representation of the Proceedings of the Governor Council & Assembly of South Carolina with respect to the disposition of the King's land etc.," July 12, 1734, TNA: CO 5/388 Part 2. For the re-emitting act, see "An Act for Calling in, Reprinting, and Exchanging the Paper Bills of Credit" [August 20, 1731], in *SLSC*, 3:305–7.

43. "The Petition of several Merchants, and others of the City of London trading to your Majesty's Province of South Carolina." For the duty act, see "An Act for Granting to His Majesty a Duty and Imposition on Negroes, Liquors, and Other Goods and Merchandizes, for the Use of the Publick of this Province" [February 23, 1722], in *SLSC*, 3:193–204.

44. "The Report of the Committee of the Commons House of Assembly of the Province of South-Carolina," 7–8.

45. Huw David, *Trade, Politics, and Revolution: South Carolina and Britain's Atlantic Commerce, 1730–1790* (Columbia: University of South Carolina Press, 2018), 17–22.

46. [Joshua Gee], *The Trade and Navigation of Great-Britain Considered* (London, 1729), 37–39, 23. See also William Wood, *A Survey of Trade* (London, 1718), 179, 190.

47. [Fayr Hall], *The Importance of the British Plantations in America to this Kingdom* (London, 1731), 67–68.

48. Quoted in M. Eugene Sirmans, *Colonial South Carolina: A Political History, 1663–1763* (Chapel Hill: University of North Carolina Press, 1966), 160–62 (quotation on 161).

49. "Address of the assembly of South Carolina," March 1, 1730, TNA: CO 5/383.

50. Governor Johnson to the Duke of Newcastle, November 15, 1731, TNA: CO 5/388 Part 1.

51. "Remonstrance of the Governor of Council and Assembly of S. Carolina to the King," April 9, 1734, in *CSP*, 41:164–80.

52. Menard, "Financing the Lowcountry Export Boom," 659–76.

53. William Wood to William Popple, July 4, 1735, in *CSP*, 42:1–18.

54. David Richardson, *The Bristol Traders: A Collective Portrait* (Bristol: Alan Sutton Publishing Ltd., 1985), 6–8, 11, 16; Kenneth Morgan, "Bristol and the Atlantic Trade in the Eighteenth Century," *English Historical Review* 107, no. 424 (July 1992): 637–40.

55. Merchants of Bristol to Mr. Wood, June 28, 1735, in *CSP*, 42:1–18.

56. William Wood to William Popple, September 10, 1734, in *CSP*, 41:196–99.

57. William Wood to William Popple, July 4, 1735, in *CSP*, 42:1–18.

58. Anthony S. Parent Jr., *Foul Means: The Formation of a Slave Society in Virginia, 1660–1740* (Chapel Hill: University of North Carolina Press, 2003), 179–80; David, *Trade, Politics, and Revolution*, 16.

59. "Council of Trade and Plantations to the Committee of Privy Council" and "Draft of H.M. Additional Instructions to Mr. Broughton," July 11, 1735, in *CSP*, 42:1–18 (quotation); "Order of Queen, Guardian of the Kingdom, etc., in Council. Approving representation of Council of Trade, and ordering that the Act of S. Carolina for appropriating £104,775 1s. 3¼d. to lie by probationary" and "Order of Queen in Council. Approving draught of an additional Instruction for the Governor of S. Carolina relating to paper money and appropriateing thereof," October 13, 1735, in *CSP*, 42:76–84.

60. "An Act to Provide a Full Supply for Subsisting Poor Protestants Coming from Europe . . ." [June 7, 1735], in *SLSC*, 3:409–11 (quotation on 409). See also [Bull], "An Account of the Rise and Progress of the Paper Bills of Credit in South Carolina," 777–78.

61. "Extract from a letter from Carolina" [July 3, 1735], in *CSP*, 42:1–18; Mr. Wood to Mr. Popple, September 3, 1735, in *CSP*, 42:49–59.

62. Menard, "Financing the Lowcountry Export Boom," 659–62.

63. For the origins of the other ships, see Littlefield, "The Slave Trade to Colonial South Carolina," 124–25.

64. David, *Trade, Politics, and Revolution*, 16–17.

65. Minutes of Council in Assembly and House of Burgesses, 1734–40, 3 March 1737, folder 8, Daniel Parish Slavery Transcripts, quoted in Gerald Horne, *The Counter-Revolution of 1776: Slave Resistance and the Origins of the United States of America* (New York: New York University Press, 2014), 94. The minutes are printed in the *South-Carolina Gazette*, November 5, 1737.

66. Jane Landers, "Spanish Sanctuary: Fugitives in Florida, 1687–1790," *Florida Historical Quarterly* 62, no. 3 (January 1984): 299; Horne, *The Counter-Revolution of 1776*, 88–90.

67. Thomas Amory to John Witton, [Boston], June 13, 1720, Thomas Amory Letterbooks, Amory Family Papers, 1697–1882, box 4, LOC.

68. "An Act for Enlisting such trusty slaves as shall be thought serviceable to this settlement in time of alarms, and for encouragement of sailors to serve the same against our enemies, and for impowering the commissioners for stamping rice orders, to pay away the same, and declaring how the forfeitures shall be recovered of persons offending against the additional act to the act commonly called the Tax Act, passed February 13th, 1719–20," in *SLSC*, 3:108–11 (quotations on 108 and 109).

69. "An Act for the Better Securing this Province from Negro Insurrections, and for Encouraging of Poor People by Employing them in Plantations" [March 11, 1726], in *SLSC*, 3:272.

70. "An Act for Regulating Patrols in this Province" [April 9, 1734], in *SLSC*, 3:395–99.

71. [Anon.], *A Scheme (by Striking Twenty Thousand Pounds, Paper Money) to Encourage the Raising of Hemp, and the Manufacturing of Iron in the Province of New-York* (New York, 1737), 1–3; Wood, *A Survey of Trade*, 166, 170.

72. *South-Carolina Gazette*, February 22, 1734.

73. "Remonstrance of the Governor of Council and Assembly of S. Carolina to the King," April 9, 1734, in *CSP*, 41:164–80; Horne, *The Counter-Revolution of 1776*, 109.

74. "The Report of the Committee of the Commons House of Assembly of the Province of South-Carolina," 25–26.

75. Eric P. Newman, *The Early Paper Money of America: An Illustrated, Historical, and Descriptive Collection of Data Relating to American Paper Currency from Its Inception in 1686 to the Year 1800* (Iola, WI: Krause Publications, 2008), 408.

76. [Anon.], *An Essay on Currency*, 21.

77. [Anon.], *An Essay on Currency*, 24.

78. [Anon.], *An Essay on Currency*, 4–5.

79. [Le Jau to John Chamberlain, April 20, 1714], in Frank J. Klingberg, ed., *The Carolina Chronicle of Dr. Francis Le Jau, 1706–1717* (Berkeley: University of California Press, 1956), 138–39.

80. Dethloff, "Colonial Rice Trade," 237.

81. Jellison, "Paper Currency in Colonial South Carolina," 138; Coclanis, "Rice Prices in the 1720s," 537; Dethloff, "Colonial Rice Trade," 234.

82. [Anon.], *An Essay on Currency*, 12, 17.

83. Jellison, "Antecedents of the Currency Acts of 1736 and 1746," 559.

84. Benjamin Franklin, "Remarks on a South Carolina Currency Scheme," printed in the *Pennsylvania Gazette* [May 31, 1733], in *Franklin Papers*, 1:322.

85. [Anon.], *An Essay on Currency*, 6.

86. [Anon.], *An Essay on Currency*, 4.

87. *South-Carolina Gazette*, February 3, 1733.

88. *South-Carolina Gazette*, March 26, 1736. The proposal called for issuing £300,000 in new bills of credit at the existing exchange rate of seven to one, £200,000 of which would be lent at 8 percent interest, with the interest payable in bills.

89. *South-Carolina Gazette*, April 3, 1736.

90. *South-Carolina Gazette*, April 3, 1736.

91. Karl Marx, *Capital: A Critique of Political Economy, Volume Two*, trans. David Ferbach (London: Penguin Books, 1992), 156.

92. Jellison, "Antecedents of the Currency Acts of 1736 and 1746," 561–62; Crouse, *The Public Treasury of Colonial South Carolina*, 30–31; "An Act for Stamping, Emitting and Making Current the Sum of Two Hundred and Ten Thousand Pounds in Paper Bills of Credit . . ." [May 29, 1736], in *SLSC* 3:423–30 (quotations on 426 and 427).

93. "An Act for regulating the Markets in the Parish of St. Philip's Charlestown, and for preventing forestalling, engrossing and regrating, and unjust exactions, in the said Town and Market" [May 29, 1736], in *SLSC*, 3:430; "An Act for the better relief and employment of the Poor of the Parish of St. Philip's Charlestown, and for the suppressing and punishing Rogues, Vagabonds, and other lewd, idle and disorderly persons" [May 29, 1736], in *SLSC*, 3:430; "An Act for appointing Commissioners to lay out a Road from the road that leads from Willtown to Charlestown, to the road that leads from Smith's Ferry, otherwise called Parker's Ferry, to Charlestown, and to keep the same in repair" [May 29, 1736], in *SLSC*, 3:436; "An Act for repairing the old and building of new Fortifications, for the security and defence of this Province from attacks by Sea, and for appointing Commissioners for carrying on such works: and for continuing New Church Street and Little Street to Ashley River" [May 29, 1736], in *SLSC*, 3:436; "An Act for Encouraging the Raising of Hemp, Flax and Silk, within the Province of South Carolina" [May 29, 1736], in *SLSC*, 3:436–37; "An Ordinance for asserting and maintaining the rights and liberties of His Majesty's subjects of the Province of South Carolina to a free, open and uninterrupted trade with the Creek, Cherokee and other Indians in amity and friendship with His Majesty's subjects, and for the better preserving those Indians in the interest of Great Britain" [June 26, 1736], in *SLSC*, 3:448–49.

94. Joseph Wragg to Isaac Hobhouse, June 9, 1736, in George C. Rogers Jr., ed., "Two Joseph Wragg Letters," *South Carolina Historical Magazine* 65, no. 1 (January 1964): 16–17. On Joseph Wragg's and Isaac Hobhouse's joint slave-trading ventures, see David Richardson, ed., *Bristol,*

Africa, and the Eighteenth-Century Slave Trade to Africa, Vol. 2: *The Years of Ascendancy, 1730–1745* (Gloucester: Alan Sutton Publishing Ltd. for the Bristol Record Society, 1987), 52–53, 57.

95. "An Act for Remission of Arrears of Quit Rents, and . . . for confirming and establishing the Titles and possessions of the several inhabitants of this Province to their respective lands, tenements, and hereditaments within the same; and for keeping the office of Publick Register of this Province from being united to other office or offices . . ." [September 8, 1731], in *SLSC*, 3:289.

96. S. Max Edelson, *Plantation Enterprise in Colonial South Carolina* (Cambridge, MA: Harvard University Press, 2006), 93.

97. Edelson, *Plantation Enterprise in Colonial South Carolina*, 92.

98. Menard, "Financing the Lowcountry Export Boom," 673.

99. "The Report of the Committee of the Commons House of Assembly of the Province of South-Carolina," 19.

100. "The Report of the Committee of the Commons House of Assembly of the Province of South-Carolina," 30.

101. Quoted in Horne, *The Counter-Revolution of 1776*, 112.

102. Martin, "Slavery's Invisible Engine," 820.

103. Stephanie E. Smallwood, "The Politics of the Archive and History's Accountability to the Enslaved," *History of the Present: A Journal of Critical History* 6, no. 2 (2016): 125.

104. Charles Hart mortgage to Thomas Ellery, August 17, 1736, Records of the Secretary of State, South Carolina Mortgages, vol. A.B. [1734–36], pp. 573–75, SCADH.

105. Hugh Tomson mortgage to William Field, August 31, 1737, Records of the Secretary of State, South Carolina Mortgages, vol. K.K. [1736–37], pp. 411–12, SCDAH.

106. Paul Marion mortgage to Isaac Holmes, September 27, 1737, Records of the Secretary of State, South Carolina Mortgages, vol. K.K. [1736–37], pp. 532–34, SCDAH.

107. Benjamin Pinder mortgage to Joseph Wragg and Richard Lambton, March 9, 1738, Records of the Secretary of State, South Carolina Mortgages, vol. N.N. [1738–39], pp. 186–87, SCDAH.

108. George Coker mortgage to Joseph Wragg and Richard Lambton, December 14, 1739, Records of the Secretary of State, South Carolina Mortgages, vol. O.O. [1739–40], pp. 266–68, SCDAH.

109. Thomas Hogg mortgage to Joseph Wragg and Richard Lambton, December 14, 1739, Records of the Secretary of State, South Carolina Mortgages, vol. O.O. [1739–40], pp. 268–70, SCDAH.

110. Mary Stanyarne mortgage to Joseph Wragg and Richard Lambton, April 1, 1736, Records of the Secretary of State, South Carolina Mortgages, vol. A.B. [1734–36], pp. 356–57, SCDAH.

111. Joan Upham mortgage to Joseph Wragg and Richard Lambton, April 7, 1737, Records of the Secretary of State, South Carolina Mortgages, vol. K.K. [1736–37], pp. 134–35, SCDAH.

112. Mary Satur mortgage to Joseph Wragg and Richard Lambton, November 2, 1739, Records of the Secretary of State, South Carolina Mortgages, vol. O.O. [1739–40], pp. 221–23, SCDAH.

113. Elizabeth M. Pruden, "Investing Widows: Autonomy in a Nascent Capitalist Society," in Jack P. Greene, Rosemary Brana-Shute, and Randy J. Sparks, eds., *Money, Trade, and Power: The Evolution of Colonial South Carolina's Plantation Society* (Columbia: University of South Carolina Press, 2001), 344–62; Martin, "Slavery's Invisible Engine," 859.

114. "Observations on an Act passed in Carolina for stamping, emitting and making current the sum of 210,000*l.* in paper bills of credit, etc.," January [19], 1738, in *CSP* 44:5–33.

115. William Wood to [Thomas Hill], February 7, 1738, in *CSP*, 44:33–43. The sterling exchange rate reached 850 percent in November 1737. John J. McCusker, *Money & Exchange in*

Europe & America, 1600–1775: A Handbook (Chapel Hill: University of North Carolina Press, 1978), 223.

116. "Council of Trade and Plantations to the King," July 6, 1738, in *CSP*, 44:156–62; "Order of King in Court directing that Act passed in South Carolina in 1736 for emitting 210000*l* in paper bills of credit is to lie by for the present," March 22, 1739, in *CSP*, 45:50–72.

117. William Wood to Thomas Hill, July 11, 1738, in *CSP*, 44:156–62.

118. "The Report of the Committee of the Commons House of Assembly of the Province of South-Carolina," 25.

119. Smith, "Some Colonial Evidence on Two Theories of Money," 1190–91.

120. "The Report of the Committee of the Commons House of Assembly of the Province of South-Carolina," 26–27.

121. "The Report of the Committee of the Commons House of Assembly of the Province of South-Carolina," 27, 29.

122. [Hall], *The Importance of the British Plantations in America to this Kingdom*, 66.

123. Charles Whitworth, *State of the Trade of Great Britain in Its Imports and Exports Progressively from the Year 1697* (London, 1776), 37–44.

124. Peter C. Mancall, Joshua L. Rosenbloom, and Thomas Weiss, "Slave Prices and the South Carolina Economy, 1722–1808," *JEH* 61, no. 3 (September 2001): 625.

125. Littlefield, "The Slave Trade to Colonial South Carolina," 125.

126. Horne, *The Counter-Revolution of 1776*, 91–92.

127. O'Malley, "Slavery's Converging Ground," 279–80.

128. "Two Joseph Wragg Letters," 17.

129. *South-Carolina Gazette*, March 2–9, 1738, [I], quoted in O'Malley, "Slavery's Converging Ground," 285.

130. As the assembly explained, "this seeming Paradox may be easily solved by considering that each Year's Produce or Export as well as Import exceeds that of the preceeding Year, reckoning in the general, and that a considerable, nay the most considerable Part of the Imports, *vizt.* Negroes, is not consumed, but converted into Stock, remains with us, and is used in the succeeding Year to pay off, by their Labour, the Debt of the preceeding Year. For as this Province the most general Way of Trading, by the fixed Traders, is by giving a Year's Credit, and so from Crop to Crop, the Province has two Crops, or the Exports of two Years to pay for the Imports of one; and altho' at the winding up of the Account, the then present Year's Imports must be paid for, as well as those of the preceeding Year, and altho' there will be then but one Crop to do it with; yet 'tis apprehended the Country will not be Bankrupt as long as they have a sufficient Stock, *to wit*, in Negroes, and other unconsumeable Commodities remaining to answer the then Balance." "The Report of the Committee of the Commons House of Assembly of the Province of South-Carolina," 15–16.

131. Richard Waterhouse, "Economic Growth and Changing Patterns of Wealth Distribution in Colonial Lowcountry South Carolina," *South Carolina Historical Magazine* 89, no. 4 (October 1988): 209–10; Menard, "Financing the Lowcountry Export Boom," 659–60. The three largest planters in St. James Parish in 1745 were Henry Izard, James Kinlock, and Sara Middleton, each of whom on average owned 220 slaves, 11,000 acres of land, and £3,500 sterling in money at interest.

132. Michael D. Byrd, "The First Charles Town Workhouse, 1738–1775: A Deterrent to White Pauperism?" *South Carolina Historical Magazine* 110, nos. 1–2 (January–April 2009): 35–52; Tim Lockley, "Rural Poor Relief in Colonial South Carolina," *Historical Journal* 48, no. 4 (December 2005): 955–76.

133. W. Robert Higgins, "Charles Town Merchants and Factors Dealing in the External Negro Trade 1735–1775," *South Carolina Historical Magazine* 65, no. 4 (October 1964): 206–9.

134. On "managerial violence," see Tristan Stubbs, *Masters of Violence: The Plantation Overseers of Eighteenth-Century Virginia, South Carolina, and Georgia* (Columbia: University of South Carolina Press, 2018).

135. Edelson, *Plantation Enterprise in Colonial South*, 87; Berlin, *Many Thousands Gone*, 146–47, 149.

136. Billy G. Smith writes of this transformation that "material standards may have followed a cyclical pattern in the low country of South Carolina and Georgia. As the former colony changed from a frontier area to one of vast plantations during the early eighteenth century, blacks lost important individual freedoms, including many of the controls they had exercised over their personal well-being." Billy G. Smith, "Poverty and Economic Marginality in Eighteenth-Century America," *Proceedings of the American Philosophical Society* 132, no. 1 (March 1988): 144.

137. "An Act for Establishing and Regulating of Patrols" [February 12, 1737], in *SLSC*, 3:456–61.

138. Philip D. Morgan, *Slave Counterpoint: Black Culture in the Eighteenth-Century Chesapeake and Lowcountry* (Chapel Hill: University of North Carolina Press, 1998), 308 (quotation), 389.

139. "An Act to empower the Honourable Thomas Broughton . . . to lay an Embargo on and to prohibit and stop from sailing, any Ships or Vessels now in any Port or place . . . and to impress at any time during the said time, any Ships, Vessels, Men, Mariners and Labourers, Horses, Arms and Ammunition, and to prohibit the exportation of Povisions therein mentioned" [February 5, 1736/7], in *SLSC*, 3:455–56; "An Act for regulating the Guard at Johnson's Fort, and for keeping good orders in the several Forts and Garrisons under the pay and establishment of this Government, and for encouraging the several officers and soldiers therein" [March 5, 1736/7], in *SLSC*, 3:465–67.

140. "An Act to enable the Commissioners herein named to stamp and sign certain Orders, to the amount of thirty-five thousand and ten pounds current money of this Province, for the putting this Province in a posture of defence, the better to enable them to support and defend the Colony of Georgia against any attacks from his Majesty's Enemies, and for the speedy finishing the curtain line before Charlestown" [March 5, 1736/7], in *SLSC*, 3:461–64.

141. In a letter to the colony's agent, Peregrine Fury, dated January 25, 1737, the assembly instructed Fury that "it will be absolutely necessary for you to represent to them at the same time the weak and defenceless condition of the province and how incapable we are of helping ourselves. Our taxes are already become almost insupportable and it will be with the greatest difficulty that we shall be able to raise new supplies since our present currency will decrease so fast and we have no hopes of more but from H.M.'s goodness in assenting to the Act passed by the late assembly." "Extract of letter from Committee of Assembly in South Carolina to Mr. Fury, agent to the province," January 25, 1737, in *CSP,* 43:1–21.

142. "An Act for granting to His Majesty the Sum of thirty-five thousand eight hundred and thirty-three pounds six shillings and eleven pence three farthings, for defraying the charges of the Government for one year . . ." [December 18, 1739], in *SLSC*, 3:527–41 (payment to Joseph Wragg is on p. 539).

143. Richard Hockley to Thomas Penn, November 29, 1739, Penn Family Papers I. Official Correspondence III, 1736–43 (hereafter Penn Papers I, Official Correspondence III), HSP.

144. Richard Hockley to Thomas Penn, February 7, 1739/40, Penn Papers I, Official Correspondence III, HSP.

145. Richard Hockley to Thomas Penn, December 12, 1739, Penn Papers I, Official Correspondence III, HSP.

146. Richard Hockley to Thomas Penn, February 1, 1739/40, Penn Papers I, Official Correspondence III, HSP.

147. Jason R. Young, *Rituals of Resistance: African Atlantic Religion in Kongo and the Lowcountry South in the Era of Slavery* (Baton Rouge: Louisiana State University Press, 2007), 68–70; John K. Thornton, "African Dimensions of the Stono Rebellion," *American Historical Review* 96, no. 4 (October 1991): 1101–13; Berlin, *Many Thousands Gone*, 72–74.

148. *Boston News-Letter*, March 11, 1736.

149. Edelson, *Plantation Enterprise*, 86–87.

150. J. H. Easterby, ed., *Journal of the Commons House of Assembly, September 12, 1739–March 26, 1741* (Columbia: Historical Commission of South Carolina, 1952), 20.

151. James Oglethorpe to the Duke of Newcastle, April 1, 1740, TNA: CO 5/654 Part 2.

152. William Bull to the Duke of Newcastle, February 11, 1739/40, TNA: CO 5/388 Part 1.

153. "An Act to enable certain Commissioners therein named, to borrow and take upon loan a sum not exceeding Two Thousand Pounds Sterling, and to enable certain other Commissioners therein named, to stamp and sign certain Orders, to the amount of Twenty-Five Thousand Pounds, current Money of this Province, for defraying the expence of certain succours and forces to assist General Oglethorpe in an Expedition against His Majesty's Enemys at Augustine and other places in Florida, and for the better preventing of Mutiny and Desertion" [April 5, 1740], in *SLSC*, 3:546–53; "An Act to enable the Publick Treasurer of this Province to Issue the sum of fifteen thousand pounds currency, out of any funds now lying in the hands of the said Treasurer, in lieu of a loan of two thousand pounds sterling . . . and also to enable certain Commissioners therein mentioned to stamp and sign a further sum in orders, to the amount of eleven thousand five hundred and eight pounds current money, for supplying the additional expences of the said Expedition, and which by the said Act are not provided for" [September 19, 1740], in *SLSC*, 3:577–79; Richard Hockley to Thomas Penn, February 7 and 18, 1739/40, Penn Papers I, Official Correspondence III, p. 101, HSP.

154. James Oglethorpe to the Duke of Newcastle, April 1, 1740, TNA: CO 5/654 Part 2; "Extract of a letter from Carolina to Mr. Wragg," May 2, 1740, TNA: CO 5/654 Part 2; "Preparations for attacking St. Augustine," April 30, 1740, TNA: CO 5/654 Part 2.

155. J. H. Easterby, ed., *Journal of the Commons House of Assembly, September 12, 1739–March 26, 1741* (Columbia: Historical Commission of South Carolina, 1952), 63–65.

156. Easterby, ed., *Journal of the Commons House of Assembly, September 12, 1739–March 26, 1741*, 377–78.

157. "An Act for the better Ordering and Governing Negroes and other Slaves in this Province" [May 10, 1740], in *SLSC*, 7:397–417.

158. "An Act for the better strengthening of this Province, by granting to His Majesty certain taxes and impositions on the purchasers of Negroes imported . . ." [May 10, 1740], in *SLSC*, 3:556–68.

159. Alan Gallay, *The Formation of a Planter Elite: Jonathan Bryan and the Southern Colonial Frontier*, 2nd ed. (Athens: University of Georgia Press, 2007), 55–59.

160. Huw David, "James Crockatt's 'Exceeding Good Counting House': Ascendancy and Influence in the Transatlantic Carolina Trade," *South Carolina Historical Magazine* 111, nos. 3–4 (July–October 2010): 151–74; "Representation to His Majesty upon an Act pass'd in So Carolina in 1746 for emitting £210,000 in Bills of Credit &c.," June 6, 1753, TNA: CO 5/402 (quotation).

161. Mancall, Rosenbloom, and Weiss, "Slave Prices and the South Carolina Economy," 630–31.

162. "Representation to His Majesty upon an Act pass'd in So Carolina in 1746 for emitting £210,000 in Bills of Credit &c.," June 6, 1753, TNA: CO 5/402.

163. Jellison, "Antecedents of the South Carolina Currency Act of 1736 and 1746," 566.

164. Newman, *Early Paper Money*, 410–14.

165. Hancock, "Capital and Credit with Approved Security," 61–84.

166. On colonial merchants as "financial intermediaries" in the New England context, see Jeremy T. Schwartz, David T. Flynn & Gökhan Jarahan, "Merchant Account Books, Credit Sales, and Financial Development," *Accounting and Finance Research* 7, no. 3 (June 2018): 154–71.

Chapter 6

1. *Pennsylvania Gazette*, December 4, 1735; *South-Carolina Gazette*, July 10, 1736; *Boston News-Letter*, November 25, 1736; *Pennsylvania Gazette*, October 20, 1737.

2. Gary B. Nash, "Poverty and Politics in Early American History," in Billy G. Smith, ed., *Down and Out in Early America* (State College: Penn State University Press, 2010), 6–9.

3. Billy G. Smith, "Poverty and Economic Marginality in Eighteenth-Century America," *Proceedings of the American Philosophical Society* 132, no. 1 (March 1988): 93 (quotation), 116.

4. Nash, "Poverty and Politics in Early American History," 12.

5. Philip D. Morgan, "Slaves and Poverty," in *Down and Out in Early America*, 93–103, 115.

6. Ira Berlin, *Many Thousands Gone: The First Two Centuries of Slavery in America* (Cambridge, MA: Harvard University Press, 2000), 5.

7. Edgar J. McManus, *Black Bondage in the North* (Syracuse, NY: Syracuse University Press, 1973), 42.

8. Jared Ross Hardesty, *Unfreedom: Slavery and Dependence in Eighteenth-Century Boston* (New York: New York University Press, 2016), 22; Christy Clark-Pujara, *Dark Work: The Business of Slavery in Rhode Island* (New York: New York University Press, 2016), 24; Leslie M. Harris, *In the Shadow of Slavery: African Americans in New York City, 1626–1863* (Chicago: University of Chicago Press, 2003), 29; Gary B. Nash, *Forging Freedom: The Formation of Philadelphia's Black Community, 1720–1840* (Cambridge, MA: Harvard University Press, 1988), 33.

9. Ann Greene's account, 1728, First Series, vol. 26, 414, Suffolk County Probate Court, Massachusetts State Archives, quoted in Whiting, "Race, Slavery, and the Problem of Numbers in Early New England," 434.

10. Clark-Pujara, *Dark Work*, 49, 114–15.

11. Gloria McMahon Whiting, "Race, Slavery, and the Problem of Numbers in Early New England: A View from the Probate Court," *WMQ* 77, no. 3 (July 2020): 433–34.

12. Clark-Pujara, *Dark Work*, 41.

13. Peter Green, John Green, and William Green v. Elisha Green, Newport, Rhode Island, July 28, 1725, in Jane Fletcher Fiske, *Gleanings from Newport Court Files, 1659–1783* (Boxford, MA: J. F. Fiske, 1998), quoted in Clark-Pujara, *Dark Work*, 41.

14. For an overview of slave hiring in the North, see McManus, *Black Bondage in the North*, 46–50.

15. Berlin, *Many Thousands Gone*, 5.

16. Venture Smith, *A Narrative of the Life and Adventures of Venture, a Native of Africa: But Resident above Sixty Years in the United States of America. Related by Himself* (New London, CT, 1798), 18.

17. *Pennsylvania Gazette*, March 5, 1751, quoted in Nash, *Forging Freedom*, 35–36.

18. W. Jeffrey Bolster, *Black Jacks: African American Seamen in the Age of Sail* (Cambridge, MA: Harvard University Press, 1997), 7–9, 26.

19. MAC, vol. 91 [Muster rolls, 1710–40], pp. 267, 274, 276, 285, 299. In another example, an enslaved man, Pompey, appears on the muster roll for Fort George in Maine for the years 1735 to at least 1740 at pay. MAC, vol. 91 [Muster rolls, 1710–40], pp. 278, 281, 291, 295.

20. "Order Impowering John Larrabee to Enlist his Servant in the Service" [April 16, 1733], in *MASS*, 11:792–93; "Order Allowing Lieut. John Larrabee Pay for a Servant" [November 26, 1740], in *MASS*, 12:712.

21. For example, the treasurer paid Captain Thomas Saunders eighteen pounds partly on "his Account of . . . his [slave's] service, dureing his own Lameness" in 1734. "Account of Jeremiah Allen, Treasurer and Receiver General, showing receipts and disbursements between May 29, 1734, and May 28, 1735," MAC, vol. 124 [Treasury, 1735–57], p. 16.

22. Zabin, *Dangerous Economies*, 59.

23. Zabin, *Dangerous Economies*, 69.

24. *Boston Gazette*, July 27, 1724; *American Weekly Mercury*, July 20, 1727; *Boston Gazette*, March 11, 1728; *Boston News-Letter*, April 16, 1730; *Pennsylvania Gazette*, December 26, 1734 and March 11, 1736; *New-York Gazette*, November 15, 1736; *Pennsylvania Gazette*, September 3, 1741, April 29, 1742, and December 25, 1750; *Maryland Gazette*, May 24, 1759.

25. *Pennsylvania Gazette*, March 10, 1743, and December 25, 1750.

26. Clark-Pujara, *Dark Work*, 39–40.

27. Hardesty, *Unfreedom*, 55–60.

28. Zabin, *Dangerous Economies*, 172n1.

29. New York Supreme Court, H.R. pleadings, Pl.K. 662, quoted in Zabin, *Dangerous Economies*, 57.

30. Manuscript minute book, New York Court of General Sessions, February 6, 1704, quoted in Zabin, *Dangerous Economies*, 64.

31. Berlin, *Many Thousands Gone*, 59–60; Hardesty, *Unfreedom*, 93–94; Harris, *In the Shadow of Slavery*, 43; Daniel Johnson, "'What Must Poor People Do?' Economic Protest and Plebeian Culture in Philadelphia, 1682–1754," *Pennsylvania History: A Journal of Mid-Atlantic Studies* 79, no. 2 (Spring 2012): 133.

32. "An Act for the more Effectual Preventing and Punishing the Conspiracy and Insurrection of Negro and other Slaves" [October 29, 1730], in *CLNY* 2:679.

33. *New-York Weekly Journal*, June 29, 1741.

34. *Acts and Laws of His Majesty's Colony of Rhode Island and Providence Plantations in New England from 1745-1752* (Newport, RI, 1752), 92–93, quoted in Clark-Pujara, *Dark Work*, 38.

35. *A Report of the Record Commissioners of the City of Boston, Containing the Boston Records from 1700 to 1728*, ed. William H. Whitmore and W. S. Appleton (Boston, MA: Rockwell & Churchill, 1883), 224.

36. *Boston News-Letter*, April 14, 1738, quoted in Hardesty, *Unfreedom*, 94–95.

37. *Boston Evening-Post*, January 14, 1740.

38. *A Report of the Record Commissioners of the City of Boston, Containing the Boston Records from 1700 to 1728*, 225.

39. Harris, *In the Shadow of Slavery*, 42.

40. "An Act for the better Preservation of oysters" (October 17, 1730), in *CLNY*, 2:655–56.

41. *Pennsylvania Gazette*, October 26, 1738.

42. Smith, *A Narrative of the Life and Adventures of Venture*, 17.

43. Warrant and Recognizance for Silas Elisha, May 3, 1727, Miscellaneous Manuscripts, MHS.

44. July 11, 1727, Bristol County Court of Common Pleas, General Sessions, 1714–38, p. 79, Bristol County Courthouse, Taunton, MA, microfilm. Accessed through FamilySearch.org.

45. *The Life, and Dying Speech of Arthur, A Negro Man; Who Was Executed at Worcester, October 20, 1768. For a Rape Committeed on the Body of One Deborah Metcalfe* (Boston, 1768); Jeannine Marie DeLombard, *In the Shadow of the Gallows: Race, Crime, and American Civic Identity* (Philadelphia: University of Pennsylvania Press, 2012), 97–101.

46. Ellen Hartigan-O'Connor, *The Ties That Buy: Women and Commerce in Revolutionary America* (Philadelphia: University of Pennsylvania Press, 2009), 110–11.

47. *American Weekly Mercury*, July 15, 1731.

48. David W. Galenson, "Demographic Aspects of White Servitude in Colonial British America," *Annales de démographie historique* (1980): 241–44.

49. *Pennsylvania Gazette*, March 8, 1732/33; *New-York Weekly Journal*, January 30, 1737; *Pennsylvania Gazette*, September 13, 1739, August 7, 1740, March 31, 1743, October 17, 1751, and July 25, 1754.

50. *Pennsylvania Gazette*, April 2, 1741.

51. On the "slaves' economy," see Ira Berlin and Philip D. Morgan, eds., *The Slaves' Economy: Independent Production by Slaves in the Americas* (New York: Routledge, 1991).

52. Douglas R. Egerton, "Slaves to the Marketplace: Economic Liberty and Black Rebelliousness in the Atlantic World," *Journal of the Early Republic* 26, no. 4 (Winter 2006): 621.

53. *South-Carolina Gazette*, March 30, 1734.

54. "Journal of the Commons House of Assembly, 31 Jul, 1746–23 Jul 1747," TNA: CO 5/452, p. 73.

55. Philip D. Morgan, *Slave Counterpoint: Black Culture in the Eighteenth-Century Chesapeake and Lowcountry* (Chapel Hill: University of North Carolina Press, 1998), 250.

56. Berlin, *Many Thousands Gone*, 157–58.

57. Berlin, *Many Thousands Gone*, 154–56.

58. Morgan, *Slave Counterpoint*, 364–65.

59. Emma Hart, *Trading Spaces: The Colonial Marketplace and the Foundations of American Capitalism* (Chicago: University of Chicago Press, 2019), 73.

60. *South-Carolina Gazette*, March 10, 1732. For additional examples, see *South-Carolina Gazette*, January 20, 1732, July 1, 1732, and October 19, 1734.

61. *South-Carolina Gazette*, November 5, 1737.

62. *South Carolina Gazette*, November 5, 1744.

63. "Journal of the Commons House of Assembly, 31 Jul, 1746–23 Jul 1747," 73.

64. Hartigan-O'Connor, *The Ties That Buy*, 53–55.

65. Roderick A. McDonald, *The Economy and Material Culture of Slaves: Goods and Chattels on the Sugar Plantations of Jamaica and Louisiana* (Baton Rouge: Louisiana State University Press, 1993), 43.

66. Alex Lichtenstein, "'That Disposition to Theft, with Which They Have Been Branded': Moral Economy, Slave Management, and the Law," *Journal of Social History* 21, no. 3 (1988): 415–16.

67. *South-Carolina Gazette*, January 20, 1732.

68. *South-Carolina Gazette*, May 6, 1732.

69. *South-Carolina Gazette*, April 8, 1732.

70. *South-Carolina Gazette*, October 7, 1732, and December 30, 1732.

71. Douglas R. Egerton, "Slaves to the Marketplace: Economic Liberty and Black Rebelliousness in the Atlantic World," *Journal of the Early Republic* 26 (Winter 2006): 632.

72. *South-Carolina Gazette*, May 25, 1734, and April 27, 1748.

73. *South-Carolina Gazette*, March 29, 1735.

74. *South-Carolina Gazette*, November 5, 1737, and November 5, 1744.

75. Betty Wood, "'White Society' and the 'Informal' Slave Economies of Lowcountry Georgia, c. 1763–1830," *Slavery and Abolition* 11, no. 3 (1990): 321.

76. *South-Carolina Gazette*, March 30, 1734.

77. *South-Carolina Gazette*, November 5, 1744.

78. McDonald, *The Economy and Material Culture of Slaves*, 34.

79. Berlin, *Many Thousands Gone*, 165–66.

80. "An Act for Licensing Hawkers, Pedlars, and Petty-Chapmen, and to prevent their trading with indented Servants, Overseers, Negroes, and other slaves" [March 11, 1737/8], in *SLSC*, 3:487–90; Morgan, *Slave Counterpoint*, 367–68.

81. M. W. Jernegan, "Slavery and the Beginnings of Industrialism in the American Colonies," *American Historical Review* 25, no. 2 (January 1920): 235–40; Morgan, *Slave Counterpoint*, 226 (quotation).

82. Edelson, *Plantation Enterprise*, 228.

83. Philip D. Morgan, "Work and Culture: The Task System and the World of Lowcountry Blacks, 1700 to 1880," *WMQ* 39, no. 4 (October 1982): 563–99.

84. "An Act for the better Ordering and Governing Negroes and other Slaves in this Province" [May 10, 1740], in *SLSC*, 7:397–417 (quotation on 409).

85. Gregory E. O'Malley, "Slavery's Converging Ground: Charleston's Slave Trade As the Black Heart of the Lowcountry," *WMQ* 74, no. 2 (2017): 294.

86. Marisa Joanna Fuentes, "Buried Landscapes: Enslaved Black Women, Sex, Confinement, and Death in Colonial Bridgetown, Barbados and Charleston, South Carolina," PhD diss., University of California, Berkeley, 2007, 143–44.

87. Justene Hill Edwards, *Unfree Markets: The Slaves' Economy and the Rise of Capitalism in South Carolina* (New York: Columbia University Press, 2021), 21, 27.

88. Edelson, *Plantation Enterprise*, 231.

89. Edward Ball, *Slaves in the Family* (New York: Ballantine Books, 1999), 137.

90. Morgan, *Slave Counterpoint*, 361–63 (quotation on 363).

91. Ball, *Slaves in the Family*, 137–38.

92. Wood, "'White Society' and the 'Informal' Slave Economies of Lowcountry Georgia," 314.

93. Benjamin Colman, *Righteousness and Compassion the Duty and Character of Pious Rulers* (Boston, 1736).

94. *Boston Evening-Post*, February 28, 1737.

95. *Pennsylvania Gazette*, June 10, 1742.

96. *Boston Evening-Post*, February 7, 1737.

97. Katherine Smoak, "Circulating Counterfeits: Making Money and Its Meanings in the Eighteenth-Century British Atlantic World," PhD diss., Johns Hopkins University, 2018, 42–43.

98. Theophilus Cotton petition and testimony [September–December 1738], MAC, vol. 101, Pecuniary [1694–1740], pp. 573–75. For other examples, see "Vote for exchanging a bill of £5 partly consumed belonging to Mrs. Tid[e]marsh, Nov. 30, 1738," MAC, vol. 101 [Pecuniary,

1694–1740], p. 572; "Account of Jeremiah Allen, Treasurer and Receiver General, showing receipts and disbursements between May 28, 1735, and June 18, 1736," MAC, vol. 124 [Treasury, 1735–57], p. 42; "Account of William Foye, Treasurer and Receiver General, showing receipts and disbursements between May 25, 1737, and May 31, 1738," MAC, vol. 124 [Treasury, 1735–57], pp. 111–12. For the decade from August 1731 to July 1741, there are seventeen petitions for replacing burned bills printed in vols. 10–12 of *MASS*.

99. *American Weekly Mercury*, August 6, 1730.

100. [William Bull], "An account of the rise and progress of the paper bills of credit in South Carolina, from the year 1700 to this present time . . ." [1739], in *SLSC*, 9:774. The other examples are in Eric P. Newman, *The Early Paper Money of America: An Illustrated, Historical, and Descriptive Collection of Data Relating to American Paper Currency from Its Inception in 1686 to the Year 1800* (Iola, WI: Krause Publications, 2008), 97, 332, 373.

101. Letter from G. Saltonstall, concerning counterfeit bills, August 27, 1724, MAC, vol. 101 [Pecuniary, 1694–1740], pp. 434–35.

102. Governor Montgomerie to the Board of Trade, August 2, 1729, TNA: CO 5/1093.

103. Governor Burnet to the Lords of Trade, November 21, 1724, TNA: CO 5/1092.

104. *Pennsylvania Gazette*, September 30, 1736.

105. *South-Carolina Gazette*, June 28, 1735.

106. *South-Carolina Gazette*, April 12, 1735, and March 31, 1733; Huw David, "James Crockatt's 'Exceeding Good Counting House': Ascendancy and Influence in the Transatlantic Carolina Trade," *South Carolina Historical Magazine* 110, nos. 3–4 (July–October 2010): 157.

107. Richard LeBaron Bowen, *Rhode Island Colonial Money and Its Counterfeiting, 1647–1726* (Concord, NH: Rumford Press, 1942), 63–68; Kenneth Scott, *Counterfeiting in Colonial America* (New York: Oxford University Press, 1957), 64–65. On women creating claims to credit through their husbands and family members, see Zabin, *Dangerous Economies*, 25–26, 36–48.

108. *Pennsylvania Gazette*, February 29, 1732; Stephen Mihm, *A Nation of Counterfeiters: Capitalists, Con Men, and the Making of the United States* (Cambridge, MA: Harvard University Press, 2007), 34.

109. Scott, *Counterfeiting in Colonial America*, 70.

110. "The Declaration of John Davis" [September 18, 1735], in *Historical Manuscripts in the Public Library of the City of Boston. Number One* (Boston: Public Library of the City of Boston, 1900), 104–6. The story was reported in the *Boston Gazette*, September 15, 1735; *Boston Evening-Post*, February 2, 1735/36, and June 28, 1736; *New-England Weekly Journal*, June 29, 1736.

111. Affidavit of Abraham Ilive, December 23, 1739, Pemberton Papers, vol. 3, p. 30, HSP.

112. "Proceedings of the Council from February 7th, 1735–6, to October 15th, 1745, Both Days Included," in *Minutes of the Provincial Council of Pennsylvania, From the Organization to the Termination of the Proprietary Government* (Harrisburg, PA, 1851), 4:429; "Journal of the Governor and Council, vol. III. 1738–1748," in Frederick W. Ricord and Wm. Nelson, eds., *Documents Relating to the Colonial history of the State of New Jersey* (Trenton, NJ, 1891), 15:119–20; Kenneth Scott, *Counterfeiting in Colonial Pennsylvania* (New York: American Numismatic Society, 1955), 42–43, 45–51.

113. *American Weekly Mercury*, August 28, 1740.

114. Smoak, "Circulating Counterfeits," 18–20.

115. *Money the Sinews of Trade* [Boston, 1731], in *CCR*, 2:438–39. Massachusetts bills were so hard to procure, the author observed, "that men are glad to catch at any thing that hath but the name of Money, if it will but pass away again."

116. [Anon.], *Money the Sinews of Trade*, 440, 443. See also "Communication Addressed to the Author of the Letter from Rhode-Island in the *Boston Gazette* of the 18th Current, from the *Boston Gazette*, February 25, 1734," in *CCR*, 3:52, inveighing against the "Rhode-Island Usurers" with "An Eye to Forty One" (the year all outstanding Massachusetts bills of credit were due).

117. [John Colman?], *A Proposal to Supply the Trade with a Medium of Exchange, and to sink the Bills of the Other Governments* [Boston, 1737], in *CCR*, 3:171.

118. *New-England Weekly Journal*, November 25, 1735.

119. Order for a committee to propose some method for detecting counterfeiters, October 3, 1739, MAC, vol. 101 [Pecuniary, 1694–1740], pp. 660–61; Order for a pursuit of counterfeiters of R.I. money, October 9, 1739, MAC, vol. 101 [Pecuniary, 1694–1740], p. 662.

120. *Boston News-Letter*, September 13, 1739.

121. *Boston News-Letter*, September 27, 1739.

122. Kenneth Scott, *Counterfeiting in Colonial Rhode Island* (Glückstadt, Germany: J. J. Augustin for Rhode Island Historical Society, 1960), 12–14.

123. *Boston News-Letter*, November 15, 1739; Petition of Cornelius Thayer relative to counterfeiters, September 13, 1742, MAC, vol. 102 [Pecuniary, 1740–52], p. 266.

124. Scott, *Counterfeiting in Colonial Rhode Island*, 27.

125. John L. Brooke, *The Refiner's Fire: The Making of Mormon Cosmology, 1644–1844* (New York: Cambridge University Press, 1994), 119–20.

126. Order about counterfeiters with a warrant for taking them, July 4, 1740, MAC, vol. 102 [Pecuniary 1740–52], pp. 70–72.

127. Scott, *Counterfeiting in Colonial Rhode Island*, 21–22.

128. Examination of Benjamin Boyce Jr for counterfeiting with papers, April 27, 1742, MAC, vol. 102 [Pecuniary, 1740–52], pp. 228–30.

129. Examination of Benjamin Boyce Jr for counterfeiting with papers, April 27, 1742, MAC, vol. 102 [Pecuniary, 1740–52], pp. 228–30, 234–35.

130. Scott, *Counterfeiting in Colonial Rhode Island*, 23.

131. *Boston News-Letter*, July 29, 1742.

132. *Boston News-Letter*, August 26, 1742.

133. Zabin, *Dangerous Economies*, 20; Scott, *Counterfeiting in Colonial Rhode Island*, 64–65; Smoak, "Circulating Counterfeits," 35.

134. Scott, *Counterfeiting in Colonial Rhode Island*, 26.

135. *Boston Evening Post*, September 10, 1744.

136. Certificate of Nathan Birdsall relating to counterfeit money, March 30, 1745, New York Colony Council papers, Series A1894-78, vol. 74, p. 202, NYSA.

137. Depositions of Augustine Hunt, William Browning, and Peter Potts relating to counterfeit money, April 4, 1745, New York Colony Council papers, Series A1894-78, vol. 74, p. 198, NYSA; Depositions of Elisha Johnson and William Russell relating to counterfeit money, April 4, 1745, New York Colony Council papers, Series A1894-78, vol. 74, p. 199b, NYSA; Certificates and Depositions relating to counterfeit money, April 5, 1745, New York Colony Council papers, Series A1894-78, vol. 74, p. 200b, NYSA; Certificate of Jacobus Swartout relating to counterfeit money, April 5, 1745, New York Colony Council papers, Series A1894-78, vol. 74, p. 201a, NYSA.

138. Letter from Governor Shirley of Massachusetts to Governor Clinton of New York relating to counterfeiters, April 27, 1745, New York Colony Council papers, series A1894-78, vol. 74, p. 196, NYSA.

139. Deposition of Robert Clark relating to counterfeit money, May 9, 1745, New York Colony Council papers. Series A1894-78, vol. 74, p. 203, NYSA.

140. Affidavit of Robert Clark relating to counterfeit money, May 9, 1745, New York Colony Council papers, Series A1894-78, vol. 74, p. 204, NYSA.

141. Governor Law to Governor Shirley, June 19, 1745, quoted in Kenneth Scott, *Counterfeiting in Colonial New York* (New York: American Numismatic Society, 1953), 65.

142. Jonathan Law to Governor Clinton, July 18, 1745, quoted in Scott, *Counterfeiting in Colonial New York*, 65.

143. Scott, *Counterfeiting in Colonial New York*, 66–67.

144. Ben Tarnoff, *A Counterfeiter's Paradise: The Wicked Lives and Surprising Adventures of Three Notorious Counterfeiters* (New York: Penguin Books, 2012), 6; Malcolm Gaskill, *Crime and Mentalities in Early Modern England* (New York: Cambridge University Press, 2000), 130; Johnson, "'What Must Poor People Do?,'" 135–38. For the Caribbean context, see Katherine Smoak, "The Weight of Necessity: Counterfeit Coins in the British Atlantic World, circa 1760–1800," *WMQ* 74, no. 3 (July 2017): 467–502. For Britain, see Peter Linebaugh, *The London Hanged: Crime and Civil Society in the Eighteenth Century* (London: Verso Books, 2006), 55–56.

145. *Pennsylvania Gazette*, November 28, 1734.

146. Scott, *Counterfeiting in Colonial America*, 82–83.

147. *New-England Weekly Journal*, June 29, 1736.

148. Scott, *Counterfeiting in Colonial America*, 67–69. For Britain, see Carl Wennerlind, "The Death Penalty as Monetary Policy: The Practice and Punishment of Monetary Crime, 1690–1830," *History of Political Economy* 36, no. 1 (Spring 2004): 154.

149. Scott, *Counterfeiting in Colonial America*, 33.

150. *Boston News-Letter*, July 27, 1713, and September 21, 1713.

151. *Boston Evening-Post*, May 17, 1756.

152. Johnson, "'What Must Poor People Do?,'" 143.

153. *Boston Evening-Post*, October 18, 1742.

154. *Boston News-Letter*, September 27, 1739.

155. Jennifer L. Roberts, "The Veins of Pennsylvania: Benjamin Franklin's Nature-Print Currency," *Grey Room* 69 (Fall 2017), 53–58 (quotation on 57–58); James N. Green and Peter Stallybrass, *Benjamin Franklin: Writer and Printer* (New Castle, DE: Oak Knoll Press with the Library Company of Philadelphia and the British Library, 2006), 55; Eric P. Newman, "Newly Discovered Franklin Invention: Nature Printing on Colonial and Continental Currency," *The Numismatic* 77, no. 2 (1964): 147–58.

156. Khachatur Manukyan et al., "Multiscale Analysis of Benjamin Franklin's Innovations in American Paper Money," *Proceedings of the National Academy of Sciences* 120, no. 30 (2023).

157. Harrold E. Gillingham, *Counterfeiting in Colonial Pennsylvania* (New York: American Numismatic Society, 1939). Accessed through Numismatics.org.

158. *American Weekly Mercury*, April 6, 1727.

159. Gaskill, *Crime and Mentalities in Early Modern England*, 127–28. On fashion, manners, and reputation replacing traditional markers of status, such as family name and landed wealth, see Phillis Whitman Hunter, *Purchasing Identity in the Atlantic World: Massachusetts Merchants, 1670–1780* (Ithaca, NY: Cornell University Press 2001), 91.

160. *Pennsylvania Gazette*, February 10, 1743.

161. Steven C. Bullock, "A Mumper among the Gentle: Tom Bell, Colonial Confidence Man," *WMQ* 55, no 2 (April 1998): 249–52.

162. *Pennsylvania Gazette*, May 18, 1738. In another example, the *Gazette* reported that Joseph Smith, a former schoolmaster and convicted counterfeiter who had been sentenced to death, broke out of a Maryland jail. The newspaper described Smith as a jack of all trades, from saddlery to clockmaking, and warned that he "may pretend he is a sailor." *Pennsylvania Gazette*, December 5, 1749.

163. *Pennsylvania Gazette*, June 8, 1738. Dean was among the dozens of coiners convicted at London's Old Bailey who were sentenced to transportation to the colonies, more than half of them women. He was probably not the only one who continued to counterfeit upon his arrival; three decades later, a newspaper article blamed the arrival of a ship in Annapolis, Maryland, carrying convicted coiners for the recent appearance of counterfeit coins. Smoak, "Circulating Counterfeits," 30–32.

164. Michael Warner, *The Letters of the Republic: Publication and the Public Sphere in Eighteenth-Century America* (Cambridge, MA: Harvard University Press, 1990), 61–62.

165. *American Weekly Mercury*, December 26, 1727.

166. *New-England Weekly Journal*, November 17, 1729.

167. Zabin, *Dangerous Economies*, 18.

168. Steven Wilf, *Law's Imagined Republic: Popular Politics and Criminal Justice in Revolutionary America* (New York: Cambridge University Press, 2010), 8–9.

169. Kristin Boudreau, "Early American Criminal Narratives and the Problem of Public Sentiments," *Early American Literature* 32, no. 3 (1997): 249, 265.

170. *Pennsylvania Gazette*, January 4, 1733.

171. *Pennsylvania Gazette*, January 25, 1733.

172. Brooke, *The Refiner's Fire*, 120 (quotation), 354n40. On the concept of "social banditry," see Eric Hobsbawm, *Bandits* (New York: New Press, 2000).

173. Brooke, *The Refiner's Fire*, 105–6, 110 (quotation), 118–20.

174. Smoak, "Circulating Counterfeits," 60.

175. Scott, *Counterfeiting in Colonial Rhode Island*, 21.

176. *American Weekly Mercury*, March 23, 1727.

177. Smoak, "Circulating Counterfeits," 73–76.

178. *American Weekly Mercury*, March 23, 1727.

179. *Pennsylvania Gazette*, December 12, 1732.

180. *Boston Gazette*, September 8, 1755 ("of the *Fair Sex*"); Joseph Bill Packer of the Albany gang, n.d., quoted in Scott, *Counterfeiting in Colonial New York*, 199 ("Miss Polly" and "distributed the ink . . .").

181. Smoak, "Circulating Counterfeits," 57–58.

182. Scott, *Counterfeiting in Colonial America*, 46–50.

183. John Styles, " 'Our traitorous money makers': The Yorkshire Coiners and the Law, 1760–83," in John Brewer and John Styles, eds., *An Ungovernable People: The English and Their Law in the Seventeenth and Eighteenth Centuries* (London: Hutchinson, 1980), 187–90; Smoak, "The Weight of Necessity," 480 (quotation).

184. Johnson, " 'What Must Poor People Do?,' " 133.

185. Gaskill, *Crime and Mentalities in Early Modern England*, 132.

186. On the "moral economy," see E. P. Thompson, "The Moral Economy of the English Crowd in the Eighteenth Century," *Past & Present* 50 (February 1971): 76–136.

Chapter 7

1. Gardner Weld Allen et al., eds., *Journals of the House of Representatives of Massachusetts* (Boston: Wright & Potter, 1928) (hereafter *JHRM*), 9:240–41.

2. J. Willard to William Clark, May 8, 1732, John Dolbeare Business Records [1718–42], Dolbeare Family Papers, box 4, folder 8, MHS.

3. May 10, 1733, *18th Century House of Commons Sessional Papers: Journals of the House of Commons* (1688–1834) (hereafter *Journals of the House of Commons*), 22:145. Digital edition of the UK Parliamentary Papers by the British Library Board and ProQuest.

4. Letter from Jonathan Belcher, September 17, 1737, TNA: CO 5/752 Part 2.

5. *JHRM*, 9:240–41.

6. Margaret Ellen Newell, *From Dependency to Independence: Economic Revolution in Colonial New England* (Ithaca, NY: Cornell University Press, 1998), 207–8.

7. Daniel Neal to Thomas Foxcroft, April 29, 1729, Benjamin Colman Papers, 1641–1806 (hereafter Colman Papers), box 1, folder 16, MHS.

8. [Anon.], *A Comparison between the British Sugar Colonies and New England, as They Relate to the Interest of Great Britain: With Some Observations on the State of the Case of New England: to Which Is Added a Letter to a Member of Parliament* (London, 1732), 8–9.

9. [Fayr Hall], *The Importance of the British Plantations in America to this Kingdom* (London, 1731), 102–8.

10. "A Modest Apology for Paper Money, Published in the *Weekly Rehearsal*, March 18, 1734," in *CCR*, 3:96–97. See also "A Few Remarks on the Present Situation of Affairs, etc. from the *Weekly Rehearsal*, April 1, 1734," in *CCR*, 3:132.

11. "State of the Trade, 1763" [Boston, 1763], in *Publications of The Colonial Society of Massachusetts, Volume XIX: Transactions, 1916–1917* (Boston, 1918), 385.

12. Daniel Vickers, *Farmers & Fishermen: Two Centuries of Work in Essex County, Massachusetts, 1630–1850* (Chapel Hill: University of North Carolina Press, 1994), 156.

13. Vickers, *Farmers & Fishermen*, 164.

14. Gloria L. Main, "Inequality in Early America: The Evidence from Probate Records of Massachusetts and Maryland," *Journal of Interdisciplinary History* 7, no. 4 (1977): 562; Christopher P. Magra, "'Soldiers . . . Bred to the Sea': Maritime Marblehead, Massachusetts, and the Origins and Progress of the American Revolution," *NEQ* 77, no. 4 (2004): 536.

15. Mr. Pigot to the Society for the Propagation of the Gospel, May 7, 1736, in William Stevens Perry, ed., *Historical Collections Relating to the American Colonial Church* (New York: AMS Press, 1873), 3:314, quoted in Vickers, *Farmers & Fishermen*, 190.

16. "A Modest Apology for Paper Money," 96.

17. "The Melancholy State of this Province Considered in a Letter, etc." [Boston, 1736], in *CCR*, 3:144.

18. [John Colman?], *A Proposal to Supply the Trade with a Medium of Exchange, and to sink the Bills of Other Governments* [Boston, 1737], in *CCR*, 3:173.

19. [John Wise], *Trade and Commerce Inculcated*, in *CCR*, 2:425–27.

20. [Hugh Vans], *An Inquiry into the Nature and Uses of Money* (Boston, 1740), in *CCR*, 3:458.

21. [John Colman], *The Distressed State of the Town of Boston Considered* [Boston, 1720], in *CCR*, 1:399, 403.

22. William Douglass, *A Discourse Concerning the Currencies of the British plantations in America. Especially with Regard to their Paper Money: More Particularly, in Relation to the Province of Massachusetts-Bay in New England* (Boston, 1740), in *CCR*, 3:328.

23. According to T. H. Breen, "There is no fully satisfactory historical account of 'Shop Notes.'" T. H. Breen, *The Marketplace of Revolution: How Consumer Politics Shaped American Independence* (New York: Oxford University Press, 2004), 188. For additional commentary on shop notes, see "The Melancholy State of this Province Considered," 143–44; [Hugh Vans], *Some Observations on the Scheme Projected for Emitting 60,000 l.* [Boston, 1736], in *CCR*, 3:204; [Anon.], "A Letter from a Country Gentleman at Boston [1740]," in *CCR*, 4:30.

24. [Vans], *An Inquiry into the Nature and Uses of Money*, 447, 458.

25. *A Report of the Record Commissioners of the City of Boston, Containing the Boston Records from 1729 to 1742*, ed. William H. Whitmore and W. S. Appleton (Boston, 1885), 121. John Colman concurred that shop notes forced "many People into such Extravagances," whereas "If Tradesmen were paid in Money they would not lay it out in such ways." [Colman?] *A Proposal to Supply the Trade with a Medium of Exchange*, 173.

26. *Boston News-Letter*, February 19, 1741.

27. *Money the Sinews of Trade* [Boston, 1731], in *CCR*, 2:444; David McNally, *Blood and Money: War, Slavery, Finance, and Empire* (Chicago: Haymarket Books, 2020), 1, 74; William M. Reddy, *Money and Liberty in Modern Europe: A Critique of Historical Understanding* (New York: Cambridge University Press, 1987), 112.

28. "The Melancholy State of this Province Considered," 143. See also [Wise], *Trade and Commerce Inculcated*, 428.

29. [Vans], *An Inquiry into the Nature and Uses of Money*, 450.

30. John L. Brooke, *The Heart of the Commonwealth: Society and Political Culture in Worcester County Massachusetts, 1713–1781* (New York: Cambridge University Press, 1989), 50.

31. *Boston Weekly News-Letter*, March 24–April 1, 1737, quoted in Jack Tager, *Boston Riots: Three Centuries of Social Violence* (Boston: Northeastern University Press, 2001), 34; Benjamin Colman to Samuel Holden, May 8, 1737, quoted in Gary B. Nash, *The Urban Crucible: Social Change, Political Consciousness, and the Origins of the American Revolution* (Cambridge, MA: Harvard University Press, 1979), 133.

32. George Minot Account Book [1732–35], Joseph Downs Collection, Winterthur Library, Winterthur, DE.

33. Douglass, *A Discourse Concerning the Currencies of the British plantations in America*, 328.

34. *Pennsylvania Gazette*, October 25, 1739.

35. Benjamin Colman to Francis Wilks, November 19, 1739, Colman Papers, box 2, folder 5, MHS.

36. *A Report of the Record Commissioners of the City of Boston, Containing the Boston Records from 1729 to 1742*, ed. William H. Whitmore and W. S. Appleton (Boston, 1885), 146.

37. Billy G. Smith, "Poverty and Economic Marginality in Eighteenth-Century America," *Proceedings of the American Philosophical Society* 132, no. 1 (March 1988): 88–90; Eric Nellis and Anne Decker Cecere, eds., "The Eighteenth-Century Records of the Boston Overseers of the Poor," *Publications of the Colonial Society of Massachusetts* 69 (2006): 973–74, 977.

38. "Note for the Treasurer to Notify Collectors of taxes, that they may receive hemp at 4 pence and flax at 6 pence for taxes," April 24, 1739, MAC, vol. 101 [Pecuniary, 1694–1740], p. 626.

39. "Extract of a Letter from a Gentleman in London, to his Friend in Boston," *New-England Weekly Journal*, November 13, 1739.

40. "Message from the House to the Council as to calling in bills of credit, &c.," January 1, 1740, MAC, vol. 101 [Pecuniary, 1694–1740], pp. 680–81.

41. Thomas Hutchinson, *The History of the Province of Massachusetts-Bay, from the Charter of King William and Queen Mary, in 1693, Until the Year 1750*, 2nd ed. (London, 1768), 2:393.

42. Letter from Jonathan Belcher, September 17, 1737, TNA: CO 5/752 Part 2.

43. *Pennsylvania Gazette*, November 8, 1739.

44. [Thomas Hutchinson], *A Letter to a Member of the Honourable House of Representatives* [Boston, 1736], in *CCR*, 3:156; [Vans], *Some Observations on the Scheme projected for emitting 60000 l. in bills of a new tenour*, 197.

45. [Colman?], *A Proposal to Supply the Trade with a Medium of Exchange*, 173. See also "A Few Remarks on the Present Situation of Affairs," 131–32.

46. [Anon.], "A Letter from a Gentleman to his Friend, from the *New-England Weekly Journal*, February 18, 1734," in *CCR*, 3:30–32.

47. See "A Letter from a Gentleman in Rhode Island to his Friend in Boston, from *the Weekly Rehearsal*, February 18, 1734," in *CCR*, 3:39; "Remarks Concerning a Late Large Emission of Paper-Credit in Boston Called Merchants Notes, from the *Boston Gazette*, February 25, 1734," in *CCR*, 3:56–57; [Anon.], "The Melancholy State of this Province Considered," 136; [Colman?], *A Proposal to Supply the Trade with a Medium of Exchange*, 168.

48. [Vans], *An Inquiry into the Nature and Uses of Money*, 459.

49. Benjamin Colman to Samuel Holden, January 6, 1735, box 1, folder 23, Colman Papers, MHS.

50. Benjamin Colman, *Righteousness and Compassion the Duty and Character of Pious Rulers* (Boston, 1736), 30.

51. Benjamin Colman to Samuel Holden, November 12, 1735, box 1, folder 26, Colman Papers, MHS. This price is close to the £532.26 metallic rate of exchange computed by John J. McCusker based on the standard price of silver for the year 1735. John J. McCusker, *Money & Exchange in Europe & America, 1600–1775: A Handbook* (Chapel Hill: University of North Carolina Press, 1978), 151.

52. *JHRM*, 11:275.

53. Alvin Rabushka, *Taxation in Colonial America* (Princeton: Princeton University Press, 2008), 454–59.

54. Bruce D. Smith, "Money and Inflation in Colonial Massachusetts," *Federal Reserve Bank of Minneapolis Quarterly Review* (Winter 1984): 1–14.

55. "A Modest Apology for Paper Money," 92.

56. "A Modest Apology for Paper Money," 97–98.

57. Benjamin Colman to Francis Wilks, November 19, 1739, box 2, folder 5, Colman Papers, MHS.

58. [William Douglass], *An Essay, Concerning Silver and Paper Currencies, etc.* in *CCR*, 3:221–22.

59. [Douglass], *An Essay, Concerning Silver and Paper Currencies*, 234.

60. Douglass, *A Discourse Concerning the Currencies of the British Plantations in America*, 336.

61. John Ashley, *Memoirs and Considerations Concerning the Trade and Revenues of the British Colonies in America* (London, 1743), 52.

62. Ashley, *Memoirs and Considerations*, 58.

63. Ashley, *Memoirs and Considerations*, 60.

64. [Anon.], *Two Letters to Mr. Wood, on the Coin and Currency in the Leeward Islands* (London, 1740), 4.

65. Alexander Spotswood to George Clarke, April 26, 1740, TNA: CO 5/1094.

66. Colonel Blakeney to the Duke of Newcastle, July 31, 1740, TNA: CO 5/41 Part 2; Colonel Blakeney to the Duke of Newcastle, August 21, 1740, TNA: CO 5/41 Part 2; Copies of letters from Governors Blakeney and Gooch to Messrs. Merewether and Manning, etc., December 14, 1740, TNA: CO 5/41 Part 2.

67. 25 April 1740, *Journals of the House of Commons*, 23:526–28.

68. *Pennsylvania Gazette*, May 29, 1740.

69. *Pennsylvania Gazette*, June 12, 1740.

70. 13 June 1739, *Journals of the House of Commons*, 23:378–79.

71. Governor Clarke to the Lords of Trade, June 13, 1740, TNA: CO 5/1094 Part 1.

72. "Report of the Lords of Trade to the House of Commons relative to Bills of Credit in the Plantations, Jan. 21, 1741," in William A. Whitehead et al., eds., *Documents Relating to the Colonial History of the State of New Jersey* (Newark, NJ: Daily Advertiser Printing House, 1882), 6:122–25.

73. Andrew McFarland Davis, *Currency and Banking in the Province of Massachusetts-Bay, Part II. Banking* (New York: Macmillan, 1901), 130–31.

74. Newell, *From Dependency to Independence*, 216.

75. "The Manufactory Scheme," September 8, 1740, Robert Treat Paine Papers, I. Family Papers, 1659–1916, B. Legal and financial papers, 1659–1867, microfilm, reel 7, Land Bank papers, 1739–49 (hereafter Land Bank Papers), MHS.

76. [Anon.], *A Letter from a Country Gentleman at Boston, etc.* [Boston, 1740], in *CCR*, 4:32.

77. [Vans], *An Inquiry into the Nature and Uses of Money*, 472–73.

78. Report of the Committee on the land bank and silver scheme, March 28, 1740, MAC, vol. 102 [Pecuniary, 1740–52], pp. 37–38; Petition that a hearing may be had in favor of the land bank, June 4, 1740, MAC, vol. 102 [Pecuniary, 1740–52], p. 39; Memorial of Salem merchants in favor of the bank, June 6, 1740, MAC, vol. 102 [Pecuniary, 1740–52], pp. 40–41; Representation in favor of the Land Bank, June 12, 1740, MAC, vol. 102 [Pecuniary, 1740–52], pp. 44–45.

79. Proclamation of Jonathan Belcher and agreement of subscribers not to take bills, July 17, 1740, Land Bank Papers, MHS.

80. Davis, *Currency and Banking, in the Province of Massachusetts-Bay, Part II*, 146.

81. George Athan Bilias, *The Massachusetts Land Bankers of 1740* (Orono, ME: University Press, 1957), 13–14; Newell, *From Dependency to Independence*, 227.

82. Proclamation against the land bank, November 6, 1740, MAC, vol. 102 [Pecuniary, 1740–1752], pp. 86–87; William Stoddard's resignation as a justice because concerned with the land bank, November 10, 1740, MAC, vol. 102 [Pecuniary, 1740–52], p. 88; Like resignation of Robert Hale, Sam'l Adams and Jno. Choate, November 10, 1740, MAC, vol. 102 [Pecuniary, 1740–52], pp. 89–90.

83. Letter to a Merchant in London, [February 27?], 1741, quoted in Joseph B. Felt, *An Historical Account of Massachusetts Currency* (Boston: Perkins & Marvin, 1839), 106.

84. Order for the court of General Sessions respecting the land bank bills, MAC, vol. 102 [Pecuniary, 1740–52], pp. 107–8.

85. List of persons in the County of Suffolk who have mortgaged their estates to the land bank, December 19, 1740, MAC, vol. 102 [Pecuniary, 1740–52], pp. 103–6.

86. List of persons in Middlesex County, who have mortgaged their estates to the land bank, December 22, 1740, MAC, vol. 102 [Pecuniary, 1740-52], pp. 109-10; A list of persons in the County of Essex who have mortgaged their property to the land bank, December 30, 1740, MAC, vol. 102 [Pecuniary, 1740-52], pp. 116-19; List of persons in Worcester County, who have mortgaged their estates to the land bank, January 1, 1741, MAC, vol. 102 [Pecuniary, 1740-52], pp. 121-26.

87. Elizabeth E. Dunn, "'Grasping at the Shadow': The Massachusetts Currency Debate, 1690-1751," *NEQ* 71, no. 1 (March 1998): 62; Newell, *From Dependency to Independence*, 218.

88. *Boston News-Letter*, February 19, 1741.

89. Davis, *Currency and Banking, in the Province of Massachusetts-Bay, Part II*, 157-58.

90. Papers respecting a confederacy with respect to the land bank, May 14, 1741, MAC, vol. 102 [Pecuniary, 1740-52], pp. 155, 163, 168.

91. Papers respecting a confederacy with respect to the land bank, May 14, 1741, MAC, vol. 102 [Pecuniary, 1740-52], pp. 159-60, 162.

92. Papers respecting a confederacy with respect to the land bank, May 14, 1741, MAC, vol. 102 [Pecuniary, 1740-52], pp. 164-65, 166-67; Bilias, *The Massachusetts Land Bankers of 1740*, 34-36; Davis, *Currency and Banking, in the Province of Massachusetts-Bay, Part II*, 153-55.

93. Hutchinson, *History of Massachusetts*, 2:395.

94. Bilias, *The Massachusetts Land Bankers of 1740*, 21-31.

95. T. H. Breen and Timothy Hall, "Structuring Provincial Imagination: The Rhetoric and Experience of Social Chance in Eighteenth-Century New England," *American Historical Review* 103, no. 5 (December 1998): 1412-13; Rosalind Remer, "Old Lights and New Money: A Note on Religion, Economics, and the Social Order in 1740 Boston," *WMQ* 47, no. 4 (October 1990): 567, 569-70; Brooke, *The Heart of the Commonwealth*, 70-71; Nash, *The Urban Crucible*, 208.

96. Davis, *Currency and Banking, in the Province of Massachusetts-Bay, Part II*, 158-59.

97. Jonathan Belcher to Richard Partridge, November 13, 1740, quoted in Davis, *Currency and Banking in the Province of Massachusetts-Bay, Part II*, 148.

98. Newell, *From Dependency to Independence*, 225-26, 228.

99. Bilias, *The Massachusetts Land Bankers of 1740*, 14-15.

100. Christopher Kilby to Thomas Hancock, September 10, 1741, quoted in Newell, *From Dependency to Independence*, 226.

101. *Boston News-Letter*, December 6, 1739.

102. [Anon.], *An Account of the Rise, Progress and Consequences of the Two Late Schemes Commonly Call'd the Land-Bank or Manufactory Scheme and the Silver Scheme, In the Province of Massachusetts Bay* [Boston, 1744], in *CCR*, 4:287-88.

103. Charles Francis Adams, *The Works of John Adams* (Boston, 1851), 4:49.

104. Charles H. Lincoln, Correspondence of William Shirley, I, 79, quoted in Bilias, *The Massachusetts Land Bankers of 1740*, 37.

105. Bilias, *The Massachusetts Land Bankers of 1740*, 37-40; William Pencak, *War, Politics, & Revolution in Provincial Massachusetts* (Boston: Northeastern University Press, 1981), 106-17; [Anon.], *An Account of the Rise, Progress and Consequences of the Two Late Schemes*, 293, 300-303, 310-11.

106. *Pennsylvania Gazette*, July 17, 1740.

107. Copy of a Speech given by Governor Shirley to the General Assembly concerning Amendments of the supply bill, and a copy of subsequent orders concerning the silver schemes and manufactory bills, October 14, 1741-May 7, 1742, TNA: CO 5/753; Eric P. Newman, *The Early*

Paper Money of America: An Illustrated, Historical, and Descriptive Collection of Data Relating to American Paper Currency from Its Inception in 1686 to the Year 1800 (Iola, WI: Krause Publications, 2008), 201–3.

108. William Shirley to Charles Apthorpe, October 17, 1741, Shirley Papers, folder 1, MHS.

109. William Shirley to the Board of Trade, December 23, 1743, quoted in Andrew McFarland Davis, ed., *Currency and Banking, in the Province of Massachusetts-Bay, Part I: Currency* (New York: Macmillan, 1901), 157–58.

110. [Anon.], *An Account of the Rise, Progress and Consequences of the Two Late Schemes*, 295–96; Hutchinson, *History of Massachusetts*, 2:404.

111. Quoted in Willard C. Fisher, "The Tabular Standard in Massachusetts History," *Quarterly Journal of Economics* 27, no. 3 (1913): 422.

112. William Shirley to the Lords of Trade, March 19, 1742, quoted in Claire Priest, "Currency Policies and Legal Development in Colonial New England," *Yale Law Journal* 110, no. 8 (June 2001): 1380–81.

113. Hutchinson, *History of Massachusetts*, 2:403–4.

114. Fisher, "The Tabular Standard in Massachusetts History," 424.

115. Priest, "Currency Policies and Legal Development in Colonial New England," 1381, 1391.

116. [Anon.], *An Account of the Rise, Progress and Consequences of the Two Late Schemes*, 296.

117. Hutchinson, *History of Massachusetts*, 2:403–4.

118. Fisher, "The Tabular Standard in Massachusetts History," 425.

119. Instructions to the Representatives of Boston elected to the General Court, Thomas Cushing, Timothy Prout, Thomas Hutchinson, and Andrew Oliver, September 25, 1744, Miscellaneous Manuscripts, MHS.

120. Newman, *Early Paper Money of America*, 204–5; Newell, *From Dependency to Independence*, 229.

121. These rates are close to those in John J. McCusker, *Money and Exchange in Europe and America, 1600–1775: A Handbook* (Chapel Hill: University of North Carolina Press, 1978), 152.

122. "Speech of Massachusetts Governor William Shirley to the General Court. Boston, February 8, 1743/44," *Pennsylvania Gazette*, March 21, 1744.

123. Nash, *The Urban Crucible*, 165–74.

124. Julian Gwyn, "Government Spending and the North American Colonies 1740–1775," *Journal of Imperial and Commonwealth History* 8, no. 2 (1980): 76–77, 79; [Anon.], *The Case of His Majesty's province of the Massachusetts Bay in New-England, with respect to the expences they were at in taking and securing Cape Breton* [Boston?, 1747], 2.

125. Nathaniel Appleton, *The cry of oppression where judgment is looked for, and the sore calamities such a people may expect from a righteous God* (Boston, 1748), 44, 50.

126. *Independent Advertiser*, March 28, 1748.

127. *A Brief Account of the Rise, Progress, and Present State of the Paper Currency of New-England* (Boston, 1749), in *CCR*, 4:391. See also *Some Observations Relating to the Present Circumstances of the Province of the Massachusetts-Bay* (Boston, 1750), in *CCR*, 4:412–23.

128. *Independent Advertiser*, March 28, 1748.

129. Mc—O—Ne—L, *A copy of a letter from Quebeck in Canada, to a pr—e m—r in France* [Philadelphia, 1747?], 1–2.

130. Mylo Freeman, *A Word in Season to All True Lovers of their Liberty and their Country* (Boston, 1748), in *CCR*, 4:358–59.

131. Vincent Centinel, *Massachusetts in Agony* (Boston, 1750), in *CCR*, 4:439.

132. *Independent Advertiser*, September 25, 1749.

133. Governor Shirley to the Duke of Bedford, January 31, 1748/9, TNA: CO 5/45 Part 5.

134. The Parliamentary debate was reported in "BOSTON, June 26, *Extract of a letter from London, dated April* 24, 1749," *Pennsylvania Gazette*, July 6, 1749; "BOSTON, July 31, *Extract of a letter from an agent of one of the colonies concern'd in the Cape-Breton expedition, dated London, May 19*," *Pennsylvania Gazette*, August 10, 1749.

135. Newell, *From Dependency to Independence*, 233.

136. Newell, *From Dependency to Independence*, 233; Hutchinson, *History of Massachusetts*, 2:438–40.

137. *Independent Advertiser*, September 25, 1749.

138. *Independent Advertiser*, February 27, 1749.

139. Hutchinson, *History of Massachusetts*, 2:440; Nash, *The Urban Crucible*, 225–26.

140. *A mournful lamentation for the sad and deplorable death of Mr. Old Tenor, a native of New-England, who, after a long confinement, by a deep and mortal wound which he received above twelve months before, expired on the 31st of March, 1750* (Boston, 1750).

141. *A Table, Shewing the Value of Old Tenor Bills, in Lawful Money, to the 15th Part of a Farthing, from one Penny to £.10,000* (Boston, 1750). Other examples include *An Exact table to bring old tenor into lawful money* (Boston, 1750); *A Table, shewing how provisions ought to be sold when the dollars pass for six shillings a-piece, as they must do, according to the act of the General Court* (Boston, 1750); *A Table for ready turning any old tenor sum into lawful money, at the rate of 6s. per piece of eight* (Boston, 1750).

142. "An Accott. of Stock Money & Debts . . . Taken Boston March ye 9th 1756," Samuel Abbot business papers, Series I. Financial Records, 1754–1819, box 50, folder 2, Baker Library Special Collections, Harvard Business School, Harvard University.

143. Nathaniel Bragg Account Book, 1741–1820, MHS; Noyes Family Papers, 1687–1949, MHS.

144. Thomas Dennis receipt, February 13, 1752, Dennis Papers, 1663–1904, MHS.

145. John Clarke Account Book, 1732–71, MHS.

146. *Pennsylvania Gazette*, May 11, 1749, and May 18, 1749.

147. Ernst, *Money and Politics in America*, 39–42.

Epilogue

1. Anon., *The Case of the inhabitants in Pensilvania* (Philadelphia?, 1744?).

2. Pennsylvania Assembly Committee of Correspondence to Richard Jackson and Benjamin Franklin, October 17, 1767, in *Franklin Papers*, 14:285.

3. Declaration and Resolves of the First Continental Congress [October 14, 1774], in *Journals of Congress, Containing the Proceedings from Sept. 5, 1774, to Jan. 1, 1776* (Philadelphia: R. Aitken, 1776), 1:27–30.

4. Edmund S. Morgan, *The Stamp Act Crisis: Prelude to Revolution* (Chapel Hill: University of North Carolina Press, 1953).

5. Jack P. Greene and Richard M. Jellison, "The Currency Act of 1764 in Imperial-Colonial Relations, 1764–1776," *WMQ* 18, no. 4 (October 1961): 485–86.

6. Robert Dinwiddie to the Board of Trade, February 24, 1756, TNA: CO 5/1328.

7. Joseph Albert Ernst, *Money and Politics in America, 1755–1775: A Study in the Currency Act of 1764 and the Political Economy of Revolution* (Chapel Hill: University of North Carolina Press, 1973), 12–16.

8. John Watts to General Robert Monckton, April 14, 1764, and to Moses Frank, June 9, 1764, Letter Book of John Watts . . . (1762–65), *Collections of the New York Historical Society* 61 (1928): 242–43, 264, quoted in Greene and Jellison, "The Currency Act of 1764," 490.

9. "Petitions of the merchants of Glasgow and Liverpool trading to Virginia respecting the paper currency there," August 1762, TNA: CO 5/1330; "The Memorials of Richard Corbin and the merchants of London trading to Virginia, with letter," December 15, 1762, CO 5/1330.

10. "An Act for relief of insolvent debtors, for the effectual discovery and more equal distribution of their estates" [November 1762], in William Waller Hening, ed., *The Statutes at Large; being a Collection of all the Laws of Virginia, from the First Session of the Legislature, in the Year 1619* (Richard, VA: Franklin Press, 1820) (hereafter *Hening's Statutes*), 7:549–63; T. H. Breen, *Tobacco Culture: The Mentality of the Great Tidewater Planters on the Eve of Revolution* (Princeton: Princeton University Press, 1985), 138–40.

11. Letter from Francis Fauquier respecting the behaviour of the Assembly, June 1, 1763, TNA: CO 5/1330; "The Petition of Merchants in London who Trade to North Carolina, and of Gentlemen and Merchants in and from that Colony," 1764, TNA: CO 5/65 Part 3; Approval of the King, by order of the Privy Council, of proposals enclosed by the Lords of Trade and Plantations, March 9, 1764, TNA: CO 5/65 Part 2.

12. *An Act to Prevent Paper Bills of Credit: hereafter to be issued in any of His Majesty's colonies or plantations in America, from being declared to be a legal tender in payments of mony; and to prevent the legal tender of such bills as are now subsisting, from being prolonged beyond the Periods limited for calling in and sinking the same. (At the Parliament begun and holden at Westminster, May 19, 1761* (London, 1764).

13. Benjamin Franklin to Richard Jackson, June 25, 1764, in *Franklin Papers*, 11:234.

14. Gary B. Nash, *The Urban Crucible: Social Change, Political Consciousness, and the Origins of the American Revolution* (Cambridge, MA: Harvard University Press, 1979), 246–48, 250, 255.

15. James Pemberton to John Fothergill, February 17, 1765, in Pemberton Papers, vol. 34, p. 137, HSP.

16. "*To the Honourable the* KNIGHTS, CITIZENS, *and* BURGESSES *of* Great-Britain, *in Parliament assembled, The* PETITION *of the* REPRESENTATIVES *of the Freemen of the Province of* Pennsylvania, *in General Assembly met*" [January 14, 1766], *Pennsylvania Gazette*, August 7, 1766; Pennsylvania Assembly Committee of Correspondence to Richard Jackson and Benjamin Franklin, October 18, 1766, in *Franklin Papers*, 13:465 (quotations).

17. Philadelphia merchants—agreements to decline receiving bills of credit as money (1766), December 8–9, 1766, James Gibson Papers Series 1, box 6, folder 1, HSP.

18. "From the PENNSYLVANIA JOURNAL, No. 1125," *Maryland Gazette*, July 5, 1764.

19. *Newbern Gazette*, November 9, 1764.

20. "*COPY of a LETTER.* MARYLAND, *October* 16, 1764," *Virginia Gazette*, July 11, 1766; Julian Gwyn, "British Government Spending and the North American Colonies, 1740–1775," *Journal of Imperial and Commonwealth History* 8, no. 2 (1980): 76–77; Andrew David Edwards, "Grenville's Silver Hammer: The Problem of Money in the Stamp Act Crisis," *Journal of American History* (September 2017): 337–62.

21. "Extract of a Letter from a Gentleman at Virginia, to his Friend in London" (October 21), *Hartford Courant*, December 30, 1765.

22. Richard B. Sheridan, "The British Credit Crisis of 1772 and the American Colonies," *JEH* 20, no. 2 (June 1960), 163–64; Woody Holton, *Forced Founders: Indians, Debtors, Slaves, and the Making of the American Revolution in Virginia* (Chapel Hill: University of North Carolina

Press, 1999), 65; Robin L. Einhorn, *American Taxation, American Slavery* (Chicago: University of Chicago Press, 2001), 36, 45; Claire Priest, "Creating an American Property Law: Alienability and Its Limits in American History," *Harvard Law Review* 120, no. 2 (December 2006): 434–35.

23. Holton, *Forced Founders*, 83.

24. *Virginia Gazette*, July 25, 1766.

25. Holton, *Forced Founders*, 60–61.

26. Francis Fauquier to the Earl of Halifax, June 14, 1765, TNA: CO 5/1345.

27. [Charles Thomson?], "A Letter from a Merchant in Philadelphia, to his Correspondent in London, dated June 19," reprinted from the *London Chronicle*, August 17–20, 1765, in *Franklin Papers*, 12:183.

28. Ernst, *Money and Politics in America*, vii–viii.

29. "The Memorial of the several Merchants and Manufacturers of Manchester," *Pennsylvania Gazette*, November 28, 1765.

30. "To the PRINTER of the Public Ledger" (October 1), *Pennsylvania Gazette*, December 12, 1765.

31. Benjamin Franklin to the Pennsylvania Assembly Committee of Correspondence, April 12, 1766, in *Franklin Papers*, 13:236.

32. Opinion of the merchants of London, regarding the issue of paper money in the Colonies [c. 1766–67], TNA: CO 5/378 Part 2.

33. Benjamin Franklin, "The Legal Tender of Paper Money in America," February 13, 1767, in *Franklin Papers*, 14:32; Benjamin Franklin to [Joseph Galloway?], [March 14, 1767], in *Franklin Papers*, 14:87; Benjamin Franklin to Joseph Galloway, June 13, 1767, in *Franklin Papers*, 14:180 (quotation).

34. For the general currency scheme, see Benjamin Franklin to [Thomas Pownall], [February 11–12?, 1765], in *Franklin Papers*, 12:47; Benjamin Franklin, "Scheme for Supplying the Colonies with a Paper Currency" [February 11–12?, 1765], in *Franklin Papers*, 12:47. For the controversy over its unexpected proposal in the House of Commons two years later, see William Strahan to David Hall, May 16, 1767, William Strahan Letters, box 1, folder 11, HSP; Benjamin Franklin to Joseph Galloway, June 13, 1767, in *Franklin Papers*, 14:180.

35. Benjamin Franklin to Joseph Galloway, August 8, 1767, in *Franklin Papers*, 14:228.

36. William Tryon to the Earl of Shelburne, February 2, 1768, TNA: CO 5/311.

37. Earl of Hillsborough to William Tryon, April 16, 1768, TNA: CO 5/332.

38. Earl of Hillsborough to the Governor of New York, February 25, 1768, TNA: CO 5/1141.

39. *Pennsylvania Gazette*, January 14, 1768.

40. "To the Printer of the PENNSYLVANIA CHRONICLE, Chester county," Dec. 21, 1767. *Virginia Gazette*, January 21, 1768. See also "Petitions of the Commons House of Assembly of South Carolina, as made to the King relative to distress caused by a late Act of Parliament prohibiting the issuing of paper currency in the Colonies as a legal tender," November 28, 1766, TNA: CO 5/390.

41. *Virginia Gazette*, April 28, 1768.

42. *Virginia Gazette*, July 11, 1766.

43. Marjoleine Kars, *Breaking Loose Together: The Regulator Rebellion in Pre-Revolutionary North Carolina* (Chapel Hill: University of North Carolina Press, 2002), 66–67, 72–73.

44. William Tryon to the Secretary of State, June 16, 1768, TNA: CO 5/328 (quotation); Kars, *Breaking Loose Together*, 137–38.

45. *Pennsylvania Gazette*, June 30, 1768.

46. *Virginia Gazette*, December 8, 1768.

47. John L. Brooke, *The Heart of the Commonwealth: Society and Political Culture in Worcester County, Massachusetts 1713-1861* (New York: Cambridge University Press, 1989), 138–40; Brendan McConville, *These Daring Disturbers of the Public Peace: The Struggle for Property and Power in Early New Jersey* (Ithaca, NY: Cornell University Press, 1999), 239–41.

48. Kars, *Breaking Loose Together*, 163, 173.

49. [Abstract of] letter from Governor Franklin to the Board of Trade, November 22, 1766, TNA: CO 5/221.

50. Peyton Randolph to the Secretary of State, 1768, TNA: CO 5/1372.

51. "Petitions of the Commons House of Assembly of South Carolina, as made to the King relative to distress caused by a late Act of Parliament prohibiting the issuing of paper currency in the Colonies as a legal tender," November 28, 1766, TNA: CO 5/390. For additional examples, see "Three copies of a petition of the Commons House of Assembly in Georgia seeking relief and repeal of the act to prevent the stamping, printing and issuing paper currency sent to the King, Parliament and citizens of Great Britain," April 6, 1767, TNA: CO 5/658; "Petition to the King from a Committee of both house of the Assembly of North Carolina," January 16, 1768, TNA: CO 5/311.

52. Green and Jellison, "The Currency Act of 1764," 517.

53. "Petition from the County of Lancaster for an Emission of Paper Money for a public loan. Presented in the House and Read January 5, 1769," January 5, 1769, Society Miscellaneous Collections, County Petitions, 1736–99, box 4b, folder 4, HSP; Nash, *The Urban Crucible*, 319.

54. Joseph Galloway to Benjamin Franklin, June 21, 1770, in *Franklin Papers*, 17:177.

55. "Petition of the Freeholders and Inhabitants of the County of Middlesex," *Pennsylvania Gazette*, October 26, 1769.

56. Governor Franklin to the Secretary of State, June 14, 1768, TNA: CO 5/1001.

57. Governor Franklin to the Secretary of State, August 24, 1768, TNA: CO 5/1001.

58. Governor Franklin to Lord Hillsborough, September 29, 1770, TNA: CO 5/990.

59. "A scheme for emitting paper currency in Virginia" [1766–74], TNA: CO 5/1372; "Representation of the Lords of Trade, to His Majesty, on an Address of the House of Burgesses of Virginia, praying Permission to issue a certain Quantity of Paper Money," June 10, 1768, TNA: CO 5/1346; Holton, *Forced Founders*, 62–63.

60. Holton, *Forced Founders*, 63.

61. Thomas D. Russell, "A New Image of the Slave Auction: An Empirical Look at the Role of Law in Slave Sales and a Conceptual Reevaluation of Slave Property," *Cardozo Law Review* 18, no. 2 (1996): 473–523; Priest, "Creating an American Property Law," 389–90.

62. Gerald Horne, *The Counter-Revolution of 1776: Slave Resistance and the Origins of the United States of America* (New York: New York University Press, 2016), 200.

63. *Rind's Virginia Gazette*, March 31, 1768, and October 27, 1768.

64. "An Ordinance for appointing commissioners to settle the accounts of the militia . . ." (July 1775), in *Hening's Statutes*, 9:61–71; Holton, *Forced Founders*, 176–80.

65. Orders of Council, July 11, 1766, TNA: CO 5/24.

66. The address of the General Assembly to the governor of New York, November 13, 1766, TNA: CO 5/1098; "The Petition of the General Assembly of the Colony of New York," December 11, 1766, TNA: CO 5/1098.

67. Address of the Assembly to Governor Moore, June 3, 1767, TNA: CO 5/1098.

68. Address of the Assembly to Governor Moore, June 3, 1767, TNA: CO 5/1098; Henry Moore to the Earl of Hillsborough, May 29, 1769, TNA: CO 5/1138; Henry Moore to the Earl of Hillsborough, July 11, 1769, TNA: CO 5/1138.

69. Lt. Gov. Colden to the Earl of Hillsborough, October 4, 1769, TNA: CO 5/1138.

70. "*To the* FREEHOLDERS, FREEMEN, *and* INHABITANTS *of the Colony of* New-York; *and to all the Friends of* LIBERTY *in* North-America" (February 12), *Pennsylvania Gazette*, February 22, 1770.

71. Letter from Lieutenant General Gage to the Earl of Hillsborough, December 7, 1770, TNA: CO 5/234.

72. Earl of Hillsborough to Lt. Gov. Colden, June 12, 1770, TNA: CO 5/1101; Greene and Jellison, "The Currency Act of 1764," 511–13.

73. Governor Franklin to the Secretary of State, June 1, 1771, TNA: CO 5/1001; William Bull to the Secretary of State, November 30, 1770, TNA: CO 5/409.

74. William Tryon to the Secretary of State, January 1, 1770, TNA: CO 5/328.

75. William Tryon to the Earl of Hillsborough, August 1, 1771, TNA: CO 5/314 Part 2; Josiah Martin to the Earl of Hillsborough, August 15, 1771, TNA: CO 5/314 Part 2.

76. Nash, *The Urban Crucible*, 320 (quotation); Breen, *Tobacco Culture*, 127; Sheridan, "The British Credit Crisis of 1772," 173–79; Ernst, *Money and Politics in America*, 313.

77. *Pennsylvania Gazette*, October 13, 1773.

78. "Petition of the General Assembly of New York to the King," *Pennsylvania Packet*, April 24, 1775.

79. "Representation and Remonstrance of the General Assembly of New York to the British Parliament, April 27," *Pennsylvania Packet*, May 1, 1775.

80. Jack M. Sosin, "Imperial Regulation of Colonial Paper Money, 1764–1773," *Pennsylvania Magazine of History and Biography* 88, no. 2 (April 1964): 198.

81. Ernst, *Money and Politics in America*, 312–13.

Index

Page numbers in italics indicate figures.

account books, 30–32, 48–49
Act for Ascertaining the Value of Money and of the Bills of Credit (Massachusetts, 1742), 205–6
Adams, John (father of the founding father), 102
Adams, John (founding father), 204
Adams, Samuel, 201
Addington, Isaac, 47, 98
Aglietta, Michel, 4
Allen, Jeremiah, 46–47, 49
America. *See* colonial governments/assemblies
American Revolutionary War (1775–83), 11, 213, 227
Amory, Thomas, 76, 80, 106–7, 132
Andover gang (counterfeiters), 172, 183
Andros, Edmund, 18–21, 25–27, 34, 35, 39, 93, 94
Appleton, Nathaniel, 208
Apthorpe, Charles, 205
Ashley, John, 197–98
assemblies. *See* colonial governments/assemblies

balance of trade, 5, 54, 74, 108, 139, 142, 188, 191, 200, 214
Ball, Edward, 165
Bank Act (South Carolina, 1712), 124–27
Bank Bill from Ipswich, Massachusetts, *203*
Bank of England, 10, 37, 67, 219
banks of credit, 34, 40, 72, 75, 90–93, 97, 102, 108, 110, 190. *See also* land banks
banks of deposit, 91, 92
Barbados, 68, 123–24
barter: bookkeeping, 2; myth of, 2, 18, 43
Bartram, Isaac, 216
Baxter, William T., 47
beaver, 16, 22; as currency, 7, 83

Belcher, Andrew, 98
Belcher, Jonathan, 171, 187–88, 192–94, 196, 201–2, 204
Bell, Tom, 181
Bellingham, Richard, 24
Berlin, Ira, 154
Bhandar, Brenda, 95
bills of credit: burning of, 33, 35, 36, 40, 78, 98, 120; compared to other forms of payment, 34; counterfeiting of, 120, 167–68, 171–77, 179, 226; earliest American, 14; incorporation into credit culture of, 48–49; in Massachusetts, 14, 29–33, *31*, 48–50, 68–70, 196–97, 207–8; in New Jersey, 49, *180*; in New York, 54–55, *55*, 83–87, 224–25; in Pennsylvania, 88–90, 112–18, *116–17*; political process for, 43–44; significance of, 8, 12; sociocultural practices involving, 44, 49–50; in South Carolina, 59–62, 68–70, 77–83, 149–50; taxes paid with, 29–33, 35, 43–44, 48, 70–72, 81–82; territorial currencies compared to, 246n110; trust essential to imposition of, 32, 41, 43–44, 49, 63; for war finance, 29–30, 42–44, 64, 79–80, 147, 207, 214. *See also* credit/loans; paper money
bills of exchange, 7, 83, 86, 110, 129, 195, 199; and banks of credit, 90, 92; compared to bills of credit, 34; demand for, 81, 106, 125, 143, 226; forgeries of, 120; prices of, 73, 76, 81, 110, 141–42 (*see also* exchange rates)
Blackstone, William, 91
Blackwell, John, 34–35, 40, 66–67, 72, 93, 96–97, 108–9, 118
Blakeney, William, 199
Blathwayt, William, 25, 60

296 INDEX

Board of Trade (England), 9, 42, 67, 68, 85, 88, 109, 111, 112, 124, 127, 129–31, 141, 187, 194–96, 199, 205–6, 214–15, 219, 223–25. *See also* Lords of Trade
Bodin, Jean, 69
Boston Caucus, 99
Boston Mint, 21–26
Bosworth, Henry, 173, 175, 202
Boudreau, Kristin, 182
Boyce, Benjamin, Jr., 173–74, 202
Boyce, Joseph, 173–76
Braddock, Edward, 214
Bradford, William, 54–55
Bradstreet, Simon, 27
Breen, T. H., 7, 105
Breintnall, Joseph, 178; nature prints of leaves, *179*
Brooke, John L., 172, 183
Broughton, Thomas, 141, 145
Brown, John, *203*
Bubble Act (England, 1720), 204
Budd, Thomas, 92, 108, 118
Bull, William, 63, 78, 80, 137, 141, 147, 225
Bullivant, Benjamin, 27
Burnet, William, 42, 85, 168
Butterworth, Mary Peck, 168–69, 183

capitalism: and agriculture, 87, 95–96; anarchic production characteristic of, 142; of British empire, 85, 119, 152, 189; features of early American, 6, 11, 55, 121–22; merchant, 47, 121–22, 127, 152; racial factors in, 5, 95, 121, 127
Charles II, King of England, 18, 24
Charles Town. *See* South Carolina
chartalism, 2, 8, 14
chattel slavery, 122, 153
Cherokee, 61–62, 79
Choate, John, 201
Choate, Robert, *203*
Clarke, George, 198–99
Clark-Pujara, Christy, 153–54
class: and access to money, 7, 65; conflicts involving, 65, 162; influence of, on monetary transactions, 30; laboring, 45, 83, 102, 189–90, 208
Clinton, George, 175–76
clothing, as medium of exchange, 7, 155–56
coins/coinage: full-bodied vs. clipped, 21–22, 66–67; Queen Anne's Proclamation on, 65–68, 84–85, 109, 141, 187, 199; standardization of, 66–67. *See also* minting of money
Colden, Cadwallader, 86, 178, 225
Cole, Michael, 60
Colman, Benjamin, 166, 192, 195, 197
Colman, John, 72–75, 96–99, 102, 119, 171, 188, 190–91, 194, 200
colonial governments/assemblies: and coinage, 65–68; fiscal powers/policies of, 8, 35–38, 64, 75–78;

infrastructure projects funded by, 47; minting of money by, 21–26; monetary role of, 1–4; monies of account in, 8, 15; and public faith, 3–4, 6, 50, 71–72, 81, 87; relief sought from, by colonial constituents, 45–46, 53–54, 143–44. *See also* early American monetary practice
colonization, money linked to, 8–9, 51–54, 119
commodity money: concept of, 1, 15; taxes paid in, 26, 33, 38, 106; tobacco as a form of, 6–7, 16
Connecticut, 21, 167–70, 174–78, 183, 185, 207, 210, 212
consumer revolution, 13, 16, 105
continental currency, 11, 219
Cooke, Elisha, Jr., 96, 99, 187
counterfeiting: backgrounds of perpetrators of, 183; of bills of credit, 120, 167–68, 171–77, 179, 226; of coins, 67; contribution of, to colonial economy, 186; difficulties in preventing and prosecuting, 169–70, 174–79, *179*, *180*, 181, 283n163; networks for, 170–77, 183, 185; of paper money, 167; popular opinion about, 176–77, 182–83, 185–86; punishments for, 170, 174, 176–79, 181–85; as response to money scarcity, 177, 183; various methods of, 166–70; women's practice of, 168–69, 185
credit/loans: book, 8, 48, 159, 211; crises involving, 106–7, 225–26; culture of, 49, 248n20; enslaved people as security for, 122–27, 138–41, 150; land as security for, 90–93, 101–2, 138; money as, 3; personal security for, 101–2; trust as form of, 1, 2; uses of, 102, 105. *See also* bills of credit; debt; loan office system
credit theory of money, 3, 236n8
Cree, 7
Creek (Muscogee), 61–62, 126
Cromwell, Oliver, 34, 66–67
Crouse, Maurice, 125
Cruger, John, 84
currency. *See* money
Currency Act (England, 1751), 10, 212, 214, 226
Currency Act (England, 1764), 10, 213–27
Currency Act crisis, 213–27
currency conversion table, *210*
Cushing, Thomas, 195

Dale, Thomas, 93
Damiano, Sara, 105
Dartmouth, William Legge, Lord, 225
Davis, Benjamin, 38
debentures, 32, 36, 40, 44, 56
debt: litigation of, 20, 106, 111, 114, 124, 206–7, 218, 220–22; public, 28–29, 34, 41, 70, 77–78, 129; transferability of, 90–92. *See also* credit/loans
Debt Recovery Act (England, 1732), 217
Denison, John, 100
depreciation: balance of trade in relation to, 5; explanations of, 69–77; inflation in relation

INDEX 297

to, 69–73; in Massachusetts, 197; in South Carolina, 80–81; taxes linked to, 69–72
Desan, Christine, 10, 36, 69
Dickinson, Jonathan, 110–12
Dinwiddie, Robert, 214, 217
disorderly houses, 156–57
Dominion of New England, 14, 18–21, 25, 35, 93
Douglass, William, 191–92, 197, 207
Draper, John, 178
ducatoons. *See* Lyon dollars
Dudley, Joseph, 25, 34, 42, 47, 68, 97
Dudley, Paul, 97–98
Dummer, William, 53–54
Dunmore, John Murray, Earl of, 224
Dutch ducatoons. *See* Lyon dollars

early American monetary practice: alternatives in, 13; debates about, 13; discourses on, 13; imperial policy vs., 9, 10; multiplicity of, 1–2, 6–9, 18, 54–59; power dynamics involved in, 3, 11–13, 50–51, 89, 191–92; scholarship on, 4–5; sociocultural practices inherent in, 6–7, 11–13
East India Company, 226
Edelson, S. Max, 138, 146
Edwards, David, 35–36
Eich, Stefan, 4
Endicott, John, 35–36
English Civil War (1642–51), 18
enslaved people: agency and power of, in relation to money, 12, 163; colonial military service of, 58, 61–62, 155, 277n19, 277n21; duty on, 127–32, 141, 148; economic/market activities of, 160–65; family separations experienced by, 123–24, 139–40; freedom purchased by, 153, 154; freedom sought by, 132–33, 146, 159–60, 162–63, 223–24; growing population of, 153; inflation blamed on, 158, 160; and informal economies, 155–60; labor issues involving, 133, 146, 148–49, 153–55, 160–65; legal and commercial restrictions on, 132–33, 145, 148, 156–58, 164–65; means of obtaining cash and credit by, 148, 153–55, 159–65; money in relation to, 4, 11; mortgaging of, 122–27, 138–41, 150; in New York, 58–59, 86; poverty of, 134, 144, 153–55; as property, 11, 59, 89, 121–24, 153, 217–18, 223; resistance activities of, 162–63 (*see also* uprisings by); sale of, 121, 124, 132, 223–24; in South Carolina, 61, 82, 121–33, 138–50; stealing by, 156–62; uprisings by, 132, 136, 146–48, 223 (*see also* resistance activities of); violence against, 144, 164–65. *See also* slave trade
Epps, Simon, 100
Ernst, Joseph, 214, 218
Essay on Currency, An, 68, 82, 125, 134–36
Eveleth, Edward, *203*
Everleigh, Samuel, 143

exchange rates: balance of trade and, 74, 108, 139, 142, 188, 191, 200, 238n25; in Massachusetts, 22, 71–73, 106, 188, 191, 200, 207; in New York, 84–86; official vs. actual, 65; paper money emissions and, 112, 128, 138, 141, 196, 214; proposals for fixing, 194, 197–99, 208, 212; in South Carolina, 79–82, 125–26, 142, 149; for sterling, 5, 65–66, 197–99, 214, 226, 255n30

Farlow, Samuel, 27
Fauquier, Francis, 217
Fearing, John, 48
financial revolution (England), 15, 37, 67
First Continental Congress, 213, 226. *See also* Second Continental Congress
Fishbourne, William, 216
Fleet, Thomas, 178
Fletcher, Benjamin, 36
floating currencies, 8, 194, 199. *See also* pegged currencies
Florida. *See* Spanish Florida
food riots, 107, 114
Fort Mose, 146–47
Fothergill, John, 215
Fourth Anglo-Wabanaki War (1722–25). *See* Governor Dummer's War
Foxcroft, Thomas, 188
Franklin, Benjamin, 10, 64, 69–70, 81, 82, 89–90, 92, 114–16, 135, 154, 178–80, 215, 218–19, 222–23; bill of credit printed by, *116–17*
Franklin, William, 222
free gifts, 208
free minting, 24–25
French and Indian War (1754–63). *See* Seven Years' War

Gallay, Alan, 61
Galloway, Joseph, 222–23
gambling, 157–58
Gardner, John, 36
Gee, Joshua, 129
General Court (Massachusetts), 14, 16, 23–24, 27–29, 35–36
Georgia, 132, 147, 149
gift exchange, 7, 50–53, 153–54
Glen, James, 141
Glorious Revolution (1688), 18, 26–27, 37, 65
gold: ignored in Queen Anne's Proclamation, 66, 68; as money, 2, 7, 9, 18; paper as substitute for, 9–10
Goose Creek Men, 59
Gordon, Patrick, 113–14, 181
government. *See* colonial governments/assemblies
Governor Dummer's War (1722–25; also called Fourth Anglo-Wabanaki War), 49, 53, 62, 75, 94
Graeber, David, 6, 57

Great Awakening, 202
Great Planters, 123, 133, 214, 217, 223, 226
Great Recoinage (England, 1696), 10, 26, 67
Green, Timothy, 168
Greer, Allan, 240n43
Grenville, George, 215, 219
Grubb, Farley, 69, 268n30

Haffenden, Philip, 35
Hale, Jonathan, *203*
Hale, Robert, 201
Hall, David, bill of credit printed by, *116–17*
Hall, Fayr, 129, 188–89
Hamilton, Andrew, 113–14, 182
Hancock, David, 127, 150
Hancock, Thomas, 208
hard money: defined as silver, 1, 65; paper money vs., 64–65, 69–77, 89, 97, 99–100, 188, 193–95, 208–10
Hart, Emma, 161
Hart, Keith, 4, 6
Hartigan-O'Connor, Ellen, 159
Hartlib, Samuel, 90–92, 183
Hat Act (England, 1732), 188
Haudenosaunee, 16, 28, 51–52, 56–57
Helleiner, Eric, 246n110
Higginson, John, 189
Hill & Guerrard, 144
Hillsborough, Wills Hill, Earl of, 219–20, 222–23, 225
Hobhouse, Isaac, 138, 143
Hobsbawm, Eric, 183
Hockley, Richard, 145–47
Houghton, John, 45
House of Commons, 10, 187, 199, 204, 209
Hoyt, John, 39
Hubbard, Nathaniel, 206
Hudson Bay Company, 7
Hull, John, 23–25
Hunt, Daniel, 175, 183
Hunt, Jeremiah, obligation bond to the trustees of Billerica, *103–4*
Hunter, Robert, 56, 59, 84–85
Hurd, Nathaniel, currency conversion table, *210*
Hutchinson, Edward, 98
Hutchinson, Thomas, 29, 40, 97–99, 193–94, 202, 206–7, 209–11

Indigenous peoples: colonial military service of, 53–54, 56, 61; colonization and, 51–54; land of, 6, 9, 34, 93–96; land deeds of, 34, 52, 93–94; money forms used by, 7, 9, 16–18, 51; in South Carolina, 59–62; violence against, 62, 94; and wolf bounties, 58–59
inflation, 5, 64–87; depreciation in relation to, 5, 69–73; enslaved people blamed for, 158, 160; in Massachusetts, 70–77, 107–108; political basis of, 68–70; in South Carolina, 79–81, 125, 142; worsening balance of trade blamed for, 74, 108
informal economy, 155–60
Ingham, Geoffrey, 3, 8, 90
Ingoldesby, Richard, 54
Innes, Mitchell, 3
interracial socializing, 157; and crime, 157–58, 183–85; and trade, 163

Jackson, Richard, 215
jailbreaks, 169–70, 174–76
James II, King of England, 18, 25, 26
Jellison, Richard, 81, 125
Jenkins, Robert, 170
Johnson, Daniel, 186
Johnson, Robert, 81, 127–30
Joseph Wragg & Co., 144, 168
Junto philosophical club, 178

Kammen, Michael, 83
Kayaderosseras Patent, 57
Keith, William, 83, 88, 109, 111–13
Keynes, John Maynard, and Keynesianism, 2, 13, 14, 15
Kilby, Christopher, 204, 205
King George's War (1744–48), 118, 208. *See also* War of the Austrian Succession
King Philip's War (1675–76). *See* Metacom's War
King William's War (1688–97; also called Nine Years' War), 27, 38, 40, 43, 45, 52, 62, 83, 109
Kinloch, James, 141, 143, 145
Knight, Sarah, 1, 12
Kuroda, Akinobu, 4, 240n42

Lambton, Richard, 140–41, 150
land, 88–119; alienability of, 90, 91, 93, 95; as backing for bills of credit, 33–34; improvement of, 95–96, 261n39; of Indigenous peoples, 6, 9, 34, 93–96; money in relation to, 9, 11; paper money in relation to, 89–92; as property, 9, 11, 89; as security for credit, 90–93, 101–2, 138; titles to, 94–95. *See also* property
Land Bank (1739–41), 94, 200–205, 208, 210
land banks, 34, 90–93, 96–99, 118, 200–205, 210. *See also* banks of credit
Laurens, Henry, 164
Law, Jonathan, 176
Lawrence, Thomas, 110–12
leaves, and safeguards against counterfeiting, 178, *179, 180*
Lee, Richard Henry, 217
legal tender laws, 2, 22, 50, 55, 65, 68, 77, 79, 82, 196, 215, 218–21, 226–27
Leisler, Jacob, 28
Le Jau, Francis, 79, 80, 125, 134

INDEX 299

Lenape, 7
liberalism: of British empire, 10, 240n49; and conceptions of money, 4, 10
Lichtenstein, Alex, 162
Lloyd, David, 111
Loan Office Act (South Carolina, 1736), 137–38, 141, 143–45
loan office system: banks of deposit vs., 92; in Barbados, 123–24; benefits of, 88–89; Currency Act and, 221–24; enforcement problems in, 101–8; introduction of, 88; in Massachusetts, 89, 97–108; in New York, 224–25; and paper money, 111–18; in Pennsylvania, 88–92, 109–18; social hierarchies reconfirmed by, 89; in South Carolina, 123–27, 135–41, 149
loans. *See* credit/loans
Locke, John, 9, 10, 67, 69, 96
Logan, George, 77–78
Logan, James, 112–14
Lords of the Treasury, 218
Lords of Trade, 18, 25–26. *See also* Board of Trade
Lovell, John, 94
Lynde, Benjamin, 50
Lynde, Samuel, 96
Lyon dollars (Dutch ducatoons), 66, 84

MacDonnell, John, 169–70, 177
Macedonian Plea, 34
Magna Carta, 20
Mann, Bruce, 106
Martin, Bonnie, 123
Marx, Karl, 11, 115, 137
Mary II, Queen of England, 26
Massachusetts: bills of credit in, 14, 29–33, *31*, 48–50, 68–70, 196–97, 207–8; depreciation in, 197; fiscal powers of, 35–38; fisheries in, 189–90; General Court, 14, 16, 23–24; hard money in, 193–95; and Indigenous money forms, 18; loan office system in, 89, 97–108; minting of money by, 21–26; money in, 14–16, 18, 187–93; money scarcity in, 39–40, 190–92; payments to Indigenous peoples by, 51–53; redemption act in (1749), 209–11; and Rhode Island currency, 171, 197, 207–8; royal charter for, 14; silver pine tree shilling, 23; sixteen-shilling bill of credit (1775), 227, *227*; taxation in, 14, 28–33; twenty-shilling bill of credit (1690), *31*
Massachusetts Bay Colony, 19, 34, 54; silver pine tree shilling, 23; twenty-shilling bill of credit (1690), *31*. *See also* Massachusetts
Massachusetts Bay Company, 14
Mather, Cotton, 29–30, 34–35, 72, 99
Mather, Increase, 14, 25, 28–29
Maxwell, Samuel, 47
McDonald, Roderick, 162
McDougall, Alexander, 225

Melyen, Jacob, 30
Menard, Russel, 127
Mendon gang (counterfeiters), 173–75, 185, 202
Meredith, Charles, 216
Mermaid (ship), 208
Metacom's War (1675–76), 19, 20, 24, 34, 93
Middleton, Arthur, 126–27, 141, 143
Miller, Perry, 89
Million Purchase, 93–94
Mingo, 224
minting of money, 21–26, 37, 243n33. *See also* coins/coinage
Mohawk, 57
Molasses Act (England, 1733), 188–89
money: agricultural and husbandry products as, 6–7, 16; colonization linked to, 8–9, 51–54; as credit, 3; credit in relation to, 2; enslaved people in relation to, 4, 11; Indigenous conceptions and uses of, 7, 9, 16–18, 51; land in relation to, 9, 11; in Massachusetts, 14–16, 18, 187–93; name vs. thing of, 15; neutrality and uniformity of, 2–4, 10; political factors in value of, 69–70; productive capacity of, 89; property in relation to, 6; traditional and recent conceptions of, 2–5, 14–15, 43; trust's role in giving meaning to, 4. *See also* bills of credit; coins/coinage; early American monetary practice; gold; paper money; silver; sterling
money of account: in ancient monetary systems, 15; in colonial governments, 8, 15; currency as, 15; significance of, 8; state-designated, 2
money scarcity: of coins, 8, 20, 22, 24, 39–40, 74; counterfeiting as response to, 177, 183; Currency Act crisis and, 213–27; exchange rates linked to, 197; inflation blamed on, 71–73; in Massachusetts, 39–40, 190–92; in Pennsylvania, 108–11; in South Carolina, 133–34, 136, 143
Montgomerie, John, 168
Moore, Henry, 224–25
Moore, James, 59–61
moral economy, 107, 113, 162, 186, 202
Morgan, David, 39
Morgan, Joseph, 96
mortgages. *See* credit/loans; private mortgage market
Muldrew, Craig, 90
Myles, Samuel, 28

Nairne, Thomas, 38, 60, 68, 78, 82
Narragansett, 20
Nash, Gary, 108
Native Americans. *See* Indigenous peoples
Navigation Acts, 19, 25
Neal, Daniel, 188
Newcastle, Thomas Pelham-Holles, Duke of, 128–29, 147, 199

Newell, Margaret, 50, 200, 210
New Hampshire, 207, 212
New Jersey twelve-shilling bill of credit, *180*
New Tenor bills of credit, 193–94. *See also* Second New Tenor bills of credit
New York: bills of credit in, 54–55, *55*, 83–87, 224–25; enslaved people in, 58–59, 86; loan office system in, 224–25; money in, 54–59; money in relation to, *55*; payments to Indigenous peoples by, 56–57
New York Slave Conspiracy (1741), 157
Nicholson, Francis, 82, 126–27, 129
Nine Years' War (1688–97). *See* King William's War
Nipmuc, 20
North Carolina, 219–21
Noyes, Oliver, 73–75, 96, 99, 102, 105. *See also* Governor Dummer's War

Oblong gang (counterfeiters), 175–76, 183
Oglethorpe, James, 147
Ojibwe, 7
Old Tenor bills of credit, 193, 205, 207, 211–12
Orleans, André, 4
Oursel, Nicholas, 76

Paagushen (alias Joseph Trask), 94
Palmer, Eliakim, 212
Paper Act (Barbados, 1706), 123–24
paper money: British attempts to control, in the colonies, 10, 199–200, 213–27; colonial rationales for, 9–10; conflicting arguments about, 13; Currency Act crisis and, 213–27; exchange rates linked to emissions of, 196, 214; hard money vs., 64–65, 69–77, 89, 99–100, 188, 193–95, 208–9; as instrument of colonization, 51–54; land in relation to, 89–92; loan office system and, 111–18; Massachusetts fisheries and, 189; meaning of, for colonial political identity, 10–11; in New York, 54–59; origins of colonial, 14–15; productive capacity of, 115, 119; role of, in everyday life, 177; in South Carolina, 60–62; state-citizen trust as guarantee of, 3–4; tearing/altering of, 166 (*see also* counterfeiting). *See also* bills of credit
Park, K-Sue, 93
Parker, James, New Jersey twelve-shilling bill of credit, *180*
Parliament, 35, 42, 65, 90, 92, 128, 147, 149, 187–88, 199–200, 204, 207–9, 211–15, 217, 219, 221–27. *See also* House of Commons
Parliamentarians, 22
Parris, Alexander, 62
Partridge, Richard, 204, 212
Paschall, Thomas, 216
pegged currencies, 10, 65, 68, 209. *See also* floating currencies

Pemberton, James, 215–16
Penn, Thomas, 118
Penn, William, 66–67, 108, 118
Pennacook, 27
Pennsylvania: bills of credit in, 88–90, 112–18, *116–17*; counterfeiting of bills of credit from, 179; loan office system in, 88–92, 109–18; money scarcity in, 108–11
pensions, 45–46, 250n42; for widows, 30, 45, 58
Pequot, 17–18
personal security, for loans, 101–2
Petty, William, 96, 115
Peyster, Abraham de, 55
Phips, William, 14, 28–29, 52
Pickering, William, 189
Pickett, Nicholas, 45–46
pieces of eight, 1, 6, 21–22, 24–26, 65–66, 84
Pike, Hugh, 45–46
pine tree shillings, 1, 6, 21–26, 23, 34, 41
Polanyi, Karl, 93
poor Protestants (European refugees), 122, 129, 131–32, 137–39
Poovey, Mary, 47
Popple, William, 130–31
popular party (Massachusetts), 97–98, 187–88, 210
Potter, John, 173, 183
Potter, William, 90–92, 183
poverty: in colonial America, 151–52; of enslaved people, 134, 144, 153–55; petitions to colonial governments for relief from, 45; in South Carolina, 144; war as contributing cause to, 151
Pownall, Thomas, 38
Priest, Claire, 206
private mortgage market, 121, 138–41
Privy Council, 9, 204
promissory notes, 27, 90, 105, 120, 216
property: enslaved people as, 11, 59, 89, 121–24, 153; land as, 9, 11, 89; money in relation to, 6. *See also* land; real property
Provoost, David, 84
public faith, 3–4
Pullen, Richard, 47

Quakers, 109, 118, 173, 183, 212, 215
quantity theory of money, 5, 69, 71
Quartering Act (England, 1765), 225
Queen Anne's Proclamation (1704), 65–68, 84–85, 109, 123, 141, 187, 199
Queen Anne's War (1702–13; also called War of the Spanish Succession), 40, 42, 45, 52, 53, 60, 62, 68, 70, 96, 109
Quit Rent Act (South Carolina, 1731), 138

Rabushka, Alvin, 71
Randolph, Edward, 24–25
Rawle, Francis, 82–83, 109, 111–12, 115, 118–19

real property, 91–92, 122
registries, public: of enslaved property, 122; of land titles and mortgages, 94–95, 101–2, 138–39, 265n138
Regulator Rebellion, 212, 220–21, 225
Rhode Island, 171–76, 197, 207, 210, 212
Rice Act (England, 1730), 128
rice production, 82, 87, 121, 128–29, 134–37, 142–45, 148–49
riots. *See* food riots
Roberts, Edward, 67
Roberts, Jennifer, 178
Robinson, John, 217
Rolfe, John, 93
Royal African Company, 124, 128–29
Royalists, 22

Saltonstall, Gurdon, 167–68
Samson, James, 39
Savage, Benjamin, 144
Savage, Thomas, 28–29
Savannah, 59–60
scalp bounties, 62, 94
scarcity. *See* money scarcity
Schermerhorn, Calvin, 121
Schuyler, Philip, 84
Schweitzer, Mary, 113, 117
Scias, John, 175–76
Scott, Kenneth, 172
Second Continental Congress, 11. *See also* First Continental Congress
Second New Tenor bills of credit, 205–6
seigniorage, 37, 41, 77
Seven Years' War (1754–63), 10, 118, 150, 212, 214–15
Sewall, Samuel, 28–32, 47, 50, 94, 99
Shawnee, 224
Shirley, William, 175, 204–10
shop notes, 7, 13, 121, 190–91
Shute, Samuel, 98–99
silver: as colonial currency, 2; as currency, 7, 9–10; hard money defined as, 1, 65; money's value based on, 71; paper as substitute for, 9–10; as Spanish currency, 1; used for British reimbursement of colonies, 208–11. *See also* sterling
silver bank: proposals for, 71, 194; rival of Land Bank (1739–41), 202
slave duty, 127–32, 141, 148
slaves. *See* enslaved people
slave trade, 121, 128–32, 138–44, 223–24
Smith, Adam, 9–10, 70
Smith, Barbara Clark, 107
Smith, Billy G., 274n136
Smith, Bruce, 80–81
Smith, Thomas, 126
Smoak, Katherine, 171

soldiers: payment issues involving, 10, 20, 27–29, 44, 198; relief claims made by, 45–46
South Carolina: bills of credit in, 60–62, 68–70, 77–83, 149–50; enslaved people in, 61–62, 82, 121–33, 138–50; exchange rates in, 142; financial collapse in (1739), 145–46, 149; and Indigenous peoples, 59–62; inflation and depreciation in, 80–81; loan office system in, 123–27, 135–41, 149; military excursions of, 59–62; money scarcity in, 133–34, 136, 143; multiplicity of money in, 121
South Sea Bubble (1720), 83, 110, 204, 225–26
Spanish Florida, 43, 59–61, 132, 146–47. *See also* St. Augustine
specie. *See* coins/coinage; gold; silver; sterling
Spotswood, Alexander, 198–99
Stamp Act (England, 1765), 10, 204, 213, 217–19
states. *See* colonial governments/assemblies
St. Augustine, 43, 60–61, 77, 127, 132, 146–47. *See also* Spanish Florida
stealing: contribution of, to conventional economy, 186; by enslaved people, 63, 148, 156–64; and informal economies, 155–60; motivations for, 152, 162–63; punishments for, 156
sterling: as British currency, 6, 8, 10, 15; exchange rates for, 65–66, 197–99, 214, 238n26. *See also* silver
Stoddard, John, 49–50
Stoddard, Solomon, 31, 49
Stoddard, William, 201
Stono Rebellion (1739), 133, 146–48, 163, 165
Story, Joseph, 93
Stoughton, William, 52
Sugar Act (England, 1764), 216, 218
Sullivan, Owen (alias John Sullivan), 184, 185

Taft, Benjamin, 173–74, 202
task system, 164
taverns, 156–57
taxation/taxes: bills of credit for payment of, 29–33, 35, 43–44, 48, 70–72, 81–82; colonists' difficulties in paying British, 216–18; commodity money for payment of, 26, 33, 38; consent and, 20; depreciation linked to, 69–72; difficulties in collecting, 38–40; in Dominion of New England, 19–21; in Massachusetts, 14; paper money's redemption via, 14–15, 70–72; resistance to, 19–21, 27, 126
Taylor, James, 33, 40, 44, 46
theft. *See* stealing
Third Anglo-Dutch War (1672–74), 24
Thomas, George, 118
Thompson, E. P., 11, 186
tippling houses, 156–57
titles, land, 94–95. *See also* registries, public: of land titles and mortgages
trade. *See* balance of trade

trust: bills of credit dependent on, 32, 41, 43–44, 63; defined, 1; in elite society, 32, 49–50; as form of credit, 1, 2; interpersonal, 4; money's meaning dependent on, 4
Tryon, William, 219–20, 225
Tuscarora War (1711–15), 61–63, 138

Usher, John, 29

Van Olinda, Hilletie, 57
Vans, Hugh, 107–8, 191, 194–95
Virginia, 214, 217–18, 223–24

Wabanaki, 20, 27, 51–53, 58, 62, 94
Wainwright, John, 100
Wampanoag, 19, 20
wampum, 1, 2, 7, 9, 16–18, 17, 22, 57, 83
Wanton, William, 172
war: bills of credit for financing, 42–44, 64, 79–80, 207, 214; British reimbursement of colonies for contributions to, 208–11; colonial financing of, 42; effects of, on laboring classes, 208; enslaved men's involvement in, 155; financing, 42–63, 147; poverty linked to, 151; soldier payments, 10, 20, 27–29, 44, 198
War of Jenkins' Ear (1739–48), 10, 134, 144, 149, 198–99
War of the Austrian Succession (1740–48), 10, 149. *See also* King George's War
War of the Spanish Succession (1702–13). *See* Queen Anne's War
Watts, Robert, 84
Webb, Benjamin, 102
Webbe, John, 92
Welke, Barbara Young, 12
Wendall, Abraham, 84
Wharton, Thomas, 216
Wigglesworth, Edward, 71–72, 74, 82, 99
Wilf, Steven, 182
Wilks, Francis, 192, 197, 205
Willard, Josiah, 187
William of Orange, 26
Winthrop, Fitz-John, 28
Winthrop, John, Jr., 91
Wise, John, 19–20, 42, 73, 96, 99, 102, 119, 190
wolf bounties, 58–59
women: contributions of, to colonial governments, 53, 57–58; as counterfeiters, 168–69, 185; as creditors, 105, 141, 153; experience of enslavement of, 122–23, 140, 164; as laborers, 107, 192; participation of, in the informal economy, 155–57, 161–63; as shopkeepers, 105–106, 113
Wood, Betty, 163, 165
Wood, William, 130–32, 141
Woodbridge, John, 34, 92, 118
Woods, Ellen Meiksins, 261n39
Wragg, Joseph, 132, 138–45, 150, 168
Wragg, Samuel, 129, 132

Yamasee, 59–61, 126
Yamasee War (1715–17), 61, 62, 78–80, 125–27, 138
Yonge, Francis, 80

Zabin, Serena, 155–56
Zelizer, Viviana, 6